# The First Year

Edited by
RICHARD N. HOLWILL

## The Heritage Foundation

The Heritage Foundation is a Washington-based, tax-exempt, non-partisan public policy research institution dedicated to the principles of free competitive enterprise, limited government, individual liberty and a strong national defense.

The Heritage Foundation publishes a wide variety of research in various formats for the benefit of decision-makers and the interested public. The views expressed in the Foundation's publications are those of the authors and do not necessarily reflect the views of the Foundation or its Trustees.

*Policy Review* is The Heritage Foundation's quarterly journal of public policy. An editorial advisory board of distinguished specialists in economics, foreign policy, defense studies, political science, sociology and other disciplines seeks out for publication original proposals and critiques addressed to the problems of our society.

Subscriptions to *Policy Review* are available for $15 for one year, $28 for two years and $38 for three years.

The Heritage Foundation Research Department frequently publishes *Issue Bulletins* and *Backgrounders:* the former are concise and timely analyses of specific, current policy issues; the later are in-depth studies of longer-range policy questions.

The Heritage Foundation Resource Bank is a clearinghouse of information useful to like-minded organizations. Its newsletter, *Insider Newsletter,* transmits news of conferences, publications and work-in-progress to interested institutions and individuals.

The Communications Network provides lecturers in both foreign and domestic policy to colleges and civic groups.

The Washington Semester Program was established to provide an opportunity for interested students to increase their knowledge by first-hand experience of Congress and the legislative process. It is an intensive, one-semester program designed to provide a balance between lectures, a congressional internship and individual research.

The Foundation is classified as a Section 501 (c) (3) organization under the Internal Revenue Code of 1954. It is further classified as a "non-private" (i.e., "public") Foundation under Section 509 (a) (2) of the Code. Individuals, corporations, companies, associations, and foundations are eligible to support the work of the Foundation through tax-deductible gifts. Background material will be provided to substantiate tax-deductibility.

Library of Congress Catalog Card Number: 81-85620
ISBN Number: 0-89195-031-1

# TABLE OF CONTENTS

## Independent Regulatory Agencies

# FOREWORD

In December 1979, The Heritage Foundation began work on a project designed to help a conservative president "hit the ground running." The result was *Mandate for Leadership: Policy Management in a Conservative Administration*, an in-depth analysis of the executive branch of government, containing more than 2,000 specific recommendations for reform, reorganization and policy revision. After the election, Ronald Reagan and his team eagerly accepted our report as they began the transition process.

Many of the individuals who contributed to *Mandate* later participated in the transition effort. When President Reagan took office, many of these individuals joined the Administration in key positions. Included among these appointments were James G. Watt, Secretary of the Interior; Norman B. Ture, Under Secretary of the Treasury for Tax Policy; and Charles L. Heatherly, the editor of *Mandate*, Executive Secretary at the Department of Education. More than thirty other *Mandate* contributors also accepted policy positions in the Administration.

Much has been accomplished in President Reagan's first year. The question we now address is simple: exactly how much? Using the recommendations contained in *Mandate for Leadership* as a guide, we embarked on an "audit" of the Administration's successes and failures since the election. This report, *The First Year*, is a culmination of that effort. It represents the combined efforts of more than 200 men and women who first began cataloging the *Mandate* recommendations in the summer of 1981. Between September and mid-November, they expended a total of nearly 10,000 man-hours on this project.

We recognized at the outset that this project would require frank assessments and occasionally sharp criticism of the Administration in some areas. We also knew that some Administration activities would deserve praise. The Heritage Foundation Board of Trustees gave clear and unequivocal instructions to the managers of the project: no criticism or praise should be altered by political pressure. The independence of the project was a paramount consideration.

Although *Mandate* provided the base line for measuring the success or failure of the Administration in the first year, the principles of conservative government were the overriding goals of our effort. Implementation of these principles, collectively called "conservatism," require continued change. This change can be effected more readily and efficiently by the occasional assessment of exactly what has been done to date and by a review of what remains to be accomplished. *The First Year* is offered as a modest contribution to the process of re-establishing a government based on personal liberty and responsibility, free enterprise, and a strong defense.

Edwin J. Feulner, Jr.

# PREFACE

This book is the product of efforts of many individuals. Not all can be named in the limited space available to us. Nonetheless, the work of each is appreciated. Particular thanks are in order for those members of The Heritage Foundation staff who, at a moment's notice, provided research, editorial, and other support to the production of *The First Year*.

Lynn E. Munn provided general editorial and research assistance and managed the confusing task of document management. Catherine England provided policy editing assistance and assisted in the writing of several chapters. Bobbie Scarff managed the final production of the audit sections and assisted in editing them. Margaret D. Bonilla, in addition to writing the chapter on Executive Orders, assisted with the research and editing of several chapters. Leonard D. Ellis proved to be one of the more remarkable research assistants I have known; his ability to gather facts was most helpful. Overall copy editing was ably done by Richard Odermatt, whose skills I admire greatly. Summer interns Dan Mahoney and Jim Walton identified, collated, and assembled the recommendations which formed the basis of the audit. Don Hall demonstrated again that his skill at word processing is unexcelled. As we approached our deadline, he was ably assisted by Charlena Turner.

Richard Holwill
Editor

# Chapter One

# THE FIRST YEAR
by Richard N. Holwill

The Reagan Administration, although headed in the proper direction, should and could have accomplished more since the election in November 1980. This assessment is based on a recognition that President Reagan's goal is to change the course of government from an expansive to a devolutionary trend, and that such a change is a monumental task. It is also based on a recognition of the fact that "major" victories often result in only minor changes. One such victory was won in the budget battle. The result was not a reduction in federal spending; it was a reduction in the rate at which spending was growing.

*The First Year* recognizes this complexity and uses standards for evaluating the performance of the President, also recognizing that change takes time. These standards are the recommendations made in *Mandate for Leadership: Policy Management in a Conservative Administration*. That book, given to the Presidential Transition Team in November 1980, made more than 2,000 specific recommendations which were collectively designed to re-establish the principles of personal liberty and responsibility, an economy freed from undue regulation, and a strengthened national defense. Implementing all of the *Mandate* recommendations in one year would have been an unrealistic proposition. However, to achieve these long-term goals, many of the recommendations should have been implemented or at least initiated. The authors of this report determined that 1,270 specific suggestions met this definition of "short term." The results of their investigation of these issues are detailed in this report along with analyses of other actions not specifically mentioned in *Mandate*.

### Personnel Problems

The principal reason for the Administration's failure to accomplish more in the first year is surprisingly consistent from department to department and from agency to agency—personnel. Almost every chapter in this report notes personnel problems typified by delayed appointments, unqualified or misqualified appointments, and by the appointment of individuals who fail to understand and accept the President's goals and policies. The importance of personnel problems prompted a separate chapter devoted solely to these issues.

The consequences of delayed appointments are extremely significant. Because qualified personnel were not put in place in a timely manner, revisions of regulations were delayed, the legislative authority for some priority changes expired, and the opposition had time to marshall its forces against important initiatives.

The problems caused by unqualified or misqualified appointees could undermine many of the Administration's long-term goals. This problem is common in the legal sections of several departments and agencies where appointees tend to be attorneys with an excellent background in banking or business law. Unfortunately, these individuals are unable to refute a career staff attorney who is opposed to the President on a particular issue. The consequence is often a continuation of an objectional program or policy and is, at best, a delay in the implementation of reform.

Many qualified appointees have already fallen into one of Washington's more frustrating traps. They appear to believe that, because they are now in control, they can make major long-term changes simply through the force of their will. Such naivete ignores the fact that this Administration, like the thirty-nine before it, has only a brief time in office. Policies, therefore, must be institutionalized through revised regulations, executive orders, and—in many cases—through legislation.

## Presidential Leadership

Because the president personally sets the tone of an administration, he too must be evaluated. Given the tendency to confuse the actions of the entire executive branch with the actions of the chief executive, the principal duties of the president are sometimes ill-defined. Refined to the essence, they are threefold: to lead the nation; to make final decisions; and to set overall policy.

The term "lead" has, in recent years, come to mean "take the lead" in drafting new laws and designing grand new government programs. This definition is the inevitable result of a national tendency to confuse action with progress. The more fundamental definition of "lead"—to cause others to follow—is actually more appropriate to use in evaluating the performance of a president. Lyndon Johnson failed, in large part, because the nation would not follow his policies in Vietnam. Richard Nixon failed in part because the nation refused to be led by a man disgraced by scandal. Gerald Ford failed to convince a majority that he could lead. Jimmy Carter could not lead, in part, because he did not know where he wanted to go.

In this respect, Ronald Reagan stands apart from all his immediate predecessors and most presidents in modern history. His greatest successes to date have been the direct result of his personal leadership on issues such as the budget, taxes, and foreign policy. He has truly led the country during this first year. This ability offers hope that he will be able to continue leading the nation in the directions promised.

Yet, in an academic sense, the need to rely on this ability as often as has been the case in the first year is disturbing. The fact the President was often required to personally save the day on many issues is an indication of poor staff work in the areas of congressional relations and in the drafting of proposals. The fight to secure Senate approval for the sale of Airborne Warning and Control Systems (AWACS) planes to Saudi Arabia is an example of this problem. First, the situation was allowed to get out of hand politically; efforts should have begun immediately to quash the Resolution of Disapproval. Second, opponents of the President seized the opportunity to turn a non-critical issue into a referendum on the President's foreign policy. Thus, the President was forced to risk his personal prestige and credibility in order to defend U.S. credibility internationally. The consequences of failure were compounded by the tactics which the Administration was forced to use.

Leadership ability is an ephemeral thing. It is easily damaged by defeat. As a consequence, the President's credibility should not be sacrificed to a fight that cannot be won. If it is risked, the rewards must have the potential to offset the possibility of long-term political damage. This President has the potential to lead the nation in a new direction. This potential should not be squandered.

Thus far, at least, the Administration seems to recognize this need for balance. It was demonstrated in their actions on the Social Security proposal. That initiative contained several provisions which were too controversial for passage. When it met bipartisan opposition, the Administration was embarrassed but wisely resisted the temptation to assume that "the President can pull it out." The basic problem was the drafting of the proposal. Had it been artful and better thought out, at least some of the less controversial provisions might have been implemented. As it happened, even these badly needed reforms have been relegated to a commission for additional study.

### Decision-Making at the White House

The President has done well in managing the day-to-day decision-making apparatus in the White House. Many previous presidents appeared to be in a quandary every time the competing interests of the various departments or agencies required a top-level referee. President Reagan has imposed a system which requires all affected departments and agencies to iron out as many problems as possible before asking for a decision from the chief executive on a dispute. This "cabinet council" system ensures a wise use of executive

3

resources, although it has also caused some rather frustrating delays in the drafting of policy proposals.

To date, however, President Reagan has not been tested with major decisions. True, he has made important decisions. However, most of these were on predictable subjects thoroughly discussed in the campaign. The true test of a president comes when he must make decisions on which he has taken a stand and which have not been discussed *ad nauseam*. For example, President Kennedy made such a decision when he challenged the Soviet move to install missiles in Cuba, an issue not discussed in the election of 1960. President Nixon made such a decision when he initiated diplomatic relations with the People's Republic of China. This subject was not even broached in 1968. Energy was not a subject discussed in the 1968 or 1972 campaigns, but in 1973, it became an issue which prompted a disastrous decision which led to seven years of counter-productive price controls.

The issues discussed in campaign debates and speeches cannot deal with the unforeseen crises of coming years. Those discussions effectively allow a candidate to say only "trust me" to make the decisions needed in the future. The American electorate does not, unfortunately, push each candidate to define the principles he would use in making those decisions. Too many candidates elected did not have a clear set of principles which could guide them in future crises. The consequence of this failure to articulate principles has been price controls, political expediency leading to government largess, and capitulation to false promises of Soviet good intentions.

Fortunately, President Reagan appears to be guided by an admirable set of principles. In his first year in office he has demonstrated a commitment to his principles, even when doing so required him to defend promises made in haste. An example is the President's refusal to support efforts to dilute organized labor's sacred cow—the Davis-Bacon Act. The threat of abandoning this promise could be used to negate AFL-CIO opposition to a key to the National Labor Relations Board. The President deserves respect for his refusal to break his promise.

**Policy Management**

The President chose his policy priorities wisely during the first year. Economic policy is key to the long-term success of all other programs and the Administration itself. Proving that a free market will work can help to ensure the "sea change" which would follow a continuation of the current conservative trend in the United States. The tax cut and budget revisions are key to the implementation of the President's economic priorities and clearly worth the effort expended during their development.

4

Although the President began the process of managing these multi-departmental policies in an admirable way, problems have become evident in recent weeks. Of these, the most serious was permitting the impression to develop that the recession which began in late 1981 was something of a surprise. It was not unforeseen. However, the Administration's failure to proclaim that fact has allowed the Democrats to blame the recession on "Reaganomics."

The President should also defend the tax cut more aggressively. The reluctance to do so has resulted in attacks on current policies from both liberals and traditional conservative economists who are primarily concerned with the size of the 1982 deficit. In the past, recessions were countered with public sector spending. The tax cut is the ideal tool to counter an economic slowdown; it will provide economic incentives necessary to revitalize the private sector. The Administration should be talking about accelerating the tax cut; instead, insidious pressure is building for counter-productive "tax enhancement" policies.

The budget revisions were handled well in the early part of the year. Thus, the President was able to decrease the rate at which federal spending was growing. However, new strategies needed toward the end of the year were not forthcoming. The Administration should not be content simply to trim the size of government largess. Such tactics will inevitably be compromised in the legislative process. Efforts should be increased to eliminate entire programs whereever possible. Eliminating programs removes the danger that they may be increased in size during future budget battles.

A continuation of the current strategy puts extreme pressure on loyal House Republicans who may have constituent pressure to support certain spending programs. If the Administration supports moves to break the spending proposals into discrete bills, the President will be better able to use his veto power. He could expect to win support to sustain a veto from Republicans who might have difficulty supporting certain cuts. Such a strategy will enable the President to work toward the goal of minimizing the role of government to those areas where it is needed and appropriate. The Administration should not be content with marginal changes in the liberal welfare state.

Foreign policy management is also a multi-departmental dilemma. It includes consideration and coordination of policies in the Departments of State, Defense, Commerce, Treasury, Agriculture, and Energy. Although the President is managing these policies better than his predecessor, coordination has been less than perfect. The Secretaries of Defense and State continue to contradict each other. The realities of European politics were largely ignored for many months. As a consequence, the Administration actually aided the anti-missile movement in many NATO countries. Moreover, little attention was paid to pending overseas issues and proposals were not drafted as alternatives to the massive Soviet natural gas sale to West Germany and to other such developments. Top-level policy management is needed to prevent a continuation of this type of problem.

The remainder of this report is devoted to discussions of policy management and decision-making on an agency by agency basis. In the course of these chapters many of these points are treated in greater detail. Chapters Two, Three, and Four analyze the functions belonging to the Executive Office of the President. Chapters Five through Seventeen focus on the Cabinet Departments. Chapters Eighteen through Twenty-two examine the executive agencies. The final eleven chapters examine the independent agencies but recognize that the President can only influence these bodies as vacancies become available and he makes new appointments.

Each chapter in this report is divided into two parts. The first is a narrative which summarizes the most important actions of the department or agency. The second part lists each recommendation and, in as few words as possible, summarizes the extent to which it was implemented or initiated. In some cases, these responses indicate that an action is "in progress" or "under consideration." These answers are used only when clear evidence of progress was demonstrated.

# Chapter Two
# OFFICE OF PRESIDENTIAL PERSONNEL
### By Willa Ann Johnson

No administration in recent history has been more conscious of the importance of the personnel selection process. When the Reagan team first considered the question of personnel in April 1980, it developed clear criteria for service: commitment to the Reagan policy goals, integrity, competence, teamwork and toughness. These criteria should have first been applied to those serving on the President-elect's Personnel Transition Task Force and in the Presidential Personnel Office (PPO) at the White House. These individuals were directly responsible for the executive personnel selection process from top to bottom.

Two essential qualities necessary in the Director of personnel efforts are administrative ability and an acute political sensitivity. An absence of these qualities causes confusion and delays. Many of the personnel problems cited throughout *The First Year* are the direct result of administrative failures. For example, the computer and candidate tracking system was ineffective; in the shift from transition office to White House continuity in the personnel staff was lost. The size of the personnel staff, the White House clearance system, and the FBI field investigations all compounded these problems.

The ineffective computer tracking and retrieval system limited consideration of qualified candidates. Once a talented individual was disqualified for a specific post in one department or agency, the name should have been, but often was not, considered for a position of similar demands and qualifications elsewhere in government. Information on identified, unplaced talent was exchanged only on a word-of-mouth basis. At mid-year, the computer system of unplaced job candidates was able only to provide an alphabetical printout of individuals recommended for service.

The lack of continuity in the personnel staff was a major problem. Of the five Associate Directors in the transition personnel office, only two went on to the White House. In the area of national security and foreign policy (Departments of Defense, State, CIA, ACDA), for instance, historical memory was lost when the associate in charge of this cluster left at the close of transition and a new Associate Director was assigned to work with these departments. Only with the Department of State was continuity and knowledge of candidate development carried over to the White House. The inadequate computer retrieval system exacerbated this problem. In the future, a one year commitment should be required of personnel staff members.

Once at the White House, the size of the personnel staff caused confusion and delay. Yet a large staff was required to compensate in order to re-create the historical sense of what had transpired during the transition and to reconstruct candidate files. From a personnel staff (including volunteers) of over ninety people, the PPO has now been reduced to forty-two.

In principle, the clearance system at the White House was structurally sound. Again, however, a disciplined tracking system in those busy days was lacking. Individuals involved in candidate approval were Martin Anderson, Richard Allen, Lyn Nofziger, and Fred Fielding. Subsequent to their approval, the nomination was then considered by "senior staff" including James Baker, Edwin Meese, Michael Deaver, and Pendleton James. Major delays were caused simply by an administrative failure to see that nominations were processed by the first group within a certain time. This could have been improved by a persistent tracking system in the PPO.

The FBI investigation of candidates began only after the President had approved a candidate's nomination. Investigations took from four to eight weeks and more. Finally, in May, representatives from the FBI and PPO met to work on the problem.

The initial goal was to have selected all Cabinet officers by Thanksgiving 1980. The last Cabinet nomination was not announced until January 7, 1981. Approximately 275 subcabinet candidates were to have been selected by January 20, 1981. Candidates for the top 400 posts were to have been selected by the end of February. Of approximately 400 top officials in the executive departments and agencies, only 55 percent had been announced, only 36 percent had been nominated, and 21 percent had been confirmed by the beginning of May 1981. Many of these positions have still not been filled. Meanwhile, personnel turnover has already begun.

The slippage in the staffing timetable created another significant problem. As time passed, and nominees to important positions remained unnamed, political pressures built and vulnerability to pressure from groups and interests not necessarily supportive of the Reagan mandate increased. This in turn prolonged the process even further. By this time, the PPO was reacting to pressures at the expense of taking the initiative.

Political sensitivity was also a major element lacking in the personnel staff. Early consultation with Members of Congress could have avoided many problems and "holds" placed on nominees in the Senate. The individual assigned to provide political guidance and alert the personnel staff to potential confirmation problems in the Senate was circumvented during transition and did not go to the PPO.

To date, most of these administrative problems partially have been resolved. Two major policy recommendations remain which must be implemented in order for this and future administrations to attract quality personnel. The Senior Executive Service pay cap of $50,112.50 should be lifted. Additionally, the Executive Schedule consisting of the five levels from Cabinet Secretaries to subcabinet officer (ELI-V) was authorized at a range from $81,000 (EL-I) to $58,550 (EL-V). Subsequently, however, funds were appropriated only for pay rates from $69,630.00 (EL-I) to $50,112.50 (EL-V). These salaries are not competitive with the private market for the quality of individuals needed. Figures from the Reagan Administration prove that this pay scale is a serious disincentive to government service for talented persons in mid-career (ages 35-45) who often have children in college and other critical financial needs. For those 46 years and older and reaching the peak of their earning power, the salary limitations are equally constraining. This must be remedied to recruit and retain talent in government service.

Finally, the Reagan Administration is the first to begin staffing under the burdensome financial disclosures and divestiture provisions of the Ethics in Government Act of 1978. This law imposes unrealistic constraints on contact with and personnel appearances before the agency at which the individual worked for a period of up to two years. This provision was designed to halt the "revolving door" through which many individuals were passing. Its effect is to require virtually total career changes for anyone entering or leaving government service. Such a system does not benefit the government and usually punishes those who are willing to give a year or two without making government service a lifetime career. The Act should be carefully reviewed and amended to remove the severe disincentives to government service.

# Chapter Three
# OFFICE OF MANAGEMENT AND BUDGET
### By Catherine England

The Office of Management and Budget had by far the most auspicious start of all agencies in the new Administration. Director David A. Stockman provided the direction to achieve a rapid transition from the mediocre management which OMB suffered in the previous administration. A great deal of credit for this must go to the staff which Stockman assembled in the substantive budget areas. From his congressional staff, Stockman retained Donald Moran and Frederick Khedouri. The budget team was completed with defense expert William Schneider and Annelise Anderson as Associate Director for Economics and Government.

By bringing in a staff with which he was familiar, Stockman was able to mobilize the permanent staff quickly. Long recognized as the most professional and talented of all bureaucracies in the executive branch, the OMB staff responded to the new leadership with enthusiasm and determination.

The early accomplishments of OMB fulfilled and exceeded the recommendations of *Mandate*. By February, the work of OMB and Treasury, with support from other Executive departments, enabled the President to deliver to the people and the Congress *A Program for Economic Recovery*. This program contained not only the *sine qua non* tax rate reduction plan but also a complete outline for reversing the growth of federal spending. In less than one month, OMB had revised the Fiscal Year 1981 and 1982 budgets previously presented by President Carter.

The outline for budget reform in *A Program for Economic Recovery* was filled out in two subsequent volumes. *Fiscal Year 1982 Budget Revisions*, delivered on March 10, and *Additional Details on Budget Revisions*, delivered April 7, provided full details of the President's budget changes for FY 1981 and 1982. In these three volumes, budget savings totaling $55 billion for FY 1981-1982 and over $203 billion through FY 1984 were presented in detail.

While compiling these budget reductions, OMB complied with another of the recommendations of *Mandate* by sending to Congress budget deferrals and rescissions in the amounts of $3.814 billion and $15.362 billion, respectively. Congressional actions on these requests were the first tests of the President's ability to achieve his goals. The President received $11.7 billion in rescissions and $3.4 billion in deferrals.

OMB also deserves praise for a willingness to view all federal programs as controllable. Entitlement programs—providing benefits to all individuals or firms meeting legislated criteria without regard to aggregate outlays—were becoming an increasing part of the federal budget. Before the new Administration took over the budgeting process, the fact that the President could propose changes in such programs and Congress could take action apart from presidential initiative had been ignored.

Having done an exemplary job in most areas, OMB is not deserving of unqualified praise. A major recommendation of *Mandate* was that federal budget policy be based on clear goals so that each federal program could be evaluated on the basis of whether it contributed to or detracted from broad economic and social policy. As a means of evaluating various parts of the budget, *Mandate* suggested OMB establish strict criteria by which to measure the many federal programs. Of the "eight basic criteria" in *A Program for Economic Recovery*, only three meet the *Mandate* recommendations for policy evaluation. The other criteria include an array of program decisions and budget outlay devices which do not facilitate the decision-making process.

Failure to implement the proper evaluation system has resulted in an emphasis at OMB on the narrowly-defined goal of balancing the unified budget. While providing recognized success criteria, this policy ignores the economic costs that may be imposed by various components of the federal budget. That the federal budget is only one measure of the drain on national resources caused by the federal government should be remembered.

Furthermore, an emphasis on the unified budget may allow other important items to escape notice. Among these are the federal allocation of capital through direct off-budget lending programs, loan guarantee commitments, and credit which is diverted through government guarantees of rates of return. These programs distort the credit markets, rewarding political rather than economic success. Their costs, therefore, ought to be considered.

Another major *Mandate* criticism of OMB was that its economic analysis was far below the standard at Treasury and the Council of Economic Advisors. This defect persists although OMB has had sufficient time to assemble an economics staff. Analysis at OMB has failed to consider the effects of changes in tax rates on savings as the OMB staff looks for ways to finance the deficits expected over the next few years. In addition, OMB has apparently failed to understand the role of Federal Reserve Board monetary policy in determining the availability of credit for both economic expansion and federal borrowing. Thus, OMB deficiencies in the area of economic expertise have led to a lack of economic perspective with which to evaluate the role of the agency in federal resource allocation.

Finally, OMB has ignored the *Mandate* recommendation that

legislation granting the President greater impoundment authority should be prepared and supported. There has been some discussion of the issue, but no action. A Senate amendment to the extension of the temporary ceiling on federal debt, which would have accomplished this goal, received no support.

## RECOMMENDATIONS
(Action taken on 5 out of 8)

- Establish spending and revenue limits for the 1982 fiscal year in conjunction with the Council of Economic Advisors and Treasury. Establish the major budget policy goals for FY 1981 concurrently.
  IMPLEMENTED PROMPTLY AND EFFECTIVELY.

- Prepare a series of appropriation deferrals during the process of preparing a substitute budget for FY 1981.
  IMPLEMENTED.

- Prepare the FY 1982 budget submission with the assumption that there are no uncontrollable expenditures.
  IMPLEMENTED.

- Prepare the budget by establishing a set of basic policy goals of the Administration and then formulate program criteria with which to evaluate specific programs.
  PARTIALLY ACCOMPLISHED.

- Gain a consensus within the Cabinet on the appropriateness of applying budget policy goals and program criteria.
  ACCOMPLISHED.

- Prepare legislation granting the President improved impoundment authority.
  NOT IMPLEMENTED.

- Choose a Director who can transcend interdepartmental rivalries, who understands the effect of government on the economy and who commands the respect of the Congress and the Cabinet.
  ACCOMPLISHED.

- Establish an economic staff, headed by a nationally recognized economist, which can operate on the same level of expertise as the Treasury and Council of Economic Advisors.
  NOT ACCOMPLISHED.

# Chapter Four
# EXECUTIVE ORDERS
### By Margaret D. Bonilla

*Mandate for Leadership* recommended that an incoming conservative president actively use the Executive Order to curtail the liberal policies of previous administrations. In this regard, *Mandate* made specific recommendations in the areas of economic policy, affirmative action programs, foreign trade, regulatory reform, and government reorganization.

President Reagan wielded this power actively, although not always in the ways recommended. In some areas, the President's use of the Executive Order was both swift and effective; in others, he did nothing at all.

President Reagan employed Executive Orders most effectively in the areas of regulatory reform and devolution of federal programs. The orders issued in these areas have emphasized a decrease in the regulatory burden upon the private sector and the redirection of federal programs to state and local governments. The order was used less to treat trade and economic issues, contrary to the suggestions in *Mandate for Leadership*. The Administration has addressed these issues through the other branches of government, effectively eliminating the need for an Executive Order.

The greatest criticism regarding the use of the Executive Order is that many issues the President treated in this manner have been addressed more appropriately by the regulatory or legislative branches. The President's use of the order was sometimes duplicative, in some cases even frivolous. The President should restrict the use of this power to those issues which demand it.

## Initial Orders

President Reagan was swift to utilize the Executive Order as a policy tool. The first was issued on January 20; three followed within ten days of the President's taking office. All of the initial orders were aimed at dismantling Carter Administration policies. The first imposed a hiring freeze on all federal employees, retroactive to the date of the general election, November 4, 1980. This initiative was followed quickly by an order postponing the effective dates of all federal regulations issued between the date of the general election and January 19, 1981. This order was particularly significant because it effectively cancelled the regulations issued by the Carter Adminis-

*The author wishes to thank Bobbie Scarff for her assistance in the preparation of this chapter.

tration after its defeat in November 1980. Many of these so-called midnight regulations were inflationary, heavy-handed, and unnecessary. Another order abolished the Council on Wage and Price Stability (COWPS) which had been created by President Carter to establish general wage and price guidelines for both the public and private sectors.

Of the initial actions, the Executive Order that abolished the price and allocation controls on crude oil and refined petroleum was perhaps the most significant. These controls dated from President Nixon's wage and price control program and were continued by succeeding presidents even when crude oil supplies were relatively plentiful. As many had predicted, oil price increases were softened and stabilized as a result of the deregulation order. Deregulation also served as an incentive for increased domestic oil exploration. Finally, deregulation of the oil industry proved to be an important reaffirmation of President Reagan's free market philosophy. Many in the business community were surprised and heartened by the President's swift action to free this industry from government intervention.

President Reagan's initial use of the Executive Order was generally well received. The first orders showed a clear commitment to easing the regulatory burden in the private sector, one of Reagan's primary campaign platforms. Moreover, the first orders were issued in a confident and determined manner, one that proved the Reagan Administration had "hit the ground running." In this sense, the initial orders were of significant political value to the President.

**Regulatory Reform**

Candidate Reagan campaigned heavily on the issue of regulatory reform. Contending that the federal government interfered excessively in the private sector, Reagan vowed to abolish or curtail those regulations and policies which inhibited investment and growth in the private sector. A year later, some progress can be noted, but these efforts have not been as succcessful as the Administration had hoped, nor as successful as they could have been.

To the Administration's credit, regulatory reform was a top priority during the first year of President Reagan's term. The President issued a number of reform-oriented orders within a few months of taking office, including:

- an order requiring the approval of all new regulations by a regulatory review group (the so-called Bush Task Force);

- an initiative requiring a cost-benefit analysis for major new regulations;

- review of all existing regulations on a regular basis; and

16

- orders reducing the amount of paperwork in the departments and federal agencies.

*Mandate for Leadership* also suggested that the Executive Order be used to initiate reforms in land use and education policies. Significant progress has been made in these areas by the Departments of Interior and Education, respectively, eliminating the need for presidential action.

In spite of the attempts at regulatory reform, the degree to which these efforts have been fruitful is questionable. Although a regulatory review board was appointed and put in place, little actual change in regulatory structures has resulted. Other review efforts have been frustrated by a lack of commitment to reform in the departments and pre-occupation with budget concerns.

In spite of the problems that the Reagan Administration has encountered in the regulatory reform area, it is fair to say that the Administration has displayed a willingness to initiate reform where it was considered most necessary. In any case, regulatory reform is arguably a long-term proposition; it is perhaps unfair to be too critical only a year into Reagan's first term, especially when economic and budgetary issues were clearly the chief priority during this period.

The Administration has not attempted to roll back affirmative action programs. *Mandate for Leadership* recommended the abolition of all references to "affirmative action" in Executive Orders; in addition, it recommended that racial classification for federal employees be discontinued. Other recommendations included changes in the minority hiring guidelines. None of these suggestions has been implemented. The only action taken in this area increased the minimum number of employees a federal contractor must have before qualifying for an exemption from affirmative action rules. This was not done through Executive Order, but through a proposed change in procurement regulations. Generally, the White House has shown little interest in stirring up old hostilities by curtailing affirmative action programs. Moreover, the Justice Department and the Equal Employment Opportunity Commission have failed to demonstrate leadership in rescinding those Executive Orders requiring excessive implementation or interpretation in the area of affirmative action.

As suggested in *Mandate for Leadership*, President Reagan has used the Executive Order to abolish a number of advisory boards and commissions. In many cases, the responsibilities of these advisory groups were returned or transferred to regional, state, or local jurisdiction. An example of this redirection was the abolition of the Lake Tahoe Regional Planning Agency; its activities were turned over to the states of Nevada and California. In addition, President Reagan abolished six river basin commissions; these responsibilities were transferred to the member-states of each commission. A number of other advisory boards were abolished, including the Advisory Board on Ambassadorial Appointments, the Circuit Judge Nominating Committee, and the Tax Court Nominating Commission.

Several advisory boards recommended for abolition in *Mandate* remain in place, including the Interagency Coordinating Council, the Energy Coordinating Council, the Federal Financing Bank Advisory Board, and the Federal Legal Council.

President Reagan created, via Executive Order, several advisory groups which are noteworthy for their intended functions. One of the most ambitious is the system of Federal Regional Councils. Representing each of the ten designated federal regions, the councils have been created to assist in the return of federal programs to local jurisdiction. In addition, the regional councils are to aid in the implementation of block grant programs, and to act as a buffer between federal and local governments during the devolution of federal services. Other commissions created by the President have been praised by *Mandate* contributors, including the Commission on Productivity, the Commission on Housing, and the Commission on Foreign Intelligence.

Some new advisory groups are of dubious importance, such as the Council on Integrity and Efficiency in Federal Programs, the Presidential Council on Federalism, and the Commission on Broadcasting to Cuba. Although the President acted judiciously in the creation of some of these councils, others may be little more than honorary advisory councils with little or no real influence. The leadership of each council will determine its effectiveness. For now, most can be viewed with healthy skepticism.

In addition to those topics already addressed, President Reagan issued orders in a number of housekeeping areas such as compensation for the Iranian hostages and water resources projects. Among those orders the following are noteworthy:

- an order related to the interdiction of illegal aliens;

- several orders dealing with personnel and retirement policies of government employees; and

- amendments to court martial policies.

Analyzing Executive Orders can be a frustrating process. A more systematic cataloging of the orders is desperately needed. Executive Orders should be codified by subject matter; the codification should be supplemented annually to reflect any changes in the status of an Executive Order.

It is essential that the President know if an Executive Order has been promulgated in a particular subject area. It is equally important that each federal department or agency be able to refer to those orders with which it must comply. Since Executive Orders can have a tremendous impact upon all federal agencies and on the public, the reorganization and codification of these orders should be a top priority in the coming year.

## RECOMMENDATIONS
(Action taken on 18 out of 45)

### Government-wide Actions

- Restrict hiring of federal personnel.
  IMPLEMENTED.

- Require that each agency head spend (in actual outlays) only 98 percent of a continuing resolution figure, or resubmit FY 1981 budget.
  BUDGET RESUBMITTED WITH CUTS.

### Regulatory Reform

- Establish a temporarary moratorium on issuance of agency regulations.
  IMPLEMENTED.

- Require approval of all new regulations by a Regulatory Review group prior to actual issuance.
  IMPLEMENTED.

- Require a specific "cost-benefit" analysis for major new regulations.
  IMPLEMENTED.

- Require each agency to submit a calendar of those upcoming regulations mandated by federal legislation.
  IMPLEMENTED.

- Review all existing regulations on a fixed schedule.
  IMPLEMENTED IN PART.

- Revoke E.O. 12092 and E.O. 12191 which implemented President Carter's wage and price guidelines.
  IMPLEMENTED.

- Revoke E.O. 11387, which prevents Americans from sending money abroad without the government's permission, and E.O. 11858, which discourages foreign investment in the U.S.
  NOT IMPLEMENTED.

- Direct the Department of Education to reconsider regulations mandating bilingual education regardless of the policy of local school districts.

  IMPLEMENTED BY DEPARTMENTAL ACTION.

- Restrict the ability of the Department of Education to control institutions which are not federally funded.

  NOT ACCOMPLISHED; SOME PROGRESS IN DEPARTMENT.

- Restrict lobbying and advocacy activities of organizations receiving federal funds; limit the type of quasi-lobbying ("informational" activity) that can be funded by federal grants.

  HANDLED UNEVENLY ON DEPARTMENTAL BASIS.

- Allow intervenor funding programs to be adopted only by those agencies that have specific statutory authority to do so.

  NOT IMPLEMENTED.

- Amend E.O. 11583 to incorporate Senate-passed prohibitions on intervention by the Office of Consumer Affairs in the proceedings of other agencies.

  NOT DONE.

- Limit the circumstances under which grants and contracts can go to groups organized primarily for lobbying and advocacy.

  HANDLED UNEVENLY ON DEPARTMENTAL BASIS.

**Affirmative Action**
- Abolish all reference to "affirmative action" or statistical reporting in all Executive Orders. Alternatively, cease racial classification of all federal government employees.

  NOT IMPLEMENTED.

- Direct the Justice Department to file "pattern or practice" cases only on proof of intent to discriminate, not on statistical appearance of discrimination.

  NOT IMPLEMENTED, BUT SPECIFIC QUOTAS FOR MINORITY HIRING WILL NO LONGER BE SOUGHT AS REMEDY IN THESE ACTIONS.

- Place reasonable limitations on requirements for retrofitting existing urban transporation systems for the handicapped.

  IMPLEMENTED BY DEPARTMENTAL ACTION.

- Redefine the scope of the term "federal contractor" under federal contract compliance requirements.

  ACTION PROPOSED; NOW PENDING.

- Permit program office heads discretionary authority to hire contractors to review FY 1981 contracts to determine if the work could be accomplished by existing personnel.
  IMPLEMENTED IN BUDGET REVIEW.

- Establish a grants index to prevent double payment for the same research project, or duplication of grants and research in the same area.
  IMPLEMENTED IN BUDGET REVIEW.

**Councils and Committees**
- Abolish the following:
  1. Interagency Coordinating Council (E.O. 12075);
     ABOLITION UNDERWAY.

  2. Energy Coordinating Committee (E.O. 12083);
     ABOLISHED.

  3. President's Economic Policy Board (E.O. 11975);
     NOT IMPLEMENTED.

  4. Federal Financing Bank Advisory Board (E.O. 11782);
     NOT IMPLEMENTED.

  5. National Productivity Council (E.O. 12089);
     REPLACED BY OUTSIDE, PRIVATE COUNCIL.

  6. Commission on National Agenda for the 80's;
     SUBMITTED A FINAL REPORT.

  7. Federal Legal Council (E.O. 12146);
     NOT IMPLEMENTED.

  8. President's Council on Youth Opportunity (E.O. 11330):
     NOT IMPLEMENTED.

  9. President's Council on Physical Fitness and Sports (E.O. 11562, as amended by E.O. 11945 and 12098).
     NOT IMPLEMENTED.

  10. Council on Wage & Price Stability.
      ABOLISHED.

**Paperwork**
- Require each department to minimize data collection.
  IMPLEMENTED IN PART.

- Require Secretaries to eliminate duplication, and ensure that no new request for information would increase private sector costs unless a comparable reduction is made elsewhere.
  IMPLEMENTED.

- Seek neither criminal nor civil penalties for non-compliance with any paperwork requirement not properly approved by OMB.
  IMPLEMENTED.

### Public Land Policy

- Issue an Executive Order declaring that for every acre "withdrawn" from public use, equivalent acreage must be released elsewhere in the federal land management system.
  SPIRIT OF RECOMMENDATION IMPLEMENTED BY DEPARTMENTAL ACTION.

- Review land withdrawals to see if the boundaries can be revised to improve availability for exploration and development of Alaska lands.
  SPIRIT OF RECOMMENDATION IMPLEMENTED BY DEPARTMENTAL ACTION.

### Energy and Environment

- Decontrol crude oil and gasoline prices immediately.
  ACCOMPLISHED.

- Revoke E.O. 12185 which requires compliance with federal energy conservation mandates as a prerequisite for federal financial assistance grants and contracts.
  NOT IMPLEMENTED.

- Prepare for abolition of Department of Energy by reorganizing its administrative functions and personnel.
  IMPLEMENTED IN PART.

- Revoke E.O. 12114, which attempts to require environmental impact statements for any activities that might affect the environment anywhere in the world.
  NOT IMPLEMENTED.

### Intelligence

- Repeal E.O. 12036, which limits our ability to protect national security against terrorism, subversion, and direct military threats.
  DRAFT COMPLETED; ACTION PENDING.

- Require agencies to exercise discretion in providing notice to persons who would be affected by release of information under the Freedom of Information Act, allowing them an opportunity to present any argument or defenses available to them.

NOT IMPLEMENTED.

## Trade

- Embargo all non-agricultural products scheduled for export to Communist countries for at least 90 days.

NOT IMPLEMENTED.

- Revise and reissue export control orders that would significantly limit the types of technology that could be exported to the Eastern bloc, and would place the burden of justification on the exporter.

NOT IMPLEMENTED.
- Revoke E.O. 12166, which allows the Export-Import Bank to deny credit on the basis of a nation's policies on human rights, compliance with environmental protection, and terrorism.

NOT IMPLEMENTED.

# Chapter Five

# DEPARTMENT OF AGRICULTURE
By William C. Bailey

During the first year of the Reagan Presidency, the Department of Agriculture was faced with three important legislative challenges: the 1982 budget, reconciliation, and the Agriculture and Food Act of 1981. Through these three initiatives, a substantial number of recommendations contained in *Mandate for Leadership* have been pursued by the Department.

Recommendations concerning departmental personnel were not specifically addressed in the legislative forum. Except for one area, the Secretary has handled personnel matters adequately. With assistance from a full-time personnel advisor, career people have been retained and utilized fully. Where required, lateral transfers have taken place to provide new leadership and avoid potentially troublesome situations. The failure to nominate an Assistant Secretary for Governmental and Public Affairs is a noteworthy shortcoming. The Department has had difficulty getting its legislation passed. A strong individual as Assistant Secretary would be of considerable value.

The primary legislative thrust of the Department has been the Agriculture and Food Act of 1981, not yet signed into law. The Act provides significant insight into the relationship between the Department and the Office of Management and Budget. OMB forced the Department to reverse its policies on reduced sugar and peanut programs because of assurances made by OMB during budget votes. Similarly, when sensing that target prices and payment limitations would be a part of farm legislation, USDA sought approval from OMB. These instances have led to the appearance that farm policy is not under the direction of the Secretary of Agriculture.

Many of the recommendations of *Mandate* were proposed by the Administration through budget reconciliation. However, many of those recommendations did not fare well in Congress.

For instance, the Department announced that it intended to discontinue guaranteed Rural Electrification Administration loans through the Federal Financing Bank. Congress prevented implementation of this *Mandate* recommendation by passing legislation requiring the Federal Financing Bank to make guaranteed loans when requested to do so by the REA.

The size and complexity of the USDA's on- and off-budget credit

*The author wishes to thank Tom Boney, Nabers Cabannis, Joseph Halow, and Burleigh Leonard for their assistance in the preparation of this chapter.

programs may well have been a factor in the Department's failure to fulfill some recommendations. As new personnel become more familiar with the vast array of credit programs, substantive changes should result.

## School Lunch and Other Nutrition Programs

Rather than suggesting a mere reduction in the meal subsidies, the Administration proposed complete elimination of subsidies for school children of middle- and upper-income families. The proposal was justified philosophically by the argument that the federal government should not subsidize those who are not in need. Nonetheless, schools contended that such a change would drive up prices to the point that many would drop out of the program, thus forcing program shutdown due to insufficient participation. Needy and non-needy alike thereby would not be served.

Congress did not adopt the Administration's proposal. Instead, it substantially reduced subsidies to non-needy children and tightened eligibility standards for free and reduced price meals. The price for these lunches was raised from 20 to 40 cents.

The debate over the elimination of the subsidy for middle-and upper-income children highlights the controversy over the mission of the school lunch program. Enactment of the Administration's proposal would have made school lunches purely a welfare program, a change from its historical purpose. Initially, subsidies were provided to all children, regardless of need; no child received a guaranteed free lunch. The transition of the program into a welfare program raised a second problem—coordination with the food stamp program. All free lunch recipients were also eligible to receive free food stamps. In essence, they are paid twice for the same meals. The Administration's proposal to eliminate this duplication of benefits also failed.

Rather than continuing a national debate on the merits of subsidizing non-needy children, the Administration should push Congress to consolidate breakfast and lunch funds and allow states to establish criteria for allocating a limited level of funding to provide meals for school children. As education is traditionally state-funded, it is reasonable that states, not the federal government, should manage the allocation of meal funds for school children. Additional savings can also be made through a dramatic reduction in funding for the summer food service program (already partially accomplished), the child care food program, and the school breakfast program.

## Food Stamps

The Administration's initial food stamp reform recommendations, and subsequent congressional action, have done little to change the fundamental structural weaknesses of the food stamp program or to restrict long-term participation increases.

Unlike Administration recommendations in other welfare-like programs, few households were actually terminated from participation as a result of proposals put forward by the Administration. Indeed, current estimates are that participation and costs for FY 1982 will be almost the same as in FY 1981—$11.4 billion going to 22 million participants—even after $1.6 billion in savings through the reconciliation process.

Approximately 23 million Americans were receiving food stamps in the spring of 1981. Estimates indicate that from 2.0 to 5.5 percent of food stamp households may be eliminated from participation by the establishment of a 130 percent gross income limit. Thus, less than a million Americans were actually removed from the food stamp program. It continues to provide monthly food stamp benefits to one in every ten Americans.

The Administration's major structural reform met significant congressional resistance from Republicans and Democrats. Its proposal to offset food stamp benefits for households with children participating in the school lunch program did not pass either House or Senate Agriculture Committee.

In place of this reform, opponents of the school lunch overlap provision succeeded in implementing a three year/three month delay in the Thrifty Food Plan indexing. Index revisions had occurred semi-annually in recent years. Last year, the system was modified to allow index revisions only every twelve months. The new change would modify the index costs every fifteen months during fiscal years 1982-1984. This provision has the effect of accomplishing short-term (i.e., three-year) savings by postponing indexing costs.

Another "savings" provision adopted during reconciliation is also essentially temporary. In the calculation of food stamp benefits, a standard deduction of $85 per month is subtracted from each household's gross income before determining benefit levels. Additionally, households may be eligible for up to $115 in additional deductions for a combination of excess shelter or child care costs. To its credit, the Administration had recommended a permanent freeze on these deductions, which have been indexed annually. The Congress adopted only a temporary freeze until July 1, 1983, at which time indexing will be resumed with consequent increased costs. Again, program costs have simply been pushed into future years by postponement rather than fundamental reform.

The net effect of the 1981 reconciliation reforms has been an across-the-board postponement in benefit increases for all participating households. Needed are targeted reductions and the elimination of certain categories of households from participation in the program.

Among such needed reductions are:

- Inclusion of housing subsidies or other "in kind" benefits in the definition of income for purposes of determining food stamp eligibility and benefits.

- Lower gross income limit, including the possibility of allowing states to determine food stamp eligibility based on income standards in the Aid to Families with Dependent Children program. Approximately 7 percent of participating households continue to have gross incomes above the poverty line.

- Establishing more stringent requirements for work registration and job search or developing mandatory workfare program for able-bodied recipients. Less than 20 percent of all households contain a working household member.

- Re-establishing a purchase requirement. Amendments were defeated in both the House and Senate which would have reinstated a purchase requirement with exemption for the elderly, the disabled and those at lowest income levels. Administration support of concept—which affects 55 percent of households—would improve chances of passage.

The establishment of a block grant in lieu of the present food stamp program would be a more fundamental reform. The food stamp program—standing alone, in combination with child nutrition programs, or included within Aid to Families with Dependent Children—is a likely candidate for block grant treatment in an Administration which believes that such program decisions can best be managed at the state or local level.

**Foreign Agricultural Policy**

Failure to define clearly foreign agricultural policy goals has led to problems for the Department. Nowhere has this been more evident than in the handling of the Soviet grain embargo.

Initially, the Administration was expected to lift the embargo immediately. It did not act on the embargo for about 100 days. Even then, action appeared to have been more a part of an effort to push farm legislation through Congress than a part of a coordinated plan to encourage U.S. exports. In addition, Administration action did not clarify policies with regard to sales to the Soviet Union.

There was, furthermore, a *de facto* embargo for an additional month or so because of the difficulty in arriving at a U.S. position on size and timing of sales. The Special Trade Representative, an individual with little or no agricultural background, headed the delegation to the Soviet Union, reducing the USDA control over the negotiations. In this instance, good rapport existed between the Office of the Special Trade Representative and the USDA. This might not always be the case.

Had the United States repealed the embargo promptly, the Soviets would have been in a more adverse negotiating position: they would not have known the size of their own crops, nor would they have had any indication of the size of the crops of other nations. In addition, they may not have entered into long-term agreements with the other countries. The delays gave the Soviets time to decrease their dependence on the United States and, simultaneously, increase U.S. dependence on the Soviet Union. As a consequence, the Soviets have now entered into contracts with other countries that are multi-year and that provide for increasing purchases.

The Soviets' long-term agreements with other countries might not affect directly the volume of grain exported from the United States, because the demand from other areas would compensate it for the lost Soviet sales. Although probably true for the first year, this sale could lead to problems in succeeding years. Other exporting nations are building their production bases and will, weather permitting, produce enough to cover their increased sales to the Soviet Union plus sales to their "traditional" customers. In contrast, the United States has instituted a fifteen percent voluntary set-aside program for wheat for the 1982 crop, and is considering similar measures for corn and soybeans.

Because the Soviet Union is clearly no friend of the United States, some may argue that providing them with food is an unwise move. This argument is counterproductive. If trade is to be exploited for diplomatic policy purposes, the consequence to U.S. farmers and the nation must also be analyzed. If the United States does not sell the grain to the Soviet Union (or to whomever wants it), then, under existing legislation, someone then pays for storing it, pays farmers to restrict future productions, and ultimately pays them for the difference between the going prices and the target prices. That someone will ultimately be the U.S. taxpayer. To further aggravate the situation, the U.S. economy will lose export revenue needed to help offset a negative balance of trade. The President did lift the embargo, but his failure to do so quickly and decisively may raise questions about his commitment to free trade. The consequences of his delays are almost as onerous as a continuation of the embargo itself.

In less controversial areas, the Administration's policy goals appear to be clear-cut and well-defined. Its position with regard to an international commodity agreement for grains is well known. The Administration has acted favorably in export areas in which it is not expected to expend funds. Export initiatives in which government funding is involved have come from Congress, not the Administration. Congress has moved to institute a revolving fund for CCC credit sales abroad; the Senate version of the farm bill includes an ill-defined stand-by authority for an export subsidy.

In its efforts to eliminate export restrictions, the Administration appears to be concentrating on the European Community's agricultural policy. This is a questionable proposition; the Community has declared that its Common Agricultural Policy, in effect for about ten years, is non-negotiable. The Community buys from the United States only what it needs and exports when and where it wishes. Strong U.S. attacks on the Community could stiffen rather than weaken European resolve.

The United States may be preoccupied with trifles. Changed policies would only lead to minimal improvements in exports. Administration efforts would be better directed at a general world-wide reduction on trade restrictions.

## Price Supports

Early this year, the Department indicated its intention to modify farm commodity price support programs to make them less dependent upon federal intervention and more responsive to signals from the market. This intent was evident in the Department's version of the 1981 farm bill, in which target prices were eliminated and the Secretary was given virtual "carte blanche" authority to tune commodity programs to the forces of supply and demand. While Congress is not expected to give the Secretary a free hand, it seems likely that he will emerge from the farm bill debate with more discretionary authority than he currently has.

The Department increased significantly the spread between the loan level and the release level for the 1981 crops of wheat and corn. The wheat spread was raised from $1.20 for the 1980 crop to $1.45 for the 1981 crop. The corn spread was raised from 56 cents in 1980 to 75 cents in 1981. Increases in the spreads for sorghum, barley, and oats also were implemented in 1981. The extent to which the Department will be able to continue this practice will depend upon the provisions that Congress includes in the 1981 farm bill currently under consideration.

The Department has done less well in providing for annual increases in commodity loan and target levels that are in keeping with the overall rate of inflation. The rates of increase in the loan and target levels for the 1981 crops of wheat and corn were considerably less than the 10.2 percent increase in the consumer price index (CPI). The rates of increase in the loan and target levels for the 1981 crops of cotton and rice were for the most part greater than the increase in the CPI. It should be noted that the Secretary's discretion to set target levels is limited by a cost-of-production formula established by law. The Department sought to correct this problem by recommending to Congress that the cost-of-production formula be eliminated in the 1981 farm bill. The Senate adopted this recommendation; the House has not.

### Dairy

The Department has labored diligently to reduce the level of the dairy price support from 80 percent of parity. In March of 1981, the Department pushed through Congress a bill that prevented the increase in the dairy price support scheduled for April 1, 1981. This successful effort was followed by a campaign to increase the Secretary's discretionary authority to adjust dairy price supports to better balance supplies with demand. The Department's recommendation to lower the minimum dairy price support from 80 percent to 70 percent of parity is expected to be enacted for fiscal year 1982.

### Interest Rates

The Department has put into practice a policy which establishes an interest rate for CCC commodity loans that covers the cost of borrowing from the Treasury. Adjustments of the interest rates are currently made every six months; the interest rate is pegged to the rate charged by Treasury during the month prior to the adjustment. A proposal to adjust interest rates on a monthly basis is under consideration within the Department.

## RECOMMENDATIONS
(Action taken on 13 out of 42)

### Personnel

- Appoint full-time personnel advisor to the Secretary.
  IMPLEMENTED.

- Move departmental budget responsibilities to Assistant Secretary for Administration.
  IMPLEMENTED.

### Trade Policy

- Promptly repeal grain embargo.
  EMBARGO LIFTED, BUT WITH DELAY.

- Exercise caution in establishing International Commodity Agreements.
  IMPLEMENTED.

31

- The Special Trade Representative should have real competence in agriculture.
  NOT IMPLEMENTED.
- Restore CCC export credit program.
  NOT IMPLEMENTED.
- Minimize import restrictions.
  IMPLEMENTED.
- Continue export promotion.
  IMPLEMENTED.
- Continue P.L. 480 with the Department of Agriculture having a stronger hand in decision-making.
  NOT IMPLEMENTED.
- USDA should become more active in international agricultural development.
  NOT IMPLEMENTED.

**Natural Resources**
- Allow the Interior Department to handle dispute on 160-acre limitation.  IMPLEMENTED. DEPARTMENT HAS NOT ENTERED THE DISPUTE.
- Resolve RARE II program.
  NOT IMPLEMENTED.
- Develop a sound policy for the Resource Planning Act.
  NOT IMPLEMENTED.

**Energy**
- Retain energy unit attached to the Secretary's office to emphasize securing of adequate fuel supplies for farmers in the event of a disruption of oil supplies.
  NOT IMPLEMENTED.
- Emphasize biomass energy production, but without subsidies (from DOE chapter).
  ADMINISTRATION REQUESTED TERMINATION OF SUBSIDIES AND LOAN GUARANTEE PROGRAM.

**Price Support**
- Widen range between the loan and release levels.
  IMPLEMENTED.

- Raise loans and targets to partially reflect inflation.
  IMPLEMENTED FOR WHEAT AND CORN, BUT NOT COTTON AND RICE.

- Adjust the farmer-held reserve to reduce excess stocks.
  REQUESTED BY ADMINISTRATION; IN CONGRESS.

- Increase the discretionary authority of the Secretary.
  REQUESTED BY ADMINISTRATION; IN CONGRESS.

- Reduce dairy price support level from 80 percent of parity.
  IMPLEMENTED.

## Payment Limitation

- Reduce payment limitation.
  NOT IMPLEMENTED.

## Low-Yield Disaster Program

- Expedite implementation of the Federal Crop Insurance Act.
  IMPLEMENTED.

- Terminate Low-Yield Disaster Program.
  REQUESTED BY ADMINISTRATION; CONGRESS HAS NOT ACTED.

## Agricultural Credit Policies

- Increase interest rate on loans to one percent above cost of money.
  NOT IMPLEMENTED FULLY.

- Cut in half total commitments to guarantee new loans.
  REQUESTED BY ADMINISTRATION; CONGRESS HAS NOT ACTED.

- Reduce interest subsidy on farm ownership and farm operating loans.
  REQUESTED BY ADMINISTRATION; CONGRESS DID NOT IMPLEMENT FULLY.

- Secretary should ask Farmers Home Administration for an audit of its activities.
  NOT IMPLEMENTED.

- Secretary should request General Accounting Office to inquire into operations of the agency.
  NOT IMPLEMENTED.

- Increase interest rates and eliminate "above moderate income housing loans" for the Rural Housing Insurance Fund.

INTEREST RATES INCREASED; GUARANTEED LOANS ELIMINATED.

### Rural Electrification and Development

- Increase interest rates, eliminate the direct telephone loan, and curtail the guaranteed loan program in the Rural Electrification Administration.

ADMINISTRATION REQUESTED; CONGRESS HAS NOT IMPLEMENTED.

- Increase interest rate on industrial development loans to cost of money.

ADMINISTRATION RECOMMENDED; CONGRESS HAS NOT ACTED.

- Increase interest rate on Rural Development Insurance Fund loans to cost of money.

PARTIALLY IMPLEMENTED.

### Consumer Issues

- The Department should require hard evidence before questioning the wholesomeness or nutritional qualities of various foods.

ADMINISTRATION EXERCISING CAUTION.

### Food Stamps

- Prevent strikers from participating in the food stamp program.

ADMINISTRATION DID NOT REQUEST; CONGRESS IMPLEMENTED.

- In computing income, all forms of income, including "in kind" income, should be included.

ADMINISTRATION REQUESTED LIMITED CHANGE. SENATE ADOPTED; HOUSE HAS NOT ACTED.

- Adjust food stamp benefits annually, rather than semi-annually.

IMPLEMENTED.

- Stiffen assets test.

ADMINISTRATION REQUESTED; CONGRESS HAS NOT YET ACTED.

- Reinstate the purchase requirement.

NO ACTION BY ADMINISTRATION. HOUSE AND SENATE DEFEATED PROPOSAL.

- Reassert the genuine nutritional emphasis of the program.
  NOT IMPLEMENTED.

- Eliminate overlap between school lunch and food stamp program.
  ADMINISTRATION REQUESTED; CONGRESS REJECTED.

### Supplemental Food Programs

- Hold FY 1982 budget at FY 1981 level for supplemental food programs while administrative adjustments are made.
  ADMINISTRATION REQUESTED FY 1982 BUDGET BELOW FY 1981 LEVEL; CONGRESS APPROVED HIGHER LEVEL.

### School Lunch

- Reduce middle- and upper-level income subsidy.
  IMPLEMENTED.

## Chapter Six
# DEPARTMENT OF COMMERCE
### By Charles H. Bradford
### and William R. Worthen, Esq.

*Mandate for Leadership* compared the Department of Commerce's organizational structure to a feudal kingdom. Its widely diverse functions—ranging from weather forecasting to measuring GNP—operate as independent fiefdoms. Nevertheless, the new Secretary has given the Department a strong sense of cohesion. Mr. Baldrige's close personal relationship with President Reagan has improved access to the decision-making process at the White House. Cooperation also seems to have been made easier by the cabinet council system adopted by the President.

A detailed audit of proposed short-term recommendations follows this overview, and reveals uneven application of forty-nine specific recommendations. Nineteen recommendations either have been adopted or are in the process of review or adoption. This overview discusses most of those recommendations specifically adopted and follows with a review of the policy problems inherent in the Administration's failure to adopt other recommendations.

## Positive Ledger

On the positive side of the ledger, *Mandate's* principal administrative recommendation for the Maritime Administration has been implemented, namely, the transfer of MARAD to the Department of Transportation. This is a very important step toward creating an integrated transportation policy, allowing consideration of the maritime alternative in the total mix of transportation systems.

In the statistical and economic areas, the Office of Federal Statistical Policy and Standards has been transferred to the Executive Office of the President, as is appropriate. The Interagency Coordinating Council, the Energy Coordinating Committee, and the National Productivity Council—all recommended for abolition—have indeed been abolished. However, the Administration plans to announce soon the creation of a National Productivity Advisory Committee made up of private sector participants. Such a committee could make a significant contribution.

The Administration did not seek repeal of the authority for a five-year population census as recommended. Nevertheless, the

---

*The authors wish to thank Leonard D. Ellis for his assistance in the preparation of this chapter.

decision not to seek budget authority for such an effort is a proper interim policy. Repeal should still be sought.

The National Oceanographic and Atmospheric Administration (NOAA) has begun to emphasize its important professional, scientific, and research missions, while playing down its political role, as recommended. The elimination of the highly politicized coastal energy impact programs and coastal zone management state grants will help in this process.

The Economic Development Administration (EDA), called by *Mandate* a "classic Great Society program" and a "boondoggle," has been dramatically reduced in size pursuant to the Omnibus Budget Reconciliation Act of 1981. The President's proposal for complete elimination was compromised in the effort to secure passage of the Budget Reconciliation Act in the House of Representatives.

The Regional Development Commissions, established pursuant to Title V of the Public Works and Economic Development Act of 1965, as amended, were abolished as recommended. The better-known Appalachian Regional Commission, which has separate statutory authority, continues to function at a reduced level of funding. The Appalachian Commission also should be eliminated.

The Administration budget proposed elimination of the United States Travel Service, largely on the grounds advanced in *Mandate*—duplication of private efforts. No other proposal under Commerce's stewardship was so completely rejected by Congress. The "Fun in the Sun" lobby not only saved the Service, it was able to secure a far broader mandate based on the spurious arguments that foreign governments are aggressive competitors and state governments use tax dollars to encourage travel. The Service now is called the U.S. Travel and Tourism Administration, and is headed by an under secretary.

In the area of international trade, a series of successes and partial successes are identifiable. The Anti-boycott Law remains intact. The Administration has supported a major broadening of the anti-trust exemption embodied in the Webb-Pomerene Act, accommodating the creation of trading companies. This bill has been approved in the Senate and now is pending in four separate House committees. In addition, private financing of major integrated systems will be made more readily available to American businesses by allowing financial institutions to have a limited equity role in the trading companies. These provisions should prove particularly valuable to U.S. businesses competing for major building contracts in the developing countries; these infra-structure projects often require major integrated package proposals.

The *Mandate* recommendations for distinguishing between developing nations using socialist and capitalist economic models were echoed in the President's presentation to the recent Summit meeting in Cancun, Mexico. Through this policy, the United States rejects the concept of global economic redistribution through grants and soft loans by both the World Bank and the International Monetary Fund. The concept of the North-South debate espoused by former Chancellor Brandt of West Germany is being wisely repudiated. Instead, the United States will be reviewing the broad picture of trade concessions; specifically, it will look at U.S. import tariffs with an eye toward their impact on developing countries.

By placing the primary emphasis on the capacity of developing countries to generate capital, the United States will implicitly favor those countries following a capitalist development model, since they have the natural advantages of local capital concentrations and more favorable investment climates. This policy replaces apologies for western economic success with a defense of a capitalist/free enterprise system. Emphasizing trade over aid encourages developing nations to adopt economic policies which at least have a chance of success. This may prove one of the most important contributions of the new Administration in the area of international relations.

The Administration has also recommended improvements in the Foreign Corrupt Practices Act. The suggested elimination of the more egregious cases of interference in American and foreign business activity should help American exporters become more competitive, particularly in the markets in developing countries. This unilateral "morality" legislation has been carefully reviewed by the Administration and has been found wanting. Consistent with *Mandate* recommendations, the President has proposed to eliminate the jurisdiction of the Securities and Exchange Commission and to repeal the accounting provisions of the Act. The Justice Department would continue to have jurisdiction for deliberate falsification of records. Action on major modifications of the Act appears imminent in the Senate; House action is less certain. While outright repeal of the politically popular prohibition on bribery remains unlikely, the elimination of unilateral export disincentives inherent in the current law might be achieved.

The Administration made proposals in the March budget for a major reduction in the capital contribution to the Ex-Im Bank. The proposals met with intense criticism and did not survive the negotiations designed to secure passage of the President's budget. Although the Administration ultimately failed to secure the major reductions, it was successful in fending off the massive increases proposed by the previous administration and recommended by many in Congress.

The Carter Administration decision to increase direct loans made by the Ex-Im Bank at substantially subsidized interest rates was a major break with past practice. As *Mandate* detailed, this approach amounted to a direct taxpayer subsidy for many of the largest American companies, made at the expense of the general economy. Federal credit subsidies of all types, which distort the marketplace, have been made a target for reform by the present Administration. It is hoped that the movement away from federal credit subsidies will be pursued with an eye toward competing with foreign credit subsidies.

The Administration also has chosen the reasonable middle course with respect to our economic relations with South Africa. Consistent with *Mandate* recommendations, the President has resisted all efforts to impose new trade and investment restrictions and at the same time has maintained the embargo on arms exports.

As a general matter, the Administration has moved toward liberalization of a number of unilateral trade restrictions. The human rights limitations have been substantially liberalized; foreign nuclear development has been freed from the overly narrow interpretation of non-proliferation concerns; and taxation of foreign income has been greatly eased. These changes show movement away from the use of trade as a method of imposing moral judgments on trading partners and are fully consistent with recommendations designed to reduce unilateral export restrictions.

Finally, also on the positive side of the ledger, the new Administration has abandoned the efforts of the Carter Administration to achieve major increases in American exports through specialized tax incentive subsidy programs. Instead, the Administration has moved aggressively to reduce regulatory impediments to economic growth. The greatest single stimulant to the American free enterprise system is the Economic Recovery Tax Act of 1981. This keystone of the Reagan economic program will promote economic growth within the United States and will enhance the position of the United States as a world trading partner.

## Negative Ledger

The largest Administration failure is in the trade field, a fact which in light of the foregoing accomplishments is ironic. Simply put, the Administration has failed to formulate a coherent policy for East-West trade. Because of the importance of this subject to a conservative administration, the *Mandate* Commerce Department report concentrated heavily on it. None of its recommendations has been implemented.

In a discussion of trade problems during October 1981 hearings, the Under Secretary of Commerce for International Trade, Lionel H. Olmer, made a damning admission: "This Administration understands these problems [of U.S. business] and will issue clear guidelines *once policy is decided*." (Emphasis added.)

Unfortunately for American security, time does not stand still while the Administration formulates policy. During the intervening period, the Soviets and our European allies have come perilously close to agreeing on the largest single East-West trade deal ever concluded: the Urengoi-Yamburg natural gas pipeline (Yamal). Belatedly, the Administration has become aware of the massive security and economic problems which this pipeline would create. The President used the forum of the Ottawa Summit of major OECD nations in July to oppose the deal forcefully.

Even more unfortunate, however, is that this opposition is fully consistent with a long American tradition—discussed in some detail in *Mandate*—of rhetoric which is completely at odds with action. During the period of policy formulation, the U.S. lifted the grain embargo and licensed the sale of Caterpillar pipe-laying equipment to the U.S.S.R. *Mandate* recommended that the lifting of the grain embargo be tied to an embargo of non-agricultural trade, particularly of high technology items. This was not done.

Since the United States has virtually no direct financial stake in the Yamal pipeline, opposition to building it costs nearly nothing. The case against the Yamal pipeline is so strong that it should dictate an American policy designed to block the deal.

The European view of the deal is based on their reliance on energy imports. According to the State Department, European reliance on natural gas increased by about 50 percent between 1973 and 1980. The increase for residential and commercial sectors, where substitution is totally impractical, was 80 percent. At the same time, European gas discoveries, largely in the North Sea, have not kept pace with demand. Current production rates do not now accommodate demand growth but, nevertheless, will exhaust known European reserves within twenty years.

Further, European interests have a substantial stake in exporting manufactured goods to the U.S.S.R. As an example, 11 percent of West German steel and machine tool production is purchased by the Soviets and, understandably, the West Germans have taken the lead in pursuing the Yamal deal. The Soviets are currently arranging purchases, at concessionary rates, of $11 billion worth of Western equipment. Some observers believe that total Soviet purchases in the West will approximate the total cost of the project, roughly $45 billion. This huge expenditure would be paid for through the sales of Yamal gas by the Ruhrgas Company (the West German distributor). Thus, the cost of these purchases will represent no drain on Soviet hard currency reserves.

From the Soviet point of view, gas sales to the West are mandatory. Of some $19.5 billion in hard currency earnings in 1979, $11.3 billion was earned through energy sales. In 1980, the proportion rose to

$23.8 billion and $15.1 billion respectively (almost two-thirds). As noted in *Mandate*, a major decline in exportable Soviet oil can be expected in the mid-1980s. Thus, massive natural gas exports represent the only viable Soviet option for securing hard currency over the long term, increasing penetration of the European energy market, and maintaining the energy dependence of satellite countries. The Yamal pipeline is the only way the Soviets can adequately ship gas in the necessary quantity within the required time.

Given both the economic interest of the Europeans in this deal and the advanced stage of negotiations, mere unilateral pressure from the United States to abandon the deal certainly would fail. Moreover, it could produce the major NATO rupture which the Soviet Union has sought for thirty years. The governments of our European allies already face tremendous internal opposition from neutralist "ban the bomb" groups; this could give these groups additional ammunition.

The President recognized this problem when he suggested an American-sponsored energy alternative at Ottawa. An American energy package, which should have included U.S. guarantees of European access to American coal and possibly African Liquified Natural Gas (LNG), was not developed in time for the Summit. This might have been rationalized before the July conference; the failure to produce such a package in the three months since July is inexcusable. Direct responsibility for this failure cannot easily be assigned. However, the major responsibility falls upon the offices headed by the Under Secretary of State of Economic Affairs, the Under Secretary of Commerce for International Trade, and, of course, the Department of Energy. The absence of concrete energy proposals emphasizes the problem of not having an East-West trade policy.

An East-West trade policy ultimately depends on overall attitudes toward the Soviet Union and its internal and external empire. The concept of detente with the Soviets has rationalized trade on grounds that involving the Soviets in a web of agreements would restrain their aggression. Evidence from Chad, Cambodia, North Yemen, Somalia, Zaire, El Salvador, and Afghanistan proves otherwise. Abandonment of detente must include a different policy on East-West trade.

The current failure to adopt a trade policy is a consequence of the continuing ambiguity in overall U.S. policies toward the Soviets. In formulating foreign policy toward the Soviets, the U.S. should consider the symbiotic nature of the Soviet political/economic system. All financing of military and economic activity is based on the five-year plans adopted by the Central Committee. Thus, all "economic" development has a military dimension. Western capital support of the Soviet economy allows the Soviets to divert resources into military expansion.

42

In the context of the Export Administration Act of 1979, no "foreign policy control" exists which applies to the Soviets. All trade with the Soviets should be viewed under the "national security control" umbrella. The Administration has failed to do this.

Such an approach should not apply to other Comecon nations. Major distinctions can be drawn between some of these countries and the Soviet Union based on the Jackson-Vanik amendment. Trade could be used to draw certain Eastern Bloc countries away from the Soviets. Such trade should not, however, involve transfers of capital into these nations, as capital transfers help the Communist countries overcome the chronic problem of socialism: capital deficits. If the United States is to approach the Eastern Bloc nations with a policy of overt competition, solving one of their greatest economic problems is unwise.

Finally, no Comecon nation should be exempted from the embargo on high technology exports. Such exemptions would only serve to undermine the entire system of controls against the U.S.S.R. Technology exports to these countries are easily available to the Soviets and represent an alarming defect in present policies.

The timing of a new East-West trade policy is very delicate, particularly in light of the troubled U.S. relations with Europe. Pressure at this time would be inappropriate and counterproductive. However, multilateral action would be a realistic response if the Soviets try to suppress Solidarity in Poland. In the meantime, the U.S. should impose this policy unilaterally as it applies to the Soviets without pressing our allies to adopt it.

## RECOMMENDATIONS
### (Action taken on 19 out of 49)

**East-West Trade**

- Trade policy should be defined by national origin and/or destination, focusing on the national security interests of the United States.

  NOT DONE UNIFORMLY.

- Embargo all non-agricultural trade with the Soviet bloc for 90 days while lifting the grain embargo against the Soviet Union.

  GRAIN EMBARGO LIFTED; NO NON-AGRICULTRAL TRADE EMBARGO. (SHOULD HAVE BEEN A PACKAGE.)

- Abolish the program of general licensing for U.S.-U.S.S.R. trade and substitute a case-by-case review.

  NOT ABOLISHED, BUT GENERAL LICENSING NOW APPLIES TO A SMALLER NUMBER OF CASES.

43

- Establish non-conclusive presumption against East-West trade.
  NOT DONE.

- Base East-West trade on political, not economic, grounds.
  NOT DONE.

- Free trade should be the dominant approach to all trade not subject to national security controls.
  SOME EXPORT RESTICTIONS REMOVED. IMPORT RESTRICTIONS REMAIN.

**General Trade Policy**

- Maintain current trade limitations with South Africa but do not impose new restrictions.
  DONE.

- Revise Foreign Corrupt Practices Act by legislation or by rescission of that part of the SEC budget applied to enforcement provisions.
  IN PROCESS.

- Maintain Anti-Boycott Law.
  DONE.

- Extend federal antitrust exemption contained in Webb-Pomerene Act to broad range of export and export-financing mechanisms.
  IN PROCESS.

- Strengthen exports by strengthening the domestic economy, e.g., lowering business taxes and reducing business regulations.
  IN PROCESS.

- Current credit policy should move away from the practice of subsidizing direct loans except where "unfair" foreign credit competition can be shown.
  IN PROCESS.

- Reject increase in Ex-Im Bank capital.
  PROPOSED. STOPPED MAJOR INCREASE.

- Design mechanism to identify foreign credit offenders.
  NOT DONE.

- Designate Comecon countries as largely non-creditworthy.
  NOT DONE.

- Reduce staff of U.S. Trade Representative (USTR) by 50 percent.

  NOT DONE.

- Either strengthen DISC or bargain it away in GATT negotiations.

  DISC WILL NOT BE STRENGTHENED. ITS FUTURE AND RELATIONSHIP TO GATT IN DOUBT.

### Import Policy

- Secure reduction in Japanese agricultural restrictions or impose import restrictions on Japanese exports.

  NOT DONE, GENERALLY. A VOLUNTARY RESTRICTION ON AUTO IMPORTS HAS BEEN ACHIEVED.

- Show greater willingness to impose import restrictions as retaliation where trading partners refuse to lower their trade barriers.

  NO EVIDENCE IN EITHER DIRECTION.

- Distinguish between socialist economic model and capitalist economic model for purposes of import restrictions on developing nations. Favor capitalist models.

  IN PROCESS.

- Do not use Orderly Marketing Agreements (OMAs) to prop up dying United States industry over a long period of time.

  OMAS STILL IN USE.

- Move away from domestic subsidies and quotas for food and animal products except where foreign competition is subsidized.

  NOT DONE.

### Executive Orders

- Repeal limit on transfers of funds abroad. Require reporting to Commerce Department.

  NOT DONE.

- Repeal restrictions on foreign investments in the United States.

  NOT DONE.

- Strengthen Cuban trade embargo.

  NOT DONE.

- Ex-Im Bank loans should be based on commercial and financial considerations except where recipient is a non-MFN or embargoed nation.

  NOT DONE.

- Ex-Im Bank loans to states suspected of harboring terrorists should be limited.

  NOT DONE.

### General Policy Problems

- Eliminate conflict between Commerce Secretary's role as chief trade advocate and chief administrator of export controls by administrative and/or legislative action.

  NOT DONE.

- Remove Foreign Commercial Service Officers from Comecon countries. Transfer duties to Foreign Service Officers.

  NOT DONE.

- Transfer East-West trade development responsibilities from Commerce to State.

  TRANSFER OF CONTROL TO DOD UNDER CONSIDERATION. IMPLEMENTATION OF THIS OPTION WOULD BE MAJOR IMPROVEMENT.

### Maritime Administration

- Transfer Maritime Administration to the Department of Transportation.

  DONE.

- Reach maritime policy decision between the alternatives of (1) phasing out shipbuilding and operating subsidy programs and deregulating the industry; (2) maintaining the present program; or (3) substantially increasing federal financial contribution to program and moving program to the Department of Defense. Shipping capacity should be viewed in the context of the entire alliance system, not just American capacity.

  NOT DONE.

### Statistical and Economic Areas

- Repeal authority for a five-year census.

  NOT DONE, BUT NO FUNDING PROVIDED.

- Remove Office of Federal Statistical Policy and Standards to the Executive Office of the President.

  DONE.

- Abolish the Interagency Coordinating Council.
  IN PROCESS.

- Abolish the National Productivity Council.
  IN PROCESS. GOVERNMENT BODY BEING REPLACED BY AN OUTSIDE PRIVATE COUNCIL.

- Abolish the Energy Coordinating Committee.
  DONE.

### National Oceanic and Atmospheric Administration

- Focus NOAA on scientific research and reduce policy role.
  IN PROCESS.

- Increase funding for National Sea Grant College program by 10 percent per year for five years.
  NOT DONE.

- Decentralize NOAA fully by regions, or close the Northwest Administrative Service Office.
  NEITHER DONE.

- Transfer oil-spill damage research and offshore oil exploration from Interior's Bureau of Land Management to NOAA.
  NOT DONE.

- Consolidate ocean pollution research by Environmental Protection Agency (EPA) and NOAA and move to NOAA or to EPA.
  NOT DONE.

- As the economic policy underlying the Economic Development Administration (EDA) is unsound, it should be abolished.
  PROPOSED DRASTIC REDUCTION IN FUNDING.

- Abolish Regional Development Program (Regional Commissions).
  DONE, EXCEPT APPALACHIAN COMMISSION (SEPARATE AUTHORITY).

- Abolish Minority Business Development Agency (MBDA) transferring any essential functions to the Small Business Administration (SBA).
  NOT DONE. MERGER TALKS GOING ON.

- The U.S. Travel Service should be abolished.
  UPGRADED, NOT ABOLISHED.

47

- Fund Patent and Trademark Office through its own fees.
  NOT DONE.

- Increase staff of General Counsel's Office while maintaining decentralized character.
  NOT DONE. STAFF DECREASED AND CENTRALIZED.

- The Department of Commerce should take the lead in two broad economic policy areas: improving productivity and lightening the burden of regulation on American business.
  NOT DONE, BUT COMMERCE IS INVOLVED IN BOTH ISSUES.

Chapter Seven
# DEPARTMENT OF DEFENSE
By William C. Green

The increasing vulnerability of our strategic deterrent forces and the decreasing readiness of our general purpose forces pose unacceptable risks for the security of the United States and our allies. Recognizing this, *Mandate for Leadership* set forth a series of policy recommendations aimed at restoring American military power to the extent necessary to meet our vital national security requirements.

After ten months in office, the Reagan Administration's record on defense policy bears little resemblance to *Mandate's* proposed agenda. The Administration has limited itself to modest increases in the underfunded Carter program and a few praiseworthy advances in procurement reform. While Soviet weapons investment over the past decade has exceeded that of the United States by over $355 billion—some 90 percent per year—and Soviet arms production yearly outstrips that of the U.S. three-to-one, the Reagan defense spending request for this fiscal year is only one percent higher than Jimmy Carter's. The FY 1982 defense budget was presented to Congress without benefit of an articulated policy framework or Reagan posture statement. There is as yet no Reagan Five-Year Defense Plan to guide our defense improvements. Although the President has pledged to close the window of vulnerability, comparative force analyses show that under the Administration's current program, the period of strategic vulnerability is growing deeper and broader.

## Strategic Forces

At the heart of the Administration's deficiencies in defense policy and planning is its failure to address U.S. strategic force vulnerability and modernization requirements in a timely or coherent fashion.

The Administration's strategic force decisions fall woefully short of the objectives in *Mandate* in two fundamental respects. First, the Administration has failed to implement critical, time-urgent quick fixes to our nuclear deterrent forces, thus perpetuating their vulnerability. Second, its key strategic initiative—MX basing—is strategically incomprehensible because it fails to respond to the need to provide for the survivability of U.S. land-based forces.

The strategic program recommendations contained in *Mandate for Leadership* stem from the recognition that our existing strategic forces have become vulnerable to a pre-emptive strike. Immediately reducing this vulnerability is a matter of the highest national priority.

49

At the same time, efforts should be made to ensure future strategic force survivability, endurance, and utility.

*Mandate* first set forth a number of strategic quick-fix solutions, including: rebasing Minuteman III in a multiple protective structure mode; rebasing our B-52 squadrons inland; increasing bomber alert rates and escape space; and accelerating production of air-launched cruise missiles (ALCMs), Trident submarines, and sea-launched ballistic and cruise missiles.

The Administration's strategic program ostensibly begins with a recognition of *Mandate's* basic premise. President Reagan stated, "today there is a very dangerous window of vulnerability," and he has spoken repeatedly and forcefully about the urgent need to close that "window." However, the specific program recommendations adopted by the Administration are inconsistent with a true concern for the present danger. None of the near-term strategic recommendations in *Mandate* was followed by the Administration. Since taking office, defense officials have systematically ignored quick-fix alternatives.

Rather than proposing solutions to the problem of near-term vulnerabilities, Pentagon pronouncements have rescheduled the arrival of the window of vulnerability. In the campaign, candidate Reagan warned that U.S. land-based forces would become vulnerable to a potential Soviet pre-emptive strike in the early 1980s. By way of contrast, Secretary Weinberger is now speaking of a projected window of vulnerability by 1985 or 1986. No explanation has been offered for this new grace period. The cynic would charge that the window of vulnerability has been officially postponed in order to justify the Administration's utter failure to redress the problem. A more charitable explanation would suggest that the present Defense leadership does not understand the meaning of strategic vulnerability, or the threat that it poses to our national security and to our ability to conduct a coherent and consistent foreign policy.

Beyond its neglect of urgently needed quick fixes, the Administration's strategic force initiatives have been characterized by delay and indecision. Upon presenting its revised Defense budget to the Congress in March of 1981, the new Administration advised that its strategic program decisions were still under review. The congressionally-mandated March deadline for decisions on the MX missiles and B-1 bomber was not met. Successive self-imposed deadlines of June, July and September were missed. Finally, on October 2, 1981, the Administration's long-awaited strategic package was announced. Although the plan included a number of vital improvements to our strategic force capabilities, it failed to address many of the nation's most critical defense needs.

On the positive side, the President's decision to produce and deploy 100 B-1B bombers, while continuing R&D on an advanced technology bomber, is in accord with the recommendation contained in *Mandate*. The strategic importance of a new survivable long-range bomber that can be deployed by the middle of this decade cannot be overemphasized. Further, the decision to deploy a scaled down Extremely Low Frequency (ELF) communications system meets the minimum essential requirement for improving the safety and survivability of SSBNs and for improving the covert operation of SSNs by allowing them to patrol at depth without losing radio reception.

Other critical elements of the Administration's strategic package are wholly inconsistent with *Mandate* recommendations. The most egregious of these is the decision to deploy the MX missile in existing silos, rather than in a survivable, deceptive-basing mode. The fundamental objective behind the ICBM modernization effort is to provide for survivability of U.S. strategic forces and eliminate the vulnerability that threatens U.S. security. *Mandate* recommended the earliest possible deployment of the MX missile in a deceptive basing mode. The Administration's ICBM modernization program calls for retrofitting MX missiles into existing silos, hardened to approximately 5,000 psi, while R&D proceeds on long-term basing solutions.

Replacing unsurvivable Minuteman or Titan missiles with equally unsurvivable MX missiles will do nothing to redress the essential vulnerability of the system, which stems from the basing of the missile, not from the missile itself.

Administration contentions that hardening planned MX silos improves survivability invite accusations of disingenuousness. Exhaustive studies unanimously concluded that it is not technologically feasible to harden silos to withstand an attack from increasingly accurate Soviet ICBMs. This realization led to efforts to find an alternative basing plan, culminating in deceptive-basing MPS designs. Secretary Weinberger recognized this fact when during his confirmation hearings before the Senate Armed Services Committee he stated, "simply putting MX into the existing silos would not answer several concerns that I have; namely, that these are well known by the Soviets and secondly that you can't harden them sufficiently to improve their *invulnerability*." [Emphasis added.] Air Force studies in the wake of the strategic package announcement reaffirm the ineffectiveness of hardening efforts against even existing Soviet capabilities.

In rejecting deceptive basing for the MX, the White House explained: "this scheme has serious military drawbacks and does not solve the current vulnerability of Minuteman and Titan forces." The strategic package announcement neither explained the drawbacks of multiple protective shelters, nor did it address what it admitted was the basic problem, current ICBM vulnerability. The Administration's failure to adopt the necessary measures to redress the vulnerability of land-based forces must be counted as its most serious shortcoming in strategic defense planning.

The decision to deploy the MX ICBM beginning in 1986 in existing Minuteman and Titan II silos is evidence of a failure to reconcile fiscal and strategic requirements. This move was combined with a decision to delete from the budget an effective, but inexpensive program to increase the number of Minuteman warheads by deploying stockpiled Minuteman IIIs in existing silos. This program would also allow the rapid retargeting of surviving missiles. If one accepts the doubtful proposition that it is sensible to deploy the MX in vulnerable Minuteman silos in 1986, it follows that one should be willing to spend far less to immediately maximize the capabilities of any surviving Minuteman ICBMs. In addition, only a few million dollars are saved by the unilateral deactivation of B-52D bombers; instead, these planes could support naval or Rapid Deployment Force missions in a cost-effective manner. The decision to retire prematurely the fifty-two remaining Titan II ICBMs saves very little money, but will significantly reduce the power of U.S. strategic forces. These decisions, based solely on cost considerations, will reduce total SNF megatonnage by 26 percent without requiring reciprocal reductions by the Sovet Union.

Other problems with the Administration's strategic package include:

$C^3I$—While important initiatives are included to improve some communication links and to begin to consider the overall survivability of critical command centers, little is being done to improve the reliability or the survivability of either existing warning systems or communication systems. Although the problems posed by nuclear effects, such as blackout and Electro-magnetic pulse (EMP), the problems of sabotage and electronic jamming, and the vulnerabilities associated with direct nuclear and conventional attack have long been known to be significant, the Administration's strategic package places the near-term emphasis on conceptual studies and analyses. Only in the far term does it contemplate concrete action to improve the survivability and endurance of the $C^3I$ systems. In fact, the diversion of funds to increase launch-on-warning capabilities may lead to an increase in the real vulnerabilities of both strategic forces and essential $C^3$ systems. While the Administration's recognition of the need for improvements in the area of $C^3I$ is encouraging, its actions are less than adequate. Decades of neglect and entrenched bureaucratic indifference to $C^3I$ must be overcome.

Bomber forces—The initial B-1 force will not be configured to carry the ALCM, and the yearly ALCM production rate has been cut from 480 to 440 missiles. Opportunities to make the existing forces more survivable and effective for the immediate future appear to have been ignored. For example, no plan to increase the alert rate of the present B-52 force has been announced. Neither effective B-52 rebasing nor other survivability enhancements (apart from a very limited EMP hardening effort) have been programmed. In fact, the 80 B-52Ds in the force are planned to be de-activated unilaterally without extracting any SALT *quid pro quo*.

Submarine forces—The Trident submarine construction rate was cut from Carter's one-and-a-half per year to only one per year. One Trident was cut from the FY 1982 budget. Completion of the new Trident base at Kings Bay, Georgia was delayed until 1992. Again, effective near-term use of existing forces is being ignored—existing Polaris submarines are being de-commissioned and scrapped faster than their capability is being replaced by the Tridents, again without regard to SALT concessions by the Soviets.

Many of the strategic program deficiencies may be largely the product of budgetary constraints, and a planning bias that favors general purpose force readiness over weapons investment and strategic modernization. In this crucial respect, the Administration's performance to date has been in direct opposition to *Mandate* objectives. *Mandate* recommended a reordering of budget priorities, doubling the share of the budget devoted to strategic programs, while reducing proportionately the funds committed to general purpose forces. Implicit in *Mandate* recommendations is the understanding that strategic forces hold the high ground in our defense posture, overshadowing all other uses of military force, especially where Soviet forces might be involved. Redressing weaknesses in our strategic force posture should assume the highest priority in defense planning and budgeting.

The specific shortcomings in the strategic package are overshadowed by the absence of any discernible strategy or plan to guide program decisions. The Administration claims that its strategic package contains a plan of historic proportions. It was presented in these words: "The Reagan program will determine, to a large extent, U.S. strategic capabilities into the next century. . . . We have used this unique opportunity to mold a strategic force that will meet the objectives of our strategy. . . . " However, no plan or strategy can be found in the Administration's actions. The Administration's strategic programs seem to have been determined more by *ad hoc* decision-making and budgetary limitations than pursuant to an integrated strategy. *Mandate's* call for the new Administration to identify U.S. defense objectives and a strategy to secure those objectives has gone unanswered.

**SALT Considerations**

The United States is unilaterally complying with the terms of the unratified SALT II treaty, a ploy begun under Carter but continued by the current Administration. In contrast, the Soviet Union has declared on several occasions that it is not bound to comply with the Treaty until it is ratified by the United States. Thus, the Soviet Union retains all the benefits of American compliance with SALT while accepting none of its obligations. This problem is compounded by as many as thirty-five well-documented Soviet violations of the SALT treaties and other arms control treaties. Despite campaigning against the SALT II treaty, the Reagan Administration has failed to challenge these Soviet actions.

Several advantages would accrue from challenging violations. Challenges would improve the prospects for more equity in SALT III talks because they would demonstrate American resolve for an equitable and enforceable SALT regime. Challenges would also provide justification for President Reagan's promised, but deferred, strategic force buildup. Additionally, they would provide sound rationale for the augmented intelligence collection and analysis capabilities needed for SALT verification. Finally and most significantly, by insisting on Soviet SALT compliance, the United States would rightly insist that existing arms control agreements be meaningful. Failure to challenge violations renders any arms control treaty a sham. Moreover, this failure surrenders the propaganda initiative to the Soviet Union, and leaves the United States in an unnecesary defensive position.

**General Purpose Forces**

While the modernization of U.S. strategic forces is the highest defense priority, the needed improvements in general purpose forces (ships, tactical aircraft and ground forces) would easily absorb an investment twice that of the recently announced strategic modernization package. General force deficiencies can be divided into problems of near-term readiness, the pace of modernization, and the basic size of the force structure. The Administration has attempted to remedy the situation in this order.

*Readiness*: Deficiencies identified by *Mandate* included funding shortages in operations and maintenance and personnel retention accounts. The recommendation for O&M funding was an increase on the order of $4 to $5 billion. The Administration's request for

54

Operations and Maintenance represents a marked improvement over the previous Administration, providing for a 4.8 percent real growth over FY 1981. Funding for flying hours, steaming days and unit training will show increases over FY 1981 levels. The realization of the increases is bolstered by the lower than expected cost of fuel for FY 1982. Increases in depot maintenance funding will eliminate backlogs for aircraft and tracked vehicles repair. The Administration also proposed significant increases for real property maintenance. However, the backlogs in this area are so large that this increase acts only to prevent the situation from getting worse instead of actually reducing the backlog itself.

The material readiness of the U.S. forces has also been degraded by a shortage of spare and repair parts. Spare parts shortages on occasion had produced severe cannibalization of certain aircraft, low unit readiness, and reduced utilization rates. The Administration has moved swiftly to fully fund Peacetime Operating Stocks for all types of aircraft. Combined with increased funding for depot maintenance activities, this represents the focus of the Administration's efforts to improve the material readiness of U.S. forces. However, actual improvements in this area remain years away. The positive effects of increased spare and repair parts funding will not be registered until sometime in the 1983-84 time frame.

To the extent that the readiness of U.S. forces can be improved in the near-term, these forces must also be able to sustain combat for some minimal period of time. The United States has placed itself in a progressively deeper hold in the area of combat sustainability. The Administration has moved to fund more missiles, ammunition and spares, but the line between essential readiness and true combat sustainability is a wholly subjective one. When budget reductions were imposed on the DOD in September, it was the consumables accounts with long-term requirements that took the more immediate cuts. Thus, while the effect on readiness may be minimal, the impact on sustainability is significant. The Administration deserves credit for what it has started. Its commitment to overcome the war reserve deficit should be renewed.

*Modernization*: The modernization of U.S. strategic forces should be the highest priority through most of the 1980s. Even with this priority, the spending total for the modernization of U.S. conventional forces will be larger and will account for more of DOD's procurement dollars during this decade.

First, the most significant pledge made by the Reagan Administration to conventional force improvements is its commitment to a 600-ship navy. This commitment parallels the recommendations contained in *Mandate*. However, as in the case of other long-term requirements, the September budget amendment reduces the likelihood that a 600-ship Navy will be achieved before the end of this decade.

Second, the modernization of U.S. ground forces ranks behind the 600-ship Navy in the Administration's list of defense priorities. There is little likelihood that the Army's share of overall defense spending will grow in the near future. Nevertheless, the Army's procurement program probably represents the most comprehensive, integrated and expensive modernization effort since World War II. For the Army, this combination of low budget priority and increasing costs means even more program stretch-outs, or more cancellations. The Administration has recommended rates of procurement for major items that exceed those programmed by the Carter Administration. However, the current pace of modernization is not sufficient to re-equip the active forces within a meaningful period of time. Despite whatever material or personnel initiatives may be undertaken to improve the near-term readiness of the Total Force, the underlying readiness trends for major Army units will not improve unless these forces are reasonably equipped.

Third, *Mandate* called for increasing procurement of all tactical aircraft programs. The Administration has responded guardedly, increasing the production of some aircraft and holding back on others until force structure options and overall budget constraints become more clear. The most significant commitment in this area has been designation of the F-16 as a potential candidate for multi-year procurement. Theoretically, this should offer more efficient production rates and a lower unit cost to the government. It is possible that budget constraints will drive down the total requests for F-16s, resulting in a multi-year contract with less than optimal rates of production. The Administration is moving in the right direction by pursuing this and other procurement reform options. Its actions in this area should be encouraged and expanded.

*Force Structure*: *Mandate* recommended four additional battle groups for the Navy, nine new air wings for the Navy and Air Force, and five additional ground force divisions. The Administration has structured its priorities so that force expansion on the scale recommended above will not take place within current force projections. The individual services and the Office of the Secretary of Defense are united in their view that the highest priority must go to correcting those deficiencies which exist within the current force structure.

The September budget review pushes force structure expansion farther into the future and accelerates the planned retirement of older weapon systems. During the period 1983-86, this may result in a slightly smaller force structure in some areas than had been planned, albeit one that is better equipped and more ready than the current one. However, this should be considered acceptable only in the short-term, since it is widely understood that today's force structure is already far short of what is needed to meet minimum defense needs.

*Manpower*: The most immediate force readiness improvements have been accomplished through improved management and Administration/congressional manpower initiatives. Two of the primary manpower problems facing the services during 1980 were poor retention among the non-commissioned officer corps, and a shortage of civilian manpower. Within the Army, certain personnel shortages were spread over more units thus improving the readiness of the non-deployed units. The Administration also responded with a pay and benefits package that, when amended by the Senate, increased basic pay for NCOs from 14 to 19 percent.

In addition, DOD was exempted from the government-wide hiring freeze. The Air Force and Navy applied modest civilian personnel increases in maintenance activities that will directly improve material readiness. The Army applied its increases to a reduction in the use of borrowed military manpower for civilian-type functions—a move which will return soldiers to their units and improve personnel readiness.

With regard to the Selective Service, *Mandate* recommended the continuation of registration, to include examination and classification. In addition, *Mandate* recommended a draft for the reserves through a six-year obligation with an optional commitment of two years in the active force. The Adminstration continued registration and appointed a Manpower Task Force to report its recommendations by December 1, 1981 on a broad range of manpower issues, including conscription. However, manpower experts are skeptical about the real purpose of the Task Force, and doubt that productive conclusions will be reached, or useful recommendations implemented.

*Strategic Lift*: For improved airlift capabilities, *Mandate* proposed cancellation of the CX program in favor of a modified C-5; additional C-130 transports; and increased funding for C-5A, C-141, and Civil Reserve Air Fleet modifications.

The Administration proceeded with the CX procurement, announcing its source selection in September. Although the CX program is regarded by DOD as a high priority, it continues to suffer a lack of support in Congress. The failure to cancel this procurement compounds other Defense budget problems.

The Administration continued the tradition of not requesting additional C-130s for tactical lift arguing that this aircraft is of insufficient priority and assuming that Congress would add them to the budget. The Administration has fully supported the C-5A wing modification program, and the C-141B (stretch) program which is now nearing completion.

The Administration's sealift program is in some disarray. The Victory Ship reactivations, proposed last March to provide prepositioned bulk storage, were cancelled in the September budget review, and the T-AKX program was also reorganized. *Mandate* recommended procurement of additional LSD-41 ships for amphibious lift. The Navy supports this program and is developing a new class of ship, LHDX, which will be an advanced version of the LHA.

Sealift, amphibious lift, and sea-based prepositioning programs remain vulnerable on two accounts. Sealift and amphibious lift do not compete well with the goal of a 600-ship Navy built around fifteen carrier battle groups. Moreover, prepositioning is very expensive and, since it is not tied to the combat capability of any particular unit, easily cancelled.

*The Rapid Deployment Force*: The Administration did not follow the *Mandate* recommendations calling for a re-evaluation of the role of the RDF. The need for improvements in the deployability of U.S. forces over long distances appeared self-evident and, for the most part, was accepted by the Administration. A disproportionate amount of time has been consumed by disputes on command relationships among the Readiness Command, the Joint Chiefs of Staff, and the Rapid Deployment Joint Task Force. The policy now in effect is to eventually create a Unified Command for the Southwest Asia/Persian Gulf region.

*Mandate* also recommended a review of the proposed size of the RDF. This question is in the process of resolution as the military demands on the RDF continue to grow. However, a variety of threat scenarios is placing an unreasonable burden on RDF planning. DOD should recognize that, at some point, RDF capabilities will be outrun, and general war planning guidelines must be applied.

The need for the re-evaluation stems from the fact that the RDF is no more than a loose coalition of separate units with no history of a coordinated command structure. These units should, at the very least, have a command patterned on the branch of service which already integrates light infantry, assault capabilities, and tactical air cover. The most desirable option would achieve increased RDF effectiveness at the lowest possible cost: give the RDF mission exclusively to the Marine Corps. Rapid deployment has been the historic mission of the Corps; any attempt to create a new such force is essentially an effort to re-invent the wheel.

Finally, *Mandate* recommended a secure overseas base structure as an essential element for permanent presence and sustainable air-ground operations in the Near East. The Administration has moved towards certain arrangements with several countries. As always, however, more rapid progress would be desirable.

## The Defense Budget

While the Soviet Union engaged in the greatest peacetime military buildup in history, the United States has systematically underfunded its national defenses. During the decade of detente (1969-1979), the United States reduced defense spending. In the early 1970s, Congress cut about $45 billion from the defense budget. The public's disillusionment with the Vietnam War made all defense spending unpopular. In the late 1970s, $38 billion was cut from President Ford's defense budget projections by the Carter Administration. The gross reduction totalled $83 billion. In 1980, defense spending as a percentage of total government spending was at the lowest point since the beginning of World War II; as a percentage of Gross National Product, it was at the lowest point since before the Korean War. The United States is still spending only about 5 percent of its GNP on defense.

In contrast, the Soviet Union is spending between 14 and 18 percent of its GNP on its military forces. Official U.S. estimates are that the Soviets have spent over $355 billion more than the United States on military investment alone since 1969. Each year, they have devoted $50 billion more than the United States to total military investments—the major determinant of future capability. The result of this gap is stark: the Soviet Union has outstripped the United States in every category except major combat ships. Soviet floor space in military-industrial plants increased by 34 percent since 1970, indicating that the trend will continue in coming years.

The costs of fully remedying U.S. military deficiencies immediately far outstrips any politically feasible allocation of funding to the Defense Department. *Mandate for Leadership* estimated these costs as approaching $160 billion. Accordingly, *Mandate* proposed a "practical and affordable" plan to redress the most serious deficiencies by increasing annual allocations for defense by $30 to $35 billion over the Carter Administration's spending estimates in each of the next five years.

The Administration came close to meeting this recommendation with its March budget amendments and future spending projections. If followed throughout the next five fiscal years, these would have probably meant defense budget increases of between $150 to $160 billion over that period. Given the fluctuating circumstances and annual uncertainties in defense programs on Capitol Hill, such an increase would have approached the *Mandate* recommendation.

In September, due solely to economic pressures, the Administration reduced its defense request. A decrease in defense outlays of $13.0 billion was adopted for FY 1982-84. The September FY 1982-1984 budget revision reduced the Reagan defense outlay increase by 43 percent and the budget authority increase by 30 percent. The proposed expenditure for FY 1982 is only one percent over the Carter levels which both *Mandate* and Secretary Weinberger termed wholly inadequate. As a consequence, much of the planned force modernization program will be deferred, since the vast majority of the defense budget reductions made for FY 1982 come from the acquisition accounts, RDT&E, and procurement. In contrast to campaign statements, it now appears that defense is clearly secondary to economic and fiscal policy.

Having shifted its political priorities, the Administration must now face the hard facts about military rebuilding programs. Reductions of the magnitude imposed in September are compounded by the timing factor. A loss of one year's spending authority translates into a loss of, at a minimum, two years in the budget cycle since it will probably take an additional year to recoup the foregone level of spending and another year to regain the recommended level of spending. Inflation further contributes to the deterioration of defense outlays; the longer the delay on major hardware expenditures, the higher the actual price.

Deferring defense expenditures is a dangerous course of action. The Soviets have repeatedly demonstrated a willingness to take risks in all parts of the world. Their increasing boldness is in part a consequence of U.S. and Western decisions not to challenge their moves with any action more decisive than symbolic boycotts of Olympic games. The Soviets embarked on this course after having been backed down during the Cuban missile crisis. They vowed they would never again be put in a position of conceding to a military threat such as the one mounted by President Kennedy. At present, no such threat can credibly be posed by the United States. Given the Administration's actions of the past year, no credible military counterforce will be available for some time to come. As a consequence, the Administration has extended the period of vulnerability in which the United States is subject to blackmail by a Soviet strategic threat.

## Alliance Burden Sharing

The Reagan Administration's efforts to obtain agreement on the part of U.S. allies to increase their level of defense spending has been ineffective. In February 1981, Secretary Weinberger noted that the outlays of the allies would no longer be measures by the "yardstick" of 3 percent annual real growth. This statement was widely misinterpreted by allies seeking to spend less. A clear statement that the Administration expected higher, not lower defense outlays should have preceded the Weinberger statement. Total NATO country defense spending (actual outlays, excluding inflation) rose at the rate of 2 percent in 1980. The implications for their economic and political sovereignty of the Soviet threat are not taken seriously in Europe. They should, nonetheless, be stressed along with a clear statement of U.S. resolve to defend the Middle East oil fields. Because these energy resources are more important to Europe than the United States, this commitment should form the basis of *quid pro quo* with the Europeans and Japanese on defense spending.

## Conclusion

President Reagan's National Security Affairs Advisor, Richard V. Allen, succinctly summarized the Soviet strategic and military threat. In a September 1981 speech, he said:

> ... The challenges which we face in the 1980's may well be the most substantial in our nation's history.... Because of inadequate defense spending in over the past decade, we find ourselves today in an extremely disadvantageous strategic position. The dangers of our present deficiencies are alarming to consider. Most alarming is the danger that the Soviet Union will miscalculate and attempt to exploit a perceived "window of opportunity" that could, in turn, generate a confrontation of cataclysmic proportions. Tough words must now be followed by substantial actions.

To date, the Administration has provided the tough words; it has not provided the policies and programs necessary to meet U.S. national security requirements.

Rectifying the problems in defense requires the development of a political coalition which is based first and foremost on the commitment to address national security needs with action—not words. This coalition should also embrace the legitimate calls for eliminating waste and inefficiency in the Department of Defense and its cumbersome procurement system. The Administration has made admirable progress in the area of procurement reform.

More can be done in this area. The Department of Defense continues to suffer from a tendency to set procurement specifications too ambitiously. The cost of equipping U.S. armed forces could be reduced significantly if DOD made greater use of off-the-shelf purchases of equipment, engineering and basic technology. Other savings could be made by including more companies in the defense procurement base. Competition must be increased through the reduction of sole-source purchasing. Instances of suspected corruption should be investigated aggressively and prosecuted to the maximum extent possible; profiteering must be eliminated.

The combined savings through an increase in competition and reductions in over-regulation, over-specification, and contract revisions could reach ten percent of total military procurement appropriations or as much as $20 billion annually in current dollars. These savings should be pursued and allocated to modernization, first of the strategic forces, and then of general purpose forces. One fundamental point must be stressed above all others: the savings realized from these steps will not accrue until the future; the Soviet threat must be addressed immediately.

## RECOMMENDATIONS
(Action taken on 46 out of 128)

**Comprehensive Defense Policy**

- Reverse the pattern of the 1970s to restore the military balance, protect sea lanes, project U.S. power, rebuild alliances, increase alliance sharing of defense burdens, and reinvigorate the intelligence apparatus.
  SOME EFFORTS BEGUN.

- Concentrate on national security concerns in the coming decade.
  NOT DONE.

- Allocate more resources to DOD.
  NOT DONE. (MODEST EFFORTS IN PROGRESS.)

- Identify defense objectives.
  SOME EFFORTS BEGUN.

- Devise new budgetary framework.
  NOT DONE.

- Devise new defense strategy.
  NOT DONE.

- Specify resources for meeting defense objectives.
  NOT DONE.

- Assess honestly the Soviet threat and U.S. deficiencies.
  NOT DONE FOR STRATEGIC FORCES.

- Develop Eight-Year Defense Plan, divided into two four-year programs.
  NOT DONE.

- Direct military departments to take the intiative for developing their own programs and budgets within Office of the Secretary guidelines.
  IN PROCESS.

- Assert a fixed, long-range commitment to substantially increased defense expenditures early in the Reagan Administration.
  IN PROCESS.

**Arms Control Policy**
- Reformulate compliance policy for SALT II.
  NOT DONE.

- Formulate new nuclear non-proliferation policies.
  IN PROCESS.

- Reformulate compliance policy and rationale for Threshhold Test Ban.
  NOT DONE.

- Reconsider the rationale for Comprehensive Test Ban negotiations.
  NOT DONE.

- Issue new guidelines for Arms Export Control.
  DONE.

- Devise new objectives for Mutual Balanced Force Reductions negotiations.
  IN PROCESS.

**Strategic Offensive Force Fixes**
- Deploy 100 stockpiled Minuteman III ICBMs.
  NOT DONE.

- Deploy a B-1 bomber variant.
  IN PROCESS.

- Re-base B-52s inland. Increase alert times, add runways, and provide hardened shelters for bombers.
  NOT DONE.

- Accelerate Air Launched Cruise Missile (ALCM) production program.
  NOT DONE.

- Deploy twenty ALCMs on each B-52G at accelerated pace.
  NOT DONE.

- Increase Trident submarine construction rate.
  NOT DONE.

- Accelerate Trident II (D-5) Submarine Launched Ballistic Missile (SLBM) R&D.
  IN PROCESS.

- Accelerate Sea Launched Cruise Missile (SLCM) deployment.
  IN PROGRESS.

- Retain Polaris submarines and arm with SLCMs.
  NOT DONE.

- Re-base part of Minuteman III ICBM force in Multiple Protective Structure at existing missile sites.
  NOT DONE.

- Speed development and deployment of MX in survivable configuration.
  NOT DONE.

- Speed deployment of the Mark 12A warhead on Minuteman III ICBMs to improve accuracy and warhead yield.
  NOT DONE.

- Increase Trident submarine production rate.
  NOT DONE.

- Speed SLCM development.
  IN PROCESS.

- Increase the funding for developing the Trident II (D-5) SLBM.
  DONE.

- Provide Strategic Force "quick fixes."
  NOT DONE.

- Improve pre-launch survivability of U.S. strategic forces.
  NOT DONE.

- Create a new strategic weapons program and accelerate existing strategic programs.
  NOT DONE.

- Accelerate initial operational capability of MX in a survivable basing mode.
  NOT DONE.

- Canisterize Minuteman III ICBMs and deploy in vertical Multiple Protective Structures.
  NOT DONE.

- Base MX in Minuteman silos with Low Altitude Defense System.
  NOT DONE.

- Refit all thirty-one Poseidon submarines with Trident I SLBMs, instead of the current twelve submarines.
  NOT DONE.

- Develop mobile Minuteman or MX.
  NOT DONE.

- Include strategic "Quick Fix" package in FY 1981 Supplemental.
  NOT DONE.

- Increase accuracy and payload of Minuteman III warheads.
  IN PROCESS.

- Deploy Mark 12A warheads on all 550 Minuteman IIIs.
  NOT DONE.

- Re-open Minuteman III production line.
  NOT DONE.

- Procure new TACAMO aircraft.
  NOT DONE.

- Continue research on ELF (Extremely Low Frequency).
  DONE.

- Increase funding for civil defense.
  IN PROCESS.

- Develop more sophisticated radar system for NORAD and deploy modern interceptors.
  DONE.

**Strategic Defense Systems**

- Accelerate development of both laser and particle beam weapons in a vigorous Ballistic Missile Defense (BMD) R&D program.
  IN PROCESS.

- Intensify ABM development with consideration of ICBM defense.
  IN PROCESS.

- Enhance civil defense program.
  IN PROCESS.

- Build 200 F-14s and F-15s.
  IN PROCESS.

## Theater Ground Forces

- Reverse trend impeding Army modernization.
  NOT DONE.

- Field five new divisions (two active, three reserves).
  NOT DONE.

- Reverse reductions in unconventional, special forces.
  NOT DONE.

- Procure additional armored vehicles such as M-1 tanks, infantry fighting vehicles (IFV), M-109 self-propelled Howitzers.
  NOT DONE.

- Procure more anti-tank and anti-air missiles.
  NOT DONE.

- Accelerate deployment of Pershing II and Ground Launched Cruise Missile (GLCM) Euromissiles.
  NOT DONE.

- Produce the neutron warhead.
  DONE.

## Rapid Deployment Forces

- Develop and procure light armored vehicles for Rapid Deployment Force.
  NOT DONE.

- Develop additional overseas base structures.
  IN PROCESS.

## Tactical Air Forces

- Establish nine new air wings (four Navy, five Air Force).
  NOT DONE.

- Increase F-15 and F-16 fighter production.
  NOT DONE.

- Increase production of F-14 and F-18 naval fighters.
  DONE.

- Increase production of A-10 and A-7 aircraft.
  DONE.

- Increase procurement of E-3A AWACS.
  DONE.

**Supply Lines and Sea Control**

- Build up U.S. mobility forces used for power projection.
  NOT DONE.

- Start construction of thirty new ships per year, at a cost of $11 billion per year, to achieve a 600-ship Navy as soon as possible.
  NOT DONE.

- Add $1 billion per year to naval budget if Soviets continue to increase their naval capabilities.
  NOT DONE.

- Continue to enhance capabilities of Civilian Reserve Air Fleet (CRAF).
  IN PROCESS.

- Establish secure base structure outside Europe by doubling capacity of Diego Garcia base; building bases in Kenya, Oman, and Somalia; deploying U.S. forces in Sinai and Negev; re-opening U.S. bases at Udorn and Sattahip, Thailand; building a major naval base on the west coast of Australia.
  IN PROCESS.

- Adopt major shipbuilding program.
  IN PROCESS.

- Procure four additional Nimitz class (CVN) nuclear aircraft carriers.
  NOT DONE.

- Create four new CVN task forces, including additional CG-47 cruisers, DDG-963 destroyers, and FFG frigates.
  NOT DONE.

- Increase production of SSN-688 attack submarines.
  NOT DONE.

- Terminate CX airlift plane.
  NOT DONE.

- Purchase additional C-130 aircraft.
  NOT DONE.

- Build the C-5B3.
  NOT DONE.

- Increase funding for C-5A, C-141, and CRAF modification programs.
  PARTIALLY DONE.

67

- Purchase SL-7 sealift ships.
  IN PROCESS.

- Acquire roll-on/roll-off ships.
  DONE.

- Build additional LSD-41 landing craft.
  DONE (IN THE FORM OF CONVERTING AND LEASING TAKX SHIPS).

## Manpower Problems

- Resume Selective Service drafting for the Reserve Forces.
  NOT DONE.

- Increase authorized military personnel levels by 300,000.
  NOT DONE.

- Increase pay by 10 percent above inflation in FY 1981.
  DONE.

- Make a commitment to increase pay 2 percent above inflation through FY 1985.
  NOT DONE.

- Stop "hemmorhage of talent" in U.S. armed forces.
  IN PROCESS.

- Institute additional combat training.
  NOT DONE.

- Increase compensation of military personnel.
  DONE.

- Increase personnel housing allowances and reimbursement for moving expenses.
  IN PROCESS.

- Develop special annual bonuses or proficiency pay for personnel with critically needed skills.
  IN PROCESS.

- Increase military pay at least $5 billion annually.
  IN PROCESS.

- Raise operations and maintenance by about $5 billion annually.
  NOT DONE.

- Add several billion dollars annually to military construction for family housing.
  NOT DONE.

## Operations and Maintenance
- Increase operations and maintenance expenditures by $4 to $5 billion.
  NOT DONE.

- Increase ammunition supply.
  NOT DONE.

- Increase readiness and sustainability of present forces.
  IN PROCESS.

- Add $11 billion per year to increase war reserve stocks, add to Operations & Maintenance, and increase fuel supplies.

  NOT DONE.

- Increase stock of spare parts.
  IN PROCESS.

## Revitalization of the Defense Industrial Base
- Develop Industrial Production Calendar.
  IN PROCESS.

- Start rebuilding military industrial base.
  IN PROCESS.

- Extend Defense Production Act of 1950 and National Emergencies Act of 1976.
  DONE.

- Prepare national defense industrial mobilization legislation.
  IN PROCESS.

## Procurement Cycle Reform
- Increase concurrency in all defense procurement to reduce lead times.
  NOT DONE.

- Require technology prototypes.
  NOT DONE.

- Revise multi-year procurement procedures.
  IN PROCESS.

- Assign high priority to long lead-time items.
  NOT DONE.

- Develop Research and Development Calendar to take into account R&D lead-times necessary for new weapons.
  NOT DONE.

- Increase RDT&E expenditures.
  IN PROCESS.

- Add $6 billion annually for enhanced staying power.
  NOT DONE.

- Add $22 billion annually above substantial increase just to amortize past procurement which has been allowed to age.
  NOT DONE.

## Foreign Military Assistance

- Pursue a vigorous arms export policy, particularly outside of NATO, and lift all ceilings on arms sales.
  IN PROCESS.

- Procure military equipment in advance of foreign military sales and assistance.
  NOT DONE.

## Nuclear Weapons Production

- Expand production of the three reactors at Savannah River, South Carolina.
  EQUIVALENT DONE.

- Restart L-reactor at Savannah River and the N-reactor at Hanford, Washington.
  IN PROCESS.

- Construct a new reactor.
  NOT DONE.

## Alliance Burden Sharing

- Pressure allies to increase defense burden sharing.
  NOT DONE EFFECTIVELY.

- Identify major conventional force deficiencies.
  DONE.

- Formulate Allied Fleet to patrol Indian Ocean, Persian Gulf, and Western Pacific.
  NOT DONE.
- Devise a two-year plan to substantially increase ammunition stocks.
  IN PROCESS.
- Increase role of Japanese Navy in sea control in East Asian waters.
  NOT DONE.
- Develop NATO naval power in Arabian Gulf.
  NOT DONE.
- Require monetary compensation from allies for the cost of U.S. forces which help guarantee them resource access.
  NOT DONE.

**Budget**
- Increase defense spending over the Carter proposal.
  NOT DONE IN ACTUAL OUTLAYS.
- Seek a Supplemental appropriation for FY 1981 of $15 to $20 billion.
  NOT DONE.
- Propose a FY 1982 defense budget with an increase of at least $35 billion.

  NOT DONE.
- Develop an Eight-Year Defense Plan for long-range planning in defense.
  NOT DONE.
- Commit to a very rapid rise in defense Total Obligational Authority (TOA) over the next two or three years, followed by a more gradual continuous increase thereafter, averaging at least a $35 billion increase in each of the next two successive years.
  NOT DONE.

# Chapter Eight
# DEPARTMENT OF EDUCATION
### By Onalee McGraw

Since the publication of *Mandate for Leadership* a year ago, there has been a tremendous change in federal education policy. Major initiatives include efforts to abolish the Department of Education and to transform federally mandated categorical programs into block grants. The purpose of these initiatives is to restore decision-making authority to state and local education agencies and to limit the federal role in education to information gathering, research, technical assistance and consultation.

## Abolishing the Department

In a memorandum to the President, Education Secretary Terrel Bell noted, "The critical signal that the overly intrusive federal role has been checked is the dismantling of the cabinet level Education Department." A separate department with Cabinet rank is inconsistent with the goal of restoration of local control. The Bell memorandum reaffirms the Administration's philosophy that the responsibility for education policy rests with state and local governments. Secretary Bell contends that cabinet departments should reflect the major constitutional responsibilities of the President. Education, he says, "is too narrow in scope, and too strongly influenced by teachers and institutional representatives to form the basis for a cabinet level agency."

Secretary Bell presented four options for the future status of the Department to the White House: creating a scaled down, non-Cabinet Education Foundation; abolishing the Department and dispersing all its functions to other federal departments and agencies; merging the Department back into the Department of Health and Human Services; or downgrading the Department into an independent agency. The last two options were considered non-viable. A Decision Memorandum, prepared for the President by a Task Force on the Education Department in November 1981, outlined the benefits and drawbacks of the two preferred options: the Foundation and dispersal of functions to other departments and agencies.

Secretary Bell favors creation of a Foundation which would retain most of the functions and programs now in the Education Department. According to the Memorandum, the Foundation would be headed by an official appointed by and responsible to the President. A non-governing advisory board would provide advice to the chairman of the Foundation on education issues. The Foundation would administer block grants, student grants and loans, compensa-

73

tory support in equal educational opportunity programs, and provide statistical and other support for educational research. The Memorandum argues that this option fulfills the President's commitment to abolish the Department, and provides an acceptable alternative for those Senators and Representatives who voted for its establishment.

The Memorandum also notes one of the greatest disadvantages of the Foundation proposal: it would continue a centralized federal presence in the education field with a great potential for future expansion of the federal role by statute and regulation. The Memorandum predicts that "conservative legislators might claim the Department has not really been eliminated, only changed in name and dropped from Cabinet status." In addition, the advisory board could be changed by legislative amendment to a governing board whose members' terms of office could extend beyond that of the President. Should this happen, special interest groups would have a greater opportunity to gain substantial control over federal education policy.

A second proposal to disperse all functions, programs and personnel to other departments and agencies does not appear to be treated seriously in the Decision Memorandum. The advantage is cited that the dispersal of programs would dismantle the Department completely. Such an option emphasizes that the federal role in education is merely to support state and local educational activities. The Memorandum does not support this option because the authors feel that it will be opposed more intensely than the Foundation proposal.

Senator Dan Quayle (R-Ind.), whose own bill abolishing the Department is a middle-of-the-road approach between the two options, is concerned about the regulatory powers which would be vested in the proposed Foundation. The Decision Memorandum does not address the question of regulatory powers. The final draft of the Administration proposal to Congress concerning the abolition of the Department is not expected until early 1982.

Any changes in the Department's status would have to be accomplished through an act of Congress. Passage of the legislation which created the Department of Education was marked by an extremely close House vote. Any attempts to dismantle the Department are sure to meet with intense opposition from the 150 education, civil rights and "children's advocacy" groups which have formed a coalition to preserve the Department. This effort is spearheaded by the National Education Association, a powerful lobby which claims to be able to marshal sufficient votes to prevent abolition of the Department of Education.

**Block Grants**

*Mandate for Leadership* recommended a major overhaul of the

Elementary and Secondary Education Act and appropriate bills to return essential decisions to states and localities through block grants. In the early months of the Administration, the Education Department and the Office of Management and Budget proposed comprehensive block grants to replace three categorical programs: Aid to Disadvantaged Children, Aid to the Handicapped, and Vocational Education.

Strong lobbying by education interests prevented block grants for the large categorical programs. Most other programs, however, were successfully consolidated into block grants. These included Consumer Education, Metric Education, Biomedical Education, Preschool Partnership, Environmental Education, Health Education, Correction Education, Population Education, and Law Related Education. Also consolidated were programs mandated under ESEA's Title IV: School Libraries and Instructional Resources, Support and Innovation, Guidance and Counseling, and Alcohol and Drug Abuse Education Act. Other programs included in block grants are Community Schools, Teacher Corps, Teacher Centers, Career Education, and Gifted and Talented. Separate statutory authority for the categorical programs consolidated into the block grants was repealed under the Omnibus Education Reconciliation Act of 1981. The Department has proposed a Reduction in Force (RIF) of approximately 150 employees who have been involved in administering categorical programs.

Despite Administration opposition, Congress extended the Women's Educational Equity Act (WEEA) as a categorical program authorized for $6 million. The congressional action to extend WEEA as a categorical program—a major priority of women's rights groups—was, surprisingly enough, partly due to the support it received in conference from conservative Republican Representative John Ashbrook, ranking minority member of the House Education and Labor Committee, and Representative Bobbie Fiedler.

The Department is preparing revisions of the Vocational Education Act, which had been scheduled to expire at the end of FY 1982 but was extended by Congress through 1984. The draft bill proposes conversion of existing federal vocational education programs into a block grant to give "broad discretionary authority" to the states.

**Deregulation**

The Education Department has embarked on a policy of deregulating virtually every major area under its jurisdiction. It hopes to return authority for decision-making to state and local education agencies to the maximum extent possible under existing law. To accomplish this objective, all Department regulations will be reviewed by the Secretary and OMB. Efforts are being made to ensure that the surviving regulations are not overly prescriptive, to reduce compliance and paperwork requirements, and to ensure that societal benefits of the regulations outweigh their costs.

During the Reagan Administration's first year, thirty sets of rules governing nineteen block-granted education programs were revoked. These regulations alone represented 118 pages in the *Federal Register*. This eliminated some 200,000 pages of grant applications, 7,000 pages of financial reports and 20,000 pages of programmatic reports submitted to the federal government annually. In March, the White House froze regulations requiring that schools provide catherization services to handicapped children during the school day. The Department is now considering changes in affirmative action requirements within Section 504 of the Rehabilitation Act. In April, the Department suspended Title IX dress code regulations. Decisions regarding attire and hair length now will be left to local school districts. Final action rests with the Department of Justice.

The Office of Special Education (OSE) has undertaken its own reviews of six sets of rules governing education of the handicapped. The reviews are expected to be complete by the end of 1981. OSE is looking at such items as due process and "mainstreaming" of handicapped children, and at requirements for Individualized Education Plans which must be reported for every handicapped child.

Although the Department withdrew regulations requiring full bilingual education for non-English speaking students, it did not resolve the problem. In the absence of major changes in either the law or relevant regulations, the guidelines established pursuant to the *Lau v. Nichols* case can be imposed on local school districts by the courts. These guidelines are as onerous as the withdrawn regulations. The Department should move quickly to initiate the changes needed to eliminate this threat.

## Title IX

Among the most controversial regulations written by the federal government were those dealing with equal opportunity (Title IX of the Education Amendments of 1972).

Secretary Bell has emphasized voluntary commitment from state and local officials to enforce civil rights laws. In a memorandum to his staff, he stated that "moral and ethical reasons rather than legal reasons ought to be more compelling if we can be more effective persuaders." At another point, Bell has observed that advancing equality of opportunity is best accomplished by cooperation rather than "specification of details of school administrative rule, regulation and curriculum." He also said, "The threat of terminating federal funding for states and localities in noncompliance with federal statutes is generally too drastic a response."

The Department has proposed that the federal enforcement role under Title IX be interpreted to cover only students, not employees of educational institutions. This interpretation has not been accepted by the Justice Department; some in the Education Department fear it will be rejected.

The issue will be heard by the Supreme Court in the case of *North Haven Board of Education v. Bell*, brought by two Connecticut school boards seeking to overturn the six-year-old job bias rules. Solicitor General Rex Lee has submitted a brief which strongly defends these rules. This action is causing friction between the two departments. Education is still considering the question of the breadth of Title IX. Although some argue that it applies to all programs in educational institutions which receive federal aid, *Mandate* recommended an interpretation which limits Title IX only to those programs that are directly funded by the federal government.

## Assistance Programs

Aid to Disadvantaged Children, formerly Title I of ESEA, has been rewritten in Chapter I of the new Education Consolidation and Improvement Act of 1981. The Department plans to keep only a small core of the Title I regulations; the remainder will be considered "nonbinding guidelines." Chapter I will take effect in the 1982-83 school year.

The main concern in the field of higher education is the various forms of student assistance, including the Pell Grants and the Guaranteed Student Loans. The Pell Grants are authorized for FY 1982 at $2.6 billion; outlays for the Guaranteed Student Loans are expected to reach $3 billion.

Some loans and grants are made directly to the student through intermediate institutions such as banks, rather than through educational institutions. The Department has proposed that educational institutions, whose students receive only such direct loans or grants, and which do not receive institutional aid, shall not be considered recipients of federal financial assistance. If finalized, these regulations would allow school officials to avert the problems of receiving federal aid without penalizing their students. This proposal has been submitted to the Justice Department but has not been approved. Many in the Department of Education fear it will be rejected.

## Personnel and Administration

The appointments in the Education Department reflect, with few exceptions, the new directions signalled by the Reagan Administration. Secretary Bell's communications to his policy-making staff emphasize deregulation, block grants, and the encouragement of high academic standards.

Several recommendations proposed in *Mandate for Leadership* relate to specific steps that might be taken to tighten up procedures for grants and insuring independent and honest evaluations. Many grant programs have now been consolidated into block grants. Those remaining are subject to new goals established by the Secretary relating to excellence and quality in education. Nonetheless, Department officials admit that the control of waste, fraud and abuse in the management of grants and contracts is a problem that will take continuous monitoring and diligent effort to overcome.

## Advocacy for Excellence

The essential problems remain. American education is in a state of crisis. The role of the federal government must be defined. Much to the consternation of those wedded to a federal subsidy for every problem and problem solver, Secretary Bell believes that the Department's role should be limited to setting an example and encouraging those at the local level who are truly responsible for actually achieving excellence and quality in education.

Secretary Bell has taken some specific actions to carry out this advocacy role on behalf of excellence. First, he has established a national commission on excellence in education charged with studying the problem in depth. The commission will submit its recommendations for reform to schools and colleges, not to the Congress or the federal government. The goals of the commission are commendable. It remains to be seen if the commission's work will be meaningful, or merely a political gesture.

Second, the Department is to review and encourage implementation of practices that the National Institute of Education research indicates will encourage higher standards. Five qualities have been identified as the key ingredients for a successful school: strong administrative leadership by the school principal, especially in instructional areas; a safe and violence-free climate that is conducive to learning; a school-wide emphasis on basic skills; teachers that demand high standards; and a system of monitoring pupil performance. It is significant that none of these qualities requires federal funding.

Secretary Bell also has recommended spotlighting outstanding schools and colleges, encouraging school boards to adopt policies that embrace higher standards, and encouraging colleges and universities to adopt admission standards that will force high schools to increase commitments to academic excellence.

The Department of Education has made a commendable change in direction. Block grants, deregulation and an advocacy of non-federally funded solutions all meet the spirit of the *Mandate* recommendations. However, the Department continues to fund numerous questionable research projects. Although the termination of many of these programs will take time, the Department would be well advised to control closely the use of these funds and to scrutinize the usefulness of their products.

## RECOMMENDATIONS
(Action taken on 17 out of 29)

### Legislation and Budget

- Eliminate Cabinet Department of Education.

  PROPOSED.

- Re-focus federal role in education on information gathering, consultation and technical assistance, and research.

  THESE ARE PRIORITIES OF THE ADMINISTRATION.

- Revise the Elementary and Secondary Education Act (ESEA), and appropriate bills.

  BLOCK GRANTS PROPOSED; PARTIALLY ADOPTED.

- Review the administration of the Higher Education Act, including comprehensive review of appropriate bills.

  CHANGES PROPOSED.

- Recommend an incremental reprogramming of money authority back to the states.

  ACCOMPLISHED THROUGH BLOCK GRANTS.

- Maintain the Basic Skills Division at its current level of support.

  INCLUDED IN BLOCK GRANTS.

- Reorganize the Office of School Improvement so that career executives will be concerned primarily with improving basic skills.

  OSI ABOLISHED. SKILLS FUNCTIONS TRANSFERRED TO OFFICE OF ELEMENTARY AND SECONDARY EDUCATION.

- Continue policy of withholding funding from divisions in the Office of School Improvement which do not now make grants, including Energy Action, Citizen Education, Health Education, and Environmental Education.

  INCLUDED IN BLOCK GRANTS.

- Review immediately the Women's Education Equity Act Program (WEEAP) and drastically reduce its budget.

  PROPOSED, BUT BLOCKED BY CONGRESS.

79

- Continue to support Teacher Corps.
  INCLUDED IN BLOCK GRANTS.

  Cut support for Teacher Centers.
  INCLUDED IN BLOCK GRANTS.

- Reduce funding for grants and conferences for the following divisions: Consumer Education, Alcohol and Drug Abuse Education, Arts in Education, Metric Education, Ethnic Heritage Studies, and Law-Related Education.
  ACCOMPLISHED THROUGH BLOCK GRANTS.

### Personnel and Accountability

- Fill positions within the Department with individuals strongly committed to the attainment and improvement of basic academic skills, and who oppose further federal support for "humanistic" or psycho-social education activities, projects or programs.
  APPOINTMENTS GENERALLY REFLECT PROPER ORIENTATION.

- Form blue-ribbon panels of distinguished citizens and educators to review all ongoing curriculum development and implementation activities being administered or supported by the federal government.
  SPIRIT OF RECOMMENDATION ACCOMPLISHED.

- Phase out or terminate promptly curricula not consistent with the objectives and policies of the new Administration.
  PARTIALLY ACCOMPLISHED THROUGH BLOCK GRANTS.

- Establish procedures within the first thirty days to interview all program managers and other department personnel involved in solicitation or approval of grant applications and disbursal of federal funds.
  NOT IMPLEMENTED, BUT MANY GRANT PROGRAMS NOW IN BLOCK GRANTS.

- Transfer personnel who advocate "humanistic" or psycho-social programs in the schools to other agencies or move them to positions where they will have no authority over policy decisions, project approval, funding, or other administrative actions involving federal financial support.
  NOT ACCOMPLISHED.

- Require that all participants/recipients of department-sponsored grants be provided a suitable and practicable means of evaluating the quality and usefulness of the service provided.
NOT DONE.

- Direct evaluation comments to an independent office within the department, and not to the office administering the grant.
NOT DONE, BUT ACCOMPLISHED IN PART THROUGH BLOCK GRANTS.

- Establish clear objective against which all education programs will be evaluated; specifically their contribution to the basic skills of reading, writing and calculation, as measured by standardized tests.
NEW PRIORITIES ESTABLISHED.

- Encourage contractor evaluation chiefs to make their conclusions in forthright, non-technical terms by guaranteeing that they will not be harrassed for reporting bad news.
NOT DONE, BUT SPIRIT OF PROPOSAL ACCOMPLISHED.

- Cut programs which cannot prove effectiveness.
SOME PROGRESS.

**Taxes and Finance**
- Devise a new system of financing measures that relieves education's dependence on direct government financing and the resulting government controls.

  1. Support legislation to extend charitable deductions to all taxpayers, regardless of whether or not they itemize deductions.
  ACCOMPLISHED.

  2. Reform government student aid programs to place maximum emphasis on direct payments to students or their families, rather than to educational entities.
  NOT DONE, BUT UNDER CONSIDERATION.

  3. Remodel research support programs to maximize emphasis on and incentives for achievement of mutually agreed-upon research objectives.
  NOT DONE DIRECTLY, BUT RESEARCH IS GOVERNED BY NEW GUIDELINES.

81

4. Coordinate activities, including financial incentives, to foster self-regulation in education as a workable alternative to government regulation.

ADOPTED AS DEPARTMENTAL POLICY.

- Limit the government's role in higher education to recognizing tax-deductible contributions, processing payments to students, families and educational entities, and obtaining proper accountings for the use of public funds.

NOT DONE.

### Civil Rights and Special Programs

- Prevent the Office of Civil Rights from using Title VI to force bilingual instruction in local schools.

UNDER CONSIDERATION.

- Presume that a school has complied with the "social justice" directives in Section 504, Title IX and E.O. 11246, unless the OCR receives convincing evidence to the contrary.

NOT DONE.

- Tailor a school's compliance with Section 504 (access for the handicapped) to its financial capacity to comply.

PRIORITY PLACED ON SECTION 504 DEREGULATION; LEGISLATION NEEDED.

- Review affirmative action regulations implementing E.O. 11246.

REGULATIONS PROPOSED; UNDER REVIEW AT JUSTICE.

- Apply Title IX regulations only to education programs receiving federal assistance.

ACTION PROPOSED AND UNDER CONSIDERATION.

- Overhaul the administration of the Bureau of Student Financial Assistance. Eliminate the waste and delays in processing student financial assistance applications.

UNDER CONSIDERATION.

# Chapter Nine
# DEPARTMENT OF ENERGY
### By Milton R. Copulos

The *Mandate for Leadership* task force on the Department of Energy stated that "the major deficiency of the Department of Energy is found in the fact of its existence." Nothing has occurred to alter the validity of this assertion. If anything, the modest steps taken by the Reagan Administration to date, such as accelerating the schedule of oil decontrol, serve to underscore this point. Where the market has been allowed to operate, it has performed well. Abolition of DOE remains a major goal.

Abolishing DOE will not be easy. In the four years since its creation, it has developed a constituency among powerful special interests and on Capitol Hill, which cannot be expected to stand by idly and allow their client agency to be dissolved. They have already begun to fight.

Of more immediate concern is the agency's performance during the period before abolition. The failure of the Administration to make timely appointments at the sub-cabinet level contributed to an uncertain initial performance, although the Department is now beginning to demonstrate a more coherent policy direction. The Secretary of Energy remained the only confirmed appointee within the Department for a period longer than prudent or necessary. This caused the Secretary to rely heavily on career bureaucrats and Carter holdovers for assistance. None of these individuals had an interest in seeing goals of the new administration fulfilled.

Most key appointments have now been filled. The appointment of an Under Secretary to act as chief operating officer of the Department was a major improvement. Previously, Assistant Secretaries reported to the Secretary, needlessly occupying his time with details rather than policy.

Although heavily criticized for lacking an energy background when first named, Secretary Edwards has worked hard. His efforts have proved successful, even if they are unrecognized by some Administration opponents.

One of the most pressing problems facing the Agency is the continuing resistance to the stated policies of the President. This lack of direction is in part attributable to poor staff work. In many instances, members of the staff in key slots appear to possess private agendas, usually in conflict with the stated policies of the President. In such circumstances, the staff involved should be removed from the policy-making process.

*The author wishes to thank Mike Boland and Jan Benes Vlcek for their assistance in the preparation of this chapter.

## Reorganization

*Mandate for Leadership* called for a three-step reorganization leading to the abolition of DOE in January 1982. The three phases would consist of: an internal reorganization using the power inherent in DOE's organizing statute; an executive reorganization under the Executive Reorganization Act of 1966; and, finally, a sunset review through which the final dismantling would occur. The lack of timely appointments to the sub-cabinet positions at DOE made it impossible to conduct an executive reorganization before the authorizing Act expired. Where *Mandate* suggestions were not followed, the reason often was the expiration of this Act.

*Mandate* suggested that the Under Secretary be the chief operating officer of the Department, freeing the Secretary for policy decisons, and that an Assistant Secretary for Finance and Administration be appointed to act as his deputy. This new position has been created. Lines of authority should now be clear.

The Department has made great strides in reducing the superfluous positions added during the Carter Administration, including the Assistant Under Secretaries and the Chief Financial Officer. Although progress remains to be made, the general direction is encouraging.

The Department also followed the recommendation to reorganize the roles of the Assistant Secretaries, so that each would have responsibility for a particular fuel type rather than a general function. The Department has also initiated its sunset review process, and has made some progress on drafting plans for the agency's dismantlement. In fairness to DOE, the Department attempted to implement the *Mandate* suggestion to eliminate the Energy Information Administration only to be overruled by Congress. On balance, compliance with *Mandate* recommendations in the area of internal reorganization is relatively high, if the expiration of the Executive Reorganization Act is considered.

## Internal Management

Internal management of the organization suffered directly from the lack of appointments. As a consequence, the Secretary had to rely heavily on career bureaucrats and Carter holdovers to perform many key policy-making tasks. Part of the problem can be traced to the incoming Administration's failure to make policy clear to employees at the outset. Several aspects of policy still remain unclear because of this confusion. Some staff members continue to be unwilling to accept policies originating in the Cabinet Council on Energy and Natural Resources. Staff level resistance must be overcome quickly, as it affects policy in many ways. Resistance has also come from the private sector, as exemplified by the pressure to continue subsidies for synthetic fuels. The President opposes such subsidies. A coalition of private firms and Members of Congress was able to force acceptance of these proposals.

The Department has excelled in moving forward to fill the Strategic Petroleum Reserve and improve its management. The SPR was one of the prime examples of poor management and confused policy under the previous administration. Secretary Edwards has taken strong steps to correct this deficiency, including the creation of an Assistant Secretary to oversee Emergency Preparedness and a Deputy Assistant Secretary with specific responsibility for the SPR.

The Department also deserves high marks for eliminating DOE funding for anti-energy groups. In years past, DOE was a primary contributor, even where the activities funded had at best a tangential relationship to energy issues. DOE now reviews contracts to ensure that any funds allocated to public interest groups are not used to finance political activism or to undercut the Administration's programs. DOE has also moved to reorient the Solar Energy Research Institute away from social activism and towards scientific research, as was intended.

The Agency's overall performance in the area of internal management has improved recently with the appointment of the appropriate Assistant Secretaries. This improvement could continue. It will not be easy; the knowledge that the Agency is scheduled for dismantling tends to demoralize the staff. However, the appointment of an Under Secretary, and a clarification of "dismantling" may help overcome this problem.

**Related Agencies and the Congress**

DOE has improved relations with the Congress. This remains a difficult task because the President's policies are not fully accepted in either the House or the Senate. The appointment of an Assistant Secretary for Congressional Affairs is to be applauded. Under the previous administration, many Assistant Secretaries and even Deputy Assistant Secretaries created their own congressional constituencies, making congressional relations extremely difficult. Although this still occurs, it no longer appears officially sanctioned.

The establishment of the Cabinet Council on Energy and Natural Resources as the primary policy-making body for energy has improved coordination between related federal agencies. While disputes among agencies still exist, and occasionally make their way into the media, these are much fewer compared to the previous administration. Also, when a policy decision is reached in the Council, all agencies have participated in it, and are fully aware of the policy.

Some progress has also been made on revision of the Clean Air

Act. Legislation is expected to reach Congress soon. A relatively high degree of inter-agency cooperation is apparent in its drafting.

Land use is an area where a surprising amount of progress has been made. In fact, the actions of the Interior Department have exceeded most expectations by a considerable margin. While DOE's role has been largely supportive, it has performed well where needed.

Overall, the DOE performance in the area of inter-agency cooperation has been quite good. This may in part be a reflection of the fact that the Secretary is a "team player" by nature, and clearly has no special agenda of his own. It can be said that this is one of the areas in which the Agency has demonstrated its best performance.

However, congressional pressure to continue the synthetic fuels subsidies and Emergency Petroleum Allocation Act regulations persists. Surprisingly, much of the congressional pressure came from the nominally conservative Senate Energy Committee, which would not be expected to endorse such interventionist measures.

**Technology, Conservation, and Energy Programs**

Although DOE has reduced the federal expenditure for "appropriate technology" and other areas of questionable merit, resistance has come from both Congress and certain career bureaucrats. The Department actually exceeded the goals recommended in *Mandate* in several areas, including the Building Energy Performance Standards, but was reversed on the latter by Congress. Congress also thwarted DOE actions to eliminate the State Energy Conservation Service as recommended in *Mandate*.

Initially, DOE moved to increase funding for basic research. However, the latest round of budget cuts, requiring a 12 percent across-the-board programmatic reduction, led to funding levels which are about equal to last year's. This may in the long run prove to be penny wise and pound foolish, as funds invested in basic research usually pay long-term dividends.

The Department performed poorly in efforts to eliminate funds for commercialization activities. The government has a role in high-risk, long-term research and development. However, subsidies for essentially commercial activities are clearly antithetical to the free market philosophy of this Administration. These efforts should be funded by the private sector.

No action appears to have been taken to eliminate the favoritism in awarding foreign firms the rights to patents developed with Department funds. During the last Administration, there were several flagrant examples of such favoritism. *Mandate* recommended that the incoming Administration make a clear statement on patent policy. This policy statement has not been issued, and remains an area in need of attention.

Considerable progress has been made toward eliminating categorical grants for various programs in favor of block grants. This resulted in *de facto* implementation of specific budgetary recommendations. The progress of the Department in the area of conservation and technology has been relatively good. Still, it must guard against efforts by both the Congress and careerists within the Agency to frustrate its plans. One criticism stands out: the funding of commercial activities should be curtailed in the future.

## Nuclear Policy

Secretary Edwards, like the President, is known to be a strong advocate of nuclear energy and, as expected, he moved forward on many nuclear energy issues. He has taken strong steps to resolve the issue of nuclear waste disposal. A recent presidential policy statement on nuclear energy included references to both the establishment of a long-term nuclear waste policy and the expediting of the Waste Isolation Pilot Program (WIPP). The Secretary also has made considerable progress in improving relations with the states on this touchy question.

The Administration has reaffirmed its commitment to the breeder reactor generally, and to the Clinch River reactor in particular. The President also lifted the ban on reprocessing which has been a force for several years. He also ordered a study to determine the feasibility of purchasing plutonium for the Clinch River facility from commercial firms, thereby helping to stabilize their market. The Administration has indicated an intention to move forward in several long-term areas which were discussed in *Mandate*. One such area is the licensing process for nuclear power plants. The President's policy statement indicated the Administration's desire to reduce the licensing process for such facilities from the present fifteen years to eight years. To accomplish this goal, the President instructed the Secretary of Energy, in cooperation with the Vice President's task force on regulation, to prepare a list of regulations which could be modified to shorten the licensing time.

The Administration also moved to maintain funds for the Converter Reactor Systems Program, to increase funding for the Advanced Isotope Separation Technology Program, and to maintain the Uranium Resource Assessment Program as recommended in *Mandate*.

No action has been taken in a number of areas relating to the Nuclear Regulatory Commission. Among the NRC programs which have yet to see Administration initiatives are: the removal of non-radiological environmental decision-making from NRC purview; the establishment of a policy to encourage standardization of plants; the combination of construction permit and operating license processes; and the restructuring of hearings on a non-judicial format. These actions are likely to require legislative action. Many of them may be included in the recommendations of the Vice President's task force.

The Administration also has failed to remove the responsibility for licensing of nuclear exports from the NRC. More important, it has not clarified its policy on nuclear proliferation. This is perhaps the only major area in which the Administration has failed to take any action. Nuclear proliferation has been a topic of considerable concern to the last several presidents. Decisions made by the previous Administration limited the U.S. effectiveness on this issue. This Administration must re-establish U.S. leadership in the peaceful use of atomic power as rapidly as possible.

By and large, the Administration's nuclear policy has been in keeping with the perceived needs of the industry. The industry's response, however, was not encouraging. Nonetheless, the Administration's domestic nuclear policy is on target; its international policy needs further attention.

### Oil, Gas, and Coal

As one of his first acts in office, the President removed the price and allocation controls from crude oil and refined products. In so doing, he made one of the most important energy policy moves of his first year in office. The controls had caused gasoline lines and shortages in the past. Their removal contributed substantially to the empirical evidence supporting a market approach for energy. The value of this contribution cannot be overestimated.

The Administration has progressed in implementing other *Mandate* recommendations as well. One of the most important was to move to settle the outstanding cases under the old price and allocation rules. These rules, patently unfair to begin with, grew out of a desire to punish the oil industry for the sins of OPEC. Recently, the Department of Energy has moved to expedite such settlements so that it can eliminate the last vestiges of those rules. This is important for two reasons. First, delay can only result in increased legal fees for both sides, and may actually weaken the government's case. Second, as long as the cases are pending, there remains a rationale for a continuing regulatory presence to monitor and supervise the cases' prosecution.

Partial progress has been achieved in a number of other areas. For example, the restrictions under Section 301 of the Fuel Use Act have been eliminated; full repeal of FUA is advocated by the Secretary. The Department's coal leasing policy has been reviewed, and has been re-oriented in a more beneficial manner. The Conrail appropriation should be of some value in expediting the transportation of coal to port. There also has been some progress (through the Department of Commerce primarily) towards improving the ability of ports to handle large coal carriers by allowing them to charge user fees to pay for deepening their channels. Although these proposals are not yet in legislative form, they may soon be introduced by some members of the Senate Energy Committee.

A number of items in the tax bill paralleled *Mandate* energy recommendations. One was to exclude newly discovered oil from the Windfall Profits Tax; another was to exempt savings from federal income taxation through a variety of means.

One specific recommendation not followed concerned the transfer of jurisdiction for multi-resource regulation from FERC to state Public Service Commissions. To date, there is no indication that this proposal has been considered. The Administration also lagged seriously in the deregulation of natural gas prices. Today, regulation of natural gas remains the single most flagrant example of federal interference in the energy market. The Administration had been expected to move on this issue in October. The announcement was withdrawn at the last moment. The official position of the Administration is that the decision has merely been deferred until sometime before the end of the year. The problem with deferral is timing. Congress will not likely tackle such a potentially divisive issue in the face of an election. Moreover, if the natural gas deregulation legislation is deferred until 1983, there will be inordinate pressure to extend controls out of fear that allowing them to expire in 1985, as would be the case under present legislation, would result in a severe shock to the economy. With delays, other distortions are institutionalized. Because of controls, some gas is selling at twice the Btu equivalent price of crude. Pipelines in the producing states do not have reserves of cheap price-controlled gas; they have long operated in a decontrolled environment. As a consequence, they cannot pay these unreasonable prices for new gas and, within a few years, could begin to experience supply shortages. Unless the Administration soon pushes decontrol, these distortions will become more serious. If that happens, those now paying the highest prices can be expected to call for continued controls to protect them, in effect, from themselves.

In summary, then, the areas of oil, gas, and coal have been characterized by both success and failure. Examples include crude oil decontrol and emphasized control of natural gas. It should be noted that the Secretary has taken a strong position in favor of natural gas deregulation.

## Conclusion

In the final analysis, the performance of the Department of Energy over the past year has been both more and less than expected. The initial months of the new Administration's tenure over DOE were characterized by a continuing dominance of the policy process by career bureaucrats and Carter holdovers. This was largely due to the failure of the Administration to make timely appointments. As more Reagan appointees began to take office, a gradual improvement was evidenced in DOE's performance.

This should not obscure the fact that much remains to be done. Lines of authority within the Department should be clarified immediately. Since the Under Secretary has been designated as chief operating officer, the Secretary should devote the bulk of his attention to policy formulation. Staff should not be allowed to circumvent normal policy-making channels to promote private agendas. Natural gas decontrol should be pursued as soon as possible. The sunset review should be completed promptly so that DOE can be dismantled next year. The Cabinet Council on Energy and Natural Resources should begin to focus on the question of nuclear proliferation, so that it will be prepared to address this issue once DOE is eliminated.

## RECOMMENDATIONS
(Action taken on 63 out of 95)

### Reorganization

- Abolish DOE and transfer essential functions to other departments.
  ABOLITION PROPOSED; TRANSFER BEING PLANNED.

- Initiate an internal reorganization of DOE.
  DONE.

- Reorganize further through executive reorganization.
  NOT DONE DUE TO EXPIRATION OF ENABLING LEGISLATION.

- Initiate Sunset Review of DOE.
  DONE.

- Restructure lines of responsibility according to fuel types.
  DONE.

- Initiate work on plan for dismantlement.
  DONE.

- Reduce the number of Assistant Secretaries from eight to four.
  NOT DONE.

- Eliminate positions of Deputy Under Secretary.
  DONE.

- Clarify lines of authority and policy direction within the Department.
  POORLY DONE; HINDERED BY LATE SUBCABINET APPOINTMENTS AND POOR STAFF WORK.

- Reduce policy role of the General Counsel to a more appropriate level.
  ACHIEVED.

- Eliminate Office of Hearings and Appeals.
  NOT DONE.

- Eliminate superfluous layer of bureaucracy added by Secretary Duncan.
  DONE.

- Redefine role of the Under Secretary as the Chief Operating Officer of the Department.
  DONE.

- Redefine role of the Secretary to assist the President in formulating energy policy, rather than having policy initiated in the Department.
  DONE THROUGH CABINET COUNCIL ON ENERGY AND NATURAL RESOURCES.

- Redefine role of Under Secretary as principal assistant to the Secretary.
  DONE.

- Eliminate the position of Assistant Secretary for the Environment and disperse functions.
  ACCOMPLISHED BY OTHER MEANS.

- Eliminate Assistant Secretary for Resource Applications.
  DONE.

- Transfer responsibility for Strategic and Naval Petroleum Reserves to Assistant Secretary for Fossil Fuels.
  ACHIEVED BY OTHER MEANS.

- Give Assistant Secretary for Nuclear Energy responsibility for all nuclear programs.
  LARGELY ACCOMPLISHED.

- Eliminate position of Chief Financial Officer.
  DONE.

- Transfer authority for oversight of the Fuel Use Act to Assistant Secretary for Fossil Fuels.
  NOT DONE.

- Introduce legislation to eliminate Economic Regulatory Administration.
  ACCOMPLISHED IN PRINCIPLE BY OTHER MEANS.

- Introduce legislation to eliminate Energy Information Agency.
  LEGISLATION INTRODUCED, BUT NO CONGRESSIONAL ACTION.

- Submit executive reorganization plan to Congress.
  NOT DONE.

## Internal Management

- Make Department policy clear to employees from the outset.
  NOT DONE; POOR STAFF WORK.

- Do not commit DOE funds for synthetic fuels projects, but rather allow transfer to Synthetic Fuels Corporation.
  NOT DONE.

- Eliminate the use of contractors to perform routine tasks.
  LARGELY ACCOMPLISHED.

- Eliminate grants to anti-energy groups.
  DONE.

- Discourage Solar Energy Research Institute from engaging in social activism.
  DIRECTOR REPLACED; PROGRESS MADE.

- Reduce overall reliance on contractors.
  MOVING TO ACHIEVE THIS GOAL.

- Improve management of the SPR.
  IN PROGRESS.

- Introduce legislation to either sell Power Marketing Authorities or transfer them to the states they serve.
  NOT DONE.

- Transfer Power Marketing Administration responsibility to Assistant Secretary for Finance and Administration.
  GOAL ACHIEVED BY OTHER MEANS.

- Eliminate funding of anti-nuclear intervenors.
  DONE.

- Eliminate Energy Information Campaigns.
  DONE.

- Select a few career bureaucrats for promotion to solidify relations with civil servants.
  DONE.

- Eliminate grants for commercialization of technologies.
  NOT DONE.

- Speed completion of the Portsmouth gas centrifuge enrichment plant.
  DONE.

- Move forward aggressively to fill the Strategic Petroleum Reserve.
  DONE.

- Reduce budget for Institutional and Intergovernmental Relations.
  DONE.

- Sharply reduce funding for Utility Programs and Regulation Intervention.
  DONE.

- Reduce by half funding for prosecution of firms for non-compliance with Price and Allocation regulations.
  INCREASED BY CONGRESS.

- Reduce staff of Fuels Regulation Program.
  REDUCED FROM 160 TO 70.

### Related Agencies and Congress
- Initiate review and amendment of the Clean Air Act.
  REVIEW IS IN PROGRESS; NO DECISIONS YET.

- Review and propose amendments to the National Environmental Policy Act.
  NO PROGRESS TO DATE.

- Orient federal land-use policy toward multiple use.

  INTERIOR DEPARTMENT MOVING AGGRESSIVELY IN THIS AREA.

- Improve coordination of energy policy with other agencies involved.

  DONE THROUGH CABINET COUNCIL.

- Improve relations with Congress.

  DONE.

- Improve coordination of energy policy in the broad sense.

  IMPROVEMENT MADE BY CABINET COUNCIL.

- Shift orientation of environmental programs from solving problems related to environmental impediments to industrialization.

  NOT DONE.

### Technology, Conservation, and Energy Programs

- Increase funding for basic research.

  INCREASED IN MARCH BUDGET; CUT IN SEPTEMBER.

- Review patent policy to eliminate favoritism for foreign companies.

  NOT DONE.

- Reduce funding for Appropriate Technology to $5 million.

  DONE.

- Eliminate federal commercialization activities in the energy sector.

  NOT EVENLY APPLIED.

- Overhaul Building Energy Performance Standards program.

  GOAL EXCEEDED.

- Sharply curtail Residential Conservation Service.

  IN PROGRESS.

- Eliminate Appliance Standards.

  IN PROGRESS; HOUSE APPROPRIATED NO FUNDS.

- Develop plan for private financing of the SPR.

  IN PROGRESS.

- Examine methods of encouraging private storage of Strategic Reserves.

  IN PROGRESS.

- Eliminate DOE role in regulating energy use of other agencies.
  DONE.

- Reduce scale of Small Business Information Program.
  NOT DONE.

- Eliminate the Analysis and Technology Transfer Program.
  IN PROGRESS.

- Maintain funding level of Industrial Conservation Program.
  DOE PROPOSED TO ELIMINATE; CONGRESS RESTORED FUNDS.

- Eliminate funding for transportation programs.
  NOT DONE.

- Turn tied grants for "state conservation plans" to block grants.
  DONE.

- Eliminate DOE regulatory and administrative role in state conservation grants.
  DONE.

- Reduce Energy Management Partnership Act funding to $90 million, and consolidate the program with state and local conservation grants.
  DONE.

- Cut funds for state Emergency Energy Conservation Act.
  RECOMMENDATION EXCEEDED.

- Eliminate State Energy Extension Service.
  DONE BY DOE; CONGRESS RESTORED FUNDS.

- Cap expenditures under State Energy Impact Program at FY 1980 levels.
  ACCOMPLISHED THROUGH BLOCK GRANTS.

**Nuclear Policy**
- Establish a national nuclear waste management policy.
  IN PROGRESS.

- Establish a new nuclear non-proliferation policy.
  NO ACTION TO DATE.

- Establish a long-term policy for nuclear waste disposal.
  IN PROGRESS.

- Fund the Breeder Reactor.
  FUNDING RESTORED.

- Initiate reforms to expedite the licensing of nuclear power plants on order.
  PRESIDENT HAS ANNOUNCED HIS INTENTION TO DO SO.

- Move forward with reprocessing of spent fuel.
  BAN ON REPROCESSING LIFTED.

- Relieve NRC of nuclear export responsibilities.
  NOT DONE YET.

- Relieve NRC of non-radiological environmental decision-making.
  NOT DONE YET.

- Encourage the use of standardized designs for new nuclear plants.
  NOT DONE YET.

- Combine construction and operating licenses for new nuclear plants.
  NOT DONE YET.

- Make licensing hearings non-judicial.
  NOT DONE YET.

- Re-orient commercial Nuclear Waste Program emphasis toward reprocessing.
  DONE.

- Continue the Waste Isolation Pilot Plant.
  DONE.

- Maintain funding for Converter Reactor Systems Program.
  DONE.

- Increase funding for Advanced Isotope Separation Technology.
  DONE.

- Maintain Uranium Resource Assessment Program.
  DONE.

**Oil, Coal, and Gas**
- Eliminate Price and Allocation Controls for coal and N6.
  DONE.

- Move rapidly to settle outstanding cases under old price and allocation rules.

  IN PROGRESS.

- Take steps to improve port facilities.

  USER FEES PROPOSAL WOULD HELP.

- Take steps to improve the ability of the rail system to move coal.

  SOME HELP IN CONRAIL APPROPRIATION.

- Repeal the Fuel Use Act.

  ACCOMPLISHED IN PART WITH SEC. 301 REPEAL; FULL REPEAL ADVOCATED BY THE SECRETARY OF ENERGY.

- Transfer jurisdiction in multi-resource regulation to state PUCs.

  NOT DONE.

- Review coal leasing policy and re-orient to encourage production.

  DONE.

- Amend Windfall Profits Tax to exclude newly discovered oil.

  ACHIEVED IN PART WITH TAX BILL.

- Exempt savings from federal income tax to encourage capital formation.

  SOME PROGRESS IN THIS AREA.

# Chapter Ten
# DEPARTMENT OF HEALTH AND HUMAN SERVICES

By Peter G. Germanis

Secretary of Health and Human Services Richard Schweiker has made considerable progress in the administration and management of the largest and one of the least efficient departments of government. He has managed to reduce the rate of growth in the HHS budget considerably and expects to trim more than 3,750 employees from its staff in FY 1982. Nevertheless, HHS survived the budget cutting process with fewer cuts than the Departments of Labor, Agriculture and others, due, in great part, to the reluctance of Congress to tamper with Social Security or Medicare. Each is part of the President's "social safety net." More fat remains to be trimmed.

Essentially, the Department is striving to achieve four fundamental goals: reduction of federal spending; reduction in the role of the federal government in the lives of individuals; return of authority for social programs to the states or the private sector wherever feasible; and reform of extraneous regulations which lead to counter-productive interference in the marketplace.

The most serious problems in HHS involve the Department's poor relations with Congress. The massive and far-reaching Omnibus Budget Reconciliation Act of 1981 achieved numerous policy changes—most of them cost saving. However, many of the provisions adopted were not those advanced by Secretary Schweiker as part of the Administration's Economic Recovery Program. The bill that finally passed was an amalgam of congressional proposals rooted in political expediency and therefore, was less than perfect.

Several priority bills were defeated or discredited to the point of retreat. Included among them was the Administration's proposal to place a cap on federal contributions to Medicaid payments. In the case of Medicare, the Secretary's recommendation for "permitting competitive arrangements for lower costs in Medicare contracting" was not adopted. Clearly, the most embarrassing episode was the mass retreat on Social Security reform. The blame for this debacle cannot be placed solely upon HHS. The White House insisted on managing the project and, because it was mismanaged, even the non-controversial reforms in the package did not receive a fair hearing. Although the block grant proposals survived in part, Congress cut less out of the program budgets than the President had asked for and attached more strings than he wanted.

*The author wishes to thank Douglas J. Antoon, Margaret D. Bonilla, John S. Eldred, Leonard D. Ellis, Lynn E. Munn, Lincoln C. Oliphant, Douglas Ross, and Robert J. Valero for their assistance in the preparation of this chapter.

## Office of the Secretary

The Secretary has failed to implement several of the recommendations in *Mandate for Leadership* which relate to the control of health care costs. Specifically, *Mandate* called for a unit to screen new surgical procedures; no such unit has been established, and no effort is evident to accomplish this important cost-control objective by other means. Moreover, the Department does not appear to have begun to wrestle with difficult, long-term questions relating to the cost-benefit trade-offs between surgery and extended therapeutic care.

One recommendation which was accepted during the first months of the new Administration may now be in jeopardy. The *Mandate* report suggested beefing up the Office of the Inspector General. Funding levels for the IG's office remained essentially unchanged through FY 1981 and the first round of FY 1982 proposals. However, the added 12 percent reductions required in late 1981 for FY 1982 seriously threaten the effectiveness of this office. Given the role of the IG in uncovering and eliminating fraud in the various aid and entitlement programs, cuts in this area are ill-advised. More could be saved by aggressively seeking out and prosecuting fraud wherever it is found. To this end, the various audit and investigation teams in HHS should be transferred to the IG's office. Although investigators need the expertise which can best be gained closer to the operational department, this expertise can be protected better if it is first gained in the field and then held in an elite office which is insulated from the operational agencies that are sometimes part of the fraud problem.

## Office of Human Development Services

The Office of Human Development Services (OHDS) has had a generally high rate of success in implementing the short-term recommendations of *Mandate*. Dorcas Hardy, the Assistant Secretary for OHDS, has moved swiftly to meet President Reagan's budget goals. Many programs that were targeted for reduction have been cut back; others have been eliminated. There has been a noticeable reduction in the number of regulations as well as a re-evaluation and clarification of those regulations considered worthwhile or essential. It should be noted, however, that many of the program cut backs suggested in *Mandate* were implemented due to the enormous budget reductions imposed on OHDS, and not necessarily because of a decision that the programs themselves were excessive.

Many of the programs within OHDS that were once federally controlled were "block granted" to the states. One notable example is the Title XX program, which was put in a block grant and sent to the states along with the responsibility for determining which Title XX

100

services the states would offer. Because the states received less money in this form, many of the Title XX programs targeted by *Mandate* were in fact cut because the individual states could not meet the funding void. The block grant program has also led to a dramatic reduction in the regulations governing these programs. Six pages of new HHS regulations replaced 368 pages for twenty-five old categorical programs in the *Code of Federal Regulations*. Substantial funding reductions were also achieved in research and grant programs, such as legal aid and child care.

One area where OHDS has had particular success is in the placement of new personnel. Both Secretary Schweiker and Assistant Secretaty Hardy have emphasized efficient management and competent staff, especially in appointive positions. However, staff reductions, both through RIFs and attrition, have streamlined the Department and reduced the number of "layers" of authority. For example, Dorcas Hardy had twenty-six individuals reporting to her when she took over OHDS; she has cut this number to six by streamlining the different branches of the Office.

### Health Care Financing Administration

*Mandate for Leadership* called for an immediate study to determine the future course of the "Talmadge Amendment," with a possible reorganization of HCFA to more effectively carry out this legislative directive. Although no team has been formed, the savings measures featured in the amendment were incorporated in the Omnibus Budget Reconciliation Act of 1981. Most of the regulations—but not all—have been written by HCFA to "implement the law."

The staff of Secretary Schweiker can also be given credit for their compliance with abortion legislation passed in recent years. The previous Secretary used every conceivable delay before notifying states of any new rules relating to abortion. In contrast, the present staff at HHS dispatched telegrams immediately upon the enactment of changes further restricting abortion funding under the Hyde amendment during the past year. In addition, the HHS staff discovered that health services through the Indian Health Services were funded through the Interior Department appropriation bill and therefore were not covered under the Hyde amendment. They nonetheless extended the regulations to that Agency and notified members of Congress of the oversight. The Department has also—not surprisingly—enforced the Schweiker amendment to the letter; the Schweiker amendment outlaws discrimination in medical schools based on an individual's views on abortion.

By and large, a great number of *Mandate for Leadership* short-term recommendations for HCFA have been addressed either directly or indirectly in the 1981 Budget Reconciliation Act. For example, *Mandate* recommended enhancing the Bureau of Quality Control and the Office of the Inspector General with the ultimate goal of fraud and abuse detection. Thus far, there has been no dramatic enhancement of either. However, in line with the Administration's overall objectives, states have been provided the incentives to beef up their detection of fraud and abuse. This was accomplished by allowing a state to win a one percent increase in its federal payment if the state's recovery of fraud and abuse equals one percent of the federal contribution to that state.

HCFA Administrator Carolyne K. Davis has realigned the upper-level management structure and assembled a team of five experienced and politically attuned managers and health care experts to report directly to her. Other structural realignments have occurred within the five new components: associate administrator for operations, associate administrator for policy, associate administrator for management and support services, director—office of external affairs, and director—office of executive operations. This streamlined arrangement should increase the efficiency of the HCFA operation and serve to promote innovation in the management of the Medicare and Medicaid programs.

Along these same lines, *Mandate* recommended investigating the possibility of increasing the physical centralization of HCFA offices to improve morale and productivity. HCFA has effectively been relocated to Baltimore, leaving approximately only 200 persons in Washington.

A major theme of *Mandate* was the reduction of the role of the federal government in the management of the nation's health care programs. This was partially accomplished in the 1981 Omnibus Reconciliation Bill. Legislation developed by the Congress in lieu of the Administration's proposals effectively returned management of the Medicaid program to the states, which may submit waivers to the Secretary for operating programs that the states feel most appropriately suit their Medicaid program needs. HCFA's responsibility will be primarily that of oversight as states develop and manage their own programs.

Increasing competition in the delivery of health care services for Medicare, Medicaid, and other government programs was stressed as a major priority in *Mandate for Leadership*. Although many of the recommendations were considered to be long-term in nature, HHS has already formed a task force to establish the ground work for enhancing the competitive forces in health care delivery system. The task force is expected to announce its recommendations late this year or early next year. Its conclusions are expected to include a program to provide greater incentives for people to select the most efficient deliverers of health care. Currently, consumers tend to be shielded from the true costs of health care through some form of insurance, which often leads to the use of unnecessary health services. The options now being considered include giving Medicare and Medicaid recipients vouchers which they could use to purchase health care in the marketplace, or a restructuring of tax incentives for health care expenditures.

Other efforts aimed at reducing government's role included recommendations for phasing out the PSRO program, while encouraging reliance on the private sector for appropriate utilization in reviewing health care services. While the intent was clear, the legislation enacted reflected the wishes of Congress and therefore the PSRO program remains in the budget to a limited extent.

As in other federal agencies, HHS is participating in the Administration's program aimed at reducing the regulatory/paperwork burden. At HCFA, the effort is twofold. Not only is there a task force established to review all burdensome regulations, but there is also an effort to attack the cost of unnecessary paperwork by reducing requirements placed on intermediaries and carriers. Contractors to HCFA will be encouraged to utilize the highest levels of technology in the performance of their contractual obligations. In day-to-day operations, carriers and intermediaries will be expected to employ paperless technologies in an effort to reduce what has been estimated to be about a $675 million administrative cost for Medicare Parts A and B alone. In addition, the Office of Health Regulation has been abolished.

In the administration of the Medicare and Medicaid programs, HCFA is expected to rely on the private sector to the greatest extent possible. Whether in the provision of Medicaid services by competitive entities such as HMOs, in carrier and intermediary competition for contracting of program management, or in competition in bidding for goods and services, the private sector will enjoy a major role. This effort will become more apparent as the Administration concentrates on Medicare through its forthcoming competition legislation.

In the past year, HCFA has concentrated on reviewing requirements which are imposed on contractor performance through contractor arrangement initiatives. Efforts to improve contractor performance are expected to continue, with competition serving as a cornerstone of the HFCA efforts.

**Public Health Service**

*Mandate for Leadership* advised the new Administration to re-evaluate the role of the federal government in the development of

103

Health Maintenance Organizations (HMOs), which have been subsidized since 1973. Not only did the Administration support the recommendations of *Mandate*, but it went one step further, arguing that federal aid to HMOs was unnecessary. Congress, however, rejected the Administration's proposal and has continued funding HMOs, albeit at a reduced level. Nevertheless, it does appear that the proposals set forth in *Mandate* have been implemented. Although there has been no official moratorium on program awards, no new HMOs have been funded. It appears that limited money now available will go to existing programs.

The original authorization for the Office of Adolescent Pregnancy has been revoked and replaced with a new adolescent pregnancy program authorized by the Omnibus Budget Reconciliation Act of 1981.

*Mandate* called for a reorganization of the program, which has been done. Further, *Mandate* called for improved integration with other initiatives so as to maximize effectiveness in reaching pregnant adolescents. In addition, efforts were to focus on developing models and testing different approaches to improve the use of authorized funds. Formally, the new statute meets *Mandate's* criteria. Whether the new statutory language will produce any real improvement cannot now be judged, but Congress has enacted new language, which has produced a legal basis substantially better than the original statute.

The new adolescent pregnancy provisions will become a new Title XX of the Public Health Service Act. The new title requires that the parents of minors be notified (in most cases) if a minor is provided with adolescent pregnancy services. Also, the new title prohibits payments to programs which provide abortions, abortion counseling, or abortion referral.

Although guidelines have been issued, no new regulations have been promulgated within the past year under Title X (Family Planning Services) as suggested by *Mandate*. *Mandate* called for studies regarding various abortion issues. These studies have not been done.

As part of the block grant approach to health service delivery, the Administration proposed ending categorical state formula grant programs for alcoholism and drug abuse and proposed rescinding the service delivery portions of the Mental Health Systems Act—placing all three programs with a Health Services Block Grant.

Congress has approved the block grant approach—altering the Administration's initial configuration, but not its intent. Public Law 97-35 established an Alcohol and Drug Abuse and Mental Health Services block grant, with funds flowing directly to the states. Several provisions contained in that block grant will help assure improved and increased emphasis upon the service and treatment needs of the chronically mentally ill—among them a specific mandate to serve that hitherto seriously underserved population, as recommended by *Mandate*. In an effort to assure that funds are utilized to provide community-based services, particularly to the chronically mentally ill, Congress required that no funds be expended for inpatient care. While benign in appearance, this provision could have the effect of restricting unduly the use of short-term, medically necessary inpatient care in the treatment of the chronic patient. In the main, however, the short-term options recommended in *Mandate* in this regard have been followed.

*Mandate* noted that a shortage of trained mental health professionals existed in 1980, and suggested a continuation of support for training programs. The Administration proposed, and Congress agreed, to terminate the single source of federal funds providing specialized residency or graduate training to address the documented shortage of psychiatric professionals.

Overall, the Department has made significant progress in halting the actual and projected growth in the health professions' education programs. Areas of special need and priority have been retained, while some of the programs with questionable value have either been reduced or eliminated.

The Secretary has quite properly recognized that while there is a significant nursing shortage in this country, solutions to correct this shortage should properly come from the private sector and not the federal government. This is an important distinction because typically when a problem such as a nursing shortage arises, the federal government has responded with some new massive federal program. In the area of nursing shortages, there is a great deal of evidence to suggest that conditions in the workplace are the significant factor rather than any special training programs.

The Administration proposed stopping new NHSC scholarships in 1982, with a projected leveling off of the corps at 2,500 members. Under the Carter Administration, the goal was to have 9,000 members in the corps by the end of the 1980s. This dramatic expansion would clearly have been out of step with the Reagan Administration's objective to allow the private sector to take care of many of the basic services in the health care area. The Secretary expressed his concern about creating a vast number of federally supported doctors to compete with those in the private sector, and took steps to slow down the growth of the corps so that it could be properly used in areas of need. The Senate agreed with the proposal not to award any new scholarships for the NHSC program, but the House Reconciliation Bill provided for 550 new scholarships per year for FY 1982, 1983, and 1984.

HHS is currently examining criteria for health manpower area designation. In September, shortage areas were de-designated for the first time in the *Federal Register*. Previously, the Carter Administration kept adding to the list without acknowledging that some areas were no longer shortage areas. This is an important step toward meeting *Mandate's* recommendation, and efforts in this areas should be continued.

The Health Services Administration and the program contained within it have undergone substantial changes in the last few months. This is in part due to modified versions of the health block grants passed by Congress in August. For example, most of the public health hospitals are being closed, and once this has been accomplished, and the block grants are fully implemented, HSA will no longer be large enough to exist by itself. The Secretary is working on an organizational plan to consolidate HSA with other areas of the Department, once the changes outlined above have occurred.

The FDA has been one agency that has been particularly burdened with regulations. Secretary Schweiker has pledged stopping "regulatory overkill" as a major goal during his tenure in office. To this end, FDA appears to be moving slowly but surely in the direction outlined in *Mandate*.

For example, Arthur Hayes, Jr., the new FDA commissioner, has assembled a task force to look for ways to reduce the time required for new drug approvals, with the hope of getting new, effective drugs on the market sooner. Similarly, FDA's new drug application (NDA) policy is being closely monitored. It should enhance the production of more generic drugs by sharply reducing the cost of demonstrating the safety and efficacy of a drug. *Mandate* also recommended seeking legislation that would provide a full 17-year patent protection once drug marketing is approved. A bill to this effect has already passed the Senate with the Administration's strong support.

The Administration, however, has done little to modify the effect of the Delaney clause, which imposes a zero-risk standard on food additives that may contain any trace of carcinogens. If enforced as written, the Delaney clause could lead to the banning of many foods. Fortunately, Senator Hatch's food safety bill (S. 1442) would allow exceptions to the present ban on cancer-causing additives, by stipulating that the restriction apply only to substances that present a "significant risk" to health.

In general, the new direction of the FDA is a positive one, aimed at reducing counter-productive government interference in the food and drug industries, thereby allowing them to better serve the public. It could, however, be accelerated.

One of the major concerns of the National Institutes of Health is the selection of a new director. The directorship has been vacant since the unexpected resignation of Dr. Donald Fredrickson in July 1981. In addition, several NIH divisions lack directors, and other key jobs remain unfilled. For this reason, two of *Mandate's* recommendations have not been fulfilled: strengthening the Director's authority over the individual directors; and, filling the vacancies on the Institute's Advisory Councils. A new NIH director is expected to be named soon and this should speed up the other appointments.

NIH is making progress in minimizing that portion of funds which goes to indirect costs rather than research itself. The NIH Director Advisory Committee has recommended that a fixed obligation grant process be attempted on a trial basis. This should reduce administrative costs for both NIH and universities since it eliminates a considerable amount of cost reporting.

The Advisory Committee to the Director of NIH has also developed an outline for patent policy guidelines. The thrust of the committee's efforts has been to examine some of the problems associated with more extensive cooperative research relationships between universities and industry. Definite policies and procedures have yet to be finalized.

The proposed budget cuts for the Public Health Service (PHS) create a no-growth situation. A new PHS Assistant Secretary was appointed promptly, and other key appointments have also been completed. Nonetheless, a few slots remain filled with "acting" appointments.

### The Social Security Administration

The Social Security Administration (SSA), now headed by John Svahn, has had a good record in complying with the recommendations set forth in *Mandate for Leadership*. A new U.S. refugee policy, which falls under the jurisdiction of SSA, has been implemented through presidential policy and refugees to this country have been processed quickly. Technically, the Cuban and Haitian immigrants were classified as "entrants," not refugees. Initially, there were some 124,900 such "entrants" of which about 122,000 have been resettled. Many of the other 3,000 have special placement problems. By the end of 1981, policies to implement the Comprehensive Refugee Act of 1980 will be in place.

Although *Mandate* made few specific recommendations for dealing with the funding crisis in Social Security, the Administration has already taken important steps to improve the financial integrity of the system. Cutbacks initiated by the President and cleared by Congress include the elimination of benefits for new post-secondary students aged 18-22 after August 1982; the $255 lump sum death benefit; and the $122 monthly minimum benefit. Recent action on Capitol Hill indicates that this last item may be restored.

The Administration's more revolutionary Social Security plan was soundly rejected by Congress. The major planks of the Administration's package included lowering future replacement rates (to compensate for the benefit over-liberalizations of the early 1970s), reducing early retirement benefits to encourage workers to remain in the labor force longer, and delaying the annual cost-of-living adjustment. The plan also had two recommendations advanced by *Mandate*: remove the earnings limitation, and reform the disability program. Unfortunately, little progress in the way of serious reform has been made due to the politically sensitive nature of this proposal. In fact, the whole issue may actually have damaged the President's image. It is reassuring to note, however, that unlike many members of Congress, the Administration recognizes that the Social Security program is plagued with serious problems and it is willing to work for a solution. To this end, it has proposed that a bipartisan task force develop permanent solutions to the problems confronting the Social Security system.

In addition, SSA has some very serious computer problems which must be addressed immediately. The current hardware and software is deficient. Commissioner Svahn is developing a plan before piecing or patching a system together. The importance of adopting a comprehensive plan in this area in the near future cannot be overstated.

### Budget

In March 1981, Secretary Schweiker presented an HHS budget of $250.7 billion for FY 1982. This was $7.5 billion less than the budget offered by the previous administration just two months earlier. With the passage of the Omnibus Reconciliation Act of 1981 in July, a large part of the Administration's efforts to reduce federal spending was in place. Table 1 compares the FY 1981 spending levels, the FY 1982 Administration request, and the House Committee recommendations with the *Mandate for Leadership* proposed budget for the Department of Health and Human Services.

House Resolution 4560, which provides the new budget authority for the Departments of Labor, Health and Human Services, Education, and other related agencies, grants $63.8 billion in new budget authority to HHS. In order to cope with larger than predicted budget deficits, however, the President has asked for additional across-the-board reductions of 12 percent in appropriation requests for non-defense programs for 1982. In accordance with the President's guidelines, Secretary Schweiker has revised his appropriation request downward to $62.6 billion. This brings it more in line with the proposed level suggested in *Mandate*.

TABLE 1

| Category | FY 1981 Appropriation | President's FY 1982 Request | FY 1982 Committee Bill | Mandate's FY 1982 Recommendation |
|---|---|---|---|---|
| | | (in millions) | | |
| Public Health Service | | | | |
| Health Services Administration | $ 1,268.0 | $ 981.3 | $ 1,051.9 | $ 1,338.3 |
| Centers for Disease Control | 279.1 | 304.2 | 326.6 | 334.5 |
| National Institutes of Health | 3,573.6 | 3,762.5 | 3,835.0 | 3,590.0 |
| Alcohol, Drug Abuse, and Mental Health Administration | 1,034.4 | 933.9 | 938.6 | 1,007.5 |
| Health Resources Administration | 489.8 | 233.7 | 292.7 | 412.9 |
| Assistant Secretary for Health | 273.7 | 297.7 | 246.2 | 262.4 |
| Subtotal | 6,918.5 | 6,513.3 | 6,691.0 | 6,945.6 |
| Health Care Financing Administration | 26,953.8 | 33,489.4 | 32,051.4 | 28,278.7 |
| Social Security Administration | 19,794.4 | 19,920.7 | 19,412.1 | 19,795.0 |
| Human Development Services | 4,667.4 | 5,313.3 | 5,338.4 | 4,923.0 |
| Total HHS | $58,557.2 | $65,498.7 | $63,791.5 | $60,874.6 |

Source: Harrison Donnelly, "House Committee Approves $87.3 billion for Health, Welfare, Education, Labor," *Congressional Quarterly*, September 26, 1981, p. 1841; House Republican Conference, *Legislative Digest*, Vol. X, No. 23, Pt. II, September 28, 1981, p. 5; and Charles L. Heatherly (ed.), *Mandate for Leadership* (Washington, D.C.: The Heritage Foundation, 1981), pp. 302-306.

NOTE: Figures do not add to total HHS because the table is incomplete. In addition, FDA is subtracted from the *Mandate* budget to make it comparable with the others.

## RECOMMENDATIONS

(Action taken on 92 out of 147)

### Office of the Secretary

- Create within the Office of the Secretary a unit to screen all new surgical procedures in light of available alternatives.

NOT IMPLEMENTED.

- Reevaluate all medical procedures in light of new procedures and standard practice.

NOT IMPLEMENTED.

- Set up a task force to review data on effectiveness of treatment modes and improve capacity to evaluate controversy of unnecessary medical procedures.

NOT IMPLEMENTED.

- Revise HHS policy on civil rights enforcement to say that the federal government must be color- and gender-blind.
  NOT IMPLEMENTED.

- Enforce the Schweiker Amendment, which prohibits discrimination at medical schools on the basis of views on abortion.
  IMPLEMENTED.

- Keep the Office of Consumer Affairs, if for no other reason than to allay congressional efforts to create a department.
  IMPLEMENTED.

- Realign the Office of Legislative Affairs with instructions to drastically improve congressional relations.
  TWO MAJOR CONGRESSIONAL SNAFUS, BUT SOME PROGRESS TOO.

- Give the new Assistant Secretary of Public Affairs authority over all HHS media efforts.
  IMPLEMENTED.

- Beef up the Inspector General's office to expose current fraud and waste within HHS, and provide a programmatic vehicle for the enunciation of new policy directions.
  FUTURE CUTS PENDING.

- Ensure that regional directors are welded into a cohesive group.
  NOT IMPLEMENTED.

- Examine the statutory requirements for various bureaus and units to see which could be amalgamated or dropped administratively.
  CONSIDERABLE PROGRESS IN HCFA.

- Foster legislation that fully implements a competitive approach in health care delivery by having HHS minimize its role as a government entity, reduce its regulation, oppose legislation that would expand its role, and devise statutes that would enable or enhance the private sector's innovative approaches.
  PROGRESS NOTED, BUT MORE WORK REMAINS.

### Office of Human Development Services (OHDS)

- Review the Child Welfare Amendments regulations, taking special care to ensure that eligibility requirements for various types of post-adoption assistance are not excessive, and that formulas for the computation of payment amounts are not overly generous.

CARTER'S "MIDNIGHT" REGULATIONS REVOKED.
REFORM REGULATIONS DRAFTED.

- Pull the Interagency Day Care Regulations pending further review if they are not yet final.

  IMPLEMENTED. FINAL REVIEW DUE ON JANUARY 1, 1982.

- Reevaluate the Rural Transportation Initiative, with an eye to eliminating duplication in transport facilities between OHDS programs, and among programs of other agencies.

  IMPLEMENTED.

- Place emphasis for Title XX on actual delivery of services, not on training for social sciences professionals, and arrange for an immediate consultation between the Secretary and the states to explore ways to correct this situation.

  IMPLEMENTED. TITLE XX SUBSUMED INTO BLOCK GRANTS.

- Reaffirm the centrality of family involvement to the success of services delivered under Head Start, and continue to emphasize extensive parental involvement as required in current regulations.

  IMPLEMENTED.

- Apply to OHDS programs the provisions of the Hatch Amendment contained in P.L. 95-561, and the Education Amendments of 1978.

  NOT IMPLEMENTED.

- Give top priority within the Administration for Children, Youth and Families to grants for provision of direct services rather than grants for theoretical research.

  IMPLEMENTED. EMPHASIS ON GRANTS FOR DIRECT SERVICES.

- Draft a reauthorization bill for the Older Americans Act with a preliminary introduction target of late March or early April.

  IMPLEMENTED. ACT RE-AUTHORIZED.

- Draft a reauthorization bill for the Child Abuse Prevention and Treatment Act, which in large part is under the aegis of ACYF/OHDS.

  PASSED BY CONGRESS, BUT WITHOUT LEADERSHIP FROM HHS.

- Draft regulations to starve out the "public interest" law firms.
  REGULATIONS LEGALLY QUESTIONABLE. GRANTS FOR LEGAL SERVICES HAVE BEEN REDUCED.

- Consider preparing a major initiative for the aged outside of the scope of traditional welfare state principles.
  PROGRESS NOTED.

- Consider the elimination of the Social Security Earnings test for another that really accomplishes the task of barring the retired from receiving unemployment insurance, etc.
  ELIMINATION PROPOSED, BUT WITHDRAWN AMID THE SOCIAL SECURITY FIASCO.

- Review the research work underway, proposed in RFP form, and in the design stage, starting before the transition and continuing throughout the first year.
  LARGELY IMPLEMENTED THROUGH FUNDING CUT-BACK.

- Redirect research and development funds to block grants to the states and to nutrition services, and reduce and eventually eliminate federal funding of social service research projects.
  SUBSTANTIAL PROGRESS NOTED.

- Oppose attempts to lift or otherwise circumvent standing authorization ceilings in programs—notably the current $2.5 billion cap on Title XX outlays and child welfare services.
  IMPLEMENTED. TITLE XX SUBSUMED INTO BLOCK GRANT PROGRAM WITH BUDGET CUTS.

- Cut the following programs below current levels:

  1. Research and evaluation across the board;
     IMPLEMENTED.

  2. Title XX training funds;
     IMPLEMENTED.

  3. "Social change" programs within ACYF;
     IMPLEMENTED. ACYF FUNDING REDUCED.

  4. Coordination activities within ADD;
     IMPLEMENTED.

- Run OHDS (whose operations consist primarily of grants administration) by a team stressing sound management as a companion of policy expertise.
  IMPLEMENTED.

- Handle the staffing of OHDS programs with an eye to retaining as many experienced "nuts and bolts" personnel as possible, unless individual considerations of competence and policy support indicate otherwise.

  IMPLEMENTED.

- Make high appointments on basis of merit rather than tokenism.

  IMPLEMENTED.

- Build strong, reliable teams to operate OHDS programs.

  IMPLEMENTED.

- Preserve credibility by using entities independent of the agency for all evaluations and most research.

  ACCOMPLISHED THROUGH CUTBACK IN FUNDING.

- Give priority to substantive rather than procedural questions in OHDS program evaluations, in initial allocations of both research and evaluation dollars.

  IMPLEMENTED.

- Attempt to make research and evaluation methods scientific (i.e., replicable), giving emphasis to fundamental evaluation of significant programs and policy variables across a wide and representative sample of sites and programs.

  IMPLEMENTED.

- Promote self-sufficiency by providing private individuals with rational incentives through work effort, family unity, and community involvement.

  DRAFT REGULATIONS AND OTHER POLICIES REFLECT THIS CONVICTION.

### Health Care Financing Administration (HCFA)

- Assemble a team to study the Talmadge Amendment to determine what must be done and when.

  NO TEAM FORMED. SAVINGS MEASURES INCORPORATED IN OMNIBUS RECONCILIATION ACT OF 1981.

- Form a small team of staff assistants to the Secretary to closely monitor the adherence of the states to limitations placed on Medicaid funding by the Hyde Amendment.

  NOT IMPLEMENTED.

- Commission follow-up studies to ensure its strong enforcement, emphasizing the detection and elimination of Medicaid fraud

113

and abuse so that Medicaid resources can be concentrated on better health care for the poor.

INCENTIVES FOR FRAUD DETECTION INCLUDED IN RECONCILIATION ACT.

- Review and modify where necessary HCFA FY 1982 budget proposals.

ADMINISTRATION PROPOSED SHARP BUDGET CUT. CONGRESS INCREASED FUNDING.

- Determine whether to request continued funding for the Office of Health Regulation and, if so, how that Office should be restructured and staffed.

OHR ABOLISHED.

- Review all regulations appearing in FY 1980 Regulation Plan to determine which are complying strictly with congressional mandate, and delay those which are being "expanded" undesirably.

IMPLEMENTED.

- Review (and put on hold) all efforts pursuant to OMB directive concerning capital constructions and efforts to further centralize health planning in the federal government.

IMPLEMENTED.

- Review the budget for new Office of Beneficiary Services. Question desirability of not acting first on a "sample" basis with respect to distribution of pamphlets and information.

REVIEW ACCOMPLISHED. PROGRAM CUT. SAMPLING NOT IMPLEMENTED.

### Administration of Medicare/Medicaid

- Improve program integrity through enhancement of Bureau of Quality Control and Office of Inspector General.

EFFORTS CONCENTRATING ON PROBLEM STATES.

- Expedite development of training programs for state agencies.

NOT IMPLEMENTED.

- Determine the desirability and feasibility of increasing physical centralization of HCFA offices.

HCFA HAS BEEN EFFECTIVELY RELOCATED TO BALTIMORE.

114

- Develop ways to improve coordination of Medicare and Medicaid through administrative and legislative proposals.

  GOAL OF ADMINISTRATION IS TO SEPARATE MEDICARE AND MEDICAID.

- Begin intensive analysis of cost-effectiveness of Medicaid program to determine why federal dollars are so hard to track and state compliance so erratic.

  NOT IMPLEMENTED.

- Implement efforts to effect the use of uniform billing forms more rapidly.

  NOT YET IMPLEMENTED, BUT APPROVED IN PRINCIPLE.

- Examine degree to which coordination exists and can be enhanced between research activities of HFCA, National Center for Health Services Research (NCHSR), National Center for Health Statistics (NCHS), and National Center for Health Care Technology (NCHCT).

  CONSOLIDATION OF NCHSR AND NCHCT PROPOSED. KILLED IN CONGRESS.

- Press the Office of Legislation and Policy to establish good liaison with key members and staffs of Congress.

  PROGRESS NOTED.

- Establish office to assist states through improved dissemination of data, relevant information, results of experiments, etc.

  NO OFFICE ESTABLISHED. INCREASED USE OF MEDICARE/ MEDICAID INSTITUTE OF TECHNICAL ASSISTANCE.

- Consider creation of Office of Exceptions and Appeals within HCFA to give providers the opportunity to seek expeditious relief from requirements that would be unduly prejudicial or improper in particular cases.

  NOT IMPLEMENTED.

- Work with Treasury and Congress to rationalize conflicts between tax and Medicare policy, or anti-trust and Medicare policy, that tend to induce less than optimal decision-making by providers from a health care delivery standpoint.

  NO GENERAL REFORM HAS YET BEGUN.

115

- Focus heavily on reducing superfluous contracts and grants awarded by HCFA.

BUDGET CUT FROM $46 MILLION TO $30 MILLION.

- Increase the number and variety of experiments and demonstrations designed to promote competition and reduce regulation, with as large a role for states and private industry as possible.

SOME GRANT MONEY DIVERTED TO THESE EXPERIMENTS.

- Examine physician reimbursement under Medicare and Medicaid; determine which, if any, alternatives to the present UCR system would be desirable and politically acceptable, and explore possible incentives to induce physicians to accept any proposed changes.

NO DECISIONS.

- Continue to explore ways to assist states to develop cost-effective prospective payment systems.

AUTHORIZED IN RECONCILIATION BILL.

- Develop methods for assuring that home health services grow in a cost-effective manner.

LEGISLATION PROPOSED IN CONGRESS. HHS HAS RESERVATIONS ABOUT COST-EFFECTIVENESS.

- Determine whether unnecessary utilization and higher costs of hospital care may be associated with the inability of physicians to practice at certain hospitals within a community because of restrictive medical staff privileges; if so, what solutions may be feasible.

NO ANALYSIS OF THIS QUESTION.

- Examine the desirability of continuing the PSRO program, and possible alternatives.

LEGISLATION TO REDUCE.

### Improving Long-Term Care Services

- Consider new ways to reimburse skilled- and intermediate-care facilities under Medicare and Medicaid, such as prospective payment systems that will help reduce the use of unnecessary hospital beds for chronically ill people.

NOT IMPLEMENTED.

- Develop realistic proposals for financing long-term care.

NOT IMPLEMENTED.

116

- Help states and communities develop more effective programs of providing long-term care to the elderly and disabled or chronically ill.

  INCLUDED IN BLOCK GRANTS.

- Reduce or eliminate the PSRO program (presently spending about $193 million a year).

  IMPLEMENTED.

- Reduce the volume of research, demonstration, and evaluation projects of HCFA.

  IMPLEMENTED.

- Exercise extreme care in choosing a Director for the Bureau of Program Policy, selecting one who is creative, knowledgeable, and shares a philosophy consistent with that of the Administration.

  IMPLEMENTED.

## Long-Term Priorities

- Develop new ways to encourage philanthropic contributions (both time and money) to health care services delivery.

  ENACTED IN TAX CODE.

- Prepare for eventual "phase-out" of both Medicare and Medicaid (perhaps HCFA itself) pursuant to development over 10 to 12 years or less of a delivery system that better serves the poor and the aged by relying on "vouchers," private health plans, and the free market.

  VOUCHER LEGISLATION PROPOSED.

## Public Health Services

- Review the federal involvement in dealing with HMOs to determine what, if any, role the federal government should play. Consider:

  1. Imposing a six-month moratorium on new program awards and extensions (beyond the six-month period) of existing awards.

     NOT IMPLEMENTED.

  2. Conducting a detailed assessment of existing projects to look at financial viability and organizational development.

     IMPLEMENTED.

  3. Determining whether the emphasis should be on continued support for existing programs or for planning and feasibility of new projects.

AVAILABLE MONEY WILL GO TO EXISTING PRO-
GRAMS.

4. Undertaking a thorough assessment of the federal role in
HMO development.

IMPLEMENTED. FINANCING CUT 1981.

**Office of Adolescent Pregnancy**

- Reorganize the Office of Adolescent Pregnancy by better
integrating it with other initiatives to maximize their effectiveness in reaching pregnant adolescents.

IMPLEMENTED.

- Focus efforts on trying to develop models, and test different
approaches which can be utilized at the local level and
integrated into more comprehensive programs.

IMPLEMENTED.

- Commission study to determine the relationship between the
provision of family planning services and the incidence of
venereal disease, adolescent pregnancy, and the choice of
abortions by unemancipated minors.

RESEARCH PROVISIONS MADE UNDER ADOLESCENT
FAMILY LIFE ACT.

**Title X of the Public Health Service Act—Family Planning**

- Propose regulations which would:
1. Condition the provision of prescriptive contraception services to unemancipated minors upon the written notification
to one or both parents or legal guardian of said minors.

NOT IMPLEMENTED.

2. Require grantees to inform patients receiving services under
Title X of the potential consequences to their health and
safety of recommended drugs and devices and of abortion.

NOT IMPLEMENTED.

3. Require grantees under Title X to provide the facts of fetal
development, as stipulated by the Secretary, to all recipients
of pregnancy testing services, abortion counseling or referral
services, or for the abortion itself.

NOT IMPLEMENTED.

4. Reserve a significant portion of Title X funds for those
organizations that provide family planning services within the
context of respect for human life at all stages of development.

NOT IMPLEMENTED.

- Commission studies to determine:
  1. Whether a woman seeking pregnancy services is more likely to choose abortion if she receives such services from a Title X grantee that provides abortions than if she receives such services from a Title X grantee that does not provide abortions.

     NOT IMPLEMENTED.

  2. The effects of abortions on the physical and mental health of women.

     NOT IMPLEMENTED.

### Alcohol, Drug Abuse & Mental Health Administration (ADAMHA)

- Assure flexibility in implementing the Waxman prevention set-aside so that some treatment services could be funded from this money, and reinstate the formula grant program.

  MOOT, NOW IN BLOCK GRANTS.

- Reinstate to formula grant program in ADAMHA/NIAA.

  MOOT, NOW IN BLOCK GRANTS.

- Strengthen the Community Support program—the current administration program dealing with chronically mentally ill—and gear up for implementation of the MHSA.

  INCLUDED IN BLOCK GRANTS. SERVICES PORTION REPEALED.

- Encourage policymakers in the Center for Disease Control to demonstrate concern for human life and the dignity of all human beings and to promulgate a policy statement to the effect that the only purpose of the Center for Disease Control is the identification and control of diseases and illnesses.

  CDC PRIORITIES HAVE IMPROVED. NO PUBLIC STATEMENT.

- Assess the impact of requiring states that receive funds through CDC to identify resources that they will commit to CDC programs, including perhaps the establishment of a minimum dollar figure or percentage and requiring reimbursement for the salaries of Public Health Service Advisors in the states.

  ASSESSMENT MADE. REIMBURSEMENT FROM STATES REQUIRED. NO MINIMUM ESTABLISHED.

- Encourage CDC to work with EPA, developing legislation if necessary, to get a clear agreement on HHS and EPA responsibilities with respect to environmental health effects.

  IN PROCESS.

119

## Food and Drug Administration

- Speed up FDA procedures so that drugs will reach the U.S. market sooner and assure companies that valuable trade secret information will be protected.

UNDER DISCUSSION, BUT NOT IMPLEMENTED.

- Allow innovative companies to retain their rights under the patent laws in order to maintain incentives for the development of new drugs.

IMPLEMENTED.

- Seek FDA legislation which will provide a full 17-year patent protection once drug marketing is approved while at the same time developing mechanisms to ensure timely submission of required data.

BILL PASSED IN SENATE. HEARINGS UNDERWAY IN HOUSE.

- Implement the 1975 Medical Devices Law in a prompt and rational manner even if changes in Bureau leadership retard FDA's progress.

IMPLEMENTED FOR MOST PART.

- Stress the need in FDA's radiological health activities to implement product safety standards and continue to improve programs aimed at helping state agencies and medical personnel eliminate unnecessary radiation exposure.

IMPLEMENTED.

- Change the leadership in the Bureau of Veterinary Medicine to alleviate problems encountered during the 1940s, such as undue industry influence, poor enforcement, and internal management cover-ups of information with important ramifications for public health.

IMPLEMENTED.

- Assess the effectiveness of FDA's "fast track" system for important new drugs.

UNDER DISCUSSION, BUT NOT IMPLEMENTED.

- Propose exemptions for a broad range of antibiotics now subject to batch certification, perhaps requiring a small number of batches to be tested at first to establish the manufacturer's track record, but then relying on other means, such as GMPs, to ensure antibiotic quality.

UNDER CONSIDERATION; NO ACTION.

- Review and implement where feasible the GAO's recommendations for improving internal management.
  NOT IMPLEMENTED.

- Examine pending proposals which would preempt state laws on hearing aids under the medical devices statute and implement a quick review of all pending regulations.
  NOT IMPLEMENTED. PROPOSALS FINALIZED INTO REGULATION WITHOUT EXAMINATION.

- Re-examine FDA conflict of interest regulations, especially with respect to outside advisors, to ensure they do not keep the agency from taking advantage of the best scientific expertise, as has been charged.
  UNDER CONSIDERATION.

- Begin to implement provisions like those in Senator Schweiker's drug bill administratively as far as possible.
  NOT ACCOMPLISHED.

- Assess scientific consensus on what constitutes adequate and well-controlled clinical trial; what standards should be for a study to be acceptable to FDA.
  NOT NEEDED.

### Health Resources Administration

- Dissolve the HRA, transferring health professions programs to the Health Services Administration and transferring health planning and health facilities functions being moved to HCFA.
  NOT IMPLEMENTED.

- Streamline the regulation writing process with regard to the programs of the Bureau of Health Planning, combined with a more restrictive view of the purposes to be accomplished by health systems agencies.
  IN PROCESS.

- Publish a comprehensive list of all members of health systems agencies so that the public and the Congress are informed as to who is making the day-to-day decisions regarding the future of American health care.
  IMPLEMENTED.

### Bureau of Health Professions Education

- Propose highly selective rescissions (with a major cut in the NHSC scholarship program, now transferred to HSA, as a centerpiece) with some of the funds reprogrammed to high priority health professions rather than just removed.

SHORT-TERM HIGHLY SELECTIVE RESCISSIONS MADE, INCLUDING NHSC.

- Focus on remedying the nursing shortage.

NOT IMPLEMENTED.

- Revamp BHPE, which designates health manpower shortage areas, with emphasis on areas whose needs are now being met and can be de-designated.

PROGRESS BEING MADE.

- Focus primarily on the Bureau of Community Health Services and the Bureau of Health Personnel Development and Services when establishing priorities within the Health Services Administration.

BLOCK GRANTS WILL RESULT IN CONSOLIDATION OF HSA.

## Bureau of Community Health Services

- Alter the goal of BCHS to assure services that are truly needed to be provided in a cost-efficient manner without interfering with the ability of the private sector to provide such services and without using these programs as a bootstrap to a national health service program.

DISCRETION TO STATES.

- Freeze all decisions that have long-term fiscal or policy implications for at least six months, including no new consultants, short-term (180 days or less) extensions of existing consulting and external contracting work, no new designations of medically undeserved areas, and no approvals for new community health centers or migrant health centers.

IMPLEMENTED.

- Develop a mechanism for updating the BCHS data base with regard to medially undeserved areas with emphasis on identifying areas for de-designation.

DE-DESIGNATION HAS OCCURRED.

- Evaluate the BCRR's usefulness both as an aggregate data source for reporting to Congress and as an instrument upon which to manage individual projects.

IN PROCESS.

- Restrain federal costs as a principal objective of the Bureau of Health Personnel Development and Services, both short- and long-term, to maintain maximum flexibility and impact on health personnel needs to underserved areas.

  IN PROCESS.

- Place a substantial number (400-500) of NHSC scholarship recipients who were ready for NHSC service on July 1, 1980 in independent practice sites.

  NOT IMPLEMENTED.

- Emphasize July 1981 placement of NHSC scholarship recipients should be away from placing individuals in Community Health Centers and other integrated sites.

  IMPLEMENTED.

- Rescind many of the appropriations for National Health Service Corps scholarships.

  IMPLEMENTED.

### National Institute of Health/Biomedical Research

- Commission a report on the extent and type of NIH drug development research and assess potential overlap with private sector activities, directing NIH wherever possible to encourage private industry to take on this work.

  NOT IMPLEMENTED.

- Strengthen the NIH Director's authority vis-a-vis the individual institute directors, for purposes of overall research priority planning and budgeting.

  NOT IMPLEMENTED.

- Examine, in cooperation with the Office of Management and Budget, the proportion of funds that go to indirect costs rather than research itself, and seek ways to minimize indirect costs.

  IN PROCESS.

- Launch an initiative to do away with unnecessary paperwork.

  IN PROCESS.

- Fill any vacancies on any of the Institute's Advisory Councils.

  NOT IMPLEMENTED.

- Review government patent policies to ensure that worthwhile NIH-supported inventions are brought through the development process, preferably by private entities picking up on NIH leads, and examine the need for changes in tax treatment of private research investment, especially in risky, innovative fields that may not seem to have much commercial potential.

NOT IMPLEMENTED.

- Establish a no-growth policy in the programs in the PHS and then move to make reductions in such programs as Health Planning, Community Health Centers, National Health Service Corps, Health Professionals Education programs, support for HMO development, and certain programs in ADAMHA.

IMPLEMENTED.

- Replace the PHS Assistant Secretary and the Carter Administration directors as soon as possible.

IMPLEMENTED, ALTHOUGH A FEW SLOTS REMAIN WITH "ACTING" APPOINTMENTS.

- Press for legislation to modify the Delaney clause on food additives and allow risk-benefit assessment.

NOT IMPLEMENTED.

- Press for new legislation to change the patent law to ensure drug companies receive the full benefit of their patent.

IMPLEMENTED THROUGH SENATE BILL (S. 255).

- Press for other new legislation where needed that could have an impact on drug development, e.g., tax treatment of research investment could be liberalized, particularly for research of "orphan drugs."

NOT IMPLEMENTED.

- Set priorities for implementing a Patient Package Insert program based on the nature and extent of use of several key drugs.

PROGRAM STAYED BY NEW COMMISSIONER.

- Consider the scope of the federal delivery system being developed which also employs National Health Service Corps personnel.

PARTIALLY ENACTED.

- Examine the size and nature of the Health Maintenance Organizations (HMOs) grant program with fewer and smaller grant awards directed to better selected sponsors.

GRANTS CUT SHARPLY.

## Social Security Administration

- Adopt a clear, concise U.S. refugee policy immediately, and quickly process refugees currently in camps within the United States.

  IMPLEMENTED THROUGH PRESIDENTIAL POLICY.

- Staff the SSA with some people who have experience in either running a state program or in working in an intergovernmental environment.

  IMPLEMENTED.

- Make the SSA Deputy Commissioner for Operations responsible for operations, and provide him with a staff independent of a mission staff to assist in dealing with subordinates.

  IN PROCESS. DEPUTY COMMISSIONER ESTABLISHED, BUT MAY NOT GET FULL AUTHORITY.

- Provide the Deputy Commissioner with all delegations necessary for performance of his responsibilties.

  IMPLEMENTED.

- Allow access to the Commissioner of these associates only through the Deputy Commissioner.

  NOT IMPLEMENTED.

- Establish an SSA Associate Commissioner for Field Operations to include the responsibility for all district office operations with responsibility for all Regional Commissioners.

  IMPLEMENTED.

- Review SSA senior staffing immediately.

  IMPLEMENTED.

- Correct the many glaring deficiencies as soon as possible. In addition to some minor reorganizational changes, personnel changes should be implemented as soon as possible.

  IMPLEMENTED, MAJOR REVAMPING.

- Refocus AFDC in the Office of Family Assistance toward providing assistance to states rather than trying to run their programs for them.

  IMPLEMENTED.

- Provide more direction for SSA's Office of Child Support Enforcement with a goal of reversing decline in collections as a percentage of total costs.

  IMPLEMENTED.

## Disability Insurance Program

- Revamp the existing disability determination process and appeals procedure.

  IN PROCESS.

- Clean up the eligibility process and the current caseload.

  IN PROCESS.

- Draw plans to take to the Congress to relieve the long-term problem of the definition of disability.

  IN PROCESS.

- Set up a program of periodic redetermination of eligibility to assure that beneficiaries are still eligible.

  BEING IMPLEMENTED.

# Chapter Eleven
# DEPARTMENT OF HOUSING AND URBAN DEVELOPMENT
### By Stuart M. Butler

The thrust of the 1980 *Mandate for Leadership* recommendations for HUD may be summarized in two words: decentralization and flexibility. In the context of a broad strategy aimed at returning discretion over the use of development and housing money to the states, the report made a number of key proposals. It recommended greater discretion for states in administering the Community Development Block Grant (CDBG), and argued that in the case of development programs retained under the direct control of HUD, the role of the field offices should be strengthened. While the report supported the idea of folding most development programs into the block grant, it did not propose the elimination of the Urban Development Action Grant program (UDAG). It did recommend that targeted federal development assistance be largely confined to UDAG, in combination with an enterprise zone program.

*Mandate for Leadership* urged the new Administration to press forward with a housing block grant, designed to consolidate housing assistance programs and to provide the states with greater discretion over housing funds. The block grant was also seen as an alternative to high-cost federal public housing and Section 8 programs. *Mandate* additionally recommended the reassessment and elimination of certain Federal Housing Administration (FHA) mortgage operations.

HUD may justly claim to have made good progress in initiating decisive change in the role of the federal government in housing and development. Some career officials are said to have described the changes undertaken and proposed as "revolutionary." While this is an exaggeration, the change already evident can be expected to gain in momentum as detailed proposals emerge from President Reagan's Commission on Housing. The Commission, created to examine and suggest solutions to the deep problems associated with housing, has recommended the adoption of a voucher system in its interim report. Such a program would provide wider but shallower rent subsidies than the expensive Section 8 program, allow tenants greater flexibility in choosing their housing, and concentrate much more on existing buildings. If it is eventually adopted by Congress—especially in conjunction with a housing block grant—HUD would virtually cease to be a direct provider of targeted housing assistance. Instead,

*The author wishes to thank L. George Griffin, David A. Hill, and Lee B. Holmes for their assistance in the preparation of this chapter.

it would focus on a strategy of income supplements designed to strengthen the general low-income rental market.

HUD Secretary Samuel R. Pierce, Jr. has been pressing hard for changes of this nature. He has given strong backing to vouchers, and the Commission's final report can be expected to strengthen the Secretary's hand when he seeks congressional approval. In addition, HUD's 1983 legislative agenda, presented to OMB in October 1981, proposes a $200 million rehabilitation block grant, to replace Section 312 loans and the Section 8 substantial and moderate rehabilitation programs. HUD also asked OMB for funds to support 40,000 housing vouchers, and requested legislation to widen the homesteading program. Throughout the HUD proposals, the emphasis is on improving the existing stock of housing, rather than on new construction programs.

While the proposals for long-term changes constitute a coherent strategy, the picture is less clear in the case of medium-term changes. Tension is building between OMB and HUD which may lead to clashes in the near future. There is resistance at HUD, for instance, to OMB pressure for the termination of elements of the FHA programs. Similarly, Secretary Pierce strongly opposed OMB's decision to eliminate UDAG in the budget request, and won a year's reprieve for the program by appealing directly to the President. Pierce now advocates that UDAG should remain under the control of HUD indefinitely, and not folded into the block grant as OMB has urged.

The Secretary's insistence that UDAG not be devolved to the states is a cause for some concern. *Mandate* did propose that the budget for UDAG be kept intact. However, that recommendation also suggested that the program include loans as well as grants, and that UDAG be combined with an enterprise zone program to stimulate private sector development in distressed neighborhoods. Simply retaining UDAG in its present form is inconsistent with the broad block grant approach and the thrust of the *Mandate* recommendations. Programs such as UDAG are inherently dangerous because they could be used by this and future administrations to exert political, rather than economic, leverage in the cities. HUD is now drafting changes in UDAG. Major improvements will be made possible by combining it with enterprise zones and by insuring that UDAG is insulated from politics.

In a second dispute between HUD and other departments over a development program, HUD is taking a line which is more consistent with the Administration's overall strategy. The enterprise zone concept was strongly endorsed by President Reagan during the presidential campaign. It has solid support among the states, several of which have enacted their own versions, and it has the backing of many minority organizations. The program is a potential showcase for supply-side economics. Although its political implications are apparent to some Administration officials, they have not pursued the idea with any vigor, and seem content to see others gain from the momentum. While virtually every organization involved in urban policy is pressing forward with the concept, the Administration has moved with embarrassing lethargy and internal discord. After nine months in office, the Administration has yet to announce its proposals, much to the irritation and frustration of zone proponents in Congress and the states. HUD officials have strongly advocated the concept in the cabinet council studying enterprise zones, and are helping to counter foot-dragging by Treasury. However, Secretary Pierce has not provided the high profile leadership necessary for success in such inter-departmental disputes, nor has he made the Administration fully aware of the broad implications of the concept.

Tension between departments is normal in every administration. Wrangling and indecision of this kind is nonetheless debilitating, and lends credence to the theory that the Reagan Administration can score stunning successes when the President takes personal charge, but flounders when there is no such central direction.

Despite the confusion surrounding some issues, HUD has made generally good progress in implementing short-term changes in the broad direction favored by the Administration and recommended in *Mandate*. Greater flexibility, for instance, has been introduced into the administration of CDBG funds. States can now operate the small cities program; the rules allow major cities greater discretion in the mix of housing and business-related expenditures. States have not universally welcomed this new power. Some governors argue that they lack the needed planning capacity to use the funds wisely. They also argue that the elimination of the federal planning program (Section 701) will make their task even more difficult. HUD believes that states will face only short-term planning problems, and, quite properly, has refused to be sidetracked in its policy of devolving decision-making to the states.

House resistance in the budget reconciliation process prevented passage of some of the short-term housing changes requested by HUD. Nevertheless, the Administration was able to amend the rules for public housing and the runaway Section 8 program. For example, tenants now will be required to contribute 30 percent of family income towards rent, rather than 25 percent, and income eligibility requirements for Section 8 are tightened. These small steps will help to reduce the depth of housing subsidies, but wide-ranging legislative reform will be required before the Administration can achieve a decisive change in the way low-income housing is provided and financed. HUD and the Commission on Housing are currently discussing policy revisions of this magnitude.

Rationalization and staff reductions in the Department are underway, although uncertainty surrounding the cuts may have unnecessarily weakened morale at many levels. No significant shift of staff to field operations has occurred, as recommended by *Mandate*. Although some field-related positions have been strengthened, a new position of Assistant Secretary for Field Operations has not been created.

The long-term changes under active discussion at HUD would constitute a decisive change in the role of the Department and in the nature of housing support in this country. Because these require congressional approval, HUD should concentrate on explaining the rationale of its policy to interested parties and on building a coalition of support. So far, HUD has done much better in debating new policy ideas within the Department than in "selling" them to the country. This has not helped the Administration. The impression is growing that, other than to cut back on existing programs, the Administration has no urban policy. HUD has done little to dispel that popular impression. The Department plays a central role in the social policy of the Reagan Administration. If its senior officials do not provide greater leadership, HUD will be vulnerable to attacks from those who charge that this Administration intends only to cut and to eliminate when it also should make efforts to improve.

## RECOMMENDATIONS
(Action taken on 26 out of 61)

### General Department-wide

- Implement hiring freeze department-wide, excluding only vital policy and advisory positions.
  IMPLEMENTED FOR OUTSIDE HIRING ONLY.

- Undertake in-depth personnel study (to be completed no later than July 1, 1981) for the Central Office and for key officials of field offices. Include:

  1. Complete evaluation and needs assessment.

  2. Review of grade structure through desk audits for functions and job descriptions.

  3. Plan for consolidation and realignment.

     ALL IN PROGRESS—INCLUDING FIELD REVIEW AND 20 PERCENT R.I.F.

- Initiate budget and program changes:

  1. Reduce travel, training, and overtime costs.
     IMPLEMENTED.

2. Develop block grant programs for all housing assistance functions and consolidate and simplify all FHA functions.
UNDER DISCUSSION BY HUD, CONGRESS, AND PRESIDENTIAL COMMISSION ON HOUSING.

3. Decentralize and deregulate Community Development Block Grant (CDBG) and Urban Development Action Grant (UDAG) programs.
IMPLEMENTED THROUGH BUDGET ACT; REGULATIONS UNDER REVIEW.

4. Appoint strong, decisive HUD Secretary and Under Secretary with executive leadership ability and experience in housing and urban areas.
SAMUEL PIERCE IS WELL QUALIFIED TO BE SECRETARY. UNDER SECRETARY HOVDE HAS CONSIDERABLE EXECUTIVE AND DEVELOPMENT EXPERIENCE.

5. Decentralize major HUD programs from Central Office to Field Offices and local governments to alleviate staff imbalance.
WILL BE ACCOMPLISHED THROUGH BLOCK GRANT POLICY.

- Reduce and realign office and staff of Secretary and Under Secretary:
  1. Abolish three of the Secretary's Special Assistant positions.
  SECRETARY NOW HAS FIVE SPECIAL ASSISTANTS.

  2. Abolish Office of International Affairs or transfer to State Department.
  NOT IMPLEMENTED.

  3. Abolish Office of Small and Disadvantaged Business or transfer it to the SBA.
  NOT IMPLEMENTED.

  4. Increase staff and importance of Deputy Under Secretary for Field Coordination.
  HAS BEEN UPGRADED.

  5. Retain Office of Labor Relations.
  IMPLEMENTED.

  6. Transfer Office of Budget from Office of Assistant Secretary for Administration to the Office of the Secretary.
  NOT IMPLEMENTED.

7. Abolish Office of Assistant to the Secretary for Growth Issues.

POSITION VACANT. NO PLAN TO FILL IT.

- Reduce FY 1981 budget request of $9.3 million by 10 percent to $8.3 million for FY 1982 (Office of the Secretary).

$8.6 MILLION REQUESTED.

- Consolidate and simplify duplicative legal offices. Drastically reduce size of legal staffs of Central and Regional offices.

EFFORTS MADE TO CONSOLIDATE DUE TO BUDGET CUTS. NO INFORMATION ON STAFF REDUCTIONS.

- Reduce Central Office budget by 10 percent from the $8.7 million FY 1981 amount to $7.8 million for FY 1982.

$141,000 INCREASE REQUESTED.

- Maintain FY 1982 request of $11.3 million for field legal services.

$158,000 INCREASE REQUESTED.

**Inspector General**

- Reinforce autonomy of the Office of the Inspector General. Encourage office to examine more serious abuses than in the past.

NO ACTION TAKEN.

- Maintain FY 1981 budget of $19.1 million for Inspector General's Office in FY 1982.

$21.3 MILLION REQUESTED.

**Assistant Secretary for Administration**

- Switch the authority and management control for all functions from the Deputy Assistant Secretary to the Assistant Secretary of Administration, who is directly accountable to the Secretary.

IMPLEMENTED.

- Undertake a thorough personnel and organizational evaluation and audit to consolidate duplicative and unnecessary offices.

IN PROGRESS; GIVEN HIGH PRIORITY.

- Evaluate in all departments the staff and operations of the Office of Automated Data Processing (ADP) operations, ADP Systems Development, and the Office of Finance and Accounting. Consider cost-effectiveness of subcontracting computer operations.

IMPLEMENTED.

132

- Reduce budget request by 20 percent from the $91 million Central Office level of 1981 to $73 million for FY 1982. Maintain $89 million FY 1981 budget for Field Administration and Operational Support for FY 1982.

  BUDGET REQUEST INCREASED $8.9 MILLION. FIELD ADMINISTRATION BUDGET REQUEST INCREASED $5 MILLION.

### Assistant Secretary for Community Planning & Development

- Reduce staff by 10 percent for 1982 through consolidation and transfer of functions.

  IN PROGRESS.

- Increase Community Development Block Grants budget request for FY 1982 from $3.8 billion to $3.9 billion. Recommend budget of $4.1 billion for FY 1983.

  $4.16 BILLION AUTHORIZED FOR FY 1982.

- Maintain budget request of $675 million for Urban Development Action Grant Program through FY 1983.

  $500 MILLION AUTHORIZED.

- Reduce FY 1982 budget request for Section 312 from $140 million to $129 million.

  NO FUNDS AUTHORIZED FOR 1982. PROGRAM CONTINUES USING PROCEEDS FROM EXISTING REVOLVING LOAN FUND.

- Maintain budget request for Section 701 at $40 million for FY 1982.

  PROGRAM REPEALED.

- Reduce budget request for Administration expenses from $68 million in FY 1981 to $62 million for FY 1982.

  $63.1 MILLION REQUESTED.

### Assistant Secretary for Housing

- Consolidate and decentralize all assisted housing programs into a community housing block grant program.

  UNDER CONSIDERATION BY PRESIDENTIAL HOUSING COMMISSION.

- Reactivate subsidy cost containment for Section 8 Fair Market Rent levels.

  UNDER REVIEW BY PRESIDENTIAL COMMISSION.

- Strictly limit contract rent approvals to a reasonableness-of-rent test.
  NOT IMPLEMENTED. RENT POLICY UNDER REVIEW BY PRESIDENTIAL COMMISSION.

- Emphasize the use of existing and moderate rehabilitation.
  IN PROGRESS.

- Realign staff toward Field Offices gradually during first year.
  PARTIALLY IMPLEMENTED.

- Reduce budget request for Assisted Housing Contract Authority from FY 1981 level of $1.5 billion to $1.3 billion through FY 1983.
  $907 MILLION AUTHORIZED.

- Reduce budget authority from FY 1981 level of $30.5 billion to $29.4 billion through FY 1983.
  $18.09 BILLION AUTHORIZED.

- Reduce Public Housing Operating Subsidies budget from FY 1981 level of $800 million to $700 million for FY 1982.
  $1.5 BILLION AUTHORIZED.

- Maintain FY 1982 budget request of $700 million for Housing for the Handicapped and Elderly.
  $850 MILLION AUTHORIZED.

- Reduce GNMA Tandem budget from FY 1981 level of $1.8 billion to $1 billion.
  $1.92 BILLION AUTHORIZED.

- Eliminate budget for Section 235 Stimulus.
  IMPLEMENTED.

- Maintain budget request for Administration expenses at FY 1981 level of $252 million through FY 1982.
  $249 MILLION REQUESTED.

- Proposed Assistant Secretary for Field Operations.
  ESTABLISHED ASSISTANT GENERAL DEPUTY INSTEAD FOR FIELD OPERATIONS.

- Retain three-tier system of Central, Regional and Field Offices. Keep Regional Offices out of processing. Strengthen Secretary's control over field operations.
  NO CHANGE.

134

- Strengthen Deputy Under Secretary, or create an Assistant Secretary for Field Operations to maintain direct chain-of-command from Secretary to field.

  DEPUTY UNDER SECRETARY STRENGTHENED, BUT DEALS PRIMARILY WITH REGIONAL OFFICES.

- Shift Central Office personnel to Field Offices to bring them to full strength.

  UNDER REVIEW, BUT NO ACTION. CENTRAL AND FIELD OFFICES UNDERGOING R.I.F.

- Provide Field Office staff with grade levels commensurate with their expanded duties.

  UNDER REVIEW BUT NO ACTION.

### Assistant Secretary for Fair Housing & Equal Opportunity

- Review FHEO's staffing and functions to streamline organization, increase efficiency, and improve coordination between this and other program offices.

  IMPLEMENTED.

### Assistant Secretary for Policy Development & Research

- Return policy development function to the Secretary.

  NOT IMPLEMENTED.

- Redirect office's mission toward real and applied research to support program objectives for housing and community development as determined by Secretary and program Assistant Secretaries.

  IN PROCESS.

- Transfer functions of the Economic and Market Analysis Division (EMAD) to the Assistant Secretary for Housing.

  NOT IMPLEMENTED.

- Cut number of full-time employees from present 200 to 175 by transfer and consolidation.

  LARGELY IMPLEMENTED.

- Reduce budget request for FY 1982 from $50 million FY 1981 level to $40 million.

  $35 MILLION REQUESTED.

- Consolidate Office of Neighborhood and Consumer Affairs within existing program offices of appropriate Field Offices, and transfer Office of Neighborhood Self-Help Development to the Neighborhood Services of America Corp., Inc.

OFFICE OF NEIGHBORHOOD VOLUNTARY ASSOCIA-
TION AND CONSUMER PROTECTION, UNDER WHICH
THESE OFFICES FUNCTIONED, HAS BEEN ELIMINATED
AND FUNCTIONS DISPERSED. OFFICE OF NEIGHBOR-
HOOD SELF-HELP DEVELOPMENT ELIMINATED.

- Maintain remaining programs within Office of Regulatory
  Functions intact.
  IMPLEMENTED.

- Eliminate funding for Neighborhood Self Help.
  IMPLEMENTED.

- Request budget of $6 million for Administration expenses in FY
  1982, down from $13.8 million in FY 1981.
  REQUESTED $8.6 MILLION.

### Assistant Secretary for Public Affairs/Legislation & Intergovern-mental Affairs

- Combine Assistant Secretaries of Public Affairs and Legisla-
  tion/Intergovernmental Affairs if new Office of Assistant Secretary for Field Operations is established.
  NOT IMPLEMENTED. LEGISLATION AND INTERGOV-
  ERNMENTAL AFFAIRS SPLIT.

- Reduce staff within Office of Public Affairs (OPA) and Office of
  Legislation and Intergovernmental Relations (OLIR).
  NOT IMPLEMENTED.

- Redirect activities within OPA (which currently overemphasize
  "public relations").
  IMPLEMENTED.

- Redirect activities of OLIR to emphasize congressional rela-
  tions.
  TITLE CHANGE TO OFFICE OF LEGISLATION & CON-
  GRESSIONAL RELATIONS. REVIEW OF ACTIVITIES
  UNDERWAY.

### New Community Development Corporation

- Do not reactivate New Communities program (not viable).
  Continue phase-out program currently in process.
  IMPLEMENTED.

- Reduce budget request by 10 percent—from FY 1981 level of
  $40 million to $36 million in FY 1982.
  $36.6 MILLION REQUESTED.

## Community Development Block Grants (CDBG)

- Remove rigid "proportionality" criterion in measuring Housing Assistance Plan (HAP) performance.

NOT IMPLEMENTED.

- Clarify distinction between administrative and program expenses so that local governments can determine whether they are complying with appropriation limitations.

NO CHANGE, BUT LOOSE DEFINITIONS AID COMPLIANCE.

## Housing Assistance

- Allow cities, counties, or states to set a lower ceiling than current 80 percent of median as cutoff to ensure that program serves intended lower-income beneficiaries.

IMPLEMENTED.

## FHA Mortgage Insurance Operations

- Retain but simplify manufactured housing and property improvement loan programs.

RETAINED, AND SIMPLIFIED THROUGH DEREGULATION.

## Regulatory Functions

- Clarify present regulations.

IMPLEMENTED.

- Establish clear and appropriate definition of a mobile home and refrain from using HUD to regulate recreational vehicles.

IMPLEMENTED.

## Real Estate Settlement Procedures Act

- Wait for completion of controlled business study before taking action. Consider impact of any action on competition and costs to the consumer.

STUDY COMPLETED SEPTEMBER 1981. NO ACTION.

## Lead-Based Paint Poisoning Prevention Program

- Develop reliable and reasonable methods to fulfill mandates of the Act and establish procedure to ensure that housing rehabilitated or sold with federal assistance does not contain lead-based paint.

UNDER CONSIDERATION BY THE SECRETARY, BUT NO ACTION TAKEN.

# Chapter Twelve
# DEPARTMENT OF THE INTERIOR
### By Robert L. Terrell

Secretary of the Interior James G. Watt has demonstrated that he has the courage and commitment to implement natural resource policies that truly represent the public's best interest. Those few coercive utopians and no-growth advocates who grew accustomed to access to the Department during the term of the previous Secretary apparently feel that a petition signed by one million people and buttons with catchy phrases will force President Reagan to yank Secretary Watt from the Interior Department. Sooner or later those same zealots will realize that Secretary Watt is simply carrying out the President's agenda, and the agenda of those who live in states where the Department controls vast amounts of land.

Watt has brought about the accomplishment of many recommendations proposed in *Mandate for Leadership*. More could have been accomplished in the first year but for the long delays inherent in nominating and confirming presidential personnel. With the changes in law brought about by the Carter Administration, the nomination process not only takes an inordinately long time, but virtually precludes hiring individuals who have ever worked for a living in the free enterprise system. Notwithstanding these problems, the Department of the Interior is, with few exceptions, staffed with highly dedicated and capable policy-makers. Unfortunately, a number of individuals who disagree with the Administration's philosophy remain in sensitive posts. Because of these "holdovers," well-meaning, right-thinking appointees quickly become too much a part of "their" office or bureau. Often presidential appointees are "captured" by holdover staff and thus become incapable of effecting change. The seriousness of this situation cannot be overemphasized. If there is to be further successful implementation of Secretary Watt's policies, these holdovers must be removed.

The Interior Department's unique composition pits development against preservation on a daily basis. The preservation elements—the National Park Service and Fish and Wildlife Service—compete for the Secretary's ear with the more development-oriented side of the Department, which includes the Bureau of Mines and the U.S. Geological Survey. Bureaus with both development and protection interests include the Bureau of Land Management and the Office of Surface Mining.

For the first time in at least a decade, the Department appears to have succeeded in reaching a balance of these conflicting interests. Secretary Watt is to be commended for attempting this most difficult balancing act. The country is well served by an Administration which both promotes the timely and orderly development of America's wealth of energy and mineral resources and, at the same time, protects and preserves the unique natural heritage of our public lands and national parks. Unfortunately, the Secretary's critics see only one fact: they no longer have dominance in the Department.

Maintaining a balance will require continued vigilance by Interior policymakers and continued active guidance from Secretary Watt. While decentralization of operational authority to bureaus and offices is generally efficient and should be continued, policy guidance from the Secretary must be evident to ensure consistency. Several recent examples of bureaus which have strayed from announced Secretarial policy should remind the Interior hierarchy that a need for increased policy audit by senior staff goes with decentralized management.

### Energy and Minerals

The Office of the Assistant Secretary for Energy and Minerals (AS/EM), through its consultant agencies, has accomplished over 58 percent of the short-term recommendations contained in the *Mandate for Leadership* report. Several of these accomplishments are worthy of note. First, implementation of an effective minerals policy is being carried out not only by AS/EM, but throughout the Department. Without compromising stringent environmental standards, procedures and regulations are being aggressively reviewed to identify those that unnecessarily hamper or restrict essential mineral development. Second, the AS/EM and Directors of the Bureau of Mines (BOM), U.S. Geological Survey (USGS) and Office of Surface Mining (OSM) were selected because of their professional background and history of advocating a workable minerals policy. Third, a significant cut in Office of Surface Mining personnel and budget was accompanied by an attendant commitment requiring states to play a more significant role in regulating surface mine operations within their boundaries. In addition, a major rewrite of the burdensome regulations promulgated by the previous zealots in OSM is currently underway.

The Bureau of Land Management (BLM) has written a paper proposing that the Conservation Division of the USGS be merged into its organization. While this had been suggested in *Mandate*, an equally attractive proposal is gaining ground; it would separate the Conservation Division from the USGS and the minerals functions of BLM and create a Bureau of Minerals Management under the Assistant Secretary for Energy and Minerals.

On the negative side, the new Director of the Bureau of Mines appears to be reluctant to effect change in the BOM's existing organizational structure. If this is not accomplished, the overall morale and professionalism within the BOM will suffer; such a development will undoubtedly adversely affect BOM's efforts to influence minerals policy. Moreover, changes are needed to assure field personnel that new policies will enhance the importance of their work. A reorganization which emphasizes minerals expertise instead of matrix management and program analysis at the top levels of the BOM will do much to accomplish this objective.

**Land and Water**

The Office of the Assistant Secretary for Land and Water Resources (AS/LWR) has accomplished over 45 percent of the short-term recommendations contained in *Mandate for Leadership*. Several of those accomplishments are worthy of note. First, the issuance of a new and aggressive five-year Outer Continental Shelf oil and gas leasing schedule not only will expand the number of leasing areas but also will increase the acreage of lease sales in the Gulf of Mexico. Second, the AS/LWR has pushed for greater coal tonnage in 1981 lease offerings. Third, the AS/LWR scheduled sales on all remaining known geothermal resource areas not previously offered for sale; all such sales were to be completed by the end of 1981. Due to the lack of priority in early months in the Bureau of Land Management, these sales will not be completed until the end of 1982. Fourth, the AS/LWR reinstituted the recognition of the "right" granted under the 1872 Mining Law to receive patent to mining claims where the requirements of that Act have been satisfied. For the last fifteen years or more, this right had been ignored because BLM was controlled by range conservationists and foresters known affectionately as "prairie fairies, stump jumpers and tree huggers." Fifth, the AS/LWR, with assistance from the Solicitor, has reversed the egregious western water policy formulated by the Carter Administration. The western states now have a greater respect for the Interior Department and are confident that their water laws will not be threatened by federal bureaucratic policies, at least for the next four years.

Notwithstanding the aforementioned positive accomplishments, there are a few negatives that should be mentioned. First, the BLM continues to maintain personnel at high policy levels that should and must be removed if the status quo is to be changed. Of all the bureaus and other agencies in the Interior Department, the BLM is, without a doubt, one where the need for change is most apparent. Once again, it appears that another presidential appointee, the new Director, has been captured by careerists whose philosophy is more consonant with that of the previous administration. If there is to be successful implementation of a truly "multiple use" policy for the nation's public lands, those individuals whose past performances continue to reflect past policy must be removed. Second, the Bureau's minerals expertise continues to be extremely weak despite the elevation of energy and minerals functions. A preponderance of "biological types" who profess to be minerals professionals are scattered throughout the Bureau. Position descriptions are written so that an individual living a few blocks from a cement plant qualifies as a minerals professional. This must be changed. Management personnel with a minerals background must be recruited.

To compound the problem of personnel quality, the Bureau has now placed a ninety-day freeze on hiring individuals outside the organization. This was done to force the Minerals Division to absorb land planners, biologists, range conservationists and others, whose jobs are threatened by recent budget cuts. These moves will result in a further dilution of the minerals function within BLM and attempts to formulate a strategic minerals policy for public lands will be threatened.

### Fish, Wildlife and Parks

The gregarious new Assistant Secretary for Fish, Wildlife and Parks is a tough and seasoned administrator, but has yet to affect significantly the day-to-day operational policies of the Fish and Wildlife Service and National Park Service. Preservationist crusaders within both constituent agencies have attempted to torpedo delicate negotiations concerning geothermal leasing in national parks, the Northern Tier Pipeline, and proposed changes to coal leasing and National Recreation Area regulations.

The AS/FWP is without a Deputy Assistant Secretary; only recently did Fish and Wildlife finally get a Reagan-appointed Director. Secretary Watt may find the AS/FWP function the weak link in program policy implementation.

### Solicitor

Despite personnel difficulties, the new Solicitor and his Deputy have made marked progress in reversing or modifying a stifling array of ill-conceived opinions and legal positions. The Solicitor appears to be in control and to have the necessary support of Secretary Watt to accomplish his legal mission. As additional senior legal staff sympathetic to the Secretary's policies are positioned, the new Solicitor will become an even more important part of Interior's new direction.

### Policy, Budget and Administration

The Assistant Secretary for "PBA" has been a serious disappointment in the Department's inner circle. While the budget, personnel, and other administrative functions assigned to this office are well-managed by professionals, the policy apparatus of the Assistant Secretary's office remains mired in liberal arguments of the past decade. An earlier criticism by *Mandate for Leadership* that AS/PBA housed too many staff with an "ivory tower mentality" remains a valid criticism. The Secretary should establish an analytical tool within the Department which more closely shares his philosophy. Without a supportive analytical staff, many of Interior's new program directions could be vulnerable in the years to come.

## RECOMMENDATIONS
(Action taken on 53 out of 97)

### Office of the Assistant Secretary—Energy and Minerals

- Restore balance to Departmental mineral policy in a review of unnecessarily restrictive policies affecting mineral development.
  ACCOMPLISHED.

- Appoint a new Assistant Secretary for Energy & Minerals who has the background and experience to be an effective advocate for the timely and orderly development of domestic energy and minerals resources.
  ACCOMPLISHED.

- Encourage cooperation between the constituent bureaus and the Bureau of Land Management, the Federal Lands Leasing Office of the Department of Energy, the Fish and Wildlife Service, the National Park Service, and the National Oceanic and Atmospheric Administration (NOAA).
  ACCOMPLISHED.

- Rebuild the decision-making responsibilities of AS/EM to sponsor a more balanced approach to resource planning among the other policy officers of the Department.
  ACCOMPLISHED.

- Review Secretarial orders which assign responsibility among AS/EM and AS/LWR regarding mineral development and land-use planning on the public lands.
  NOT ACCOMPLISHED.

- Assert increased minerals advocacy to other executive branch agencies with surface land management responsibilities and to the Executive Office of the President.
  ACCOMPLISHED.

- Devote particular attention to the appointment of Directors for

Bureau of Mines, U.S. Geological Survey, and Office of Surface Mining.
ACCOMPLISHED.

- Direct the new AS/EM to ensure that constituent bureaus reflect their respective missions in reports and recommendations to AS/EM.
ACCOMPLISHED.

- Structure the analytical function within the U.S. Geological Survey to emphasize those functions which affect minerals development on federal lands and the Outer Continental Shelf.
NOT ACCOMPLISHED.

- Broaden lines of communication among the states, the AS/EM, and bureaus and open bureaus' lines of communication to private sector.
ACCOMPLISHED.

- Implement, with substantive assistance from the Bureau of Mines and the USGS, the mandate of the Mining and Minerals Policy Act and other statutes which direct the executive branch to implement national minerals and materials policy.
ACCOMPLISHED.

- Increase number of Deputy Assistant Secretaries to permit attention to the proposed expansion of energy and minerals function.
NOT ACCOMPLISHED. LIMITED BY FY 1982 BUDGET.

**Bureau of Mines**

- Place Office of Minerals Policy and Research in the Bureau of Mines as the generator of policy input to the AS/EM.
ACCOMPLISHED.

- Revise Bureau of Mines budget upward to reflect the higher priority given by the new Administration to ensuring an adequate supply of critical minerals.
BUDGET CUT, BUT MINERALS POLICY WAS GIVEN PRIORITY.

- Employ minerals experts for policy analysis, rather than administrative or generalist personnel.
REORGANIZATION IN PROGRESS. FULL IMPLEMENTATION DOUBTFUL.

144

- Increase policy role for minerals experts and increase budget (phased-in over several years) to improve morale and to install professional expertise at the management level at the Bureau of Mines.

  NOT ACCOMPLISHED. REORGANIZATION MAY BE ONLY COSMETIC.

- Review grade levels to attract and retain professionals within the Bureau.

  ACCOMPLISHED.

- Stress the expertise of Bureau employees; contracting should be minimal.

  NOT ACCOMPLISHED. CONTRACTING IS BEING MINIMIZED ONLY BECAUSE OF BUDGET CUTS.

- Initiate review of internal Bureau practices which govern responsiveness to mandates of mineral resource assessments and to congressional and agency requests.

  NOT ACCOMPLISHED.

- Review all outstanding efforts at the Bureau of Mines and identify clear priorities so that staff understands the importance of their work output.

  NOT ACCOMPLISHED.

- Formulate and implement a nonfuel minerals policy overseen by the AS/EM, with detailed analysis provided by the Bureau of Mines.

  ACCOMPLISHED THROUGH THE CABINET COUNCIL.

- Re-examine approach to land-use policy regarding mineral-rich federal lands. Access for mineral exploration and potential development must be protected to assure exploration for domestic strategic and critical minerals.

  ACCOMPLISHED.

**Office of Surface Mining Reclamation and Enforcement**

- Review contested or unnecessarily stringent rules within ninety days.

  NOT ACCOMPLISHED PROMPTLY. CURRENTLY UNDERWAY.

- Eliminate obstacles to the approval of state reclamation plans.

  ACCOMPLISHED.

- Move quickly to reduce OSM enforcement staff and cut budget requests significantly in the regulatory program.

  ACCOMPLISHED.

- Replace current OSM senior staff and regional directors with professionals more attuned to a rational program of ensuring rehabilitation of mined lands.

  ACCOMPLISHED.

### U.S. Geological Survey

- Emphasize selection of new Director and other senior officers to promote domestically and internationally the expertise of the Survey.

  ACCOMPLISHED.

- Review mineral resource evaluation procedures utilized by the Conservation Division in assisting the BLM to derive fair market value for the sale of onshore and OCS minerals.

  NOT ACCOMPLISHED.

- Review the Conservation Division's mineral resource mapping and information support for the Bureau of Land Management's land-use planning with a view toward the production of maps and narratives more useful to BLM land-use managers.

  NOT ACCOMPLISHED.

### Mineral Leasing and Outer Continental Shelf

- Issue a new proposed five-year leasing schedule with no Environmental Impact Statement (EIS).

  ACCOMPLISHED. TO BE PUBLISHED IN MARCH OF 1982.

- Reverse decisions that limit the size or composition of 1981 and 1982 and future sales.

  ACCOMPLISHED.

- Revise the following decisions:

  1. Sale 53 (Central and North California). Issue notice of proposed sale in October 1980.

     ACCOMPLISHED. COURT RULING FORCED SECRETARY TO WITHDRAW FOUR OUT OF FIVE BASINS.

  2. Sale 68 (South California) and Sale 67 (Gulf of Mexico). Advance to 1981.

     NOT ACCOMPLISHED.

146

3. Sale 68 (South California). Add now in order to allow for an adequate EIS.

NOT ACCOMPLISHED.

4. RS-1 (Reoffering Sale 1). Cancel this sale, scheduled for June 1981 in order to conserve administrative resources.

NOT ACCOMPLISHED; SALE HELD IN JUNE.

- Terminate geohazard surveys/studies.

ACCOMPLISHED.

- Order NOAA to cease prohibitions of oil and gas operations in marine sanctuaries.

NOT ACCOMPLISHED.

- Increase size of sales in the Gulf of Mexico from 1.2 million acres to 2 million acres or more.

ACCOMPLISHED.

## Coal Leasing

- Issue a Solicitor's opinion that the payment of advance royalties in lieu of continued operations can be imposed only at the time that pre-Federal Coal Amendments Act leases come due for readjustment.

NOT ACCOMPLISHED. RULEMAKING CURRENTLY BEING PREPARED.

- Issue a Solicitor's opinion stating that the unsuitability criteria do not apply to leases issued before enactment of the Surface Mining Control & Reclamation Act (SMCRA) and that retroactive application of such criteria is unlawful.

NOT ACCOMPLISHED.

- Issue a Solicitor's opinion holding that the test applied for determining "commercial quantities" should be the test in use at the time the permit was issued, or when the permit was extended.

NOT ACCOMPLISHED.

- Issue a Solicitor's opinion holding that the 1976 regulations are not to be applied to pre-1976 leases; that the statute does not grant the Secretary the authority to automatically declare each lease an LMU; and that the Secretary has no authority to require the formation of an LMU until lease readjustment, or until the lessee voluntarily consents to such formation.

PROPOSED RULEMAKING DUE FOR *FEDERAL REGISTER* PUBLICATION IN NOVEMBER 1981.

- Issue a Solicitor's opinion holding diligent development and continuous operation regulations to be inapplicable to leases existing at the time the regulations were issued.

  NOT ACCOMPLISHED.

- Issue Solicitor's opinion concluding that 1872 Mining Law claims existing at the time coal prospecting permits were issued should not be declared null and void *ab initio* but should be applied prospectively, if at all.

  ACCOMPLISHED.

- Permit the 1981 coal lease sale to take place and attempt to guarantee its immunity from challenge.

  ACCOMPLISHED.

- Protect the viability of the initial sale by the preparation of a Solicitor's review of the coal program.

  NOT ACCOMPLISHED.

- Issue regulations subsequent to the initial lease sale instituting specific changes in the coal management program including: deletion of the requirement that only high- and medium-potential coal lands be evaluated; retention of all coal lands through the process despite declared applicability of the various screening criteria; elimination of the "threshold development" concept; restriction of the "unsuitability" criteria.

  DUE FOR PUBLICATION IN THE *FEDERAL REGISTER* DECEMBER 1981.

- Eliminate the sixty-day cooling off period.

  NOT ACCOMPLISHED.

- Issue regulations providing that all annual rental payments received within 20 days after the anniversary date and mailed before the anniversary date automatically meet statutory requirements.

  NOT ACCOMPLISHED.

- Lift the moratorium and reinstate all applications to their order of priority of filing, whether before or after the effective date of the regulations.

  ACCOMPLISHED.

- Initiate a withdrawal review since the review being conducted by BLM under Section 204 of the Federal Land Policy and Management Act is not likely to be adequate.

  NOT ACCOMPLISHED.

- Open the National Wildlife Refuge System lands immediately to geophysical exploration.

NOT ACCOMPLISHED.

## Mineral Impact Review

- Issue lease on all applications filed before 1980 by the end of 1981, with no exceptions.

ACCOMPLISHED.

- Schedule and complete sales on all remaining known geothermal resource areas not previously offered for sale by the end of 1981, without exceptions.

TO BE COMPLETED BY END OF 1982.

- Endorse adoption of legislation such as H.R. 6080 as passed by the House of Representatives during the 96th Congress.

NOT ACCOMPLISHED.

- Issue a *Federal Register* notice that the proposed rules of the Carter Administration are scrapped.

NOT ACCOMPLISHED.

- Recruit minerals professionals by upgrading the grade levels at which they are hired and by creating a meaningful career ladder on a par with other resource professionals.

NOT ACCOMPLISHED.

- Curtail the continuing growth of minerals professionals within the National Park Service.

NOT ACCOMPLISHED.

- Expand the Bureau of Land Management's minerals expertise so that mineral patent applications, many of which have been pending over fifteen years, may be processed expeditiously.

NOT ACCOMPLISHED.

- Honor the "right" granted under the Mining Law of 1872 to receive a patent if the requirements of that Act have been satisfied.

ACCOMPLISHED.

- Adopt the Forest Service regulations (surface management regulations).

NOT ACCOMPLISHED.

- Permit a reasonable level of surface disturbance before requiring a filing with BLM provided the disturbances do not trigger the significant surface disturbance regulations.
ACCOMPLISHED.

### Wilderness Policy

- Suspend enforcement of the "valid existing rights" portion of the Solicitor's opinion and the Wilderness IMP for all outstanding leases and permits issued prior to October 21, 1976, and for all mining claims located prior to October 21, 1976, and subsequently recorded in a timely manner with BLM.
ACCOMPLISHED.

- Reinterpret Section 603 of FLPMA regarding "valid existing rights," in order to maximize the number of leases, permits, and mining claims which are not subject to the non-impairment criteria.
ACCOMPLISHED.

- Revise the Solicitor's interpretation of "manner and degree" to protect grandfathered rights.
DRAFT OPINION AWAITING SOLICITOR'S REVIEW.

- Issue a Solicitor's opinion revising and clarifying the exploration provisions of the Wilderness Act which declare that such exploration constitutes the dominant use of such lands.
DRAFT OPINION AWAITING SOLICITOR'S REVIEW.

- Recommend legislative amendment of the Wilderness Act to provide for exploration of wilderness system lands until the year 2000, and for wildernesses created after 1980 for a period of twenty years.
NOT ACCOMPLISHED.

- Announce immediately that there will be no net increase in lands withdrawn by the Executive Branch from operation of the mining and mineral leasing laws.
NOT ACCOMPLISHED.

- Restore at least 10 percent of existing withdrawals to operation of the mining and mineral leasing laws by 1983.
NOT ACCOMPLISHED.

### Eastern States Office

- Do not require environmental assessments for oil and gas lease applications involving reserved mineral estates with private surface, and where the parcel is surrounded by non-federal mineral estates, if the well-spacing requirements exceed the size of the tract applied for.

ACCOMPLISHED.

- Do not require environmental assessment for applications for fractional mineral interest leases.

ACCOMPLISHED.

- Review the coal trespass program to ensure that the cost of prosecuting coal trespass does not exceed the damages received; prosecute only significant coal trespass.

NOT ACCOMPLISHED.

- Sell all fractional federal mineral estates to the private holder of the other fractional interest.

NOT ACCOMPLISHED.

- Dispose of all lands (60,000 acres or less) where the government owns surface and subsurface, and which are determined not essential to a minerals management program.

NOT ACCOMPLISHED.

- Order the ESO to post all available lands on the simultaneous oil and gas lists before the end of 1981.

ESO INSTRUCTED TO ACCOMPLISH THIS BY THE END OF 1982.

**Water Policy**

- Assure westerners that they have a substantive role in governmental decisions affecting their area.

ACCOMPLISHED.

- Repudiate and abandon federal policies which threaten state water laws.

ACCOMPLISHED.

- Repudiate the June 25, 1979 Opinion and request the new Solicitor to re-examine the issues involved.

ACCOMPLISHED.

- Do not support changes in the Reclamation Act of 1902 which would result in a major restructuring of the long tradition of western agriculture.

ACCOMPLISHED.

### Fish, Wildlife, and Parks

- Require an immediate and complete revision of the Fish and Wildlife Coordination Act regulations.

  RULES AND REGULATIONS FROM THE PREVIOUS ADMINISTRATION WERE REJECTED, BUT NOT PROMPTLY.

- Initiate planning necessary to begin intensive seismic activity in the William O. Douglas Arctic Wildlife Range.

  ACCOMPLISHED.

- Introduce legislation to amend the Land and Water Conservation Fund, allowing the enhancement programs with federal side funds to offset present "Threats to Parks" problems.

  ACCOMPLISHED.

- Use the Land and Water Conservation Fund (LWCF) to preserve existing parks rather than only for the acquisition of more and more land.

  ACCOMPLISHED.

### Indian Affairs

- Initiate contacts with key congressional leaders, Indian organizations, and tribes to discuss candidates for BIA posts.

  ACCOMPLISHED.

- Appoint a qualified Indian as Assistant Secretary for Indian Affairs early in the first year to improve representation of Indian interests in DOI budget preparations.

  ACCOMPLISHED, BUT APPOINTMENT CAME LATE.

- Reaffirm present policy of self-determination.

  ACCOMPLISHED.

- Pledge cooperation with Congress on Indian legislation, particularly efforts to achieve economic self-sufficiency and resource development.

  ACCOMPLISHED.

### International and Territorial Affairs

- Appoint as head of the Office of Territorial and International Affairs within DOI a person who has both administrative experience and subject matter background.

  ACCOMPLISHED.

- Abolish the Office of Micronesian Political Status Negotiations

152

as an interagency office and incorporate it under the Office of Territorial and International Affairs.

NOT ACCOMPLISHED.

- Implement necessary measures to enhance the security of the Kwajalein Testing Facility in the Marshalls.

ACCOMPLISHED.

- Initiate meetings with key congressional leaders.

NOT ACCOMPLISHED.

- Delineate the roles of White House staff and DOI staff.

ACCOMPLISHED.

- Institute meeting with territorial officials to discuss areas of concern and commitment.

NOT ACCOMPLISHED.

- Aggressively pursue funds to exercise the lease option for a military facility on the island of Tinian, NMI.

ACCOMPLISHED, BUT FUNDS WERE DELETED IN HOUSE.

### Policy, Budget, and Administration

- Insure the integrity and security of official Departmental files and decision papers by adding physical security and applying appropriate debriefings.

ACCOMPLISHED.

- Review the multi-agency participation in OCS leasing process, and consider options to reduce the number of involved agencies and the time required for the sale process.

NOT ACCOMPLISHED.

- Coordinate and manage Environmental Impact Statements through the Office of Environmental Project Review and monitor performance closely through the AS/PBA.

NOT ACCOMPLISHED.

### Office of the Solicitor

- Regard the Solicitor and his top associates as important personnel who can advance Administration policies.

ACCOMPLISHED.

- Review and reissue all opinions which counter productive development of the public lands and those which curtail or diminish private property rights, including:

153

1. M-36889, May 1977; considers the effect of failure to record in a timely manner under Section 314(b) of the Federal Land Policy and Management Act (FLPMA).

   NOT ACCOMPLISHED. AFFIRMED BY TENTH CIRCUIT.

2. M-36895, July 14, 1977; considers the applicability of the mitigation concept to federal agencies' activities which adversely affect the critical habitat of listed endangered species.

   NOT ACCOMPLISHED.

3. M-36914, June 25, 1979; considers non-reserved water rights—specifically the federal water rights of the NPS, FWS, USBR, and BLM.

   ACCOMPLISHED.

4. M-36893, August 2, 1977 (and supp. November 19, 1979); considers effect of mining claims on Secretary's authority to issue coal and phosphate prospecting permits.

   ACCOMPLISHED.

5. M-36894, July 21, 1977; considers Secretary's authority to grant extensions of outstanding coal prospecting permits under the Federal Coal Leasing Amendments Act of 1976.

   RESOLVED THROUGH LITIGATION.

6. M-36905, July 19, 1978; considers requirements for cumulative impact analysis under Section 7 of the Endangered Species Act.

   ACCOMPLISHED.

7. M-36910, September 5, 1979 (86 I.D. 89); charts a general course for interpreting Section 603, the wilderness study requirements of FLPMA.

   MANY OF THE ISSUES HAVE BEEN RESOLVED AND OTHERS ARE UNDER REVIEW.

8. The June 25, 1979, memorandum of Leo Krulitz, Solicitor, to Secretary of the Interior Andrus on federal water rights of NPS, FWS, USBR, and BLM.

   ACCOMPLISHED.

# Chapter Thirteen
# DEPARTMENT OF JUSTICE

The Department of Justice has been a major disappointment during the first year of the Reagan Administration. It has implemented only a few recommendations made in *Mandate for Leadership*; it has not taken the lead in revising regulations, opinions and executive orders; it is actively blocking reforms proposed by other departments. A number of indicators suggest that improvements at Justice are unlikely.

The problems begin with personnel. The Department resembles a Wall Street law firm. Top appointees are business lawyers who have little or no experience in the constitutional or public policy issues with which Justice deals on a daily basis. In addition to lacking important expertise, these officials are accustomed to using junior associates for legal research. Thus, they are ill-equipped to challenge staff attorneys who propose to undertake actions in violation of conservative principles. The staff attorney will produce an impressive list of lower court decisions to support his contention that "case law demands action." The Reagan appointee is likely to be unfamiliar with all aspects of the issue and too willing to accede to lower-court authority without reviewing, awaiting, or seeking a Supreme Court decision. Consequently, no effective control is placed on staffers who would pursue personal crusades on social issues. Moreover, the cautious nature of corporate lawyers makes them unlikely candidates to lead a jurisprudential counter-revolution. The whole history of the common law system rests on a cautious advance from past precedents. Liberals have never been impeded by precedent in their quest to advance the frontiers of judicial activism, but conservatives have been all too hesitant to roll back those frontiers by seeking to erase those erroneous precedents. The conservatism of the Reagan Justice Department, therefore, all too often constitutes a simple defense of the status quo, no matter how liberal existing law might be.

The extent of this problem is evident in a number of areas where major differences exist between the public pronouncements of Justice officials and the activities undertaken by the Justice Department. For example, Attorney General William French Smith delivered a major speech opposing judicial activism. Describing the courts' past and present adventures in constitutional creativity, the Attorney General said, "Using the due process clauses, unelected judges substituted their own policy preferences for the determinations of the public's elected representatives." He argued that, "the application of these principles has led to some constitutionally dubious and unwise intrusions upon the legislative domain." He denounced federal judges who had sought to administer everything from school systems to prison systems to sewer systems, and he announced that the Justice Department would resist this judicial intrusion into the political realm. These ideas are perfectly sound, but they require action. The Attorney General did not propose a judicial retrenchment; he merely stated, "We will resist expansion." On the day following this speech, Solicitor General Rex Lee was quoted by *The New York Times* as saying that the Department would not seek to overturn prior decisions, but would simply ask the courts to go no further. When the Attorney General was interviewed by *The Washington Post* a month later, he still failed to make a single specific recommendation for turning his ideas into reality.

One of the most potent tools for restraining activism is the power of Congress to restrict the jurisdiction of the federal courts in those areas in which they have abused their authority. Despite the Constitution's plain authorization of this approach, Assistant Attorney General William Bradford Reynolds told the Senate Judiciary Committee that he believed such restrictions to be unconstitutional. Reports have circulated for months that other Reagan appointees in the Department share his view.

More direct conflicts exist in the Department's Civil Rights Division. Assistant Attorney General Bradford Reynolds announced that he would impose the dilution test developed under the Voting Rights Act in an even-handed manner. Nonetheless, when Indianola, Mississippi, attempted to annex both predominately black and predominately white suburbs, the Department objected. Annexation was allowed only of the black suburbs. Instead of preserving approximate racial balance, the town became overwhelmingly black. Despite complaints, Reynolds backed the staff attorney's interpretation of "case law" and refused to allow the annexation of the white suburbs.

A classic example of adherence to past practices and lower court authority took place just recently in the Civil Rights Division. Acting under Section 5 of the Voting Rights Act, Assistant Attorney General Reynolds objected to a 1968 North Carolina constitutional amendment forbidding the division of counties in legislative and congressional redistricting. Only limited portions of North Carolina are even covered by the Voting Rights Act. No Supreme Court decision supports the submission of state-wide applications. Reynolds simply followed the prior practice of the Department as advocated by his career advisors. On the merits of the decision, moreover, he relied upon the tenuous theory of "dilution" of the strength of the minority vote, holding that it might one day be necessary to cross county lines in order to create gerrymandered seats specifically designed for minority candidates. While this sort of approach has long been advocated by the Department, and sometimes endorsed by the lower courts, it has never been approved by the Supreme Court and is contrary to President Reagan's policy of minimizing federal intrusion into local affairs.

Prison cases further illustrate the failure of Justice officials to enforce public policies at working levels. The Department has indicated its opposition to overly detailed judicial standards for the operation of prisons. This position is consistent with that of the Supreme Court which has recently reversed excessively burdensome requirements in prison cases. Justice Department field lawyers, however, continue to harrass state and local prison officials with briefs seeking unnecessarily burdensome standards for the operation of prisons. Because Justice officials are not effectively monitoring these cases, state congressional delegations and state officials must continue the on-going battle simply to keep local situations under control.

The Department recently promised improvements in two important areas. Reynolds has promised that Justice will not ask for goals, quotas, or timetables when attempting to resolve employment discrimination suits. He also stated that in the future, such suits will be based on hard evidence and not on statistical pattern and practice data. The Attorney General has promised that the Department will raise the issue of "standing" in environmental cases. This reverses the Carter Administration's refusal to challenge environmental groups whose opposition delayed development projects even though they could not show personal damage. If this reform is adopted, much frivolous litigation can be eliminated and both the Department and the courts will be able to concentrate on those cases which are truly significant. Available evidence is insufficient to determine the sincerity of Department reform efforts, and cynicism may be appropriate. As in the other cases listed, the Department has not issued formal orders or regulations, and has failed to pursue Executive Orders which would bind staff attorneys to these positions.

One major recommendation in *Mandate* called for the enhancement of a system to control and review all litigative activity in the Department. The examples above indicate that Justice has not accomplished this goal. Department officials have stated a number of commendable policies. They must now demonstrate their commitment to implement these policies by controlling career staffers who do not share the Administration's goals. If Department officials are to do this, the following list of objectionable Justice Department actions will surely grow. Since January 20, the Department:

- Pursued a suit a compel Yonkers, New York, to build low-income housing on sites chosen by the Department.

- Entered a suit to force Mobile, Alabama, to abandon its at-large system of elections.

- Supported the constitutionality of the extension of the deadline for ratification of the Equal Rights Amendment.

- Challenged the constitutionality of a proposed legislative veto of agency regulations.

- Entered into a settlement agreeing to terminate use of the Federal PACE exam and, potentially, any future employment test which fails to produce an acceptable number of minority job candidates.

- Blocked Department of Education efforts to provide that the sex discrimination provisions of Title IX do not apply to employment relations but only to relations with students.

- Delayed, so far successfully, efforts by the Department of Education to overturn previous policies which applied onerous federal regulations to colleges whose students receive federal aid, even though the colleges themselves do not.

The Department of Education is not the only department that has had its intentions frustrated by the Justice Department. The Department of Interior has been involved in a water rights suit in Nevada, which it inherited from the Carter Administration. A group of Indians have been trying to reclaim water rights, but were rebuffed by the lower courts. The Interior Department did not wish to appeal the decision, and apparently the Lands Division of the Justice Department agreed. Nevertheless, Solicitor General Rex Lee disagreed and decided on his own to appeal the decision.

*Mandate* also recommended that the Department exert better control over those staffers who have worked actively to undermine the official policies and actions of the Department. Justice officials report that this has been done in several areas by transferring uncooperative staffers to non-sensitive positions. According to Justice officials, some individuals have even been fired from the Department. This drastic action has been taken only occasionally because it usually results in extended and often costly disputes with the employee; thus, they argue, a cost-benefit test is appropriate before proceeding with a major housecleaning. Nonetheless, the abuse of internal information continues, as evidenced by frequent press leaks on sensitive issues.

Despite its manifest shortcomings, the Department has scored a few gains in its early months. Most notable is the Attorney General's report to the President on the Voting Rights Act. Each of the

158

alternatives proposed by Justice offers a reasonable opportunity to escape the pre-clearance provisions of the Act. The Department firmly rejected the House effort to apply, on a nationwide basis, an "effect test" for discrimination which could easily have led to a racial quota system in apportionments at all levels of government. In the face of sustained pressure from White House aides to accept the House bill, the Attorney General held his ground and convinced the President to support changes.

In litigation, the Civil Rights Division has retreated from some of the more outrageous positions of its predecessors. The Division reversed its previous position and is now supporting the constitutionality of a Washington law prohibiting local school boards from busing in the absence of a court order. The Division has adopted a position of neutrality in a case in which it previously sought to force Texas to educate illegal aliens in its public schools. Many of these decisions have come about as a result of outside pressure rather than internal conviction, but they should not escape notice.

*Mandate for Leadership* recommended revamping the procedures for selecting judicial nominees. The Department argues that it has made major improvements in this area in that all opinions and other papers of nominees are now carefully studied before submission to the White House for final selections. Many individuals and groups concerned with the appointment of judges with strong opinions on right-to-life questions are not impressed. They are extremely disappointed with the appointment of Sandra Day O'Connor to the Supreme Court, and with several apparent candidates for lower court positions. The Administration should realize that this issue is critically important to a number of groups which are essential to the coalition which elected the President. Unless the Department is careful to ascertain the position of potential nominees on issues important to these groups before nominations are made, the President may lose the support of a demonstrably influential political force.

*Mandate* also made a number of recommendations concerning specific attempts to redraft the Criminal Code. Virtually all of these recommendations were ignored, as the Department prematurely endorsed the current omnibus bill, S. 1630. The President's top advisors convened a meeting immediately upon learning of this action. Consequently, the entire series of criminal code reform bills was reviewed by the Justice Department; the result was only marginally different. In testimony on October 28, 1981 Attorney General Smith continued to support the bill but did ask for "improvements" in bail reform to prevent the release of dangerous offenders, in the development of effective means to counter sophisticated financial manipulations by criminals, in the sentencing system to set minimum time requirements in the law, in the imposition of forfeiture provisions to make crime less profitable, and in provisions allowing for coordinated federal, state, and local prosecution.

Smith went on to endorse several provisions which were specifically challenged in a recent Heritage Foundation *Issue Bulletin* on the Criminal Code Reform Act of 1981 authored by Nicholas E. Calio of the Washington Legal Foundation. Smith praised the "intent" section of the code; Calio pointed out that this section confuses the issue and could increase the difficulty of obtaining convictions. Smith was pleased that the code strengthened the ability of prosecutors to fight "white collar" crime; Calio contrasted the crackdown on businessmen with the almost uniform reductions of penalties for non-business criminals. Calio also noted that the Criminal Code could be interpreted as giving grounds to prosecute corporations for the unauthorized actions of non-officers who act only on an "apparent" or "implied" authority.

Smith endorsed the notion of revising the code comprehensivly; Calio warned that the Act is so far-reaching that no one, not even the drafters, seems to understand fully the impact of the proposed revision. Finally, Smith contends that the bill would result in a conservation of judicial resources. Calio stated a different concern: "the bill replaces statutory language, enhanced and illuminated by hundreds of years of common law development, with new words and definitions subject to *de novo* interpretation by a modern federal judiciary which is already unable to keep pace with its caseload." Clearly, this Act will cause an increase, not a decrease in the work of the courts. The Administration is ignoring the recommendations of *Mandate* with regard to criminal code reform. It is also ignoring a continuing body of analysis which warns of the dangers inherent in wholesale revisions of the laws governing all aspects of life in the United States. This position should be considered carefully.

Improving the performance of the Department of Justice hinges on finding a way to control the career staff and to improve the performance of Reagan appointees. The former simply do not share the Administration's goals; the latter have been ineffective in their efforts to manage policy and too often have required months of on-the-job training. The best solution to the continuing problems at Justice is to recruit policy-level and staff-level individuals with an understanding of the proper role of government in a free society.

Prospects in this area are not good. Experienced lawyers with excellent and conservative credentials are available for positions in the Department. The Administration, however, has apparently chosen to look in areas other than the conservative legal community to staff the Department of Justice. The Department is proceeding with job offers to 100 young lawyers selected by the Carter

Administration through the Honors Law Graduate Program. This is a major mistake.

Department officials should, at the very least, take actions to ensure that their policies are implemented after they have gone. The present method of implementing new policies—delivering speeches and testimony before Congress—is inadequate. The Justice Department is currently hampered by opinions, memoranda, and Executive Orders issued by previous administrations. It should learn from this lack of flexibility. Instead of a case-by-case effort for change, Justice should immediately implement the *Mandate* recommendations, calling for revised opinions by the Legal Counsel, revisions in regulations, and suggestions to the White House for new Executive Orders. Only when these steps are taken will this Administration begin to develop an institutional legacy.

## RECOMMENDATIONS
(Action taken on 16 out of 44)

### Personnel and Organization

- Fill every Assistant Attorney General position with conservative personnel.

  ONE CARTER APPOINTEE REMAINS; SEVERAL NOMINEES NOT CONSERVATIVE.

- Replace every Deputy Assistant Attorney General with conservative personnel.

  SOME CARTER APPOINTEES REMAIN.

- Remove every Schedule C and replace them with conservative personnel.

  MANY CARTER APPOINTEES REMAIN.

- Reorganize the Department to place the Deputy Attorney General immediately below the Attorney General on the organization charts.

  ACCOMPLISHED.

- Propose legislation to create a new Associate Attorney General to handle the functions formerly fulfilled by the Deputy Attorney General.

  NOT DONE.

- Give the Deputy Attorney General direct responsibility for the functions of the Executive Office for U.S. Attorneys, the Office of Intelligence Policy and Review, the Justice Management Division, and the Office for Legal Policy.

  FULLY IMPLEMENTED.

- Consolidate physically the Antitrust and Land Divisions in order to improve control.

  NOT DONE.

- Enhance the Department's centralized system for monitoring major litigation so that central policymakers are aware of what each division is doing.

  NOT DONE. FIELD ATTORNEYS CONTINUE TO PURSUE CASES WITHOUT CONTROL.

- Control or fire those employees who have put the desires of special interest groups ahead of impartial administration of the law.

  SOME IMPROVEMENT, BUT ABUSE CONTINUES.

### Judicial Appointments and Litigation Management

- Push for judicial candidates who understand and can articulate the limits of the judicial function.

  NOT DONE IN ENOUGH CASES.

- Establish a mechanism, either through the appointment of appropriate merit commissions or through some other suitable screening process, which will guarantee that judicial candidates are ideologically compatible with the President.

  NOT DONE. INTERNAL SCREENING DOES NOT ALLOW FOR SUFFICIENT INPUT.

- Enter into negotiations with other departments and agencies to try to consolidate the litigative function on behalf of the federal government.

  UNDERWAY.

- Prepare a memorandum giving comprehensive guidance to federal agencies concerning the ambit of the political question doctrine.

  ARTICULATED IN SPEECH.

- Revise the government's position in litigation on the constitutionality of the ERA extension.

  NOT DONE.

- Prepare a memorandum rescinding the Harmon brief and forbidding the establishment of public interest intervenor programs not specifically authorized by Congress.

  NOT DONE, BUT NO INTERVENOR REQUESTS GRANTED.

- Move to limit the reach of the *Enmons* case, insulating unions from extortion prosecution under the Hobbs Act.

  NOT DONE.

- Oppose attempts to expand felony penalties for violations of simple regulatory statutes.

  NOT DONE. ATTORNEY GENERAL TESTIFIED FOR INCREASED PENALITIES.

- Move to reverse *U.S. v. Thodarson*, insulating unions from certain organized crime prosecutions.

  NO LEADERSHIP FROM DEPARTMENT OF JUSTICE.

- Develop and push a bill to protect federal undercover agents from disclosures of their identities.

  ACCOMPLISHED.

- Develop a conservative and workable system of criminal sentencing in the form of a legislative proposal.

  DOJ SUPPORTING CRIMINAL CODE REFORM.

- Work for the re-enactment of the death penalty in federal law.

  DEPARTMENT OF JUSTICE SUPPORTING SUCH LEGIS-LATION.

- Develop an effective proposal for pre-trial detention.

  DOJ SUPPORTING SENATE LEGISLATION.

- Take measures to prevent the publication of prosecution standards issue.

  ACCOMPLISHED.

- Issue an interpretation of 5 U.S.C. 7532 which would broaden the definition of "national security" and thereby give the Administration broader discretion in checking "leaks."

  NO OCCASION TO DATE.

- Enact, by new interpretations or by legislation, a revised reading of the Freedom of Information Act which would:
    1. expand the protection for "investigatory records";

    2. expand the meaning of disclosures "[interfering] with enforcement proceedings" to include disclosures interfering with law enforcement;

    3. exclude all non-citizens from both access to classified information and access to summaries of such documents and information concerning the maintenance of such records;

163

4. establish an agency-wide procedure for giving notice to private submitters of information requested under FOIA;

5. establish an agency-wide procedure for private submitters to challenge demands for information;

6. limit FOIA to apply only to citizens and permanent resident aliens;

7. lengthen the time period for the disclosure of records;

8. modify exemption 7 to apply to all investigatory records, exempt disclosures tending to reveal confidential sources or ongoing investigations, exempt disclosure to persons who would use the information to threaten the safety of any person, and allow a court to examine *in camera* any sealed requested information;

9. give submitters access to federal courts for *de novo* review of an FOIA request;

10. modify exemption 4 to specifically exempt information which "would not customarily be released to the public by the person from whom it is obtained," to specifically exempt information which the agency has in good faith obligated itself not to disclose, and to make exemption 4 mandatory; and

11. bring information covered by the Trade Secrets Act within the ambit of FOIA.
PARTLY ACCOMPLISHED.

- Promulgate and implement a more aggressive policy of challenging standing in environmental litigation.
ADVOCATED IN ATTORNEY GENERAL'S SPEECH.

- Promulgate and implement a policy against "sweetheart suits" and stipulated judgments in conflict with the law.
ADVOCATED IN ATTORNEY GENERAL'S SPEECH.

- Implement an effective proposal to combat the influx of illegal aliens.
POLICY INEFFECTIVE AND LEGALLY QUESTIONABLE.

- Enter into cooperative efforts with allies to deal with the refugee and asylum problem.
POLICY IMPLEMENTED; ENFORCEMENT INEFFECTIVE.

- Appoint a chief of the Civil Rights Division who has a broad background and firm ideological commitment in the area of civil rights.

  NOT DONE.

- Propose legislation to put an end to racial quotas, goals, and guidelines.

  ANNOUNCED A POLICY OF NOT PROSECUTING FOR QUOTAS. DID NOT ASK FOR LEGISLATION.

- Replace Section 202(1) of E.O. 11246 with language absolutely forbidding any racial preference whatsoever by government contractors.

  NO LEADERSHIP FROM JUSTICE.

- Propose repeal of Section 203 of E.O. 11375, relating to maintenance and submission of compliance reports.

  NO LEADERSHIP FROM JUSTICE.

- Amend E.O. 11375 to require that complaints filed with the EEOC and the Department by the Department of Labor be based on intentional *de facto* discrimination.

  DOJ SUPPORTED THIS POSITION BUT DID NOT SEEK EXECUTIVE ORDER.

- Repeal sections 101 and 105 of E.O. 11246, mandating reverse discrimination, quotas, and affirmative action.

  NO LEADERSHIP FROM JUSTICE.

- Propose legislation to repeal 29 U.S.C. 793, requiring affirmative action for the handicapped by government contractors.

  NO LEADERSHIP FROM JUSTICE.

- Modify E.O. 11914, relating to the employment of the handicapped, to prevent reverse discrimination.

  NO LEADERSHIP FROM JUSTICE.

- Propose legislation to reverse *Fullilove*.

  DOJ SUPPORTING SUCH LEGISLATION.

- Issue Executive Orders to require proof of intent in discrimination cases.

  NO LEADERSHIP FROM DOJ.

- File *amicus* briefs opposing efforts by private parties to obtain equitable relief involving preferential treatment on the basis of race.

  NOT DONE.

- Issue an Executive Order requiring that no federal agency terminate funding to any private program unless there is clear proof of discriminatory intent.

  DOJ TESTIMONY TO CONGRESS SUPPORTED THIS POLICY.

- Support Freedom from Quotas legislation.

  NOT DONE.

- Decrease the 1982 DOJ budget by 9 percent over the projected 1981 figures.

  BUDGET CUT 12 PERCENT.

- Eliminate Office of Justice Assistance Research Service.

  NOT DONE, BUT BUDGET CUT DRASTICALLY.

# Chapter Fourteen

# DEPARTMENT OF LABOR
### By George Pritts

The White House failed to staff the top levels of the Labor Department in an expedient manner during the early months of the Administration. As a result, the management of the Department was hindered, innovative restructuring was impossible, and many of the specific recommendations listed in *Mandate for Leadership* were not adopted. This general statement is not intended to imply that the Department did nothing of value during the past year. Secretary Donovan skillfully implemented large budget cuts, and initiated reforms in several areas.

In addition, those appointments that have been made promise improvements at Labor during the remainder of the Administration. Under Secretary Malcolm Lovell has a strong background in administration and appears qualified to manage the day-to-day operations of the Department. Assistant Secretaries Angrisani and Auchter are well qualified to preside over reforms at ETA and OSHA respectively. In addition, Deputy Assistant Secretary Collier is well-qualifed, and early indications promise reform proposals in areas such as Black Lung, FECA and LHWA.

One area of early disappointment is the Office of the Solicitor. The Department's interpretation of Executive Order 11246 discussed in detail later in this chapter is contrary to the *Mandate* recommendations and should be reconsidered. If re-interpretation is not feasible, the Solicitor should take the lead in asking the White House for amendments. The mission of this office could be refocused toward reversing the excesses of previous years. This should be done partly through careful selection of new Associate Solicitors from the ranks of those who share the Administration's priorities and philosophy. Although these positions only open through attrition, the Solicitor has failed to capitalize on current vacancies and should do so as quickly as possible.

### Employment Standards Administration

The Davis-Bacon Act has received the attention of both the Congress and the Administration. One of the first moves of Labor Secretary Donovan was to postpone the regulations proposed by the Carter Administration. Subsequently, the Reagan Administration proposed a complete overhaul of the Davis-Bacon and Service Contract Act regulations. Over 2,000 comments on the proposals have been submitted to DOL. Final regulations are expected to be implemented in the spring of 1982.

*The author wishes to thank Charles T. Carroll, John Florez, and Richard C. Lawson for their assistance in the preparation of this chapter.

Among the beneficial changes sought by the Administration are:

- Elimination of the 30 percent rule for pre-determining wage scales. Instead utilize a majority rule, or in the absence of an identifiable majority, a weighted average.

- Elimination of the practice of "importing" urban wage rates into rural areas.

- Classification of helpers whenever wage surveys are taken and wage determinations are issued. (It must be noted that the proposed ratio of one helper to five journeymen will defeat the purpose of these regulatory changes.)

- Elimination of useless and costly weekly payroll reporting requirements.

On balance, the Reagan Administration has courageously confronted the Davis-Bacon monster. New regulations proposed by the DOL have failed, however, to eliminate the helper-ratio requirements. This failure will probably negate many of the positive effects of other regulatory changes made by the DOL. Current ratios prevent indigenous contractors from bidding on federal or federally-assisted work because regulations prohibit utilization of their work forces. The DOL should recognize prevailing local practice as the standard in this area, as the original Davis-Bacon act required.

Despite proposed regulatory changes, many in Congress still favor repeal of the Davis-Bacon Act. To date, opponents have made one unsuccessful attempt to eliminate Davis-Bacon requirements for military construction projects. Senator Thurmond's amendment, added in the Armed Services Committee, was defeated by a 55-42 vote. Future attempts to repeal or reform Davis-Bacon are almost certain. The success of these efforts is in doubt as long as the President's opponents persist. To date, he has stood by his campaign promise to defend the Act. Given this fact, the Reagan Administration should concentrate its efforts on reforming the way in which the Act is implemented rather than actively seeking its repeal. This course of action would allow President Reagan to fulfill his campaign promise to organized labor but would also provide an opportunity for much-needed reform.

## Labor Management Services Administration

Many of the short-term suggestions for the Labor Management Services Administration (LMSA) deal with the special privileges granted unions and the abuses that have arisen from them. Because most of these special privileges are written into current law or result from judicial interpretation of existing statutes, correcting the problem requires new legislation in most cases. The 97th Congress has been active in this area. Leadership on these issues interestingly is coming from the Hill and not the Administration.

A bill introduced by Senator Nunn and co-sponsored by Senator Nickles, addresses internal union corruption by increasing the penalities for misleading union pension funds and for labor extortion, bribes, and kickbacks. Senator Nickles introduced and Senator Nunn co-sponsored S. 1182 which amends the Longshoremen's and Harbor Workers' Compensation Act to eliminate from the current law those provisions which attract organized crime. Senator Nickles also introduced S. 1541, aimed at treating pension abuses by amending ERISA. These three bills represent a significant step toward the goal of eliminating corrupt union practices.

In addition, legislation has been introduced by Senator Thurmond which would amend the Hobbs Act to forbid union violence committed as a result of collective bargaining disputes. This legislation will probably not be considered until changes in the Criminal Code are taken up by Congress. A student right-to-work bill has also been introduced, though it is not expected to receive much serious consideration. The Administration should make it a point to actively support the legislative changes underway—particularly in the case of the Hobbs Act.

The Reagan Administration has made some very good appointments at Labor. For example, while *Mandate* suggested repeal of the Landrum-Griffin Act, the Department recognizes that accomplishing this goal is not politically feasible in the short-run. However, Don Dotson, the new Under Secretary of the LMSA, is sensitive to the past problem. He is wisely shifting the focus of LMSA investigations under Landrum-Griffin from campaigns and internal union elections to racketeering. Many of the problems associated with union corruption can be corrected with proper enforcement of the current law. In general, the new people at the Labor Department should be able to effect other needed changes in policy and program applications.

### Office of Federal Contract Compliance Programs

The Office of Federal Contract Compliance Programs (OFCCP) attempted some modest changes in its regulations during the initial days of the Reagan Administration. As a consequence of the poor timing and patchwork nature of the proposal, it possibly caused more problems for the Administration, causing a delay in needed reforms in federal contracting regulations. The proposal would have increased the exemption from affirmative action plan regulations from a $50,000 to a $250,000 threshold. This proposal has drawn fire from civil rights groups, Administration opponents and even from such strong supporters of the Administration as Senator Orrin Hatch. Unfortunately, the proposal does not address the real problems with contract compliance programs. Those problems are based in the eight factor analyses required in the development of affirmative action programs. None of these factors was addressed in the proposed rulemaking.

This rulemaking also ignored the most onerous facet of current contract compliance rules, the unlimited back pay provisions. Title VII of the Civil Rights Act allows for penalties to be assessed against employers convicted of discriminatory pay practices which are limited to the equivalent of two year's pay differential. An Executive Order published by the Carter Administration removes that limit in cases under the jurisdiction of OFCCP. As a consequence, OFCCP complaints have routinely asked for five years back pay. In one case, it asked for eleven years back pay and, in the most offensive example of administrative abuse, asked for thirty years back pay differential. Although this last case has not yet been settled, the position of the Department has not been altered by the current Administration. The Department should immediately press for a change in the Executive Order allowing this type of administrative "overkill."

OFCCP is continuing to view itself as a purely punitive agency. It has failed to follow *Mandate* recommendations calling for the development of incentives and encourage creative programs to improve opportunities for women and minorities in the work force. The current system of coercive training may achieve some cosmetic results, but the development of effective non-coercive training and recruiting programs will better serve the needs of both employees and employers.

### Equal Employment Opportunity Commission

Considerable overlap continues to confuse the jurisdiction between OFCCP and the Equal Employment Opportunity Commission (EEOC). Although several letters of understanding have been drafted to minimize these conflicts, the problem has not been resolved. All authority for Title VII complaints and all findings of "affective class" should be transferred to the EEOC. The result will be an elimination of duplication and a reduction in overhead and costs. This savings can be accomplished administratively and should be initiated quickly.

The problems at EEOC are equally severe. The Administration has compounded this situation by deferring appointments and making appointments which have been less than effective. EEOC is beset with both managerial and financial problems which are contributing to poor morale at the Commission.

New leadership initiatives are needed to revitalize the Commission.

Delays in processing complaints should be eliminated. The standards for prosecution evaluation established by the Carter Administration should be abandoned. These called for 45 percent "success" rates and benefit settlements averaging $1200 per case. This prosecution "quota" smacks of a small town speed trap, implies a presumption of guilt and demeans the legitimate work done by the Commission. The agency should pursue legitimate cases of discrimination quickly, effectively, and without prejudice. It should also acknowledge that unequal results do not constitute *prima facie* evidence of discrimination. The keyword in this entire process should continue to be "opportunity".

In addition, the Commission should limit systemic investigations of possible violators. At present, EEOC has not ended the practice of investigating companies at random and is continuing to review employment patterns which are several years old. In the future, systemic investigations should be limited to those agencies where evidence of discrimination is developed through other means (including convictions in individual cases). The investigations should be limited to the most recent two years, the limit for damages under Title VII.

### Occupational Safety & Health Administration

The short-term goals set by *Mandate for Leadership* for OSHA included: 1) deemphasis of the adversarial approach, which was the hallmark of the previous Administration, and promotion of more cooperative relationships with business and labor; 2) retargeting inspections toward workplaces with proven hazardous conditions; and 3) expansion of enforcement responsibility by the states.

Assistant Secretary Thorne Auchter has demonstrated a strong commitment to achieving these objectives, both in his public statements and in testimony before congressional committees. The agency has sought to establish a better relationship with the private sector in several ways. A "code of professional responsibility" directive was sent to all compliance officers. The directive requires that enforcement officers, who are often the public's only contact with OSHA, do their job in a professional manner by being courteous, helpful, and neutral. Organizationally, OSHA is increasing the utilization of joint labor-management safety committees, of training grants, and consultation activity. All of these activities seek to harness the resources of the private sector in monitoring and promoting health and safety in the workplace.

Positive steps have been taken to target inspection resources. A directive was issued in the summer of 1981 governing routine safety inspections. Revised procedures governing health inspections and inspections initiated by employee complaints must still be developed.

171

The timing of these revisions is uncertain. The leadership in OSHA is frustrated at the slow pace at which the bureaucracy reviews, ruminates, and regurgitates fundamental policy changes before final approval.

OSHA has attempted to fulfill the Reagan Administration's commitment to increase the states' role in governing America. This is evidenced in giving states greater independence and responsibility in state plan enforcement. However, the states need the incentives offered under OSHA which provide the funding for state plans. The added budget cuts being contemplated by the Administration will lower the funds available to the states, decreasing the incentive to assume an enforcement role under OSHA.

The major risk facing the Administration in implementing these short-term goals is that fatalities and injuries may increase in number and frequency. This may be causally linked with the changes implemented by OSHA. To the opponents of these changes, such as the unions, the causes will not matter. Political demagoguery can be expected in the event of any increase in work-related death or injury. The consequences could be a slowdown in the pace at which the Administration would impose additional policy changes.

### Mine Safety and Health Administration

*Mandate for Leadership* did not set forth any specific short-term program recommendations for the Mine Safety and Health Administration. MSHA has been plagued by the same problems which haunt OSHA: an adversarial approach to safety and health enforcement, a misallocation of inspection resources, and a tendency at times to promulgate regulations which are costly but ineffective. A major cause of the problems is the Federal Mine Safety & Health Act of 1977. The Act is punitive in structure and approach; it requires minimum mandatory inspections, mandatory citations for every violation of the Act, mandatory penalties, and unrealistic training requirements. The Act leaves the agency with little flexibility in directing its resources toward the proven high-hazard mine sites.

The solution to MSHA problems centers on legislative change. Reform proposals have been developed by the private sector, and some have been introduced in Congress. Congress cannot realistically proceed with comprehensive reform legislation with input from the Administration. This was not possible during the first ten months of 1981 simply because an Assistant Secretary of Labor for the Mine Safety and Health Administration was not confirmed until the end of October. Assistant Secretary Ford B. Ford has indicated that he is eager to support reform efforts and to provide the congressional committees with the Administration's views on needed changes. The Department of Labor could fulfill the short-term goals of *Mandate for*

*Leadership* if it submits legislative recommendations by February 1982.

### Employment Training Administration

ETA is struggling to redirect its efforts to emphasize block grant and private sector initiatives. ETA staff have begun the program reviews and planning procedures necessary to effect changes in line with broad Administration objectives. Some progress has been made in emphasizing private sector participation in the achievement of public policy employment and training objectives, but this area needs improvement.

The failure of the Administration to nominate and confirm an Inspector General until late September inhibited a more rapid improvement in the audit and evaluation process. However, by the end of November, ETA had completely cleared its audit blacklog. ETA has acknowledged the need to upgrade the Management Information System, but progress has been slow. Achievement of this and other communications-related objectives largely hinges on the definition of general policy goals and a major overhaul of ETA planned by both the Department of Labor and Congress.

The Administration has not communicated its policy goals for ETA, except to propose budget cuts which would eliminate the Public Service Employment and Maintenance of Effort requirement sections of the Comprehensive Employment Training Act (CETA). This apparent inaction may reflect a prudent strategy. CETA is a politically sensitive program, and the Administration budget proposal has not been finalized by the House and Senate appropriations committees. The Administration may deliberately be avoiding policy battles and strong public interest lobbying efforts in the months prior to CETA's reauthorization hearings, scheduled for the end of 1982. Few redirected employment and training programs could be implemented successfully in the next year; major efforts are probably being saved to establish a new focus for the agency without interference from outside interests. Congress is currently preparing for the CETA reauthorization process, when it will consider consolidation of programs, the active involvement of private industry in job training, and a redefinition of eligibility requirements for CETA programs. These legislative proposals would result in a reduction in funding for CETA programs to below current levels, and improve their viability.

### Benefits Review Board

The Benefits Review Board was singled out for attention because of the serious backlog of cases. *Mandate for Leadership's* only short-term recommendation was to evaluate the possibility of temporarily expanding the size of Board membership. Consideration has been given to this option within the Department of Labor, but the Department does not have the authority to appoint additional, temporary members. Legislation, either by a substantive amendment to the Longshoremen's & Harborworkers' Compensation Act, or by authorization through the Labor-HHS appropriations, would be needed to effect changes. The Labor Department has not sought such an authorizaton from the Appropriations Committees. When the Administration appeared before the Senate Labor Subcommittee in October 1981 to testify on a reform proposal (S.1182), it did not seek any changes in the size of the Board. In short, the Administration appears not to have taken affirmative steps to reduce the increasing case backlog. The Department did endorse the reform proposal, which includes changes designed to discourage frivolous claims and expediting case processing. This would eventually reduce the amount of the backlog.

This inaction may be attributable in part to the nature of the programs over which the BRB has jurisdiction: the Black Lung Benefits Act and the Longshore Act. The former provides disability benefits for coal miners with black lung disease, and the latter provides workers' compensation benefits for longshoremen and other selected workers engaged in maritime employment. Both programs have become abominations in terms of costs and the violence done to traditional workers' compensation principles. These programs are in need of substantive reform. Their defenders, principally in the House, can be expected to beat back any drastic reform proposals. The relatively narrow, procedural issue of the size of the BRB cannot be separated from the more controversial substantive issues. The likelihood of addressing the problem of case backlog legislatively is somewhat remote.

**Pension and Welfare Benefits**

All three aspects of federal retirement policy—Social Security, personal savings, and private pensions—are receiving close scrutiny from the Reagan Administration. The Economic Recovery Tax Act, signed into law by President Reagan in August 1981, contains provisions expanding the availability of, and encouraging contributions to Individual Retirement Accounts (IRAs) as one means of strengthening personal savings.

Private pension plans raise problems in more than one area. For example, in October 1981, the General Accounting Office released a report which concluded that most of the paperwork filed under ERISA requirements was never reviewed and was often lost. The extensive paperwork requirements represent one of the biggest obstacles faced by small businessmen who want to establish a pension plan.

## National Labor Relations Board

President Reagan has had the opportunity to make two appointments to the National Labor Relations Board (NLRB). The first of these was Robert Hunter (author of the DOL chapter in *Mandate*). Hunter has been confirmed by the Senate and has taken his seat on the Board. Reagan's choice for the second opening on the NLRB, the Chairman's position , was John Van de Water. While clearly qualified, Van de Water's nomination has run into serious problems in the Senate.

The fight to stop Van de Water's Senate confirmation is being led by the AFL-CIO. Publicly, their opposition is based on the contention that those attorneys who have worked in management positions, as Van de Water has, are tainted and cannot exercise fair judgment. Privately, it is believed the AFL-CIO and some Democratic Senators want to ensure they are consulted about future appointments to the Board. Van de Water's confirmation is, therefore, in some doubt.

There has been little action on other short-term recommendations made in *Mandate*. These are primarily administrative actions that can only be implemented through changes made by the Board and the General Counsel with the NLRB. Until Reagan is able to name a majority of the Board and ensure the cooperation of the General Counsel, these changes will have to wait. The Senate Labor Subcommittee intends to hold oversight hearings concerning the impartiality of the NLRB staff in the spring of 1982.

## Bureau of International Labor Affairs

The AFL-CIO designation as the U.S. Employee Representative to the International Labor Organization is consistent with ILO constitutional provisions, but it results in a distortion of the representation of U.S. workers internationally. Executive Order 12216 has not been revised to allow greater input from more representative worker and employer groups as suggested in *Mandate for Leadership*. The Order should be revised to establish a method for a more fair and realistic selection of worker representatives. In addition, ILAB reorganization is still needed. Although the ILAB staff has been reduced, this is due to an earlier reassignment of trade adjustment assistance activities outside of the ILAB structure, and not to a major restructuring of the agency. A more efficient organizational structure could further reduce ILAB personnel requirements. Finally, despite the *Mandate* recommendations, ILAB continues to administer programs contracted for and financed by foreign governments. These programs should be transferred to the Treasury Department, which currently administers similar programs for Saudi Arabian developments. Ideally, the U.S. government should promote private sector programs to replace present government initiatives.

# RECOMMENDATIONS
(Action taken on 53 out of 115)

## Employment Standards Administration

- Repeal or effect comprehensive review of Davis-Bacon Act; examine implementing regulations. Include careful examination of methods used by DOL in making wage determinations.

  NOT IMPLEMENTED. MOST CHANGES COSMETIC ONLY.

- Suspend requirements of Davis-Bacon Act as authorized by the Act in times of national emergency.

  NOT IMPLEMENTED.

- Decentralize enforcement responsibilities and give contracting agencies final authority to resolve disputes under the Davis-Bacon Act.

  NOT IMPLEMENTED.

- Impose a moratorium on amendments to prevailing wage determinations.

  NOT IMPLEMENTED.

- Bar DOL from requiring non-union contractors to use work rules and classifications on federal work.

  PENDING REGULATION. EFFECT IS TO RECOGNIZE LOCAL PRACTICE.

- Include "helper" or "trainee" classifications in order to encourage entry of minority and youth employees into the labor market.

  PENDING REGULATIONS LEAVE MUCH TO BE ACCOMPLISHED.

- Reduce burdensome paperwork requirements. Limit weekly payroll reports to submissions of statement regarding wages paid.

  ACCOMPLISHED THROUGH REGULATION.

- Insure that wage scales determined in larger, municipal areas are not applied to rural counties where the true prevailing wage generally is much lower.

  ACCOMPLISHED THROUGH REGULATION.

- Halt efforts by DOL to expand application of the Davis-Bacon Act beyond the actual intent of the Congress.

  NEW PROPOSED REGULATIONS HAVE BEEN ISSUED.

## Labor Management Services Administration

- Shift investigation focus from organizing campaigns and internal union elections to racketeering. Coordinate such action with the Department of Justice.

  IN PROGRESS.

- Revoke the rule exempting certain unions with "small" budgets from LM-2 reporting requirements.

  NO ACTION TAKEN.

- Push provision in proposed criminal code reform bill to close the loophole the *Enmons* decision put in the Hobbs Anti-racketeering Act, which basically exempts union violence if committed in furthering a collective bargaining dispute.

  LEGISLATION PENDING BEFORE HOUSE AND SENATE JUDICIARY COMMITTEES TO EFFECT THIS CHANGE THROUGH OMNIBUS TITLE 18 REWRITE.

- Repeal Landrum-Griffin Act except for LM-2 and LM-3 financial reporting by unions.

  NOT IMPLEMENTED.

- Eliminate special union privileges and immunities to reduce likelihood of union racketeering:

  1. Repeal sections of Landrum-Griffin Act which force government intervention in private labor and trade associations.

  2. Repeal National Labor Relations Act provisions which place collective rights precedent to individual rights.

  3. Repeal arbitrary feature of NLRA Section 14(b) as well as federal promotion of compulsory unionism in Railway Labor Act, providing that existing contracts be left in force.

  4. Repeal exclusive representation feature of NLRA and Railway Labor Act to alleviate union's burden of the free rider.

     NOT IMPLEMENTED.

- Amend the Constitution to prohibit discrimination on the basis of membership or non-membership in a labor or other organization:

  1. Amend exclusive representation provision in Postal Service Act to allow unions composed primarily of ethnic minorities to bargain collectively with themselves.

  2. Amend the Railway Labor Act to allow deauthorization

177

elections by employees who do not want to be fired for lack of union membership.

3. Amend the NLRA to eliminate compulsory hiring hall arrangements.
   NOT IMPLEMENTED.

- Enact student right-to-work bill which sets a minimum wage below which compulsory union membership could not be imposed.
  LEGISLATION PENDING. NO ACTION ANTICIPATED.

- Enact a Free Press Right-to-Work Bill for broadcasters and journalists not wishing to join a labor union.
  NO BILL INTRODUCED.

- Apply laws to union officials as they would apply to anyone else. Curtail federal pre-emption of state civil and criminal laws. Apply equally the laws of agency for state torts.
  NO ACTION TAKEN.

- Eliminate union exemption in Hobbs Anti-racketeering Act.
  LEGISLATION INTRODUCED.

- Eliminate judicial anti-trust exemption for union anti-competitive monopoly power.
  LEGISLATION INTRODUCED.

- Eliminate the new judicially-created exemption from punitive damages against union officials.
  NO ACTION TAKEN.

- Require that pensions under collective bargaining agreements be free from union retaliation for unfavorable representation votes as they are now free from employer retaliation.
  NO ACTION TAKEN.

- Refrain from subjecting public sector to direction of union officials (avoid strikes, compulsory arbitration, political activity, and political spending).
  NO ACTION TAKEN.

- Consider deletion of all funding from LMSA, or at least delete funds earmarked for the investigation of union organizing campaigns pursuant to Landrum-Griffin Section 203(b).
  NOT IMPLEMENTED. NO ACTION ANTICIPATED.

- Require complete "house cleaning" of staff of labor-management

178

departments, which currently are pro-union and political in presentation.

NO ACTION TAKEN.

- Appoint personnel to appropriate policy positions in DOL to effect needed changes in policy and application of programs, especially in the labor standards section.

GOOD MANAGEMENT TEAM ABOARD.

- Amend National Labor Relations Act to make "hot cargo" agreements between unions and governmental agents and authorities unlawful.

NO LEGISLATION INTRODUCED.

- Abolish pre-hire labor agreements in construction industry.

NOT IMPLEMENTED.

### Office of Federal Contract Compliance Programs

- Allow contractors to exclude from their affirmative action programs minority groups which are represented in the labor force in such significant numbers that affirmative action efforts would be meaningless.

REGULATIONS PROPOSED.

- Limit contractor's "labor force" for a particular job to qualified individuals located in the reasonable recruitment area for that job.

REGULATIONS PROPOSED.

- Exempt contractors which employ women and minorities at a ratio equal to at least 80 percent of their availability in the labor force from preparing AAPs.

REGULATIONS PROPOSED.

- Do not require contractors to perform a utilization analysis for any job group which has so few incumbents that the results would not be statistically significant.

REGULATIONS PROPOSED.

- Require contractors to consider only individuals who are qualified for, and interested in, a particular job in calculating "availability" figures.

REGULATIONS PROPOSED.

- Designate contractors "underutilized" only when women and minorities are not found in job classifications in reasonable proportion to their presence in the qualified labor force.

REGULATIONS PROPOSED.

- Establish voluntary goals and timetables as one method of demonstrating good faith efforts to ensure equal employment opportunity.

  OFCCP RECEIVING COMMENT. MAY CORRECT PROBLEM.

- Establish voluntary training programs to demonstrate good faith efforts to ensure equal employment opportunity.

  REGULATONS PROPOSED TO CORRECT THIS PROBLEM.

- Establish a standard requiring contractors to engage in good faith efforts to employ women in construction.

  UNDER CONSIDERATION.

- Review E.O. 11246 to determine whether the program should be continued in light of the remedial authority established by Congress under Title VII of the Civil Rights Act.

  UNDER CONSIDERATION BY OFCCP AND SENATE LABOR COMMITTEE.

- Do not require alternative recruitment sources be utilized if female and minority applicant flow is sufficient to generate qualified applicants for job openings.

  REGULATION PROPOSED.

- Define a contractor's nondiscrimination obligations in accordance with the standards applicable to Title VII.

  REGULATION PROPOSED.

- Bar OFCCP from affording retroactive relief to aggrieved individuals as a condition of government contracting.

  REGULATION PROPOSED.

- Deny OFCCP authority to impose quotas.

  NOT IMPLEMENTED.

- Do not disclose information submitted to OFCCP pursuant to a complaint investigation or compliance review to third parties—including charging parties, employees or other government agencies—without the written consent of the party submitting the information.

  NOT IMPLEMENTED.

- Subject administrative requests or rulings requiring the production of witnesses or documents involving allegedly confidential information to immediate judicial review.

  NOT IMPLEMENTED.

- Do not predicate violations of E.O. 11246 either directly or indirectly upon conduct which occurred during a period of time encompassed by a letter of commitment, conciliation agreement, or consent decree.
  NOT IMPLEMENTED.

- Eliminate wasteful, "sweetheart" consulting contracts.
  PROGRESS IS MUCH TOO SLOW.

- Consider a major overhaul of the agency—perhaps re-establishing its entire administrative structure along functional lines.
  UNDER CONSIDERATION.

**Equal Employment Opportunity Commission**

- Review all existing and pending regulations to determine whether they are consistent with Title VII as enacted by Congress.
  UNDER REVIEW.

- Define the extent to which third parties harmed by actions taken by persons relying on Commission guidelines may seek relief from EEOC itself.
  DEPARTMENT NOT TAKING LEAD.

- Establish in law that any action not prohibited by Title VII cannot be made unlawful through an Executive Order.
  DEPARTMENT NOT TAKING LEAD.

- Insure that no liability will attach for actions taken in reliance on Commission rulings.
  DEPARTMENT NOT TAKING LEAD.

- Liberalize the present standard used to award attorney's fees to the prevailing party in Title VII litigation.
  NO ACTION.

- Clarify and limit procedural rules regarding discovery in Title VII cases.
  NO ACTION.

- Reform the EEOC's regulatory procedures by:
  1. Clarifying authority to issue guidelines;
  2. Establishing standards governing their development;
  3. Authorizing challenges prior to enforcement;
  4. Specifying standards for review; and

5. Specifying that these actions not have a presumption of validity.

NO ACTION TO DATE.

- Revise class action procedural rules.

NO ACTION TO DATE.

- Strengthen protections against improper disclosure of employee data.

NO ACTION TO DATE.

- Establish procedures to elect remedies and encourage resolution of Title VII claims through binding arbitration.

NO ACTION TO DATE.

- Clarify existing law to state that a complainant must file a charge of employment discrimination with either the EEOC or a state 706 agency within 180 days of the discriminatory act.

NO LEADERSHIP FROM DEPARTMENT.

- Require that any suit brought in federal court must be filed within two years of the filing of a charge by a private party.

NO LEADERSHIP FROM DEPARTMENT.

- Require that a private plaintiff Title VII suit be filed within two years of the time from which the plaintiff was eligible for a right-to-sue letter.

NO LEADERSHIP FROM DEPARTMENT.

- Clarify Section 713(b) of Title VII to make clear that when an employer relies upon the provisions of a consent decree entered into with the government, such actions cannot form the basis for later Title VII liability.

NO LEADERSHIP FROM DEPARTMENT.

- Adopt amendments correcting the problems caused by the guidelines issued by the EEOC under the Pregnancy Discrimination Amendments to Title VII.

NO LEADERSHIP FROM DEPARTMENT.

### Occupational Safety & Health Administration

- Encourage OSHA to develop cooperative programs involving government, business, and labor.

PROGRESS NOTED.

- Redirect OSHA's enforcement activities so as to target, as precisely as possible, work places with poor safety records.

PROGRESS NOTED.

- Revise OSHA's approach to state OSHA programs.
  PROGRESS NOTED.

- Appoint task force to examine how OSHA can establish more cooperative relationship with business and labor through:

  1. Safety committees

  2. Expert consultations

  3. Training grants

  4. Reconstituting National Advisory Committee

  5. Demonstration projects.
     NOT ACCOMPLISHED, BUT ASSISTANT SECRETARY SUPPORTS THESE GOALS.

- Appoint task force to redesign policies on targeting of inspections.
  SAFETY TARGETING SUPPORTED THROUGH DIRECTIVE. HEALTH DIRECTIVE PENDING.

- Revise state plans program through appointment of task force.
  NOT ACCOMPLISHED. BLOCKED BY FUNDING CUTBACK AND FEDERAL COURT DECISION *(AFL-CIO V. MARSHALL)*.

- Maintain stable appropriations levels, in keeping with government budget policy guidelines of no growth.
  ACCOMPLISHED.

### Mine Safety and Health Administration

- Appoint a study commission to evaluate current enforcement of the MSHA and to make recommendations for administrative and legislative changes.
  NOT ACCOMPLISHED. EVALUATION BEING DONE BY MSHA ITSELF.

### Pension and Welfare Benefit Programs

- Expand availability of Individual Retirement Accounts (IRAs), effectively strengthening personal savings.
  ACCOMPLISHED THROUGH PRESIDENT'S TAX BILL.

- Review current regulations under Code Section 410 and 411 with a view to simplification.
  S. 1541 PROPOSED CODIFICATION.

- Revise DOL disclosure regulations, permitting more flexible communication of benefit plans. Review reporting requirements with a view to permitting more self-administration.

  S. 1541 CONTAINS STREAMLINED REPORTING REQUIRE-MENTS.

- Promulgate regulations under the new Multiemployer Plan Bill to provide reasonable and inexpensive methods for administering those plans.

  IN PROGRESS.

### National Labor Relations Board

- Require new chairman of NLRB and all future Board members to have substantial private sector experience in labor-management relations.

  ACCOMPLISHED.

- Require that oral arguments take place before the full NLRB one week during every calendar quarter.

  NLRB INTENDS MORE ORAL ARGUMENT.

- Eliminate trial by surprise in Board proceedings.

  NO ACTION TAKEN.

- Require consistent rule on witness sequestration.

  NO ACTION TAKEN.

- Streamline procedures to be utilized by NLRB in carrying out its mandate under Section 10(1).

  NO ACTION TAKEN.

- Require Board to design specific affirmative guidelines for the use of its powers under Section 10(1) of the Act.

  NO ACTION TAKEN.

- Require NLRB to defer to decision of the U.S. Circuit Courts of Appeals when the decision reverses the Board in the region covered by that circuit.

  NO ACTION TAKEN.

### Bureau of International Labor Affairs (ILAB)

- Revise E.O. 12216 to redesignate membership on the International Labor Organization (ILO). Membership should consist of:

  1. Secretary of Labor

  2. Secretary of State

3. Designate from the Executive Office

4. Head of the U.S. Chamber of Commerce

5. Head of the National Federation of Independent Business

6. Two labor representatives named by the President, one a union president and one an employee who is a worker and not a union member.

NOT ACCOMPLISHED. ADDITIONAL INPUT FROM REPRESENTATIVE WORKER AND EMPLOYER GROUPS NEEDED.

- Reorganize ILAB to reflect need for only five offices:

1. International Labor Organizations;

2. Foreign representation group (labor attache program, relations with ministries);

3. Research group (data and analyses of foreign labor conditions);

4. Exchange group (formal/informal visits by labor leaders); and

5. Trade group (to analyze impact of trade on employment).

TRADE ADJUSTMENT ASSISTANCE TRANSFERRED. NO OTHER ORGANIZATIONAL CHANGES MADE.

- Refrain from administering programs contracted for by foreign governments and financed by them (i.e., manpower project in Saudi Arabia).

PROGRAMS STILL ADMINISTERED.

- Reduce ILAB staffing, particularly through reassignment of trade adjustment and foreign aid activities elsewhere. Emphasize foreign experience/background as well as competence.

GREAT REDUCTION IN TOTAL ILAB EMPLOYEES OCCURRED UPON REASSIGNMENT OF TRADE ADJUSTMENT ASSISTANCE ACTIVITIES, BUT LITTLE OTHER REDUCTION EFFECTED.

### Bureau of Labor Statistics

- Appoint a Federal Commission on Statistics to ensure public's confidence in the impartiality of economic and labor statistics. BLS Task Force should evaluate:
1. Applicability of SES career-reserved categories to all program chiefs.

NOT ACCOMPLISHED.

2. Transfer of preparation of Consumer Price Index and monthly employment statistics to Department of Commerce.
ACCOMPLISHED.

3. Accuracy of Form 2441 on union associations and membership.
NO ACTION.

4. Transfer of Davis-Bacon wage rate responsibility from Employment Standards Administration to Bureau of Labor Statistics.
TRANSFER PROPOSED.

COMMISSION NOT CREATED, BUT RECOMMENDATIONS ACTED ON THROUGH CABINET COUNCIL ON ECONOMIC POLICY.

- Reduce BLS budget:
  1. Consider transfer of Cost of Living Survey preparation to Bureau of the Census.
  NOT DONE.

  2. Initiate independent publications and data audit to identify other areas of long-term savings.
  NO AUDIT INITIATED. REAGAN REQUESTED $108 MILLION, DOWN FROM CARTER'S $115 MILLION; HOUSE PASSED BILL FOR $123 MILLION, SENATE ACTION NOT COMPLETE.

### Office of the Solicitor

- Appoint Associate and Regional Solicitors sympathetic to labor goals of the Administration. (Opportunities normally will arise only through attrition.)
PARTIALLY ACCOMPLISHED THROUGH APPOINTMENT OF FIVE ASSOCIATES. SIX REMAINING IN OFFICE ARE CARTER "HOLDOVERS."

### Employment and Training Administration (ETA)

- Establish an agency mission for ETA.
IN PROGRESS.

- Appoint an experienced manager/policy person as Assistant Secretary for ETA, who has had both local and national experience.
MARGINALLY ACCOMPLISHED.

186

- Fire all existing top-level personnel.
CERTAIN CHANGES MADE, BUT NO WHOLESALE DISMISSAL.

- Appoint a good congressional relations person.
NOT IMPLEMENTED.

- Establish clear lines of responsibility and authority within the Department.
NOT IMPLEMENTED.

- Replace all top-level people with people of sound management credentials.
PARTIALLY IMPLEMENTED.

- Provide clear missions and goals for all departmental personnel. Performance goals and standards must be set up at all levels.
IN PROGRESS.

- Restore sound management practives at all levels: goals/mission, planning, executing, review, and replanning.
IMPROVEMENT CAN BE NOTED.

- Re-examine the role of National Office vs. Field Offices.
NOT IMPLEMENTED.

- Improve public relations, particularly to encourage private sector participation.
STILL ROOM FOR IMPROVEMENT, BUT SOME PROGRESS MADE.

- Revamp Office of Management Assistance to provide high quality technical assistance.
NOT IMPLEMENTED.

- Review and revise Audit Evaluation and Enforcement.
REVISION IS MOVING TOO SLOWLY.

- Upgrade Field Representatives. They are the key link between DOL and local governments.

- Coordinate policies and regulations among all ETA's agencies.
NOT IMPLEMENTED.

- Upgrade the Management Information System.
PROGRESS SLOW, BUT GOAL ACKNOWLEDGED.

- Clean out the Office of National Programs.

  ELIMINATION UNDER CONSIDERATION.

- Re-evaluate CETA Title III programs.

  DONE. CUTS MADE IN TITLE III.

- Consolidate the Office of Youth Programs under CETA.

  NO PUSH FOR NECESSARY LEGISLATION.

- Re-evaluate ETA's enforcement role and the relation between ETA's employment and training responsibilities and the negative effects of ETA's EEOC and other enforcement responsibilities.

  MAJOR OVERHAUL UNDERWAY.

- Submit a CETA re-authorization bill no later than the end of the first session of the 97th Congress.

  BUDGET CUTS PROPOSED AND PASSED.

- Examine Private Sector Initiative Program (PSIP) as possible alternative to CETA.

  MARCH OMB RECOMMENDATIONS INCLUDED A HEALTHY INCREASE FOR PSIP.

- Re-evaluate U.S. Employment Service statutes.

  IN PROCESS.

- Initiate welfare reform.

  PLANNING HAS BEGUN.

- Eliminate aspects of Trade Adjustment Assistance that are no more than glorified unemployment benefits.

  IN PROGRESS.

- Consider legislation for economic development such as the Kemp-Garcia "Enterprise Zone" bill.

  IN PROGRESS.

**Benefits Review Board**

- Evaluate the case backlog and, if necessary, expand the size of the Board temporarily to speed reduction of the backlog.

  NOT ACCOMPLISHED.

- Promulgate procedural rule changes relative to the DOL's appearance in cases.

  NOT ACCOMPLISHED.

# Chapter Fifteen
# DEPARTMENT OF STATE
### By Jeffrey B. Gayner

In reviewing the management problems of the U.S. foreign policy system in late 1980, *Mandate for Leadership* concluded on a pessimistic note. "The nation is still waiting," the study maintained, "for an administration both willing and able to bring coherence, management and precision to the operation of the U.S. foreign policy system." Nobody who studies these issues today would contend that the Reagan Administration has been able to completely iron out the deficiencies in the machinery for making and conducting foreign policy. To the readers of the Heritage report, this should come as no surprise. Nor should this reflect necessarily upon the personnel or the policies of the Reagan Administration.

The central theme of the Heritage study documents the near insoluble difficulties that all administrations since Truman have had in coping with the human machinery of foreign policy. The study notes that over a period of thirty years there have been at least 65 major reports on foreign policy-making in Washington, with few concrete results. Each administration has had to proceed slowly; after a time it evolved its own unique "style" as defined by the habits and personality of the President. The Reagan system is still in a fairly early stage of evolution, but there are signs of improvement.

After nearly one year, the pattern of decision-making is already a notable improvement over the incoherence which marked the Carter Administration. President Reagan's national security goals are clear, and the political skills of the White House personnel are good. The President has been able to command a great deal of support and unity from his staff. His decisions have been firm and clear and they have been communicated lucidly—and supported—by his main subordinates in the bureaucracy.

True to his campaign promises, the President has upgraded the role of the State Department, and the National Security Advisor has remained largely out of the public spotlight on policy matters. Both of these changes were recommended by the Heritage report. The system which has evolved has been centralized in a series of inter-departmental committees, run mostly by the State Department. A National Security Planning Group has been formed, composed of top-level Cabinet and White House officials and presided over by the President himself. This is an informal body, but it allows the President to discuss the most serious issues at the highest echelon. Thus, both the timing and definition of important policy choices come—as they should—from the top of the bureaucratic structure.

Despite these encouraging signs, persistent problems remain. The institutional and personality difficulties of the Reagan presidency have been a nagging embarrassment. These began on Inauguration Day, when Secretary of State Haig prepared a memorandum designed to make the State Department pre-eminent in policy decisions. The clashes between Haig and National Security Advisor Allen have continued since then. As a first priority, the Administration should end this problem by establishing a clear and meaningful role for the National Security Advisor. *Mandate* contained suggestions on the crucial relationship between the White House and the State Department. They were not followed. This recommendation refers to the institutions in question without regard to the personal problems of any particular official.

A related problem is the confusion of authority throughout the foreign policy bureaucracy. Different public statements by competing officials have created a perception of mismanagement. Secretary Haig alluded to a "cacophony of voices" in the Administration. "If you're asking me would I like to see greater discipline in this regard," he told a reporter, "my answer is yes." The Secretary's comment is consistent with the *Mandate* recommendations. Although the main thrust of Reagan's management has been constructive, the Administration still has not resolved this key institutional issue.

In a philosophical sense, the top foreign policy leadership in the Reagan Administration has generally presented a coherent conservative view of the world. But while unity of purpose exists, profound problems have also arisen in the implementation of publicly declared policy. As indicated above, clashes between some of the principal personalities have had a debilitating effect upon policy. However, possibly the greatest problem has been the absence of a sufficient number of key leaders at all levels of the State Department devoted to the Reagan philosophy of foreign policy. Rather than make maximum use of the personnel appointments allowed, the Secretary of State has minimized the influx of new thought into key State Department positions.

The Secretary decided to rely on career Foreign Service officers with whom he has worked over the years, instead of conservative experts from outside government. For example, of the sixteen top "political" positions in the four regional bureaus of the State Department, only two of these crucial jobs went to individuals who are not career Foreign Service officers. Other key international posts continue to be occupied by Carter holdovers and career liberals. A thorough housecleaning was recommended in *Mandate* and continues to be a major priority. Thus, any significant change of policies promoted from the top of the Administration is stymied at the bottom. More important, no drive for innovation or change arises from the levels of the Department that should have and could have had devoted conservatives in office.

After nearly one year, the Administration has made substantial progress in reformulating the national security decision-making process. Much remains to be done. In addition to the institutional and personality problems already mentioned, long-range coordination and planning are lacking within the bureaucracy. The AWACS issue was badly mishandled by the Department; major improvements are needed in congressional relations. There is evidence of misuse of important expertise in the decision-making process, sloppy staff work, and continuing internal quarrels over policy-making authority. The Administration should have addressed these problems sooner, as solutions will require time.

The great successes achieved in domestic and economic matters prove that the Administration can make historic decisions when necessary. After over thirty years of mismanagement, the foreign policy decision-making system still requires more streamlined guidance from the White House.

## Policy Directions

*Mandate for Leadership* suggested that the United States should adopt a comprehensive, coherent but flexible foreign and defense policy which would both reassure our allies and reassert U.S. influence in the world. To date, the overall foreign policy as outlined by the Reagan Administration embraces the following basic elements:

- Beyond simply asserting its leadership of the free world, the United States must act responsibly as a leader.

- America's military position must be improved and strengthened in order to compensate for the dramatic buildup of Soviet military power during the past two decades.

- America seeks to moderate and restrain Soviet adventurism throughout the globe.

- Cognizant of the significant interrelationship between the domestic and the international economic order, the United States seeks first to restore viability, productivity and balance in its own economy.

In emphasizing such elements, the Reagan Administration has stated its intention that foreign policy be conducted with balance, clarity and consistency. Furthermore, American policy efforts must be focused, as Under Secretary of State for Political Affairs Walter J. Stoessel, Jr. has already stated, "within a framework which permits actions and policies in one region to be mutually reinforcing in another region."

*Mandate* focused on two key issues in foreign policy that required immediate attention from a conservative administration: human rights and Law of the Sea. In both these areas, the United States has pursued policies in recent years which neglect our own vital interests by unnecessarily catering to the interests of other countries who often do not share our fundamental objectives in foreign and economic policy.

Immediately upon assuming office, the Reagan Administration dramatically reversed the more extreme aspects of the policies on the Law of the Sea. Rather than proceeding with negotiations that probably would have led to an unsatisfactory treaty, the Reagan Administration promptly called for a complete review of the process.

The Administration has undertaken a detailed review of the Law of the Sea negotiations and the vital economic interest of the United States is expected to remain a principal concern of the State Department. Any new treaty quite likely will contain the incentives necessary for private enterprise to risk capital investment in deep seabed mining operations. Similarly, the United States has taken the position, particularly in the Cancun meeting, that the Third World must pursue economic policies that encourage real growth and welcome private investment. The massive transfers of funds and technology represented by the initial Law of the Sea Treaty have been wisely rejected by the Reagan Administration. The Administration has also generally discouraged continued Third World reliance on all forms of international wealth redistribution. A coherent approach to both domestic and foreign economic policies has become evident in the initial year of the Reagan Administration.

James A. Malone, Assistant Secretary of State for Oceans, International Environmental and Scientific Affairs, effectively summarized a sound position for the Administration on the negotiations, in testimony before the Senate Foreign Relations Committee on June 4, 1981:

> We think that the world community too, will be better served, if we return to the Conference with a realistic assessment of what will satisfy our people and our Congress. The Administration does not wish to be in a position of misleading other countries into concluding a treaty they will expect us to ratify, a treaty which in many respects is believed by them to satisfy our national interests, and then find us unable to participate in the final results.

The Administration has taken a similarly courageous position in its approach to the human rights problem. As recommended in *Mandate*, the Administration has continued to reaffirm the U.S.

192

commitment to human rights while effectively using quiet diplomacy to promote adherence to human rights.

In both the initial statements by the Reagan Administration on human rights and in its conduct of bilateral and multilateral diplomacy, the Reagan Administration has exhibited a far more sophisticated understanding of the problem of human rights than previous administrations. Rather than narrowing the concern of the United States for human rights, as charged by its critics, the Reagan Administration has actually broadened the definition and consequent coverage of human rights. In three specific areas, the Administration expanded human rights coverage to include abuses by non-governmental groups, violations by terrorists and explicit support for economic rights of individuals.

Under the previous administration, only human rights violations by governments were condemned. Similar actions by non-governmental groups, such as guerrilla forces and so-called liberation forces, were judiciously ignored. Terrorism has not previously been regarded as a violation of human rights. In a comment often misquoted, Secretary of State Haig asserted that "International terrorism will take the place of human rights, [as] our concern, because it is the ultimate abuse of human rights." Finally, the Administration recognized the interrelationships between economic liberty and civil and political liberty. Michael Novak, the head of the U.S. delegation to the U.N. Commission meeting in Geneva stated: "We believe that when citizens have economic liberties, inevitable pressures lead toward greater political and civil liberties."

Although frequently reiterating its support for human rights, the Reagan Administration has consciously avoided the kinds of unproductive confrontation politics in this area that characterized the previous administration. Thus, the Administration clearly has followed the advice of *Mandate* to use "quiet diplomacy" to "nudge friendly and allied regimes in the direction of greater respect for civil and political rights." Similarly, the Administration has attempted to prevent the worst abuses of human rights by aiding governments threatened by totalitarian regimes. The Administration has realized that the pursuit of human rights is often a delicate diplomatic balancing act, and that "human rights are not advanced by replacing a bad regime with a worse one, or a corrupt dictator with a zealous communist politburo."

If a significant fault exists with the Reagan Administration's pursuit of human rights, it has been its inability to compellingly articulate its views. This has partly derived from the absence of an effective spokesman for the policy in this area as a result of the failure to secure Senate confirmation of the first nominee for the Assistant Secretary for Human Rights and Humanitarian Affairs. With Senate confirmation of Elliot Abrams as Assistant Secretary, the Administration will have someone who should ably carry out human rights policy.

## U.S./Soviet Relations

In the past decade, U.S.-Soviet bilateral relations were referred to under the rubric of "detente," and were conducted under the assumption that a major change had taken place in the nature of the Soviet state. The Soviet Union was judged to have dropped its goal of promoting revolution, and to have become a "status quo power." Soviet involvement in a variety of Third World conflicts was explained as being the result of its "legitimate aspirations as a superpower." This illusion appears to have dissolved as a result of the Soviet invasion of Afghanistan. Unfortunately, the major detente initiatives appear to have acquired a life and motivation of their own.

The most important issue in the detente policy is arms control, which Henry Kissinger referred to as the "litmus test of detente." The Reagan Administration has taken a considered and deliberate approach to this issue, refusing to rush into negotiations until it has reconsidered America's goals and methods in conducting arms control. Top officials of the Administration appear to recognize that arms control has been successfully used by the Soviets to gain nuclear superiority and to make America's deterrent force vulnerable. Any agreement the United States would consider "meaningful" (i.e., contribute to strategic stability) would be objectionable to the Soviet Union for that very reason. Therefore, U.S. arms control policy should be built upon the assumption that negotiations should be carried out for diplomatic reasons, rather than with any hopes of achieving major reductions in military forces.

Important voices both outside and within the Administration, however, are asserting that the failure of the United States to achieve meaningful arms control is not due to Soviet policy, but instead to the incompetent appointees and policies of the Carter Administration. They assert that a combination of firm negotiating techniques and a willingness to build major weapons systems for use as "bargaining chips" will result in arms control treaties of real significance. These views can be summed up in a pre-election statement by Alexander Haig, that the destiny of Ronald Reagan is to negotiate an equitable SALT treaty with the Soviet Union.

A second major pillar of the detente process is the use of trade to cement U.S.-Soviet ties. In recent years, however, there has been a growing realization of the degree to which this subsidized the Soviet military build-up. U.S.-Soviet trade falls into two major areas: the sale of U.S. grain to the Soviet Union, and the sale of U.S. high technology to the Soviet Union. *Mandate* recommended prompt termination of the grain embargo in conjunction with an embargo of non-agricultural goods. The grain embargo was lifted but only belatedly; the Administration is now moving to eliminate credit subsidies. No general sales embargo has been imposed. Moreover, the Administration has not been effective in extending the ban on the sale of military-related items to the Soviets. The recent authorization of Caterpillar Tractor manufacturing equipment is evidence of a failure to adopt this *Mandate* recommendation. The Administration has also failed to close the loophole in the high technology trade embargo which results from sales to non-Soviet Comecon nations. The sale of high technology items to these countries contributes to the vulnerability of U.S. strategic forces. Finally, the large loans extended by the United States government and financial community have become hostage to continued good relations between the superpowers.

A third important element in U.S.-Soviet bilateral relations under the detente process is human rights. The Reagan Administration has formulated a sound policy in this area. It realizes that emigration, family contacts, and lessened pressure on dissidents are important to the United States not only on principle, but also because a large number of Americans have personal ties in the Soviet Union. The Administration also recognizes that official U.S. rhetoric in this area gives the Soviet Union leverage over U.S. policy. It has returned to the practice of making quiet representations on behalf of individual cases; at the same time, it has condemned the general lack of respect for human rights displayed by the Soviet Union. An important part of this policy is the increased role of Voice of America and Radio Liberty/Radio Free Europe in presenting an alternative source of information to the Soviet people.

The Reagan Administration has improved on the naive policies of its predecessor in dealing with the Soviet Union. It is free of the illusion that in the final analysis the United States can rely on the Soviet Union to exercise "restraint" in international affairs. Yet it appears to share another illusion that has crippled American policy: the belief that the Soviet Union is impressed by American symbolic gestures and rhetoric. The Soviet Union does not respect gestures and speeches. The Administration should proceed rapidly to develop a coordinated policy toward the Soviets which is based on vigilance, a willingness to challenge Soviet expansionism, and peaceful competition on both an international and economic basis.

### Europe

From the outset, the Reagan Administration believed that to deal effectively with its European partners it would have to project an image of national strength and confidence. It has done this fairly successfully these past months, in sharp contrast to the image of ambivalence and weakness projected by the preceding administration. Strength and confidence alone are insufficient tools with which to lead the varied NATO countries. Although they still look to the United States for leadership, they expect those who exercise that leadership to show consideration and sensitivity to certain of Western Europe's political problems.

The Administration's priority in Europe is to strengthen the NATO Alliance in the face of growing Soviet military capabilities. To this end, it has pressed its European partners to reaffirm their support for NATO's December 1979 decision to modernize theater nuclear forces by adding 572 long-range Pershing II and ground-launched cruise missiles to their arsenal. The Reagan Administration also implored the Europeans to renew their commitment to the Carter-inspired, three-percent real increase in annual defense spending. In a matter not directly related to NATO's European defense commitments, the Administration requested that the allies assist the United States in fielding its "quick reaction force" for use in the Persian Gulf and other areas that are particularly important to Europe's economic well-being.

The Reagan Administration has been successful in obtaining NATO agreement on all three requests. Nonetheless, European support for these proposals has not been specific, an indication of the underlying European apprehension about the extent of the Reagan defense initiatives. For example, reaffirming their general support for the three-percent defense spending guideline, NATO defense ministers revealed that the Europeans interpreted the figure as more of a maximum target, rather than the minimum one the Reagan Administration considered it to be. The Ministers responded to the U.S. request for assistance to its Rapid Deployment Force by agreeing only to coordinate assessments of the threat and identify common objectives. They declined to assure the use of ports and overflight rights for the RDF in such crises, noting instead that common objectives "may require members ... to facilitate out-of-area deployments in support of the vital interests of all."

On the political front, the Reagan Administration has less to show for its efforts. An early Administration casualty was its campaign to dissuade the West Germans, in particular, from participating in the Yamal pipeline project with the Soviet Union—an initiative no doubt injured by President Reagan's decision to end the Carter-imposed U.S.S.R. grain embargo. In more general terms, European political leaders were obviously dismayed by conflicting signals from the State and Defense Departments during the early months of the Administration. Although contretemps have been largely eliminated, European heads of state must wonder if departmental infighting will eventually force Secretary Haig from government. Finally, the Reagan Administration's clumsy handling of the decision to go ahead with full production of the "neutron bomb" exacerbated political problems in Western Europe by strengthening the hands of pacifist and anti-American political elements throughout Europe.

The election of Socialist governments in France and Greece may well prove a harbinger of tougher times ahead for President Reagan's European policies. The new Administration may perceive an increasing Soviet threat; convincing European governments of the danger will be increasingly difficult given the Socialist commitment to detente. The Reagan Administration is faced with the delicate but critical task of strengthening NATO's defenses without undermining political support for the Alliance itself. To date, its overall performance has been less than fully effective. The Administration should now concentrate on improving its ability to handle sensitively the problems posed by European politics.

**Central America**

*Mandate* named Central America as the most pressing problem area in the Western Hemisphere. One year later, this assessment remains unchanged. The government of El Salvador may not be able to resist the mounting pressure on it to negotiate with its leftist opponents. Such negotiations will be perceived as a prelude to the installation of a leftist government and new leftist political and military challenges in Guatemala, Honduras, and Costa Rica.

The Reagan Administration has pursued the broad outlines of policy toward El Salvador recommended in *Mandate*. In particular, the Administration has effectively discouraged any change in the leadership of El Salvador by elements which may, out of frustration with the continuing war, have been tempted to forcibly topple the government.

Nonetheless, the situation has continued to deteriorate in recent months. The State Department has not effectively monitored or responded to events in the country. Meanwhile, the White House has been absorbed with domestic budget and fiscal matters and the sale of AWACS to Saudi Arabia.

The essential problems continuing in El Salvador relate to some of the issues raised in the *Mandate* study:

- The Salvadorean armed forces have been unable to get the upper hand over the guerrillas. The guerrillas appear to be achieving their strategic objective of establishing themselves as a force which cannot be beaten militarily and, hence, must be dealt with through negotiation.

- The essential political process in El Salvador is getting underway despite the continuing high profile of violence. Nevertheless, serious questions remain about the timing of the elections, and even more so about the logic of the assumption that elections, however honest, can result in an improved military and security climate.

- The Salvadorean agrarian reform program, while of some political benefit, is rife with incompetence and corruption. Under its present government management, it is discouraging private sector investors whose investments are needed in the Salvadorean economy. It is also helping to diminish the Salvadorean earnings from cash crops, thus adding to a deficit which will have to be borne in part by the U.S. Treasury.

The Reagan Administration has failed in two critical areas:

(1) It has failed to articulate and defend its policy in Central America before the Congress and the American public. U.S. liberals are taking advantage of this failure by organizing themselves into a grass-roots lobby in opposition to aid to El Salvador.

(2) It has failed to put genuine supporters of the Reagan philosophy into key positions in the State Department. Regardless of high-level rhetoric, the policy that finally emerges is similar to that of the previous Administration.

In addition to addressing these matters, the Administration should also follow the *Mandate* recommendation and encourage certain other Latin American governments to aid El Salvador with a concerted military advisory effort—particularly with intelligence experts and experienced non-commissioned officers. The two or three years which our embassy in San Salvador believes it will need to "professionalize" the Salvadorean military is longer than domestic and international political constraints may allow.

U.S. policy toward Nicaragua only gradually evolved into the position recommended in *Mandate* to limit assistance only to private, non-governmental groups unless the government indicates genuine interest in creating a free and pluralistic society. The Sandinistas have instead further consolidated power, suppressed nearly all opposition, and created the largest army in Central American history. Only recently has the Reagan Administration attempted to terminate all aid to the Sandinistas, including assistance provided by multilateral banks and other institutions. The United States must expand efforts both to isolate Nicaragua and to assist its threatened neighbors.

Elsewhere in Central America, the Administration has developed excellent relations with most governments by curtailing public attacks on their systems of government, and by attempting to eliminate self-defeating restrictions, particularly on arms sales. The United States has encouraged the private sector approach to development in the area. Promotion of human rights has proceeded

198

through quiet bilateral diplomacy, in contrast to the ineffective public lecturing of previous years. In particular, the Administration has demonstrated greater sensitivity to the terrorist problem confronting countries such as Colombia. Although U.S. policy in South America has attracted only minimal public attention, it has begun to develop broad support for common security, political, and economic interests.

## The Middle East

The Reagan Administration's strategy for the Middle East, as articulated by Secretary of State Haig, is to crystallize an anti-Soviet "strategic consensus" among the pro-Western and moderate states in the region—Israel, Egypt, Saudi Arabia, Jordan, Turkey, Sudan, and Oman. Although each of these states has a pronounced interest in limiting Soviet influence in the region, the group as a whole is divided on a long list of issues and particularly on the best means of resolving the Arab-Israeli dispute. In order to encourage and strengthen a fragile consensus among so many states with such diverse interests, the Administration has attempted to trumpet the Soviet threat while glossing over divisive Arab-Israeli issues. However, many Arab states have publicly warned that they consider Israeli actions to be more of a threat than Soviet actions. The Israelis, for their part, remain extremely suspicious of American ties to the Arab world.

If the strategic consensus policy is to have a chance for success, then the Palestinian problem must be addressed to the satisfaction of both Israel and its Arab neighbors—an extremely difficult task. The Reagan Administration remains committed to the Camp David framework for peace between Egypt and Israel, but has not yet been able to expand the negotiating process to include other Arab states who do not believe that the Israelis are willing to grant "meaningful" autonomy to the Palestinians. President Reagan, who entered office as a stronger supporter of Israel than President Carter, thus far has not applied as much pressure to Israel in the negotiations as did his predecessor. President Reagan also has altered American policy by declaring that Israeli settlements recently built on the West Bank were "not illegal" with respect to the Camp David accord.

The Administration effectively handled the three Middle Eastern mini-crises that have threatened its policy of strategic consensus in recent months. Diplomatic troubleshooter Philip Habib successfully negotiated a partial resolution of the Syrian missile crisis with Saudi help. The temporary suspension of F-16 deliveries to Israel in the wake of Israel's pre-emptive strike against the Iraqi nuclear reactor put the Begin government on notice that American support for Israeli military operations could not be taken for granted unless Israel was acting to preserve its vital defense interests. The prompt and decisive

American response to the assassination of President Sadat strengthened Egyptian confidence in Washington and Israeli confidence in Cairo.

The Administration's ability to push the controversial AWACS sale through a balky Congress was not a major victory for its Middle Eastern foreign policy, but merely a successful effort to maintain the viability of its strategic consensus policy. Congressional rejection of the sale would have critically damaged U.S.-Saudi relations, undermined the U.S. strategic position in the Persian Gulf region, and deflated the perceived value of an American security commitment in the eyes of moderate Arab states such as Egypt, Sudan and Jordan. Although congressional acceptance of the AWACS sale was a psychological blow to Israel, it poses only a limited threat to Israeli security which can easily be neutralized by offsetting U.S. military assistance to Israel. The White House is expected to offer such assistance in the near future.

While President Reagan quickly moved to assuage Israeli anxieties over the completion of the AWACS sale, he inadvertently angered Israel by commenting favorably on the eight-point Saudi peace plan originally proposed by Crown Prince Fahd in August. This proposal called for return of all territory captured by Israel in 1967 and the establishment of a Palestinian nation with East Jerusalem as its capital. This was an important step forward by the Saudis because it tacitly recognizes Israel by guaranteeing the right of all countries in the Middle East to live in peace. While the Saudi proposal is a step in the right direction, it contains several points that are unacceptable to Israel and the United States, and thus is not a realistic basis for discussion. The Begin government, which totally rejected the Saudi proposal, immediately launched a public information campaign focused on the White House, Congress, and the American media in order to lobby for American rejection of the plan. The Reagan Administration, seeking to calm Israeli concern, reiterated its commitment to the Camp David accords and pointed out that it had never endorsed the Saudi plan, but merely acknowledged its potential promise.

In summary, the Reagan Administration, by and large, has pursued a consistent, coherent, and flexible approach to Middle Eastern policy. It has moved to strengthen America's strategic position in the region by increasing American influence in moderate Arab states without diluting the American commitment to Israel. In the long run, this policy can only be successful if the Arab-Israeli conflict is resolved peacefully. The Administration has not yet formulated its position on how best to facilitate the realization of a comprehensive peace plan based on the Camp David process. Such a delay was to be expected given the Israeli elections in June, the diversion of the AWACS debate, and the death of President Sadat.

The single glaring flaw in the Administration's handling of Middle East policies was its handling of the AWACS controversy. The case for the sale was not presented fully in enough time to forestall the lobbying efforts by opponents to the sale. The Administration's efforts to educate Congress were conducted initially in a piecemeal, poorly-coordinated fashion. Although President Reagan was able to salvage the sale through his personal political skills, it is apparent there was poor staff work or inadequate congressional relations resources in the NSC and State Department. The exact nature of the problem should be identified and corrected before more of the Chief Executive's valuable time is required to fight congressional battles that should have been easily won.

### Africa

President Reagan's foreign policy team has not yet expressed a broad series of well-defined policies for the African continent. This looseness of policy, however, is the product of events and developments within Africa itself rather than of any failing on the part of the Administration. Several key African states are in a condition of flux and any attempt to implement rigid U.S. policies toward them would be premature and ill-advised. Flexibility will enable the State Department to deal with problems as they arise and to deal with individual states as separate entities with their own unique problems.

Assistant Secretary of State Chester Crocker has long argued for greater flexibility in U.S. relations with the Republic of South Africa. His policies now seem to be bearing fruit in the negotiations for the independence of South West Africa/Namibia. Negotiations are currently being conducted in great secrecy, but both Pretoria and Washington have let it be known that they are closer to a final settlement than ever before. South Africa's recent military successes against SWAPO guerrillas and the presence of a semi-friendly administration in Washington may well have persuaded the leadership of the National Party that now is the time to yield. A successful conclusion to the Namibia negotiations would give greatly increased credence to the new policy of constructive involvement and would strengthen the hands of those figures in Washington who are willing to speak out on behalf of the Republic.

The repeal of the Clark Amendment and, it is hoped, the passage of the Foreign Aid bill, should remove Pretoria's fear of the effect of a Cuban force on the northern border of the new state. Should the ruling MPLA faction in Luanda break its word and allow the Cuban forces in Angola to stay behind after the signing of a Namibian settlement, the U.S. would be in a position to begin supplying military assistance to Dr. Jonas Savimbi's UNITA forces and thus negate the effects of the Cuban presence while putting increased pressure upon Havana's scanty resources.

To all intents and purposes, the Administration has decided to wait upon events in Zimbabwe. Prime Minister Mugabe has been informed that if he allows Zimbabwe to continue its democratic, multi-racial, free economic course, he can expect economic aid and assistance from the United States. It cannot be presumed that Mugabe will necessarily be swayed by financial considerations. The Prime Minister's actions to date have constituted a peculiar mixture of pragmatism and ideology and it is difficult to assess which consideration is uppermost in his mind at the moment. He has already given several indications of his desire to transform Zimbabwe into a one-party state, and recent developments suggest a threat to the financial integrity of the white minority. The United States is not in a position to influence Mugabe directly. The Administration seems to have adopted the safest course, waiting to see which course Mugabe chooses before deciding whether to treat him as a friend.

The withdrawal of all but emergency food aid from Mugabe's neighbor, Samora Machel of Mozambique, was well-advised. Machel had already demonstrated his deeply committed opposition to the U.S. on several occasions. His Marxist economic policies have proved that all recent foreign aid has been wasted. Machel's arrest of several U.S. Embassy officials provided the Reagan Administration with an acceptable excuse to terminate Carter's ill-advised rapprochement with Mozambique.

Zaire is not currently in a state of conflict, but the government of President Mobutu Sese Seko appears to be more unstable than ever, particularly since France's new president, Francois Mitterrand, announced that his government would no longer provide African states with military assistance in times of emergency. Mobutu can no longer depend upon his protector in Paris to save him from assaults from Angola. The Reagan Administration has wisely decided to build up a strategic supply of cobalt, Zaire's primary resource. The United States is now able to countenance short- to medium-term disruptions in its supply of this vital mineral with more equanimity than before the purchase.

Secretary of State Haig has seen to it that King Hassan II of Morocco continues to be supplied with arms to fight the Polisario guerrillas in Western Sahara. He has not, however, made any notable effort to become involved in the projected negotiations between the two parties. Such involvement may prove to be possible and desirable.

The assassination of President Sadat has further exacerbated the already tense situation in northeast Africa. Colonel Qaddafi has been pursuing blatantly imperialistic foreign policies, invading his neighbor, Chad, threatening Sudan and Egypt, and eliminating his enemies abroad. The United States has demonstrated its displeasure with Qaddafi. The downing of two Libyan planes over the Mediterranean was an excellent demonstration of resolve.

Libya has now begun to threaten the Sudan. Egypt cannot be expected to tolerate a Libyan move against the Sudan since this would leave the country with hostile forces on both its western and southern borders. Moreover, Sudan's control of a long stretch of Red Sea coast makes a Libyan takeover of that country a direct threat to U.S. national security interests. The situation may yet be resolved without direct U.S. involvement. Egypt boasts an army of 320,000 men and Sudan 60,000, compared to a Libyan force of only 42,000. The supposed superiority of Libyan equipment has been greatly overestimated. Vital U.S. interests are served by maintaining a reliable flow of spare parts to Egypt and Sudan.

**Asia and the Pacific**

In evaluating the Reagan Administration's foreign policy approach with respect to the Asian-Pacific theatre, it is critically important to determine: 1) whether or not that policy has been comprehensive, coherent and flexible; and 2) whether that policy reinforces our overall foreign policy objectives.

The specific objectives of the Administration's policies toward the Asian-Pacific region may be summarized as follows:

- Alerting the Asian-Pacific community to the current Soviet threat in the region.

- Curbing the growing Soviet military presence and influence throughout the region.

- Restraining the aggressive ambitions of Soviet surrogates in the area, notably Vietnam.

- Encouraging closer cooperation—political, economic, and military—with our Asian and Pacific allies and friends.

- Strengthening our relationship with the People's Republic of China.

On the whole, the Administration's foreign policy objectives have not been universally applauded by Asian and Pacific leaders. This is in part due to what some Asian and Pacific leaders conceive as an excessive and one-sided preoccupation with the Soviet threat. Similarly, while many leaders approve of America's reassertion of leadership in the region, they are withholding or reserving judgment until specific and concrete recommendations are forthcoming from

Washington to deal with as yet unaddressed questions and problems such as trade and U.S. arms sales to the PRC and Taiwan.

The Reagan Administration perceives the threat of Soviet hegemony as the paramount concern in the Asian theater. This perception is not shared by the majority of U.S. allies in the Pacific. The Japanese government, for example, views the threat as political in nature, rather than military. The Suzuki government has therefore emphasized both a gradual military build-up and an intense effort to aid other countries in the region in their nation-building efforts.

Initially, the Reagan Administration demanded that Japan move quickly to increase its defense power. Recently, however, there have been conflicting signs within the Administration as to the proper course of action to be taken. In early September 1981, U.S. Deputy Assistant Secretary of State Michael H. Armacost noted that it was not prudent for the United States to criticize the Japanese government publicly in this regard. In fact, he stated that Washington had decided not to press Japan officially to strengthen its defense capability. In late September, U.S. Deputy Secretary of Defense Frank C. Carlucci urged Foreign Minister Sunao Sonoda to press for prompt improvement of defense capability to cope with the growing Soviet military threat. Such statements provide evidence that U.S. policies are neither coherent nor unified.

Other nations, particularly Indonesia, agree with the American perception of the Soviet threat, but have lingering doubts concerning U.S. policy *vis-a-vis* the PRC. From their perspective, the PRC poses a similar threat to the overall stability of the region. Given the fact that historically China has always regarded Southeast Asia as a legitimate sphere of influence, and given the continuing party-to-party relationship that China has with rebellious communist forces throughout the region, the apprehension of these Southeast Asian leaders is understandable.

To curb the growing Soviet military presence and influence throughout the Asian-Pacific region, *Mandate for Leadership* called for an increase in U.S. military presence in and assistance to the region. The Reagan Administration has stressed that U.S. naval forces would be significantly enhanced and increased, but no specifics have been forthcoming on their actual deployment. It does appear that the Administration will place top priority on improving naval mobility to allow quick deployment of forces to the Indian Ocean and southwestern Asia. Only marginal increases are expected in U.S. troop deployments in the Western Pacific theatre. Nonetheless, U.S. interests require a critical increase in the visibility of both land and sea forces in the Pacific.

The Administration has made a series of moves which can contribute to curbing Soviet influence:

- Military assistance has been increased to the ASEAN nations. In particular, Foreign Ministry Sales (FMS) credits have been increased to Thailand, Indonesia, the Philippines and Malaysia. Similarly, Economic Support Funds (ESF) and International Military Education Training (IMET) have been enlarged.

- The United States has publicly renewed its security commitments to Australia, New Zealand, Thailand and the Philippines.

- ASEAN has been encouraged to foster better bilateral military relations among its member states even though the prospects of a "multilateral defense agreement" appear bleak.

- Increased joint military exercises between the United States and our Asian and Pacific allies are becoming more frequent.

The Reagan Administration, working closely with the ASEAN nations, has taken a strong and effective stance with respect to Vietnam. The continued diplomatic and economic isolation of Vietnam should be the hallmark of U.S. policy. United Nations Resoluton 35/6 should be supported steadfastly until a UN-supervised withdrawal of Vietnamese forces from Kampuchea occurs and Khmer self-determination is restored.

The Administration acted well in cancelling troop withdrawal from Korea and in offering increased military assistance to the Seoul government. The Administration should nonetheless emphasize greater coordination, planning and execution of military operations between the respective governments.

Although the Administration has made a special effort to emphasize the value it places on ASEAN and each of the countries concerned, greater attention must be placed on solving some of the economic problems that exist within ASEAN and between individual ASEAN nations and the United States. These include market access, congressional restraints, and terms of trade.

Our relations with the People's Republic of China must be predicated on the practical realization that the Soviet threat in both Asia and around the globe is such that cooperation is in the interest of each country. Cooperation must be mutual. The United States should be ready to assist the PRC in its developmental program, both through economic and cultural interaction, but should move very cautiously in establishing military relations with the PRC. The Reagan Administration recently announced that it would remove "in general" munitions list restrictions on arms to the PRC and would consider "a much broader range of requests on a case-by-case basis." According to Secretary of State Haig, "specific Chinese requests will be considered in conjunction with appropriate consultation with the Congress and, where necessary, appropriate consultation with affected allies." The Administration must not allow these arms sales to be seen as the beginning of a military alignment with the PRC, or as a United States assumption of the responsibility for the defense of China. Arms sales to the PRC should be treated as a strategic issue demanding consensus with U.S. allies in Europe and Japan.

In developing an effective policy toward the People's Republic of China, the Reagan Administration has failed to address effectively relations with the Republic of China (Taiwan). Although properly criticizing the Carter Administration for totally capitulating to the PRC's conditions for establishing a U.S. Embassy in Peking, the Reagan Administration has done nothing to rectify the one-sided China policy. As the *Mandate* study warned one year ago, "We must reject a normalization process that means the eventual demise of the ROC as a viable economic, social and political entity." Rather than halting this process, the State Department has effectively scuttled even minimal pledges of support for Taiwan, apparently promised by the outgoing Carter Administration and explicitly stated in the Taiwan Relations Act.

The Reagan Administration should have demonstrated decisiveness in reconstructing Asian policy by restoring Taiwan to an integral role in the security system of the Western Pacific, even if at a level below that of the previous treaty relationship. Instead, the Administration has refused to sell advanced fighters to Taiwan, and has granted a tacit veto power to Peking over U.S. policy toward Taiwan. The sale of the planes properly assumes psychological dimensions broader than their defense capabilities. Only through such a discernible sign of support for Taiwan can the United States prevent a continued slide of Taiwan to political oblivion. A coherent and credible security policy in Asia cannot be predicated on satisfying Peking.

During the Carter Administration, many Asian and Pacific leaders questioned the capability and durability of U.S. commitments to the region. The Reagan Administraton is making an attempt to restore U.S. credibility and leadership, but many Asian and Pacific leaders are withholding judgment. Conflicting policy statements and unanswered questions could erode the Administration's efforts. If the Reagan Administration wishes to adopt a comprehensive, coherent, and flexible American foreign and defense policy towards the Asian and Pacific theatre, it must address the following questions and problems:

- the sale of arms to Taiwan and the "future" relationship between the PRC and the Republic of China on Taiwan;

- trade issues with Japan, including the Japanese trade surplus, non-tariff barriers, and high technology transfers;

- the extent of military sales to the PRC; and

- the nature of America's defense commitment to the Pacific.

Only when these policy questions have been resolved will U.S. Asian and Pacific policy reflect our basic foreign policy objectives.

## Conclusion

The Reagan Administration has not, thus far, pursued the kind of conservative foreign policy outlined in *Mandate for Leadership*. Most indicators suggest that the principal architects desire to establish a conservative foreign policy. Sound objectives are not being transformed into concrete and coherent policies. This failure is due to the inability of the Administration to focus sufficient attention on international problems at the same time it is dealing with drastic changes in domestic economic policy.

In the one noteworthy triumph, the AWACS sale, an inordinate amount of energy was expended to prevent an embarrassing defeat. This same energy level is needed to sustain domestic and international support for conservative policy initiatives to address major issues, such as the growing Soviet threat, the deteriorating situation in Central America and European misunderstandings of U.S. policy.

The conclusion of *Mandate* suggested strategies for "taking control of foreign policy." Despite sometimes dramatic leadership by the Secretary of State, control of the State Department has remained largely in the hands of people who are not devoted to a conservative foreign policy. Although some excellent appointments were made in the Department, no real "housecleaning" took place. The Administration refused to use discretionary appointment powers with the necessary intensity to dramatically change the operation and direction of the Department. Thus, new policy initiatives at top levels became only minor modifications in policies at the operational level.

On some specific issues, such as the Law of the Sea and human rights, effective changes have been made, albeit awkwardly. Despite significant improvements over the previous administration in the conduct of foreign policy, a more impressive overall record should have been achieved. The Administration has seized the opportunity to substantially change U.S. foreign policy. As domestic problems are resolved, the Administration should pursue as its priority implementation of a conservative foreign policy.

## RECOMMENDATIONS
(Action taken on 26 out of 56)

### Policy Formulation and Management

- Define clearly lines of authority between the NSC and State

Department and make the Secretary of State paramount in foreign policy.

ACCOMPLISHED.

- Make the foreign affairs bureaucracy more effective by appropriately using both the NSC and State.

ATTEMPTED BUT NOT DONE.

- Restrict the NSC to certain specific roles in the foreign policy process.

ACCOMPLISHED.

- Discourage the NSC from being publicly prominent or advocating policy.

ACCOMPLISHED.

- Encourage the State Department to lead, but not dominate, the foreign policy process.

ACCOMPLISHED.

- Enhance the role of the State Department in economic matters, including the creation of new bureaus and procedures.

NOT ACCOMPLISHED.

- Enhance the authority of Secretary of State at the State Department by giving him greater control over the bureaucracy.

ACCOMPLISHED ONLY FORMALLY.

**Personnel**

- Reform the system of Foreign Service appointments.

NOT DONE; APPARENTLY NOT CONTEMPLATED.

- Increase the number of personnel assigned to collection and analysis of information.

THE NUMBER OF PERSONNEL HAS ACTUALLY DECREASED.

- Establish and use an "outside wing" of "wise men."

LIMITED USE OF OUTSIDE EXPERTS.

- Fill as many of the available "political" or "non-career" positions as possible.

NOT IMPLEMENTED.

- Effect a thorough "housecleaning" of existing political and other non-career appointees who can be removed at the discretion of the President.

NOT IMPLEMENTED.

208

- Devote particular attention to the positions at the DOS which involve the flow of material, information, and authority to make decisions.
ONLY PARTLY IMPLEMENTED.

- Encourage each Assistant Secretary or Bureau Director to hire a reliable aide to monitor all reports and information and oversee the implementation of policy by the bureaucracy.
NOT IMPLEMENTED, PARTLY DUE TO BUDGET CUTS.

- Restructure policy-making and policy-directing responsibilities to reduce narrow bilateral consideration of issues.
SPORADICALLY IMPLEMENTED.

- Move swiftly to instill new leadership throughout the Department so that new policy directions can be implemented with a minimum of friction and maximum impact.
NOT DONE AT ALL; APPOINTMENTS VERY SLOW.

- Establish efficient procedures to answer congressional requests for information.
NOT DONE.

- Adopt legislation to provide for a comprehensive system of classification.
NOT DONE.

- Create a Joint Committee on National Security.
NOT DONE. MUST BE A CONGRESSIONAL INITIATIVE.

- Assign personnel with a knowledge of Congress and strong beliefs in the value of a congressional policy role to the Congressional Relations office.
IMPLEMENTED.

- Assign one individual at a senior level in the NSC or White House to deal with national security issues in the Congress.
NOT DONE.

### Latin America

- Attempt to change the current Sandinista government in Nicaragua by supporting the free labor unions, the Church, the private sector, the independent political parties, the free press, and genuine human rights organizations.
DONE.

- Cease all financial support of the Sandinista government.
  NOT DONE.

- Improve the management of the economic reforms announced in 1980 by the Salvadorean Junta.
  SOME INTEREST, BUT NOT YET IMPLEMENTED.

- Cancel Phase II of the Salvadorean agrarian reform program.
  POSTPONED.

- Discourage significant changes in composition of the Salvadorean Junta, whether through coups or through external pressure.
  POLICY ADOPTED.

- Encourage the Salvadoreans to form alliances with Guatemala, Honduras, and other nations in the hemisphere.
  NOT DONE.

- Be prepared to stand by anti-Communist allies in meeting the Cuban challenge, and do nothing that would strengthen or lend respectability to Marxist-Leninist liberation movements.
  DONE.

- Take political, economic, and para-military steps to contain Cuba's activities and influence to its own island.
  ONLY LIMITED STEPS TAKEN.

- Increase U.S. arms sales and military programs in South America.
  DONE WITHIN CONGRESSIONAL RESTRAINTS.

- Design an aid program to promote the growth of the region's private sector rather than the region's governments.
  NOT DONE.

- Encourage Venezuela to take a leading role in supplying oil to its neighbors under favorable terms.
  DONE.

- Develop aid programs based on person-to-person contact, including cultural programs, rather than funding low-visibility projects.
  NOT STRESSED AND PROGRAM HURT BY BUDGET CUTS.

- Devise a vigorous joint effort between the U.S. and Colombia to control drug smuggling.
  NOT DONE.

- Support efforts by the Colombian government to deal with the country's Marxist-Leninist guerrillas.
  LIMITED EFFORTS MADE.

- Assist both Peru and Ecuador to stabilize the democratic process and to promote free enterprise.
  DONE.

- Design policy to preserve Bolivia's pro-U.S. orientation, maintain the country under respectable leaders, and work with the Bolivian government authorities in the control of drugs.
  PARTIALLY IMPLEMENTED.

- Improve relations with Chile and Argentina and provide them with military equipment to provide security assistance to the hemisphere.
  RELATIONS IMPROVED; LEGISLATION PROPOSED.

### Law of the Sea and Human Rights

- Indicate impatience with "Third World" posturing on the Law of the Sea Treaty to break deadlocks that effect our vital interests.
  DONE.

- Consent to the Law of the Sea Treaty only if an incentive system for extracting minerals from the sea-bed is included.
  POSITION ADOPTED.

- Re-affirm commitment to human rights and remain an example for the world to follow in this field.
  DONE.

- Use quiet diplomacy to persuade friendly governments to show greater respect for human rights and avoid moralistic preaching on the problem.
  DONE.

- Support allied states under siege by totalitarian forces.
  DONE.

- Name to head the Bureau a prominent figure who has a sophisticated understanding of human rights, and who will expose the most serious violations of human rights.
  DONE.

### Africa, Asia, and the Third World

- Deal directly with the threat of terrorism and subversion in

211

Third World countries in order to create a climate conducive to foreign investment.
DONE.

- Focus U.S. policy in Africa on economic development through the encouragement of private investment.
DONE.

- Use friendly advice rather than strong-arm tactics to persuade South Africa to change its racial policies.
DONE.

- Require reciprocal concessions from the People's Republic of China, particularly regarding Taiwan.
NOT DONE.

- Increase air and naval forces in the Pacific.
NOT DONE.

- Continue to upgrade the Korean armed forces and rule out any withdrawal of American forces from Korea.
DONE.

- Reaffirm our security commitment to Australia and New Zealand and encourage greater participation by them in Indian Ocean military maneuvers.
NO CLEAR POLICY IN THIS AREA.

- Increase military assistance to Thailand.
POLICY ADOPTED, BUT CONGRESSIONAL SUPPORT NOT FORTHCOMING.

- Encourage Japan to raise its defense spending.
DONE INITIALLY; NOT FOLLOWED THROUGH.

- Oppose recognition of the Vietnamese-supported Heng Samrin regime in Cambodia.
DONE.

- Increase support for refugees from Indochina in Thailand.
NOT DONE.

- Reaffirm commitment to the people of Taiwan and approve the sale of military equipment they need for self-defense.
NOT DONE.

# Chapter Sixteen
# DEPARTMENT OF TRANSPORTATION
### By Jack R. Wimer

Andrew Lewis, Reagan's choice for Secretary of the Department of Transportation, faced four significant tests during his first months in office: the air controllers' strike, increasing automotive regulation, foreign car import quotas, and mass transit accessibility for the handicapped. The Reagan Administration, and Secretary Lewis in particular, passed three of these tests handily. On the question of foreign car imports, however, the actions of the Secretary and the Administration are open to dispute.

Secretary Lewis, and ultimately President Reagan, opposed free trade advocates in the Administration, and publicly supported automobile import restrictions. The restrictions which the Administration negotiated with Japan are defended by some as being far less stringent than those Congress might have imposed had the President and Secretary Lewis been unwilling to compromise. This contention is questionable in light of the Administration's series of extraordinary legislative successes.

The Administration's action on import curbs is troublesome because free trade often lacks a concentrated, politically powerful domestic constituency. While consumers benefit from free trade, their interests are diverse, and difficult to forge into a coalition strong enough to counteract effectively the organized and concentrated opposition to free trade. Free trade is a good test of how well the federal government can promote the broad public interest. The Secretary's actions in the years when the quotas on Japanese cars are to be renegotiated will be worth watching.

The import issue is only one of four. DOT's actions during the air controllers' strike demonstrated firmness in the face of a crisis that seemed capable of tying the nation's air traffic in knots. The rescission of regulations requiring passive restraints in cars and wheelchair accessibility to buses and subways removed some expensive problems left over from the previous administration. Three out of four is a commendable record. Other actions indicate that this record will improve with time.

*Mandate for Leadership*, recognizing the varied nature of DOT programs and functional areas, made few major recommendations concerning organization of the Department or the Office of the Secretary. Instead, *Mandate* highlighted personnel and management as the key to successful DOT administration. While some broad policy changes might be justified in theory, the political ramifications would likely render them not worth the cost. The first several months of the Reagan Administration's impact on DOT has generally reflected the pragmatic organizational approach suggested by *Mandate*.

*Mandate* recommended structuring the Office of the Secretary (OST) to minimize the bureaucratic and administrative dimensions of the job and to emphasize the strong role the Secretary would play in policy issues. DOT Secretary Lewis has played an effective role in several key policy issues.

Another major short-term recommendation was to continue to expand a Department commitment to regulatory analysis as a self-help tool for regulatory reform. Executive Order No. 12044 has been replaced and strengthened by the Reagan Executive Order No. 12299, which requires cost-benefit analysis of major new regulations. The DOT has followed this direction enthusiastically. The agency appears to be committed to reviewing not only new regulations, but also those already on the books.

*Mandate* suggested that there was a duplication in mission between the Federal Highway Administration (FHWA) and the National Highway Traffic Safety Administration (NHTSA), but that consideration of a merger or bureaucratic change should be deferred if a responsible and conservative official can be found to head NHTSA. Raymond Peck seems to fit that bill admirably. His commitment to judicious regulatory procedures is a welcome change.

*Mandate* mentioned that any long-term look at reorganization should focus on the opportunity to bring within DOT various aspects of air, surface, and maritime regulation now housed in separate federal agencies: Civil Aeronautics Board, Interstate Commerce Commission, and Federal Maritime Commission. The Reagan Administration recently has recommended to Congress early abolition of the CAB, transferring some of its functions to DOT. That type of proposal should be followed with the FMC and ICC as well. Both are agencies whose commitment to deregulation has been subject to public question. These moves ought to result in one rationalized structure capable of accomplishing the phased deregulation of the U.S. transportation industry.

**The National Highway Traffic Safety Administration**

Under the Carter Administration, the NHTSA created a war-like atmosphere between itself and the automobile industry. Administrator Joan Claybrook claimed to be fighting her battles on behalf of the consumer, but it is doubtful that consumers were well served by her crusade. What is certain is that consumers footed the bill, and that bill grew with each passing year.

The new Administrator, Raymond Peck, has turned things around. One of his earliest actions was to announce a full-scale regulatory review to reduce the regulatory burden on the automobile industry. While the announced deadlines have not all been met, the review is making steady progress. NHTSA has rescinded its proposal to set post-1985 fuel economy standards, allowing market forces and consumer choice to determine optimal fuel economy. Bumper standard regulations have been revaluated; substantial evidence indicates that current regulations governing bumper production result in an economically inefficient product. The savings in reduced collision damage are more than offset by the higher costs of production and increased fuel consumption. A number of unsubstantiated regulations are now being reconsidered, including standards regulating visibility and a requirement that a highlighted 55 m.p.h. figure be displayed on car speedometers. While the previous administration had concocted a safety rationale for this last requirement, its real effect was to irritate the American driver with a visible reminder of petty federal power.

In conducting this regulatory review, NHTSA has made one mistake. It cast the justification for its action in terms of aiding Detroit. The main beneficiary will be the American consumer.

Administrator Peck's most significant action has been the rescission of the passive restraint standard. This regulation was issued under the Carter Administration, with promises that it would lead to the installation of front-seat air bags in most new cars. Manufacturers chose to satisfy the standard with automatic seat belts rather than air bags. The belts provided no more protection than conventional belts, but cost considerably more. Because the automatic feature can easily be overridden, its additional cost would not necessarily result in any increase in belt usage. Despite substantial pressure, Administrator Peck decided to revoke the standard. In so doing, he removed a costly and inefficient regulation which would have become a symbol of unbridled government paternalism. Automatic belts will probably continue to be available to the public as an option in some car lines. This will allow buyers to choose the type of protection they desire.

NHTSA's data collection capability was significantly expanded during the previous administration. It is NHTSA's most important tool for determining which problems of vehicle safety can be addressed by government. The data collection program fared relatively well under present budget cuts. This is a wise decision. The emphasis on this program should be continued.

Administrator Peck's decision to retain several high-level Claybrook appointees raised some doubts during his first months in office, and to an extent, these doubts still remain. When NHTSA first proposed to delay the passive restraint standard, the proposal was written so poorly that it suggested either incredible carelessness or the deliberate sabotage of a top-level decision. The Agency subsequently did an excellent job in defending its proposal, and it appears that later policy decisions have not encountered such internal roadblocks.

## The Federal Highway Administration

FHWA has the unhappy task of managing the declining balance in the Highway Trust Fund through an era of mounting maintenance demands and escalating construction costs. Decisions regarding the allocation of funds and the source of future revenues are largely up to Congress. At congressional request, FHWA is currently developing a Highway Cost Allocation Study which will be the basis for much of this future decision-making.

FHWA has acted to increase local flexibility in utilizing the federal funds that are allocated to the states. The Agency is expected to rule soon on a proposal, made near the end of the previous administration, to increase local flexibility in federally-assisted "RRR" work (resurfacing, restoration, and rehabilitation) on non-freeway highway projects.

FHWA has also taken some steps toward deregulation in the trucking industry. In September 1981, the Agency decided against a proposal to further restrict work hours for interstate shippers. A similar decision is expected on the regulation of minimum cab size, leaving that issue to Congress when it considers the problem of national weight and size standards for trucks. Proposals to reduce the regulation of driver record-keeping, qualification, and cab check-out have either been issued or are under study.

## Federal Railroad Administration

The new administration at DOT focused on the serious deficiencies at FRA and immediately set out to promote drastic administrative as well as legislative changes. The result has been a tremendous benefit to the federal Treasury in tandem with improved rail and freight passenger service in the northeast and a rational approach to the dispersion of federal railroad financial assistance nationwide.

The Administration worked with Congress to develop an improved approach for the dispersion of state railroad financial assistance. Projects in geographic areas demonstrating the most need will now receive the lion's share of funds. The former program, under which all states were guaranteed financial minimums regardless of need, virtually has been discontinued.

The Federal Railroad Administration deserves credit for tackling the massive $2.5 billion Northeast Corridor Improvement Program and weeding out projects which did not pass a cost-benefit test. The Northeast Corridor is essentially a rail passenger corridor which stretches between Washington, D.C. and Boston. FRA deleted a 166-mile electrification project between New Haven and Boston, which would have resulted in only minimal benefits to the whole

216

program at a cost in excess of $200 million. Combined with other modifications to the Northeast Corridor Program, this will result in a savings of $300 million to the Treasury. These desperately needed funds can now be channeled to other transportation programs. As *Mandate* pointed out, the Northeast Corridor program is extremely sensitive politically and is not easily altered. The challenge to the Administration is now to resist political pressure to restore these costly and unwise components of the program.

The Administration's approach to rationalizing the Amtrak System was designed to enable Amtrak to operate as a private sector enterprise free of as much government intervention as possible. Although its plan was commendable, the Administration failed to provide a financial recommendation to support it. A substantial portion of the Administration's program on Amtrak was implemented into law. The result is that Amtrak will be operating essentially the same system in FY 1981 as in FY 1980 with a 25 percent reduction in funds. The savings to the Treasury is close to $250 million under the recommendation of the previous Administration.

The Consolidated Rail Corporation (Conrail) has continually failed to meet its profitability projections since it began operations on April 1, 1976. This became the priority rail transportation program of the Administration early in 1981. A detailed legislative program was designed to permit an immediate sale of Conrail to the private sector. The Administration's proposal was altered in part, but essentially approved. The legislation entails relief from mandatory labor protection, substantial concessions from railroad labor groups on existing working practices, and regulatory freedom to relieve the system of many unprofitable lines. If Conrail does not improve quickly, the system will be subject to sale to the private sector in a fashion almost identical to that originally proposed by the Administration.

Rail safety is the only area actually regulated by the Federal Railroad Administration. The Administration to date has not attempted to change the rail safety programs unilaterally. Rather, it has worked with a labor/management task force to seek a consensus change. This effort has resulted in success for the first time in the history of the industry. The agreed-upon program will be implemented in 1982.

**The Urban Mass Transit Administration**

UMTA's chief regulatory action under the new Administration was its rescission of regulations governing access by the handicapped to federally-assisted mass transit systems. These regulations, promulgated under the Carter Administration, required that all components of a mass transit system be accessible to a person in a wheelchair. For many transit systems this would have entailed prohibitively expensive retrofitting of subway stations and buses. The option of providing special services to the handicapped, such as door-to-door van service, was expressly ruled out. Yet in many cases such special services would have provided far greater mobility for the handicapped at a fraction of the cost. Clearly, buses equipped with wheelchair lifts are useless for those handicapped persons who cannot get to a bus stop.

In July 1981, UMTA issued new interim regulations which allow communities to choose the manner in which they will provide transportation services for the handicapped. These regulations, and the permanent rules which eventually will replace them, should resolve this issue. It took UMTA six months to issue the interim regulations; whatever the reason, this delay was excessive.

In recent years, proposals for new mass transit systems have grown despite the inability of existing systems to meet their operating costs. UMTA has formulated a new federal policy on aid to mass transit. Operating assistance grants to mass transit systems will be phased out, and a moratorium has been placed on capital grants to new transit systems pending the review of these proposals. Capital assistance to existing systems will continue. While this new policy should produce substantial reductions in federal expenditures, it will only postpone consideration of the basic question of why mass transit should not pay its own way.

The most fruitful area for UMTA's efforts may be in removing those federal policies which are responsible for some of mass transit's high cost. The new handicapped access regulations are one step in this direction. Another step already taken is the phasing out of UMTA's "White Book" procurement regulations for new buses. These extensive design requirements limited local purchasing flexibility and drove up costs. New York and other cities purchased buses built to these standards only to have the bus frames crack after a few months of use, demonstrating the futility of federal design requirements. The next area for cost-reduction efforts should be the labor force, where federal regulations often give undue bargaining power to transit unions. While these regulations are handled chiefly by the Department of Labor, UMTA could play a very beneficial role in pushing for massive changes in this area.

Finally, UMTA could attempt to experiment with decentralized and essentially unregulated jitneys. This would entail finding a metropolitan area willing to scrap its taxi licensing and fare-setting apparatus and to allow unregulated private car or van service. While such a project would encounter substantial political and bureaucratic hazards, it nonetheless offers a private solution to what is becoming an increasingly expensive public issue.

**The Federal Aviation Administration**

The Federal Aviation Administration survived a baptism of fire during the first nine months of the Reagan Administration. The FAA faced problems more severe, complicated, and politically explosive than any other agency, with the possible exception of the Office of Management and Budget. The success of the FAA in solving its technical problems and defusing its political problems is envied among other agencies. This success has forged a stronger agency now capable of serving as a standard-bearer for the Executive Branch.

When the newly-appointed FAA administrator, J. Lynn Helms, took over the Agency:

- Air traffic controllers were threatening to shut down the nation's airways with an illegal strike.

- Professional pilots were threatening a walkout over aircraft crew complements.

- Airline crashes had shaken the FAA's image as the world's foremost technical authority on aviation safety.

- A high level of reported near collisions and a frightening rate of air traffic control computer failures plagued the Agency and worried the public.

- Cooperation between air controllers and pilots was deteriorating, as was morale among FAA's more than 50,000 employees.

- FAA was fighting for power within the Department of Transportation, squabbling for turf with NASA, and bickering over silly policy matters with the National Transportation Safety Board (NTSB).

Nine months later, most of these inherited problems have been either solved, defused, or addressed sufficiently by the FAA. Only sticky relations with the NTSB remain an insurmountable problem.

**PATCO**

Contrary to the belief of union leaders and Washington headline writers, the PATCO strike is over. FAA now has a serious manpower shortage on its hands, but the level of air traffic operation without those 11,500 controllers is near normal. The FAA is beginning to believe what some aviation groups have said for years—that the air traffic control system was bloated. Not all the credit for the swift, sure handling of this explosive situation can go to Administrator Helms. The lion's share must go to President Reagan and the American public, both of whom stood firm on the ground that an illegal strike was intolerable. Secretary of Transportation Drew Lewis also deserves praise for his action in this area.

219

### Three-Pilot Crews

Although the Administration took a gamble in establishing the President's Commission on Aircraft Crew Complement, it scored a clear victory. The pilots union agreed to abide by the decision of the Commission, and then honorably kept its word when the decision favored the Administration. The pilots later became valuable allies in the air traffic controller strike. The FAA now has a much better working relationship with the Airline Pilots Association.

### Technical Expertise

Administrator Helms has taken a number of steps to re-establish the FAA as the world authority on aviation safety. He has retained and improved upon the "lead region" concept initiated by the former administrator. This concept allows the FAA to take its best engineering talent in a particular field—air carrier aircraft, for example—and concentrate it into a single region, thereby improving the overall technical abilities of the Agency. Now, all large aircraft are certified in one region, all agricultural aircraft are certified in another, avionics are certified in a third, and so on.

### Near Collisions

The FAA's greatest fear following the PATCO walkout was that computer failures would complicate the problem of manning the air traffic system with too few employees, and that a serious disaster might occur. Fascinating statistics show a singular consequence of the PATCO strike: the computers are failing only about half as often as they did before the strike, and the number of near-collisions is also down by approximately 50 percent from the time just before the strike.

### Air-Ground Cooperation

Pilots and remaining controllers alike report heretofore unheard-of cooperation between pilots of aircraft of all sizes and FAA controllers. Most agree that the system would not work nearly so well were it not for this spirit, which had been missing for years on FAA radio frequencies. FAA morale received a boost as well. While the inner workings of the agency have never been smooth, an improved worker attitude now prevails.

### Interagency Relations

The argument about whether FAA belongs in DOT will not be solved for years. For now, the only answer is to patch up relations between the two. The heat taken by Secretary Lewis and Administrator Helms over the PATCO strike seems to have forged close bonds. Lewis recently made the ultimate gesture of friendship: he ordered giant "FAA" letters to be placed on a sign at FAA headquarters. For the past fourteen years, the FAA building has been nameless, a reminder of its lack of autonomy.

The matters at hand with NASA are not so simple. A turf fight, mostly involving aeronautical research, has existed for several administrations. In the past, both agencies have charged ahead, sometimes working on the same project at the same time. Administrator Helms is now holding peace talks, and the two agencies are attempting to match NASA's technical expertise and facilities with FAA's programs and needs. Progress has been made, but only Congress can totally sort out the matter through the appropriations process.

Relations with the NTSB may be hopeless given the personalities of current leaders. This matter probably will not be resolved until the two agencies agree to communicate through a medium other than the press.

## The Future

Now that the FAA has shown that it can walk the high-wire, it needs to prove that it can walk the neighborhood beat with equal grace. The FAA must provide the basic services to the air transportation system to allow it to continue its efficient operation. Three needs stand out:

1. The FAA's incomprehensible maze of regulations must be put into reasonable order.

2. The Airport Development Air Program must cease to be a political whipping boy.

3. The private pilot must not be crowded out of America's airspace.

Progress is being made in reducing regulations. Administrator Helms boasts about turning a 1,000-page regulation into eight lines. In this process, safety regulations need not be abandoned, but should be revised to work in concert with other regulations. A comprehensive effort to consolidate and coordinate all aviation regulations is in order.

Airport development is in a colossal mess. About $3.5 billion sits in the trust fund. Some of this money was paid in aviation gas taxes by the Wright Brothers. Very little is being used to improve the nation's airports and airways, although the need is tremendous: FAA planners estimate a 100 percent increase in instrument flight operations in the next ten years. If this traffic is to be handled safely, improved facilities are mandatory. Administrator Helms privately admits he would like to spend more of the funds collected over the past three administrations, but he is under great pressure to hold back on spending. Congress and the Administration cannot decide if they should give the money to big airports or small ones, so nobody gets it. Each year, the surplus funds lose purchasing power and airport safety projects go unfunded. Spending the surplus is politically ticklish. FAA needs to take the lead before inflation further reduces the buying power of the fund.

The high cost of flying and the regulatory morass has spawned an entirely new aviation industry based on man's desire to fly without federal strings. Ultralights, hang gliders, home-built and experimental aircraft are enjoying previously unimagined popularity. This growth in relatively unregulated sectors of aviation serves to highlight a potential danger of increasing FAA regulation. As history has shown, man will not be deterred from the pursuit of flight. As one form of aviation becomes too heavily regulated, albeit through a well-intentioned pursuit of safety, men will find other, less regulated forms of flight. Without regulatory reform, the result may be less, not more, safety.

## RECOMMENDATIONS
(Action taken on 60 out of 79)

### Office of the Secretary

- Expand commitment to cost-benefit analysis.
  IMPLEMENTED.

- Tighten up OST salaries and expense accounts as much as possible.
  IMPLEMENTED; $35.68 MILLION IN FY 1981 AND $35 MILLION IN FY 1982.

- Maintain lowest possible funding level for the limitation on Working Capital Fund account.
  IMPLEMENTED; $70 MILLION LIMITATION IN FY 1982.

- Eliminate funds for the Cooperative Automobile Research program.
  FUNDING ELIMINATED.

- Fund approximately $15 million for the Office of the Inspector General.
  IMPLEMENTED.

### National Highway Traffic Safety Administration

- Revise basic approach to regulation of the auto industry.
  IMPLEMENTED IN PART.

- Reduce Operations and Research budget to about $10 million.
  NOT DONE; $82 MILLION AUTHORIZED IN FY 1982.

- Rescind passive restraint standard.
  IMPLEMENTED.

- Base proposed safety standards on "real world" data rather than mere laboratory testing.
  IMPLEMENTED.

- Conduct cost-benefit evaluations of proposed standards.
  IMPLEMENTED.

- Issue deadlines for forthcoming decisions.
  NOT IMPLEMENTED.

- Reorganize docket materials to increase public accessibility.
  NOT IMPLEMENTED.

- Base automotive recall decisions on collected traffic data, rather than on individual complaints.
  TOO EARLY TO DETERMINE.

- Utilize cost-benefit analysis in recall proceedings.
  TOO EARLY TO DETERMINE.

- Increase the consideration given to market forces and feasibility in setting fuel economy standards.
  IMPLEMENTED.

- Give high priority to collection of accident data.
  IMPLEMENTED.

- Open research and testing decisions to public comment.
  NOT IMPLEMENTED.

- Initiate regular public reviews of past agency research.
  NOT IMPLEMENTED.

- Reduce funding of demonstration projects.
  IMPLEMENTED.

- Fund State and Community Highway Safety account at $25 million.
  NOT IMPLEMENTED; $77 MILLION PROPOSED FOR FY 1982.

## Federal Highway Administration

- Review minority business enterprise regulations.
  IMPLEMENTED IN PART AT DEPARTMENT LEVEL.

- Continue the Highway Cost Allocation Study.
  IN PROCESS.

- Review overlapping regulations.
  IN PROCESS.

- Have adequate basis for any regulated shortening of work hours for truckers and shippers.
  IMPLEMENTED. WORK HOUR RULES UNCHANGED.

- Defer to new Congress in any rulemaking on minimum cab size.
  IMPLEMENTED.

- Reconsider proposed regulation of "on premise" signs.
  IMPLEMENTED.

## FHA Budget

- Maintain General Operating Expenses Account at FY 1981 level.
  IMPLEMENTED.

- Maintain Motor Carrier Safety funding at FY 1981 level.
  IMPLEMENTED.

- Maintain FY 1981 funding level for the Highway Research Development accounts.
  IMPLEMENTED.

- Eliminate funds for the Highway Beautification account.
  FUNDS ELIMINATED.

- Fund Highway-Related Safety Grants account at level not to exceed $20 million.
  IMPLEMENTED.

- Reduce appropriation for Territorial Highways to funding level below $5 million.
  IMPLEMENTED.

- Fund Safer Off-System Roads account at recommended level of $75 million.
  FUNDS ELIMINATED.

- Eliminate funds for Access Highways to Public Recreation Areas.
  FUNDS ELIMINATED.

- Fund the Federal Aid Highways Account and National Scenic and Recreational Highway Account at combined level of approximately $8.52 billion.
  IMPLEMENTED.

- Maintain emergency relief at minimum level.
  IMPLEMENTED.

- Eliminate funds for the Auto Use Management program.
  FUNDS ELIMINATED.

### Federal Railroad Administration

- Submit rail safety omnibus report on priority safety programs by January 31, 1981.
  IMPLEMENTED.

- Design a legislative plan under which each rail carrier would formulate its own railroad safety plan, subject to agency approval, and would be responsible for its implementation.
  IMPLEMENTED IN PART.

- Give high priority to pursuit of uniform state safety laws.
  NOT IMPLEMENTED.

- Prepare phased rationalization of AMTRAK, emphasizing cost-effective routes.
  IMPLEMENTED, RESULTING IN CONGRESSIONAL ACTION.

- Fund Rail Service Assistance and Improved Financing Fund accounts at combined level not to exceed $1 billion.
  IMPLEMENTED; $127.8 MILLION PROPOSED.

- Fund the Northeast Corridor Improvement program at level not to exceed $400 million.
  IMPLEMENTED; $176 MILLION PROPOSED.

- Fund no more than $900 million for AMTRAK.
  IMPLEMENTED; $539 MILLION PROPOSED.

- Fund Alaska Railroad at level not to exceed $9 million.
  IMPLEMENTED; $6.2 MILLION PROPOSED.

- Eliminate funds for Rail Labor Assistance account.
  FUNDING ELIMINATED.

### Urban Mass Transit Administration

- Rapidly appoint top UMTA policy officials.
  IMPLEMENTED.

- Establish a task force to review regulations.
  IMPLEMENTED.

- Declare a moratorium on grants for new rail starts.
  IMPLEMENTED.

- Revise regulations governing public transit accessibility for the handicapped.
  IMPLEMENTED.

- Reduce administrative expenses for UMTA to $15 million.
  NOT IMPLEMENTED.

- Reduce funding for the Research, Development and Demonstrations program to a level of approximately $35 million.
  NOT IMPLEMENTED.

- Fund Urban Discretionary Grants at level not to exceed $1.5 billion.
  IMPLEMENTED.

- Fund Non-Urban Formula Grants account at level not to exceed $70 million.
  IMPLEMENTED.

- Eliminate funds for the Waterborne Transportation Demonstration project.
  FUNDS ELIMINATED.

- Maintain funding for the Interstate Transfer Grants program at level not to exceed $700 million.
  IMPLEMENTED.

### Federal Aviation Administration

- Inform public about congressional role in negotiations with the Professional Air Traffic Controllers Organization (PATCO).
  IMPLEMENTED.

- Work with Justice Department on tough stance on illegal PATCO strike.
  IMPLEMENTED.
- Launch Blue Ribbon study group to investigate ATC computer problems.
  IMPLEMENTED.
- Increase productivity of lobbying effort.
  IMPLEMENTED.
- Prepare for next major air disaster.
  PARTIALLY IMPLEMENTED.
- Patch up relations with National Transportation Safety Board.
  NOT IMPLEMENTED.
- Adopt policy of expanding aviation capacity through use of Airport Development Aid Program funds.
  POLICY ADOPTED.
- Reverse trend of FAA engineering inferiority.
  POLICY CHANGES MADE, AND GOALS SET.
- Establish centralized FAA engineering facility.
  IMPLEMENTED IN EFFECT.
- Establish two technical advisory boards.
  NOT IMPLEMENTED.
- Choose technically qualified FAA Administrator.
  IMPLEMENTED.
- Better utilize NASA's technical talents.
  PARTIALLY IMPLEMENTED.
- Prevent regulatory overreaction to major crashes.
  POLICY ADOPTED.
- Defuse the three-pilot crew issue raised by the Air Line Pilots Association.
  IMPLEMENTED.
- Improve relationship between FAA and DOT.
  IMPLEMENTED.
- Examine FAA's relationship with DOT's Transportation Research Center.
  UNDER ACTIVE CONSIDERATION.

- Achieve greater flexibility with Civil Service regulations.
  NO ACTION.

- Implement an expedited contract procurement cycle.
  NOT IMPLEMENTED.

### FAA Budget

- Fund FAA Facilities and Equipment Account at level not greatly exceeding that of FY 1981.
  IMPLEMENTED.

- Maintain funding level of Research, Engineering and Development Account close to that for FY 1981.
  IMPLEMENTED.

- Increase funding of the Airport and Airway Trust Fund to $800 million.
  NOT IMPLEMENTED; $450 MILLION PROPOSED.

- Fund Operations and Maintenance Account for Metropolitan Washington Airport at level similar to that for FY 1981.
  IMPLEMENTED.

- Lower the Aircraft Purchase Loan Guarantee Program funding from FY 1981 level.
  IMPLEMENTED; CUT FROM $388 MILLION IN FY 1981 TO $100 MILLION IN FY 1982.

# Chapter Seventeen
# TREASURY DEPARTMENT
### By Bruce R. Bartlett

The original *Mandate for Leadership* study recognized that the Treasury Department's greatest contribution to a conservative administration would be in the area of tax policy. Hence, the greatest proportion of the recommendations regarding Treasury Department policy were directed toward taxation.

By and large, Treasury has done an exceptional job of implementing the specific proposals made in *Mandate*. Treasury led the fight for the Economic Recovery Tax Act of 1981 (Public Law 97-34). From an economic point of view, this legislation is far and away the best piece of tax legislation passed by the United States Congress since the early 1960s, and probably since the 1920s. It is solidly based on the principles of supply-side economics and will make a major contribution to the correction of the tax-inflicted economic problems the United States has experienced in recent years.

This is not to say that Treasury deserves all the credit for the supply-side features of the tax bill. Many of these originated on Capitol Hill, rather than within the Administration. In some cases, Treasury actually opposed efforts by Members of Congress to insert supply-side tax measures into the tax bill. Much of this had to do with political strategy. It was the Administration's initial position to oppose all amendments to the President's bill, which called simply for a ten percent reduction in individual income tax rates for three years, combined with 10-5-3 depreciation reform. This provision allows businesses to depreciate their investments in buildings in ten years, equipment in five years, and motor vehicles in three years. Problems continued even after it became clear that amendments would have to be accepted.

In the final analysis, the tax bill enacted into law implemented a very high percentage of the specific recommendations made in *Mandate for Leadership*. For example, the Economic Recovery Tax Act of 1981 was notable for the following reasons:

1. It was written almost exclusively with an eye toward the impact of tax policy on economic growth, in contrast to most tax bills enacted in recent years, which emphasized redistribution of income.

2. It focused on the long-term, rather than short-run economic and political cycles.

3. To a large extent its focus was kept on incentive effects, rather than aggregate dollar size.

4. It indexed the tax code to inflation beginning in 1985, so that taxpayers will not be pushed up into ever higher income tax brackets by inflation.

5. The tax rate reductions were applied across the board and not targeted toward specific income groups.

6. The bill partially reduced the tax bias against personal saving by authorizing financial institutions to issue certificates which will allow taxpayers to earn up to $1,000 in interest ($2,000 for a joint return) exempt from federal taxation. The bill allows taxpayers to exclude up to 15 percent of net interest from taxation after 1985 (up to $3,000 for an individual and $6,000 for a couple), and substantially expands the use of Individual Retirement Accounts (IRAs) and Keogh Plans.

7. The top marginal income tax rate for individuals was reduced from 70 percent to 50 percent on January 1, 1982.

8. Business depreciation allowances were reformed along a 15-5-3 basis.

9. The tax bias against Americans working overseas was substantially reduced.

Other supply-side tax measures enacted which were not explicitly discussed in *Mandate* include:

1. Institution of a tax credit for research and development expenditures.

2. Tax credits and exemptions for oil producers against the so-called windfall profits tax.

3. Reductions in the corporate tax rate for small firms.

4. Reinstatement of capital gains treatment for stock options which meet certain conditions.

5. A substantial reduction in the estate and gift tax, which will aid capital formation and help preserve family farms and businesses.

In addition to its recommendations regarding tax policy, *Mandate* made many other recommendations about administrative aspects of the Treasury Department and general economic policy as affected by Treasury.

*Mandate* urged that there should be no expansion or extension of the New York City or Chrysler bailout programs. Thus far, no such actions have been taken, although many proposals are being considered to bail out the savings and loan industry, which is suffering from the effects of high interest rates. Ironically, it was the savings and loan industry which was responsible for including the tax-free savings certificate provision in the tax bill, saying that this would save them. It is now clear that these certificates will not save the S&Ls; they are now asking for more government favors to save them from their own mistakes.

One very important area where the Treasury has rejected a *Mandate* recommendation is in the area of debt finance. *Mandate* urged that the Treasury suspend issuing long-term debt until interest rates decline. This is important for two reasons: first, issuing long-term debt at a time when interest rates are temporarily high saddles the taxpayer unnecessarily with enormous interest payments for many years into the future. Second, and more important, it is like advertising that the Treasury does not believe the Reagan program will work. If Treasury believed its own interest rate forecasts, there would be no sense in issuing long-term debt today when interest rates are expected to fall soon. By issuing long-term debt under such circumstances, Treasury is sending a signal to financial markets that it does not believe its own forecasts and that interest rates will rise. As one can see from the following Treasury Department statistics, it has been issuing very substantial amounts of long-term debt:

| | |
|---|---|
| Increase in federal debt outstanding January through July 1981 | 6.3% |
| Increase in amount of federal debt maturing within one year | 1.3% |
| Maturing within 1 to 5 years | 9.3% |
| Within 5 to 10 years | 14.3% |
| Within 10 to 20 years | 10.7% |
| 20 years and over | 16.5% |
| Average maturity of federal debt, January 1981 | 3 years, 9 mo. |
| Average maturity of federal debt, July 1981 | 4 years, 0 mo. |

Considering that current yields on Treasury bonds are more that 14 percent, the extent to which the taxpayer is losing is evident. That 14 percent interest will have to be paid out every year for the next thirty years on some bonds even if long-term interest rates fall to their historic average of four to five percent. This is one important reason why interest on the federal debt is the third largest item in the federal budget, amounting to more than $90 billion in the current fiscal year.

For these reasons, many prominent economists have suggested that the Treasury issue only short-term debt until interest rates decline, so that the taxpayer is not locked into paying high interest rates far into the future. In lieu of this, others have suggested that the Treasury issue indexed bonds, whose interest rates would fall if inflation falls, or to issue callable bonds which the Treasury can redeem before maturity if interest rates fall. Another proposal, advanced by Senator Roger Jepsen of Iowa, would be to issue gold-backed bonds, which could be sold at lower interest rates, since their principal would be backed by a specific quantity of gold.

In other areas, the Treasury has not supported increasing interest paid on U.S. savings bonds because it believes that it would only cost more money without increasing sales of savings bonds. This is unfortunate because it perpetuates a double standard whereby large financial institutions and wealthy individuals can obtain high returns on their investments in Treasury bills or notes. Small savers, many of whom are elderly, are denied a market rate of interest on their savings. This is discrimination and ought to be eliminated.

*Mandate* also suggested that Treasury refrain from concerning itself about the balance of trade deficit and avoid intervening in foreign exchange markets unless absolutely necessary. Under the leadership of Beryl Sprinkel, Under Secretary of the Treasury for Monetary Affairs, this recommendation has become Treasury policy.

In the area of foreign trade, the Treasury section of *Mandate* urged that trade be encouraged through the elimination of legal obstacles to trade, rather than through export subsidies. Although the Reagan Administration asked for reductions in appropriations to the Ex-Im Bank, which subsidized exports through low-interest loans, Congress rejected the proposal. Further efforts need to be made in this area. On the negative side, the Administration supported curbs on the import of Japanese automobiles. This was a misguided move. One can only hope there will be no repeat performance when the steel industry or the textile industry makes its pitch for protection. The result could be a trade war with devastating effects on U.S. and world economies.

On a more positive note, the Treasury appears finally to be adopting a more realistic attitude toward foreign aid. As Professor Peter Bauer has argued for decades, in books such as *Dissent on Development* and *Equality, the Third World, and Economic Delusion*, foreign aid's major effect has been to strengthen the government sector in recipient nations, enrich a number of petty dictators, and ultimately interfere with the adoption of market-oriented policies, which are the only hope of the underdeveloped world. The Treasury now seems to be coming to this realization. For the first time in decades, some restraints are being placed on U.S. contributions to multilateral development banks, such as the I.M.F. and the World Bank, which are the main conduits for foreign aid. Moreover, at economic summit meetings, such as the one recently in Cancun, Mexico, the United States has supported forcefully the adoption of free market principles in Third World nations. This is a development which is to be encouraged and applauded.

Finally, with regard to the administration of the Treasury Department, *Mandate* urged the establishment of a new Under Secretary position at Treasury to oversee tax and economic policy, to be filled by a person with a strong background in these areas. This recommendation was perfectly executed through the appointment of Dr. Norman B. Ture, principal author of the Treasury section of *Mandate for Leadership*, as Under Secretary of the Treasury for Tax Policy. Dr. Ture is one of the fathers of supply-side economics. It is doubtful that any other person in the United States is better qualified for the job he now holds.

## RECOMMENDATIONS
(Action taken on 25 out of 42)

### Tax Policy

- Revise the tax code, with emphasis on the economic aspects of tax policy.
  ACCOMPLISHED.

- Emphasize long-term economic growth and ignore short-run economic and political cycles when evaluating tax policies.
  SO FAR, SO GOOD.

- Emphasize the incentive aspects of tax rate changes rather than their aggregate dollar size.
  DONE.

- Restructure the tax code to end the bias against saving and growth.
  PARTIALLY ACCOMPLISHED.

- Protect the tax system against future inflation.
  DONE.

- Cut tax rates across the board. Do not target specific income groups.
  DONE.

- Tax earned and unearned income separately, each starting at the lowest tax rate.
  NOT DONE.

- Establish top tax rate on unearned income at no more than 50 percent.
  DONE.

- Exclude a certain percentage of interest or dividends from gross income.
  INADEQUATELY DONE.

- Allow taxpayers to "roll over" their gains in all investments as they are currently allowed to do with gains on owner-occupied housing.
  NOT DONE.

- Liberalize Keogh and Individual Retirement Accounts.
  DONE.

- Review business tax treatment of capital recovery allowances.
  DONE.

- Allow firms to expense their investments in real capital.
  NOT DONE.

- In lieu of expensing, allow firms to depreciate physical capital along a 10-5-3 approach (10 years for buildings, 5 for equipment, and 3 for cars and trucks).
  ALMOST ENTIRELY ACCOMPLISHED.

- Propose an initial tax bill which contains three simple elements: an across-the-board marginal tax rate reduction for individuals, 10-5-3 depreciation reform, and corporate tax rate reduction.
  VIRTUALLY DONE.

- Propose tax policy changes, to be accomplished in future years, which include:

  1. Targeted savings incentives.
     ACCOMPLISHED.

  2. Reform of high implicit marginal tax rates on low income workers resulting from means-tests for welfare and other unemployment benefits.
     NOT YET DONE.

  3. Tax rates should apply to real income, capital gains and profits, rather than illusory inflationary incomes, capital gains and profits.
     PARTIALLY ACCOMPLISHED.

### Loan Guarantees

- There should be no expansion or extension of the New York City or Chrysler loan guarantee programs and no further such programs established.
  DONE.

- Establish a "credit budget" to monitor and control government "off-budget" credit activities.
  PARTIALLY DONE.

- Reform revenue sharing to modify distortions.
  NO ACTION YET TAKEN.

- Move toward an auction method for all Treasury debt.
  NOT DONE.

- Suspend issuing long-term debt until interest rates decline.
  NOT DONE.

- Review the savings bond program to give investors a market rate yield.
  NOT DONE.

- The Treasury should not concern itself with the balance of payments.
  DONE SO FAR.

- Require Fed to pay more attention to the dollar's exchange rate as an indicator of monetary policy.
  NOT DONE.

- Refuse to support establishment of a substitution facility in the International Monetary Fund.
  DONE.

- Reappraise U.S. policy towards the taxation of U.S. citizens working abroad and foreign operations of U.S. business.
  PARTIALLY DONE.

- Liberalize tax laws affecting foreign earned income of U.S. citizens working abroad.
  DONE.

- Deter efforts to eliminate or restrict deferral and the foreign tax credit.
  DONE.

- Avoid imposing disincentives for foreign trade or investment.
  TOO EARLY TO EVALUATE.

- Re-examine current legal obstacles to U.S. exports, including the Foreign Corrupt Practices Act and the Webb-Pomerene Act.
  FOREIGN CORRUPT PRACTICES ACT UNDER REVIEW IN CONGRESS.

- Cease subsidization of exports through the Export-Import Bank.
  REAGAN REFORMS BLOCKED BY CONGRESS.

- Encourage exports by making the U.S. more competitive through supporting modernization of U.S. industry.
  SO FAR, SO GOOD.

- Support further reductions in tariff and non-tariff barriers to trade.
  NO ACTION YET TAKEN.

- Oppose further cartelization of raw materials in international trade.
  NO ACTION YET TAKEN.

- With regard to multilateral aid and institutions:
  1. Discourage further appropriations to multilateral lending authorities over which the U.S. has no control.
     NOT YET DONE.

  2. Re-evaluate the need for such multilateral development institutions as a means of funneling capital to less developed nations.
     IN PROCESS.

  3. Stop making low interest loans to such multilateral development banks.
     NOT YET DONE.

- Rethink U.S. commitment to foreign aid.
  NOT YET DONE.

- Designate an Under Secretary to oversee tax and economic policy, with the Assistant Secretaries for Tax Policy and Economic Policy and the Commissioner of Internal Revenue reporting to him.
  DONE.

- Require this Under Secretary have a strong background in tax and economic affairs.
  DONE.

- Combine the U.S. Customs Service with the Bureau of Alcohol, Tobacco and Firearms.
  NOT DONE.

- Encourage closer cooperation between the Tax Division of the Justice Department and the Treasury Department.

  TOO EARLY TO EVALUATE.

- Require that the IRS confine itself to the enforcement of tax law, rather than the making of tax law.

  SO FAR, SO GOOD.

- Compensate liberally taxpayers who win suits against the IRS for court costs.

  NO ACTION YET TAKEN.

# Chapter Eighteen
# SENIOR EXECUTIVE SERVICE
### By Robert M. Huberty

In November 1980, the Senior Executive Service (SES) was barely a year old and little could be said of its performance. The careful design of the legislation creating SES and the support of federal executives who joined it in overwhelming numbers provided reasons for thinking it would have a major and positive effect on policy administration. Some even said that SES, one of the few notable achievements of the Carter Administration, would best serve the incoming Reagan Administration. Members of the Senior Executive Service would constitute a cadre of seasoned and motivated executive talent, free to transfer within and between departments with rank and pay determined by individual performance, not by a designated position. SES procedures for performance appraisal and the awarding of bonuses, in turn, would provide the Reagan Administration with ways to reward and punish executives charged with carrying out its new policy initiatives. The SES could ensure the "responsiveness" of the bureaucracy to the new Administration. Those who carried out the Administration's mandate could expect to receive their due.

One year later, it is clear that SES has not lived up to the expectations of those who wrote the law and of federal executives within it. What expectations the Administration can have of SES is unclear. As long as Congress tampers with the structural arrangements necessary for SES to work according to plan, its future is in doubt.

The failure of SES to satisfy its members can be summed up in one word: money. In November 1980, the four highest pay ranks of SES—90 percent of the 6,900 members—had reached the pay cap of $50,112.50 imposed by Congress for FY 1980. That situation has worsened in the past year. Currently, all six SES pay levels have reached the pay cap, as have many middle management GS-15s and GS-14s. An ES-6 who may administer a staff of thousands and a budget of hundreds of millions of dollars is paid the same as an incoming ES-1 with limited program responsibilities. There is no incentive to motivate executives to assume greater management responsibilities. Indeed, without the promise of pay rewards, there is little incentive for experienced GS-14s and GS-15s to assume the greater career risks of joining SES. A recent Merit Systems Protection Board (MSPB) survey of GS-13s through GS-15s found that only 30 percent said they were likely to join SES if they were offered a job they liked.

On September 30, 1981, Congress failed to extend to senior executives the 4.8 percent pay raise granted all other civil servants. The Senate, in conference, refused to approve the House measure. This SES pay raise, which was supported by the Reagan Administration, would have raised the ceiling to about $52,000. While granting the raise to senior executives would have done little to alleviate the problem of "pay compression," not approving it has only exacerbated the problem. Because GS-14s and GS-15s did receive raises, the number of those who now are paid the same salary as the government's most senior career executives has increased from 28,000 to about 40,000.

In the longer term, Congress and the Administration will have to brave the displeasure of voters and recognize that different pay for differing job responsibilities is as appropriate a reward for government employees as for those in the private sector. The question of determining pay comparability is a knotty one. The Administration has the matter under study. It must realize that without the hope of pay raises tied to career advances, members of SES will continue to leave government service.

Attrition rates at SES are worsening. Assistant Secretary of Defense Lawrence Korb has observed that statistics show the SES attrition rate in the Defense Department was 17.5 percent in 1980 and 1981, double the 1979 Navy Department rate. The Office of Personnel Management (OPM) Director, Donald Devine, testified that in 1980 the retirement rate of eligible SES members was 38 percent. According to the GAO, the retirement rate of 1980 eligibles who were at the pay ceiling was 57 percent. The Comptroller General has figured that each pay-capped 55-year-old senior executive who retires with thirty years' experience costs the government about $30,000 per year in pensions which, unlike capped pay, are supplemented by cost-of-living increases. This does not include the cost of training and paying a replacement. Some will conclude that attrition may well rid the bureaucracy of its most tenacious time-servers. This is perhaps the least efficient way for government to weed out unsatisfactory executive performance.

The Senior Executive Service was set up with formal mechanisms for handling the assessment of executive performance. An annual performance appraisal was intended to identify unsatisfactory performance. A bonus award system was established to reward exceptional performance. The problems faced by both systems have not been sufficiently addressed in the past year.

In hearings held in the spring of 1981, the House Subcommittee on Civil Service found no evidence to validate the fears of the opposition that the Reagan Administration might turn the performance appraisal system against career executives. GAO and MSPB surveys show that

SES members have a high level of confidence in the performance appraisal system. SES members generally believe they have participated in developing realistic and achievable performance objectives by which they are evaluated, and they believe they are evaluated fairly. However, it should be noted that 99 percent of all SES executives received "fully satisfactory" performance ratings. As of July 1981, only one career executive has been removed from SES for poor performance.

Some have argued that these figures are not surprising because SES members could not have achieved their high rank unless they were demonstrably competent. To accept this thesis or the antithesis—that SES is government of, by, and for inept bureaucracy—is to accept speculation as evidence. The research to determine whether SES performance appraisal systems are well-devised and well-administered simply has not been completed. Only when this is accomplished can the performance of senior executives be judged "fully satisfactory."

The charge that agency performance appraisal systems are inadequately supervised has been made against OPM by the GAO. OPM responded that it has less authority to prescribe performance appraisal standards for government agencies since passage of the 1978 Civil Service Reform Act. This Act created SES and decentralized the process of senior executive selection, training, classification, appraisal, and reward. OPM, which does not want the responsibility, argues that agencies are better able to determine their own appraisal standards. It cites as evidence those GAO opinion surveys showing executive satisfaction with agency performance appraisals.

This argument is inadequate. Other GAO surveys of actual agency practices have found that most agencies failed to pre-test their performance appraisal standards and provided inadequate guidance for those administering the standards. GAO has urged OPM to take a more active role in monitoring and assisting the agencies. The Reagan Administration can hold executives accountable for their performance in carrying out government policy only if agency appraisal systems are trustworthy. OPM would be well-advised to oversee more carefully the implementation and administration of the system.

While SES executives have a high opinion of the performance appraisal system, they have a low opinion of the system for awarding bonuses. Various opinion surveys find that large numbers of SES members believe they have little chance to receive a bonus despite high performance ratings; they suspect management favorites are the ones to receive bonuses; and they see bonuses going disproportionately to executives at the top of the agency and to those who, as members of SES performance review boards, make the bonus decisions.

A cynic might conclude these dark thoughts are the inevitable results of the fact that not more than 20 percent of SES executives can receive bonuses. With 99 percent rated "fully satisfactory," 79 percent of all eligible SES members are certain to be disappointed.

The extent of dissatisfaction with bonuses needs to be understood in the light of two factors: Congress' restrictions on the awarding of bonuses, and the pay cap which made bonuses appear to be means to its circumvention. In July 1980, an outraged Congress cut from 50 percent to 25 percent the number of career SES members in an agency who could receive annual bonuses of up to 20 percent of base pay. Congress acted following disclosures that the first agencies to take advantage of the system, NASA and the Small Business Administration, had gone to the 50 percent limit in the number of executive bonuses they awarded. OPM, fearful of losing the bonus system altogether, then administratively reduced the percentage limit from 25 percent to 20 percent. Hardly a year after the start of SES, senior executives charged that Congress and OPM had reneged on the promise of bonuses which had persuaded 98.5 percent of them to join and to accept the risks of performance appraisal. In September 1981, Congress exacerbated the problem. Besides denying senior executives a 4.8 percent raise, Congress mandated the 20 percent limitation after OPM had allowed the number bonuses to climb back to the 25 percent limit set by Congress in July 1980.

This sequence of events soured both Congress and senior executives on the bonus system. Some in Congress and in SES would welcome repeal. Whatever the outcome, the system's credibility will not easily be restored.

The battle over percentages is, of course, a money struggle. But it also reflects, in part, a difference in understanding the purpose and effect of bonuses. Many senior executives, using the private sector as their model, see bonuses as part of a total compensation package to be extended to the greatest number of executives who are motivated to fulfill performance objectives. Giving bonuses to 50 percent of an agency's executives is then a desirable goal, not an outer limit. Congress, on the other hand, clearly regards bonuses as performance awards. Fewer bonuses are therefore desirable in order to distinguish between levels of performance. Large numbers of bonuses appear to be raids on the public purse.

The Reagan Administration is caught in the middle. If it wants the bonus system to work, it must demonstrate that bonuses motivate employees. But many bonuses or few? From an academic standpoint, this requires a theory of motivation and of a psychology of work; on this, there is no agreement. From a political standpoint, executive

242

expectations clash with congressional suspicions. Only the foolhardy would try to settle a quarrel between a bureaucrat and a Congressman.

The bonus muddle is made worse by the pay cap. Congressional suspicions that bonuses are awarded to circumvent the pay ceiling and supplement executive income raise questions about the purpose of bonuses.

Although it is the source of much bad feeling and public controversy, the exact percentage of bonuses awarded is of minor significance. A functioning SES requires that senior executives believe that their willingness and ability to carry out the Administration's policy directives are the criteria which will determine career advancement in government service. Pay-for-performance is the central premise of the Senior Executive Service. Unless the Administration can re-establish that premise, SES will fail.

### RECOMMENDATIONS
(No action taken on the single recomendation)

- Lift the pay cap.
  NOT DONE.

# Chapter Nineteen
# THE INTELLIGENCE COMMUNITY
### By Samuel T. Francis

The first year of the Reagan Administration has been an ambiguous one in the area of intelligence policy reform. No dramatic reforms have been implemented, although some promising incremental reforms have been promised or started. There are several reasons for the lack of dramatic change. The Administration has given priority to domestic budgetary, fiscal, and economic issues. Issues concerning national security, defense, foreign policy, and intelligence policy have suffered from inattention. The higher councils of the Administration in these areas are divided and appear indecisive. The controversial nature of intelligence activities and policies in general, in conjunction with controversies surrounding particular individuals in the intelligence community, have contributed to the failure to implement *Mandate* recommendations. The prospect for the implementation of these intelligence reforms in the near future appears remote.

The heart of the reform program consists of three major steps: 1) the separation of the clandestine branch of the Central Intelligence Agency (the Deputy Directorate for Operations or DDO) from the analytical branch (the Deputy Directorate for Intelligence or DDI) into autonomous agencies; 2) the upgrading and establishment of a centralized counterintelligence (CI) data bank; and 3) the upgrading of the analytic process. Only in the third area has there been any significant progress. There is little support or constituency for the separation of DDO from the analytical branch. Director Casey stated at his Senate confirmation hearings that he had considered this idea some years previously and was not disposed favorably toward it. Several former intelligence officers favored it, but perhaps more from animosity toward the analytical branch than from any consideration of its policy implications. In retrospect, it may be that the original *Mandate* chapter on intelligence did not thoroughly express the exact relationship which would develop between clandestine collection and analysis under the proposed reforms. Clearly, the former function cannot simply submit raw intelligence data to policy-makers without analysis, and both analysts and collectors must collaborate closely if they are to perform their functions competently.

In terms of counterintelligence, the Administration appears to be moving at a glacial pace to lay the basis for a redevelopment of this essential function. Before it can do so, there must be considerable legislative revision of the Freedom of Information Act and Privacy Act. Such revisions were advocated in *Mandate*. To date, the

Administration has taken the position that FOIA must be amended to prevent it from impeding law enforcement or intelligence collection by the FBI. It has not endorsed similar proposals for the CIA. There is no serious effort at this time to amend the Privacy Act.

In the area of intelligence analysis, the Administration has undertaken two measures that are promising. One is the appointment of John McMahon, formerly DDO, to head the DDI. This is the first time in the history of the CIA that the head of DDO has taken over the analytical branch, and this step may in itself resolve many of the problems that have afflicted the relationship between the two branches. McMahon's reputation for competence and honesty make his appointment one of the most noteworthy in the new Administration.

Second, the Administration has restored the President's Foreign Intelligence Advisory Board (PFIAB), which will have the power to commission an alternative source of analysis. PFIAB, abolished by President Carter, had commissioned the now famous "A" team and "B" team competing analyses of Soviet strategic strength. Its restoration promises a much-needed second look at estimates which have become notoriously inaccurate in recent years.

In Congress, the Administration has strongly supported passage of the Intelligence Identities Protection Act (S. 391/ H.R. 4), a measure introduced in February but still not passed. The delays in passage of this Act have been caused by opposition from liberal elements in both Houses and both parties and by a certain amount of disorganization among supporters in Congress. Revealing the identity of U.S. intelligence personnel, if the identity is classified information, would become a federal crime under the Act. Given the activities of the anti-intelligence lobby—exposing intelligence identities and defending those who do—clandestine collection or covert operations have been seriously compromised. One CIA Chief of Station was murdered after his illicit exposure; at least one other was the victim of an armed attack. The careers and professional activities of others have been disrupted. The inability or unwillingness of the U.S. government to provide protection for its intelligence operatives also has weakened the morale of its officers and their collaborators. This lack of commitment to an intelligence program subverts the confidence of allied intelligence services and causes them to share intelligence with the CIA only reluctantly.

If the enactment of intelligence identities legislation promises to improve the morale of the clandestine branch, the appointment of Max Hugel by Director Casey to head the DDO appeared to lower it. Hugel's appointment was the subject of vitriolic criticism by former members of the clandestine branch. This criticism appeared to be justified by subsequent allegations about his business conduct. The principal problem appeared to be Hugel's complete lack of experience in clandestine intelligence activities. His appointment had been justified on the basis of his political activities and his personal friendship with Director Casey. These relationships called into question the DCI's judgment and, coupled with later allegations about Casey's own business conduct and associates, undermined public confidence in him.

The investigation of Director Casey by the Senate Select Committee on Intelligence itself inspired little public confidence in this oversight mechanism. The Committee Chairman, Senator Goldwater, called for the Director's resignation before the investigation had been completed; he was later obliged to retract his demand. Goldwater reportedly sought to promote his friend, Admiral Bobby Inman, Deputy Director of the Agency, into the position of DCI by forcing Casey out. To date, none of these issues has been completely resolved.

The Casey-Hugel incident raises important problems of intelligence policy and administration. First, it raises the problem of the adequacy of CIA and other governmental security investigations of prospective employees. This matter is closely related to the erosion of the Federal Employee Security Program, which was also discussed in *Mandate for Leadership*. Second, the prevalence of leaks and rumors concerning the Casey-Hugel investigation and an alleged CIA covert action plan indicates a continuing lack of respect for confidentiality among certain Administration and congressional personnel. The Administration is reported to be devising techniques to trace security leaks. Third, the Casey-Hugel matter suggests the politicization of the intelligence community and of the congressional oversight mechanism. The Hugel appointment, the allegations against Casey and Hugel, and the congressional handling of the subsequent investigations indicate priorities other than a concern for the integrity of the intelligence community. Politicization may be an inevitable consequence of congressional oversight of intelligence matters, although it was not unknown prior to the establishment of the intelligence committees. The past year gave no indication that politicization of intelligence institutions and policy is diminishing.

Casey is reported by knowledgeable observers to be one of the better Directors of Central Intelligence in the history of the CIA. He has brought to his position both professional (though somewhat dated) credentials in intelligence work through OSS and extensive managerial experience. This combination has been rare among past directors. The latter quality is felt to be more relevant to the work of the DCI than the former. Admiral Bobby Ray Inman, as Deputy Director, is a most widely respected government official. The most serious criticism of him made to date is that, as former Director of the

National Security Agency (NSA), he is too wedded to technical forms of intelligence and continues to have too little appreciation for human intelligence (HUMINT). Many critics of the CIA and the authors of the *Mandate for Leadership* Intelligence chapter argue that the CIA should make efforts to improve HUMINT. Hugel's replacement as DDO by John Stein, a career clandestine officer, has also been widely praised. Stein apparently is open to the increased use of human intelligence.

*Mandate for Leadership* also included recommendations for the reform of internal security policy, an area closely related to intelligence matters but overlapping also with law enforcement. Although there has been an almost complete erosion of the internal security apparatus, three areas continue to stand out in their need for reform: revision of the Attorney General's Guidelines for Domestic Security Investigations (the Levi Guidelines); restoration of at least one standing committee in Congress for internal security matters; and restoration of the Federal Employee Security Program.

The Levi Guidelines currently are under review by the Administration and the Department of Justice. The attempted assassination of the President in March generated controversy about the Guidelines, as has the recent surfacing of terrorist activities in the form of armed robberies and bombings by the Weather Underground and allied extremist groups. The General Counsel of the Department of the Treasury (having authority over the U.S. Secret Service) issued a report in the summer of 1981 calling for revision of the Guidelines. Director Webster, however, publicly opposed changing them. The most important single measure that the Administration could perform in the field of internal security is the revision of the Levi Guidelines to allow the FBI to investigate extremist groups that have ties with underground violent organizations or which may develop into violent organizations themselves. The Guidelines forbid all investigations unless the subject is believed to have committed or is about to commit violence or a federal crime. As was pointed out in *Mandate*, many extremist groups, while not involved in criminal activities themselves, have close ties with those secret or underground groups that do commit crimes of a political nature. Investigation of above-ground sympathizers, now effectively barred by the Guidelines, would do much to restore an adequate internal security program.

Internal security is a necessary function of the government. The U.S. Congress should possess a mechanism to review and investigate internal security problems, enact or amend internal security legislation, and oversee the enforcement of this legislation. The Subcommittee on Security and Terrorism of the Senate Judiciary Committee was established under the chairmanship of Senator Jeremiah Denton of Alabama at the beginnning of the 97th Congress. This congressional action, which was supported by the Administration, fulfills this aspect of *Mandate*. The chief counsel of the Subcommittee is Joel S. Lisker, formerly with the FBI and the Foreign Agents' Registration section of the DOJ. Both Denton and Lisker bring much-needed skills and experience to the Subcommittee.

The Subcommittee has made an effort to begin inquiries into the present extent of the Federal Employee Security Program. The Administration has done little to re-develop an ability to exclude from federal employment personnel of dubious security or loyalty. Under the restrictions discussed in *Mandate*, it is almost impossible to assure the American people that their public servants are loyal or secure and that classified information is secure. The continuing flood of leaks from the Reagan Administration to the press include the draft intelligence estimate on terrorism and a draft Executive Order on the intelligence community, to name only the more significant. These facts illustrate part of the problem and underline the difficulty of effective decision-making in the absence of confidentiality.

Perhaps the most promising new direction of the Reagan Administration in the area of intelligence and security policy has been its emphasis on Soviet and Soviet-bloc support for international terrorism. This emphasis is manifest in three documents: Secretary of State Haig's speech on January 28, 1981, which was the first official confirmation of the Soviet role in support of international terrorism; a White Paper on "Communist Interference in El Salvador" issued on February 23, 1981, which documents Soviet-bloc aid to the El Salvadoran terrorists; and a CIA research paper issued in June 1981, that for the first time publicly discusses and acknowledges the Soviet role in terrorism. However, subsequent controversy over these allegations, erroneous press accounts, and a weak response from some Administration officials diluted the public impact of the official statements. If the Administration wishes to have its intelligence analyses taken seriously, it must undertake a far more strenuous effort to defend them.

The main problem of the Reagan Administration in intelligence policy during its first year is closely related to this weak defense. The Administration does not yet appear to have resolved in its own mind the continuing controversy about the role of intelligence and internal security in a free society. Massive House and Senate support for a strong Intelligence Identities Act indicates that both the public and the Congress share the concern over the emasculation of the CIA and the FBI and wish to see them rebuilt. The Administration, from the President down, should respond to this mood positively, seize the opportunity for improving intelligence and internal security institutions, and initiate a vigorous and well-informed public dialogue to defend its commitments in this area.

In addition, the Administration's top priority at the CIA should be an intensive re-building of the clandestine branch that will lead to an increased and improved capacity for clandestine collection and covert action and not an elaborate structural reform. While technical means can, at least under optimal conditions, provide more extensive and more concrete intelligence, HUMINT alone can provide data on motivations and intentions, and only through human assets can the capacity for covert action be rebuilt. Before the Administration can develop a more efficient clandestine service, however, it must resolve lingering and deeply-rooted doubts about the willingness of the government to commit itself to supporting intelligence activities and removing them as much as possible from the political winds.

## RECOMMENDATIONS

Because of the nature of the original proposals for the Intelligence Community—some proposals were for long-term consideration and many, if implemented, would remain classified information—it is not feasible to discuss all the proposals of the original *Mandate for Leadership* in this area. The following list represents the most important proposals that can be discussed in a public document. (Action was taken on 5 out of 16.)

### Legislation

- Enact legislation to prohibit the unauthorized disclosure of the identities of clandestine agents and their case officers.
  DONE.

- Enact legislation to separate the Deputy Directorate of Operations (DDO) as an independent agency.
  NOT DONE.

- Enact legislation to create a counterintelligence office staffed by specialists from all the intelligence agencies where central files could be kept, central counterintelligence analysis carried out, and pursuit of cases could be coordinated.
  NOT DONE.

- Modify the Foreign Intelligence Surveillance Act (FISA) to dis-establish the special court (Foreign Intelligence Surveillance Court).
  NOT DONE.

- Propose legislation to exempt the FBI from the Privacy Act and the Freedom of Information Act.
  PROPOSED IN PART.

- Support restoration of at least one standing committee of the Congress for the investigation of internal security problems and the oversight of the enforcement of the internal security laws.
  DONE.

- Support legislation to establish a Director of National Intelligence in the Executive Office of the President and Director of the National Foreign Assessments Center (NFAC) with a fixed term.
  NOT DONE.

## By Executive Action

- Upgrade the Defense Intelligence Agency (DIA) to produce competitive analyses with NFAC.
  NOT DONE.

- Increase the number of Counterintelligence personnel in the FBI and CIA.
  PROPOSED FOR THE FBI; NOT FOR THE CIA.

- Revoke Executive Order 12036 and issue a new Executive Order for the intelligence community.
  ORDER DRAFTED BUT NOT YET RELEASED.

- Restore the Federal Employee Security Program (FESP) and the Attorney General's List of Subversive Organizations.
  NOT DONE.

- Revise the Attorney General's Guidelines for Domestic Security Investigations (Levi Guidelines).
  NOT DONE; HOWEVER, GUIDELINES ARE CURRENTLY UNDER REVIEW AND ARE TO BE REVISED.

- Appoint an Attorney General who understands and appreciates the importance of internal security issues.
  DONE.

- Appoint as Director of the FBI an individual who understands and appreciates the importance of internal security.
  NOT DONE.

- Restore the internal security division of the Department of Justice as an independent division.
  NOT DONE.

- Reform intelligence analysis by altering career patterns of analysts.

  NOT DISCUSSABLE IN DETAIL; NFAC HAS BEEN REOR-GANIZED UNDER THE NEW DIRECTOR.

# Chapter Twenty
# ENVIRONMENTAL PROTECTION AGENCY
### By Louis J. Cordia

Delays in appointments impeded the implementation of regulatory reforms at EPA. Anne McGill Gorsuch was not nominated until February 21 and was not confirmed by the Senate until May 5, 1981. All in all, the appointment process has been excruciatingly slow at the lower levels as well. The last of the six Assistant Administrators was not named until early November. To date, only two have been confirmed. The Agency has been forced to make do with acting officials, special assistants, and consultants.

These problems were compounded by the resignation of two senior officials over policy differences. Administrator Gorsuch is to be commended for handling these resignations wisely. Rapid personnel changes may present an image of instability but such an image is far better than maintaining policy level staffers who do not share the Administration's policy goals.

Before Gorsuch arrived at the Agency the Reagan Administration had already taken some significant steps to start the regulatory reform process. The Regulatory Relief Task Force headed by Vice President Bush has announced a goal of "cutting away the thicket of irrational and senseless regulation." Executive Order 12291 provides clear guidelines for judging the effectiveness of regulations. In a memorandum to all department and agency heads, the President asked for a sixty-day freeze to allow for reviews of the last-minute regulations proposed by the Carter Administration.

The task force designated two EPA regulations for full regulatory review. One affected pre-treatment standards for industrial discharges into municipal wastewater treatment facilities, and another determined best conventional technology (BCT) in the permitting process. EPA regulations not affected by this sixty-day review were postponement of record-keeping requirements for manufacturers in the pesticide industry, limited exemptions from hazardous waste regulations under the Resource Conservation and Recovery Act, two air pollution permits using the "bubble" concept, and a one-year deferral of truck noise standards.

The Vice President's Task Force also sent a letter to the business community, state and local governments and federal agencies, soliciting their help in identifying regulatory priorities. Over 300 groups, associations and companies responded with approximately 3,000 comments on regulations of some forty federal departments and agencies. EPA rules, regulations and policies received at least four times as many comments as did those of any other single government department or agency. The definition of hazardous wastes, standards for new and existing facilities, financial responsibility requirements, and rules for small waste generators under the Resource Conservation and Recovery Act received the most attention from respondents on hazardous waste rules. On a single hazardous waste issue, the majority of comments recommended that EPA exempt from the rules wastes that are used, reused, recycled or reclaimed, and industrial byproducts that are burned for energy recovery. Many comments recommended that mixtures containing *de minimis* quantities of hazardous wastes be excluded from the regulations as well. Another proposal was to incorporate the degree of hazard approach into standards for facilities.

"Superfund"—the Comprehensive Environmental Response, Compensation, and Liability Act of 1980—was also discussed by these correspondents. Issues most frequently mentioned included the reportable quantities requirements, the feedstock taxes, and the cost of cleaning up hazardous waste dumpsites. Many comments expressed concern that the EPA and the Department of Justice appeared to have agreed that cleanup orders to industry will not be limited by the cost-effectiveness and cost-benefit policies in the national contingency plan. Many companies voiced reservations about the use of the MITRE Corporation's priority system to list sites for remedial action. They also questioned the risk assessment procedure.

Turning to the Clean Water Act, many objected to the general pre-treatment regulations for existing and new sources, estimating that compliance would require $4 billion in capital cost and $1 billion in annual operating costs. The stringency of proposed effluent limitations under the National Pollutant Discharge Elimination System (NPDES) and the administrative and monitoring tasks required under the permit program were severely criticized. Recommendations to the consolidated permit program ranged from revamping to eliminating it.

The Prevention of Significant Deterioration (PSD) program in the Clean Air Act drew considerable attention. One trade association called for its elimination, while others thought that Class I and II increments could be eliminated if mandatory Best Available Control Technology (BACT) requirments would be maintained. A variety of comments were received on the visibility requirements for National Parks and Wilderness areas. Some argued that these standards should apply only to congressionally-designated Class I areas, while others felt that no visibility requirements should be imposed until an adequate scientific basis can be developed for analyzing and measuring visibility impairment. Some were in favor of the "bubble" concept, and of states managing their own air pollution control plans based on generic rules rather than site-specific state implementation plan provisions.

Subsequently, the Department of Commerce compiled a list of the twenty most burdensome regulations based on comments received by the Task Force through June 8. EPA's hazardous waste management regulations under the Resource Conservation and Recovery Act (RCRA) headed the list. Criteria and standards for the National Pollutant Discharge Elimination System (NPDES) under the Clean Water Act were second; and pre-treatment standards under the Water Act were fourth. The Department of Commerce chose not to include Clean Air Act issues in this exercise.

The Administration announced a schedule for completing review of twenty-seven existing regulations the task force had targeted for review in March. At the same news briefing, James C. Miller III, Administrator of Information and Regulatory Affairs at OMB and Executive Director of the Regulatory Relief Task Force, said, "EPA has been the subject of most comments and they were generally very critical." However, to be fair, Miller added, "EPA has the largest number of statutory schemes and mandates to carry out."

On June 12, 1981, the Administration announced that it had taken action on 181 regulatory relief proposals. The largest potential savings were from relief initiatives undertaken by the Environmental Protection Agency and the Department of Transportation. Potential savings from these EPA actions is estimated at $3.4 billion in one-time costs, and $1.3 billion in recurring costs. These figures do not include the $800 million savings from a regulatory revision designed to help the ailing auto industry, nor do they include the $1.2 billion savings that would result from a thorough review and revision of the hazardous waste regulations.

Late in the summer, the Regulatory Relief Task Force released a second list of regulations to be reviewed. On August 12, it listed thirty-nine additional regulations and paperwork requirements, including two issues of high priority: EPA's pre-manufacture notice exemption policy under the Toxic Substances Control Act (TOSCA) and the Agency's consolidated permit program under RCRA.

The President's regulatory reform program has increasingly stressed the importance of scientifically credible risk assessments; this point was also stressed in *Mandate for Leadership*. In October, Dr. George Keyworth, the Director of the Office of Science and Technology Policy in the White House, was appointed to the President's Task Force on Regulatory Relief. He will chair a task force work group on science and technology, of which EPA Administrator Anne Gorsuch will be a part. In the Vice President's announcement on October 9, 1981, credible science was emphasized as a need to "improve the regulatory process. The agencies having primary responsibility for environmental health and safety regulations must work together to enhance the scientific basis of their regulatory decisions." The National Academy of Sciences, the General Accounting Office, the EPA Science Advisory Board and other scientific bodies have stressed the value of independent review in assuring that agencies draw accurate conclusions from scientific data. Dr. John W. Hernandez, the Deputy Administrator of EPA, is heading the effort at the Agency to increase the use of the Science Advisory Board, and an independent scientific review panel to improve regulations to be promulgated and those that are under review. Dr. Keyworth's Working Group should offer an important ingredient to risk/benefit/cost assessments.

To date, the EPA, in conjunction with the Bush Regulatory Relief Task Force, the Office of Management and Budget, and Keyworth's Scientific Working Group, has begun an extensive review of environmental rules and regulations. As commendable as the effort has been, it has only begun. The "new beginning" has been delayed.

The Environmental Protection Agency chapter in *Mandate for Leadership* offered 150 administrative and legislative options. These were designed to begin a market-oriented discussion of environmental issues in the 1980s. This philosophy was lacking during the confrontational decade of the 1970s and its plethora of "quick fix" regulations. Many policy initiatives from *Mandate* were used by EPA as starting points in the review process. Some have been discarded; others have been continued. The audit section of this review treats responses such as "under consideration" as "not done" unless evidence of genuine progress has been demonstrated. Although such answers may be sincere, good intentions are not a substitute for action.


## RECOMMENDATIONS
(Action taken on 48 out of 146)

### Air Quality: Administrative Options

- Delegate detailing authority of State Implementation Plans (SIPs) to the states after the federal government sets policy guidelines.

  NOT DONE.

- Reconsider (with an eye toward suspending) EPA regulations detailing new instrumentation, monitoring station siting and quality assurance by the states.

  NOT DONE.

- Defer final publication of new criteria documents for the National Ambient Air Quality Statements (NAAQS) pollutants until an independent, objective (internal and external) review has been conducted.

INITIATED IN PART.

- Limit EPA "overview responsibilities" to SIP approval, with no option for permit-by-permit review of the Prevention of Significant Deterioration new source program.

NOT DONE.

- Review the full impact on society of setting mobile source guidelines for diesel emissions exhaust controls.

NOT DONE.

- Require independent scientific review of the adequacy and validity of air diffusion models used in regulatory actions in the absence of adequate monitoring devices and data.

NOT DONE.

- Review carefully recommendations of the National Commission on Air Quality (NCAQ) to Congress to develop possible amendments to the Act.

INITIATED.

- Review the scientific basis upon which revised standards for oxides of nitrogen, carbon monoxide, sulphur dioxide, and total suspended particulates are set, and revise the standards on the basis of credible data, especially in light of the mandatory review of all NAAQS required in 1980-81.

PARTLY INITIATED. FULL IMPLEMENTATION EXPECTED.

- Retain changes previously adopted in New Source Performance Standards (NSPS) to increase flexibility, including the average time for emission measurements, "bubble concept" and emission trade-off and, where possible, develop other new ideas.

INITIATED.

- Propose and promulgate emission standards for heavy and light duty trucks, both diesel and gasoline powered, which are based on scientifically credible technical data.

NOT DONE.

- Review and redirect the goals of research and development towards more objective regulatory goals.

INITIATED.

257

- Acquire more knowledge on visibility monitoring and modeling before carrying out the statutory mandates.

NOT DONE.

- Implement the primary Nonferrous Smelter Order Program, and streamline its procedures and requirements.

NOT DONE.

- Provide a positive delineation of requirements under Lowest Achievable Emission Rate (LAER), Best Achievable Control Technology (BACT), Reasonably Achievable Control Technology (RACT) and New Source Performance Standards (NSPS), or delete the requirements.

INITIATED.

- Consider allowing the use of tax-exempt Industrial Development Bonds (IDBs) for process changes which reduce air pollution emissions to provide early roll-over of facilities, and promote manufacturing efficiency.

NOT DONE.

**Air Quality: Legislative Options**

- Propose amendments to the Clean Air Act:

  1. Direct states to evaluate all major fuel burning sources on a plant-by-plant basis, to determine the environmental requirements appropriate to each, and to set emission limitations accordingly, and abolish SIP requirements which apply to all sources within the state.

  NOT DONE.

  2. Allow a Governor to provide emergency orders to extend variances up to five years, and to extend the variances to other applicable emission limitations in cases where significant local or regional economic disruption or unemployment exists.

  REJECTION ANTICIPATED.

  3. Provide that a state, in computing emissions for enforcement purposes, shall in all cases employ the "30-day rolling average" concept.

  REJECTION LIKELY.

  4. Direct the EPA to re-evaluate periodically and revise modern data on airsheds and airstreams.

  NOT DONE.

5. Require review of Agency criteria documents on proposed standards by scientific experts from outside the EPA to ensure that regulations and standards are based on objective scientific evidence which has received extensive peer review.

   INTIATED IN PART.

6. Authorize the President to designate agencies outside EPA (e.g., the National Oceanic and Atmospheric Administration (NOAA) and the National Bureau of Standards (NBS)) to review air quality monitoring and modeling activities of the EPA, and provide federal grants to other entities to develop or carry on such efforts.

   NOT DONE.

7. Require the EPA to develop and implement cost-benefit and risk-benefit analyses of all new regulatory proposals.

   INITIATED IN PART.

8. Increase federal funding in other agencies for research on biomedical and environmental effects relating to the burning of coal.

   INITIATED IN PART.

9. Provide extensions for meeting NSPS emission limitations for those existing sources which voluntarily convert to coal usage, consistent with the provisions required by the Department of Energy order under the Energy Supply and Environmental Coordination Act (Section 113(d)).

   NOT DONE.

10. Consider providing a ten-year period of protection against further regulatory change for all facilities constructed or modified to meet existing requirements.

    UNDER CONSIDERATION.

11. Allow the states to set secondary standards.

    REJECTION PROBABLE.

12. Allow the use of intermittent or supplementary control strategies in conjunction with control equipment technology to achieve standard compliance in appropriate circumstances.

    NOT DONE.

13. Restrict the application of the PSD permit approval program to only those facilities which might affect mandatory Class I

areas and the remaining portions of the country where the air is currently cleaner than the NAAQS.

INITIATED IN PART.

14. Include a method to obviate the need for offsets and substitute the requirement for LAER and BACT.

NOT DONE.

- Provide a comprehensive package of financial incentives, including expanded use of the Internal Revenue Code, to encourage the voluntary retirement and replacement of environmentally inefficient industrial facilities.

NOT DONE.

## Water Quality: Administrative Options

- Focus national resources selectively on critical problem areas where municipal, industrial and non-point sources adversely affect water quality.

INITIATED.

- Review and revise immediately rules, regulations, program requirements, policy memoranda, and guidelines of the water quality office.

NOT DONE FULLY.

- Issue ocean discharge permits under the variance provided in the 1977 amendment; reassess the mandate to stop ocean disposal of residuals.

PARTIALLY DONE.

- Require EPA staff to set reasonable deadlines of respondents and to respond promptly to all filings at the Agency.

NOT DONE.

- Advise citizens of the cost of any project to be funded through a federal construction grant.

REJECTION EXPECTED.

- Publish cost estimates of each rule, regulation, and guideline promulgated by the EPA.

INITIATED IN PART.

- Request states to identify the issues they would like resolved and establish priorities among these issues.

INITIATED.

- Revise Best Available Technology (BAT) guidelines to represent the capability of an average plant operating technology, which is shown to be continuously operable under the conditions for which it would be prescribed, and revise Best Practicable Technology (BPT) to be the technology generally in use.

NOT DONE.

- Accelerate construction of municipal wastewater treatment plants and reduce costs by removing steps I and II from construction grant eligibility and by making each state solely responsible for review and approval.

NOT DONE.

- Initiate plans for an in-depth review of Section 208 and Section 303 planning as a basis for recommending possible legislative change.

NOT DONE.

- Establish an independent forum of scientists to recommend scientific methods for defining when and if substances should be designated hazardous, toxic, carcinogenic, or otherwise classified.

NOT DONE.

- Require that all guidance and requirements be cleared through a policy coordinating committee to ensure continuity between the program and the evaluation of its impact.

PARTIALLY ACCOMPLISHED.

- Require an independent scientific review of the validity of water "models" utilized in the absence of adequate monitoring data.

NOT DONE.

## Water Quality: Legislative Options

- Establish a total environmental management concept to prevent narrowly focused regulatory initiatives and misconceptions.

INITIATED.

- Transfer the responsibility, personnel and funding for collecting and evaluating data on water quality, air quality and health to the other federal agencies which have demonstrated long-term competency in these areas.

NOT DONE.

- Revise the toxic pollution section (Sec. 307) to require a determination of risk/benefit in the adoption of standards.

NOT DONE.

261

- Re-establish the goals of the Act to be consistent with the earlier legislation that protected designated water uses.
  NOT DONE.

- Emphasize the present law's requirement of considering use and value in the adoption of water quality standards and delete the present goal of "fishable/swimmable, wherever attainable."
  NOT DONE.

- Clarify that new legislation need not be introduced to protect ground-water.
  NOT DONE.

- Establish funding for municipal construction grants at a predictable, uniform rate with a practical time period for completion of the program.
  PARTLY COMPLETED.

- Adopt scientifically credible standards for the principal objective of environmental legislation (the protection of human health) and transfer responsibility for development and interpretation of data to NIH.
  NOT DONE.

## Solid Waste: Administrative Options

- Retain a hazardous waste system, expanding it to include a classification of wastes according to degree of hazard, requiring that such a program deal with testing of truly hazardous wastes, notification of their existence, and tracking their whereabouts until final disposal.
  PARTIALLY ACCOMPLISHED.

- Dispose of a number of significant issues currently in litigation which remain unresolved.
  NEGOTIATIONS IN PROGRESS.

- Consider seriously abandoning design standards in favor of flexible performance standards which can reflect existing technology, enabling the EPA to determine the effectiveness of the standards before imposing huge costs without any proven results.
  INITIATED.

- Ensure that the public is aware of environmental situations which are likely to have a serious adverse effect on their health through a policy of factual public relations with sufficient distribution. Avoid publicity campaigns coordinated with litigation or investigations.

IN PROCESS.

- Direct efforts to ensure that waste generators are aware of the laws and regulations applicable to their activities by communicating directly to the party involved and by attempting to achieve solutions without litigation where technical violations of regulations occur through misunderstanding or ignorance.

INITIATED.

- Consider disposal site conditions when applying methods to determine whether a waste is or may be hazardous.

NOT DONE.

- Revise the existing "extraction procedure" for measuring the toxicity of wastes, which fails to assess the characteristics of various types of wastes.

NOT DONE.

- Initiate a concerted siting program at the state level at the earliest opportunity to reduce the pressure on existing sites and the temptation to dispose of such wastes improperly in their absence.

INITIATED.

## Toxic Substances: Administrative Options

- Set priorities and develop a simplified procedure to implement the Toxic Substances Control Act (TOSCA) and establish regulatory priorites.

INITIATED.

- Establish an outside study to assist administrative and organizational aspects for streamlining operations in the Office of Pesticides & Toxic Substances.

INITIATED.

- Administer a single set of regulations since TOSCA interrelates, but cannot pre-empt, the air, water, and solid waste regulations.

NOT COMPLETED.

- Add a small business advocate to the EPA's Office of Industry Assistance.

NOT DONE.

- Establish an independent (non-governmental) team of scientists

who will review contested decisions for their scientific merit—both on a regulatory and enforcement basis.
INITIATED.

- Consider determining substantial and unreasonable risk based on actual data from comprehensive studies.
INITIATED.

- Retain Pre-manufacture Notification (PMN) as an early notification procedure and base notification of high risk on the volume of material, type of exposure, non-litigatory solutions.
NOT DONE.

- Encourage a strict interpretation of Section 14(a) of the statute to eliminate confidentiality problems.
NOT DONE.

- Limit testing only to those chemicals which significantly call for testing to insure proper risk determination.
NOT COMPLETED.

- Develop international coordination of toxic substance laws.
NOT DONE.

- Revise present reporting and record-keeping proposals, which are not cost-effective for either the EPA or industry.
NOT DONE.

- Review the EPA's continued attempts to propose broad and vague reporting rules.
INITIATED.

### Toxic Substances: Legislative Options

- Review TOSCA for its cost and effectiveness.
INITIATED.

- Commission a scientific advisory group of non-federal experts to review contested data and regulations for scientific accuracy and interpetation.
NOT DONE.

- Initiate a serious inspection of the management and structure of the system which includes a review of data requirements to distinguish between real value and cost, and a review of the actual handling and use of data.
INITIATED.

264

- Evaluate industry costs of providing data and government costs of handling data.

  INITIATED.

- Review TOSCA and all of the other environmental laws for possible combination into one comprehensive environmental statute.

  NOT DONE.

### Pesticides: Administrative Options

- Recommence the registration process mandated by the 1978 Amendments.

  NOT DONE.

- Review carefully the problems of acquisition and review of validated safety and health test data and scientific judgment in evaluating data.

  NOT DONE.

### Radiation: Administrative Options

- Require the head of the Office of Radiation Programs (OPR) to be technically competent in radiation and skilled in management of radiation professionals.

  SEARCH FOR COMPETENT PERSON CONTINUES.

- Define the proper scope of radiation issues needing ORP actions (if any).

  NOT DONE.

- Define, support, and utilize the Radiation Policy Council operation within the EPA, or establish it as a separate Executive Department advisory committee.

  REJECTION EXPECTED.

- Establish priorities for EPA's radiation efforts that are underway and are still needed, or set aside such programs if they are not needed.

  NOT DONE.

- Develop an early study toward establishing a *de minimis* regulatory approach to radiation.

  INITIATED IN PART.

### Radiation: Legislative Options

- Examine the initial and subsequent EPA legislation (particularly the 1977 amendments to the CAA) to determine if radiation programs within the EPA should be strengthened, clarified, or eliminated, and initiate congressional review of the word "environment" to determine its scope and future action priorities.

  NOT DONE.

- Determine if EPA radiation programs that would continue are adequately funded and staffed, and if Congress should define required professional levels of staff training.

  NOT DONE.

- Consider combining the health functions within EPA with other health-related agencies in an overall "health" agency and the adoption of congressional and Executive Branch agreement to act upon the review recommendations.

  NOT DONE.

- Determine what measures are needed for regulatory action above the *de minimis* level.

  NOT DONE.

- Commission a federal study panel on public health perspectives.

  NOT DONE.

### Noise: Administrative Options

- Review new emission regulations for railroad facilities, buses, automobiles, motorcycles, low noise emission products, and the Interstate Rail Carrier regulation for cost-benefit effects and limit regulations to the statutory minimum where available health effects studies indicate no evidence of health problems.

  PROGRESS NOTED.

- Consider a major redirection of effort with respect to economic impacts of the noise program that the EPA has now adopted.

  NOT DONE.

- Support attitudinal survey data by direct evidence or omit from future budgetary and programmatic efforts.

  ACCOMPLISHED.

- Require all federal agencies which have regulatory authority over noise sources to meet regularly and pool research data toward defining a *de minimis* level of noise exposure.

  NOT DONE.

### Noise: Legislative Options

- Consider legislative revision that would reduce or eliminate the EPA noise control program.

  INITIATED.

- Provide states with the necessary technical assistance to evaluate, and where necessary to regulate, noise levels in the interim.

  NOT DONE.

### Research and Development: Administrative Options

- Replace appointees with people having technical and managerial background and experience in the field.

  VACANCIES REMAIN.

- Transfer research functions to, or involve other knowledgeable agencies in, projects including: atmospheric chemistry (ozone function), acid rain, groundwater contamination, hazardous waste detoxification, and relationship of levels of detectability and basis for standards to health and environmental protection.

  INITIATED IN PART.

- Define R&D projects with a view toward establishing long- and short-term priorities; and descriptions of the problem, impact, cost, value, anticipated use, and project resource and time requirements.

  INITIATED.

- Re-evaluate the role of R&D as it relates to the support of regulatory strategy.

  INITIATED IN PART.

- Separate the recognized requirements for supporting basic research on environmental and health sciences from the more pragmatic needs of regulatory program development.

  NOT DONE.

- Undertake an independent outside review of R&D requirements for each of the major research areas with an objective of clearly defining the role of research, both in the development of regulatory strategies and in evaluating the success of regulatory efforts.

  NOT DONE.

- Set up a "blue ribbon" group to determine the best way to administer R&D necessary for environmental improvement.

  NOT DONE.

- Determine feasibility and problems of putting air research under NOAA, water research under USGS, health and aquatic organism research under NIH.
  NOT DONE.

- Evaluate all aspects of the "new" research program proposed for the EPA to ascertain whether it can fit under another organization, leaving the EPA free to propose guidelines and set regulations, and be the federal enforcement authority.
  NOT DONE.

- Change to an impartial R&D philosophy which has no preconceived conclusions.
  NOT DONE FULLY.

- Develop risk/benefit/cost parameters and methodologies for all mandates and then publish for peer review. Rectify the misconceived policy of a need for zero discharge, zero emission, or zero risk in order to have a healthy and productive nation.
  NOT DONE.

- Review and, if necessary, revise existing regulations on the basis of the most sound scientific information available, and revoke regulations based on "quick and dirty" studies, predictive research, and/or inadequate data.
  INITIATED.

- Eliminate the federal control of land-use aspects from major environmental laws and return unconditionally to the states the discretionary authority for dealing with pollution at levels below those shown by good scientific research to be hazardous to public health or environment.
  NOT DONE.

- Encourage development of greatly improved and more effective pollutant control technology, especially in the field of toxics and toxic mixtures.
  NOT DONE.

- Encourage development of less expensive tools for monitoring or testing.
  INITIATED.

- Encourage the participation of independent and university labs in the fulfillment of the SAB's research "wish list."
  INITIATED.

- Support NIH and others in conducting in-depth epidemiological studies and other needed studies that assess the applicability of regulatory actions in protecting the public health and the environment.
INITIATED.

**Enforcement: Administrative Options**
- Construct a reasonable process to develop cases and decide referrals to the Department of Justice (DOJ) for the filing of judicial actions.
INITIATED.

- Establish a formal procedure for filing administrative complaints and the conducting of administrative adjudications prior to referral to the DOJ, basing referrals upon genuine risks to the public health and safety, and not upon policy decisions such as putting pressure on local officials.
NOT DONE.

- Conduct a joint EPA/DOJ review of all enforcement actions pending in the district courts to separate those actions which have been brought for various policy reasons from those which have been brought to protect direct threats to the public health and safety.
INITIATED.

- Consider placing a much lower priority on or dismissing those actions which were not brought for public health and safety reasons.
NOT DONE.

- Conduct a special review of pending and proposed enforcement actions to identify those in which a state enforcement action has been initiated or an Agency fault is discovered.
INITIATED.

- Develop an effective administrative mechanism for the consideration of variances.
NOT DONE.

- Create an administrative deferment through the exercise of prosecutorial discretion.
NOT DONE.

- Develop an administrative deferment program to protect the individual.
NOT DONE.

- Develop administrative guidelines to restrict the use and misuse of grants and planning and research funds.

  NOT DONE.

- Deny lower level EPA officials the power to withold funds on vital and needed projects in order to pressure local officials who have an honest dispute over regulatory requirements.

  NOT DONE FULLY.

- Prohibit any activity by EPA officials or contractors to attempt to pressure or otherwise influence local legislators.

  NOT DONE FULLY.

- Develop strict guidelines concerning requirements for accuracy and honesty in communications with local officials.

  NOT DONE FULLY.

- Generate administrative instructions directing EPA officials to narrowly construe their jurisidiction and eliminate the growing tendency of the Agency to expand its activities into areas clearly not intended by its authorizing statutes.

  NOT DONE FULLY.

- Stop utilizing enforcement pressures to induce cities and industries to agree to actions for which there are no legal requirements while "forgiving" other actions required by law or regulation.

  NOT DONE FULLY.

- Cooperate and coordinate enforcement activity with the states and curtail the federal review of state enforcement activity.

  INITIATED.

- Re-evaluate and revise existing EPA penalty policies to assure flexibility which would aid rather than impede settlement of pending litigation.

  INITIATED.

- Offer penalty policies and guidelines to states, but not as mandatory requirements which would trigger federal enforcement if the state elects not to use them.

  NOT DONE.

- Examine the existing memorandum of understanding between EPA and DOJ to reflect new policy direction and to cover all enforcement referral actions.

  NOT COMPLETED.

- Review and revise the consolidated permitting regulations to remedy procedural aspects which do not fully recognize the rights of the permitee.

UNDER CONSIDERATION IN NEGOTIATIONS.

- Adopt regulations which would change the context of EPA's regulatory efforts from focusing on technologies to focusing on end-results.

NOT DONE FULLY.

- Initiate modifications to allow flexibility and innovation in control strategies.

INITIATED.

- Initiate a special effort to test and expand concepts of self-regulation and consensus rulemaking.

INITIATED.

### Enforcement: Legislative Options

- Define the major environmental laws in greater detail as to what is expected from each of these laws to help guide not only the adoption of policies by the EPA but also its enforcement activities.

NOT DONE.

- Amend environmental laws to insert both economic feasibility and cost/benefit analysis as an implementing program to be developed by EPA in setting standards and in resolving enforcement actions.

NOT DONE.

- Require environmental laws to clearly authorize the adoption of variance programs by the EPA, especially when there is no immediate threat to the public health and safety that would require full implementation of the restrictions established by the laws and regulations.

NOT DONE.

- Require further detailing within the statute to clarify the exact use and limitations on use intended by Congress and require cost-effectiveness and cost-benefit considerations in all grant programs.

NOT DONE.

- Consider tying compliance with federal standards to the availability of federal funds to offset the cost of achieving such

271

standards. Prosecute publicly-owned dischargers when they present clear threats to the public health and safety.

NOT DONE FULLY.

- Restore in the environmental laws the concept of federalism.

  INITIATED.

- Eliminate various political considerations built into the laws, such as the special restrictions on clean areas imposed to stop the relocation of industry in an effort to protect the Northeast.

  INITIATED.

- Place the full burden of the program on the federal government when states refuse to assume the burdens established under the federal regulatory program.

  NOT DONE FULLY.

## International Activities: Administrative Options

- Cancel present "White House" policy development on export of hazardous materials.

  NOT DONE.

- Limit EPA concern for exports to legislative intent under TOSCA and the Federal Insecticide, Fungicide and Rodenticide Act (FIFRA), which is information only.

  NOT DONE.

- Refer to and rely on multi-national studies.

  NOT DONE.

- Develop new legislation or policy statements providing due process requirements in establishing multi-national agreements.

  NOT DONE.

- Require an Executive Branch review and a delineating policy statement to define the relationship betwen EPA and the State Department.

  NOT DONE.

- Encourage full public and industrial participation in developing international positions.

  INITIATED.

# Chapter Twenty-One
# ACTION, LEGAL SERVICES CORPORATION AND COMMUNITY SERVICES ADMINISTRATION
### By Stephen Markman

The Administration deserves great credit for its achievements during its first nine months in office with respect to the agencies discussed in this chapter. None of its victories, however, can yet be termed absolute. The Administration has proposed abolition of the Legal Services Corporation. It has abolished the Community Services Administration and transformed it into a block grant program. It is in the process of phasing out the VISTA program, the most abused of domestic ACTION programs. In this process, the Administration has made early inroads toward permanently undermining the influence of professional anti-poverty lobbyists.

While the aggregate budget of these agencies is relatively insignificant—it only recently exceeded $1 billion, well below one percent of the total federal budget—the impact of these expenditures has been multiplied many times over through the targeted funding of individuals and organizations possessing a common ideological agenda.

Rather than fulfilling their mandate of assisting poverty-stricken individuals with the mundane problems associated with indigency—inadequate legal services, lack of technical skills, lack of access to basic social services—these agencies have too often assumed a mission of social and political advocacy. Those intended as program beneficiaries were perceived, too frequently, as victims of a wrongly-structured society rather than as individuals in need of specific economic and social resources.

The Legal Services Corporation has indulged frequently in exercises of "clientless lawyering" in which class actions and new legal precedents are pursued at the expense of assisting the indigent client with his or her domestic, contract, or civil problems. Its attorneys have worked to overturn laws imposing limitations and obligations upon recipients of public welfare. They have participated in suits directed at establishing innovative claims of Indian rights. They have litigated new constitutional theories of the scope of capital punishment under the Eighth Amendment. They have argued creative claims of student rights, tenant rights, and minority rights. In their pioneering efforts in "rights-creation," the Corporation has been on the cutting edge of the litigation explosion that has burdened the courts, delayed the administration of justice, and undermined traditional notions of the limited role of the judiciary in resolving social problems.

273

The Community Services Administration, through funding a network of nearly one thousand local anti-poverty agencies (Community Action Agencies), has provided seed money for countless efforts at organizing welfare recipients, apartment tenants, food stamp beneficiaries, and other groups of indigent and semi-indigent community residents. In place of traditional programs designed to provide social counselling, job training, nutritional assistance, and welfare information to individual beneficiaries, local Community Action Agencies instead have funded lobbying efforts opposed to food stamp reform, national "strategies" directed at farmworkers and minority groups, "experiments" in community reform, and policies encouraging confrontation between the "haves" and "have-nots." The CSA's Community Development Program, designed to provide capital to local businesses employing the poor, simply has been involved in proselytizing policies.

Finally, ACTION, the agency housing an assortment of federal government volunteer programs, has provided funding and encouragement to a variety of local organizations conducting militantly political activities. Particularly through its Volunteers in Service to America program (VISTA), ACTION has given taxpayer funds to "volunteer" workers in partisan political campaigns. It has financed state and national legislative lobbying efforts. It has assisted in union organizing campaigns. It has aided local initiatives to secure tax reform, utility rate reform, and welfare reform. In place of traditional anti-poverty activities aimed at assisting the poor individual to develop skills and attitudes necessary to obtain an adequate income, VISTA has substituted the notion of social reorganization as a prerequisite to overcoming poverty. Much of this same ideology has dominated the policies of the Peace Corps, a semi-autonomous agency within the ACTION structure.

*Mandate for Leadership* recommended that the objective of a conservative administration (or indeed of any responsible administration) with respect to these agencies be more than a policy of simple economizing. While there is no question that the programs administered by these agencies have been subject to an unusual amount of waste and abuse, with grossly inadequate accounting and oversight procedures, this nevertheless is a secondary problem. Instead, *Mandate* recommended the elimination of public subsidies to individuals and organizations with a narrowly ideological view of the causes of, and the means for eradicating poverty.

The Administration clearly has demonstrated that it recognizes the need not only to save dollars, but also to transform the entire focus of the anti-poverty debate in this country. It has demonstrated this through its emphasis upon tax reductions and economic incentives as a means to generate economic wealth; private sector voluntarism

274

instead of public largesse as a means to provide basic services to the poor; and the explicit articulation of new principles and policies to underlie United States international anti-poverty and economic aid efforts.

The Administration has further recognized the need to do more than simply institute funding for conservative programs and beneficiaries in place of previous funding policies and priorities. Such a policy has a superficial appeal. This option would leave the present institutions in place for the time (which inevitably must come) when a non-conservative administration returns to power. Such a policy would implicitly sanction the politicization of these agencies and would deny conservatives the right to object if subsequent administrations reinstituted the policies of the Carter ACTION agencies. To its credit, the Administration has resisted adopting a number of policies that might be logically dictated by the short-sighted "Reagan Administration is the last administration we will have" view of public policy.

Instead, the Administration has proposed major institutional reforms with respect to each of these agencies. These reforms are designed to eliminate funds for political advocacy, re-orient the anti-poverty debate, and create new structures for channelling new kinds of assistance to the poor. While the ultimate legislative fate of these proposals remains uncertain, the Administration, in its first 300 days, has made remarkable progress in achieving some of the most important domestic policy recommendations of *Mandate*.

## Legal Services Corporation

The Reagan Administration did not seek reauthorization of funding for the Corporation in its FY 1982 budget. An original recommendation was made that the program be consolidated into a single, large social services block grant to the states. Individual Administration spokesmen have criticized the Corporation for its social activist policies and have suggested that the private bar, supplemented by state and local legal assistance programs, could adequately fill the void left by the abolition of the Corporation. They pointed out that an additional $50 million in sundry legal services programs remains available through other agencies of the federal government.

The ultimate fate of the Corporation remains highly uncertain. The massive reconciliation bill, which establishes new programs of block grants to the states, does not contain the legal services function, as recommended by the Administration. Both the House of Representatives and the Senate Labor and Human Resources Committee have approved legislation which would re-authorize the Corporation for at least two years, although at significantly different levels of funding. House-passed legislation would provide $241 million for the Corporation for FY 1982 and FY 1983, a significant reduction from FY 1981 funding of $321 million. In addition, it would establish a number of apparent limitations upon the litigative activities of the Corporation and its attorneys. The Senate committee-passed legislation contains none of these limitations (although they may be added on the floor), but would authorize only $100 million for each of the next three fiscal years.

The Administration has thus far stated its objections to retaining the Corporation at any level of funding. Proponents who have already rejected relatively sure funding of $100 million in the context of the omnibus budget resolution, are now gambling that the Administration will not veto any measure authorizing or appropriating funds for the LSC. If the Administration retains its apparent determination to refocus the delivery of legal services to the poor, a veto would appear to be a feasible option. Test votes in both the House and Senate (despite an absence of high level White House lobbying, particularly in the Senate) suggest that prospects are at least fair that any veto of the LSC could be sustained.

On balance, the Administration has done extremely well to date. Its most difficult task lies ahead. Any veto of Corporation funding will meet substantial opposition from the organized bar, bipartisan support for the Corporation in both Houses of Congress, maudlin media coverage, and claims that further abuse of the Corporation's mandate is unlikely because of new legislative restrictions upon its statutory authority. These restrictions are largely cosmetic and likely to be as effective as past "restrictions." To maintain the structure of the Corporation at any level of funding is to perpetuate the notion that there is some appropriate role for the federal government in the provision of legal services. Continuation also maintains a focal point for activity by an increasingly influential legal services lobby. The Administration should maintain its resolve.

### Community Services Administration

The Community Services Administration is the first major federal government agency since the Second World War to be totally abolished. In March, the Administration proposed that CSA activities be consolidated into a social services block grant to the states beginning in FY 1982. While House-Senate conferees on the budget reconciliation legislation refused to adopt this specific proposal, they did abolish the CSA and transfer most of its activities to a less comprehensive Community Services Block Grant (CSBG).

While the FY 1981 appropriation for the CSA was approximately $526 million (taking into account rescissions during the fiscal year), the new block grant will be funded at a significantly reduced level.

276

The continuing appropriations resolution provides $363 million for the program; the Administration's latest budget recommendations call for only $225 million in funding. It appears likely that final funding for FY 1982 will be in the vicinity of $300 million.

The Administration's efforts to eliminate the CSA greatly exceeded most of the recommendations made in *Mandate for Leadership*. Much of this credit should go to personnel placed in key policy positions by the Administration. The final CSA Director, Dwight Ink, played an important role as a low-key caretaker/administrator, attempting to ensure as efficient and non-controversial a phase-out as possible. He carefully avoided criticizing the agency and was clearly a major factor in averting any unusual public focus upon the dismantling of CSA. In addition, the presence of a number of committed "Reaganites" in leadership positions at CSA seems to have ensured that the effort to abolish the agency would be maintained on a direct and unwavering course.

It has been suggested that delays in the appointment of an Administrator contributed to the few transitional difficulties that developed, such as the confused efforts to assist in the relocation of CSA personnel. A federal court is currently considering whether the federal government is obliged to give priority to these individuals for a smaller number of new positions at the Department of Health and Human Services.

In addition, concern has been expressed that the final Community Services Block Grant program contains a number of restrictions upon the discretion of the states that mitigate somewhat the value of the new block grants. These restrictions include the requirement that current CSA grantees be entitled to 90 percent of the block grant allotment for FY 1982; the requirement for FY 1983 and beyond that 90 percent of the allotment go to political subdivisions of a state, or to non-profit community anti-poverty agencies; and the requirement that public hearings be conducted for FY 1983 and subsequent years on the "proposed use and distribution" of block grant funds. The latter requirement could provide a basis for litigation by disaffected anti-poverty agencies and their clients.

A number of other remnants of the CSA will operate for the foreseeable future. HUD has been invested with new authority to use certain funds for what were formerly CSA Community Development programs. A small Office of Community Services has been established within HHS to administer a new discretionary program consisting of nine percent of the annual allotment of CSBG funds. The statutory structure of the Community Action Agencies (one-third representatives of the poor, one-third local government, one-third representatives of community groups) also remains largely intact.

Of paramount importance is that CSBG funds are not likely to be employed as part of a practice to fund organizations possessing a common ideological agenda. The focus of the anti-poverty effort has been shifted from Washington to the states. The influence of the anti-poverty complex will be limited in the process, as their efforts must now be dispersed over fifty states. While the Administration should consolidate this victory, and eliminate any residual entitlement to public funds by CAAs, CSA's achievement to date is genuine and impressive.

## ACTION

Although the Administration has proposed a much less radical restructuring for ACTION than for either the Legal Services Corporation or the Community Services Administration, the effort to de-politicize funding is well underway. This is reflected primarily by the pending phase-out of the VISTA program and by the renewed emphasis within the agency upon genuine volunteer activities in contrast to paid "volunteer" activities.

While final congressional action has not been completed on the VISTA phase-out, proposed funding for FY 1982 has been reduced by more than one-half from FY 1981, with the objective of terminating the program by FY 1983. ACTION already has adopted new practices and procedures to strengthen prohibitions against political and organizing activities by VISTA volunteers under existing contracts, and has refused supplemental funding in every instance for National Grants Program recipients. In the process, the effective phase-out of VISTA may occur even before its scheduled FY 1983 demise.

Largely because of the reduction in spending for the much-abused VISTA program, the total ACTION budget (currently $153 million) is likely to be down in FY 1982 by as much as ten percent—apart from the recently proposed 12 percent across-the-board reduction in agency spending. Funding for VISTA for this period should be reduced from approximately $32 million to $16 million.

With the amputation of VISTA, ACTION is left with an assortment of volunteer agencies that (with the exception of the Peace Corps) have proved largely non-controversial. Particularly with respect to the volunteer programs for senior citizens administered by ACTION, praise has come from many conservatives in recent years. First Lady Nancy Reagan, for example, after exposure to the Foster Grandparent program remarked, "I've always felt that most programs benefit only one side. . . . But here was a program in which both sides benefitted." This and other Older American programs, such as the Senior Companion Program (providing opportunities for senior citizens to assist their incapacitated

278

contemporaries) and the Retired Senior Volunteer Program (matching senior volunteers with needy community organizations), will be maintained in their present form by the Administration, and are slated for modest increases in funding.

ACTION Director Thomas Pauken has demonstrated a particular commitment to enhance the genuine volunteer component of ACTION programs. A conscious decision has been made to move away from reliance upon federal employee-volunteers, who receive between $5,000 and $10,000 in salaries, to true community volunteers. In this respect, ACTION could represent the cutting edge of the Reagan Administration's proposed reliance on a "new spirit of volunteerism," a campaign reflected by the establishment of the Presidential Task Force on Private Sector Initiatives.

Director Pauken, even prior to the creation of the Presidential Task Force, repeatedly cited the need to spur "greater private voluntarism," and has apparently undertaken significant efforts to involve the philanthropic community much more deeply in areas of ACTION activity. This kind of effort, as well as other Administration initiatives to involve churches, families, volunteer organizations, and ethnic associations more deeply in the social welfare process could have important implications for the future evolution of the welfare system in this country.

Not all of the new ACTION initiatives are without cost. Concern has been expressed that a number of extremely small and currently non-controversial new programs could blossom into larger and more permanent programs. Among the present initiatives in varying stages of development at ACTION are the new Vietnam Veterans Leadership Program, a Literacy Initiative Program, and Young Volunteers in ACTION. While each has laudable objectives, control should be exercised to ensure that these initiatives do not develop into larger, less manageable, and more costly programs. Because the objectives of these programs are so widely supported, ACTION would be well-advised to ensure that it does not develop the kind of self-interested constituencies that so easily attach to public spending measures. The "sunsetting" of the Vietnam Veterans Leadership Program is a commendable step in this regard.

The major congressional controversy relating to ACTION during the early months of the Reagan Administration has involved the question of "separating" the Peace Corps from ACTION. While the Peace Corps was established as an independent agency in 1961, it was merged with ACTION through an Executive Order issued by President Nixon in 1971, following the creation of ACTION in that year. A subsequent reorganization by President Carter in 1979 granted the Peace Corps the somewhat confusing status of an "autonomous" agency within ACTION. At present, the Peace Corps is largely free of the direction of ACTION, although these agencies do share a number of administrative functions, such as recruiting and public affairs.

A congressional effort to establish the Peace Corps as a totally independent agency outside of ACTION will likely be approved this session. According to the congressional leader in this effort, Senator Alan Cranston (D-Cal.), "much of the impetus for the separation arose out of the nomination of an individual with a background in military intelligence to serve as Director of Action." Senator Cranston has expressed strong concern that the integrity of the Peace Corps and its volunteers will be compromised because of the intelligence work (a decade ago) by the new ACTION director. While the issue of ACTION/Peace Corps separation is not inherently ideological, it has been transformed into one by by Senator Cranston. Clearly Mr. Pauken's conservative politics, at least as much as his intelligence background, has generated much of the Senator's concerns about the scope of Mr. Pauken's administrative authority. A previous Deputy Director of the Peace Corps with a similar intelligence background served the agency with no apparent difficulties. Moreover, Senator Cranston was a firm opponent of the Peace Corps' "autonomy" during the 1978 debates on the issue.

Administration efforts to retain the present relationship between ACTION and the Peace Corps have been subject to some criticism. While the Administration has been explicit in its opposition to separation, this matter clearly has been a low priority. It has engaged in little serious congressional lobbying on the issue.

More important, confusing signals have come from the Administration. Reports persist that the new Director of the Peace Corps, Loret Ruppe, has tacitly (and occasionally not so tacitly) indicated her own agency's lack of opposition to separation. While Mrs. Ruppe has strongly denied these reports, many Members of Congress continue to labor under the view that the Administration is not of one mind on this issue. This perception may well be responsible for the imminent separation decision by Congress.

The Peace Corps remains a troublesome problem. No evidence has been offered to suggest the Peace Corps has moved in a direction contrary to that of the Administration generally. More to the point, there does not seem to be much clear direction to the agency. There has been no major organizational overhaul. Indeed, the Peace Corps can be criticized for maintaining far too many personnel holdovers from the previous Administration. There have been no major changes in policy direction or emphasis. Given the efforts of the previous ACTION director, Sam Brown, to transform the Peace Corps into a distinctly ideological vehicle, this inaction is not reassuring.

Director Ruppe has made a sincere effort to develop enthusiasm

280

for the Peace Corps among the Reagan constituency—describing it, for example, as a "person to person, pull-them-by-the-bootstraps type of program." She has failed to develop support, in part, because of her lack of sensitivity to some important symbols of conservative philosophy. She has spoken, for example, of the "obligations" of the United States to the Third World in a way that indicates that the nations of the North have some imagined "obligation" to the nations of the South. She has failed to institute procedures for instructing volunteers about the "menace of communism" pursuant to the statutory charter of the agency. Her conferences tend to feature such speakers as Robert Mugabe, Cardinal Kim and Senator Paul Tsongas (the latter was particularly vocal in his opposition to the nomination of Thomas Pauken as ACTION director). The Peace Corps continues to work under tha auspices of the United Nations Development Fund to send volunteers to the People's Republic of China.

Perhaps none of these actions is of conclusive significance. Each does, however, communicate the notion that it is business as usual at the Peace Corps, an agency whose style and rhetoric have never been those of conservatives.

The Peace Corps cannot be criticized for any affirmative undertaking by Director Ruppe that has gone awry; rather, it can be criticized because she has failed to seize the opportunity to transform the Peace Corps into a program of more permanent value. The new leadership at the Peace Corps has not been inclined to ask difficult questions about the mythology that has grown around the agency, nor has it explored hard-headed means of assessing the actual contributions of the Peace Corps over its two decades of existence. The easy rhetoric of the Peace Corps as an "investment in world peace" continues without pause or much apparent introspection. It would be tragic if the Administration lost its opportunity to revitalize this agency by reviewing its past achievements and its past failures with an eye toward re-articulating its benefits for the U.S. taxpayer, and the foreign policy interest of this country.

The Administration has proposed to reduce the FY 1982 budget for the Peace Corps by approximately $8 million, down from a FY 1981 budget of approximately $104 million. As a result, the Peace Corps already has had to eliminate operations in countries such as South Korea, Colombia, Nicaragua, and the Ivory Coast. As Director Ruppe promised, the greatest impact of the reductions was felt by the administrative operations of the agency in Washington.

# RECOMMENDATIONS
(Action taken on 29 out of 35)

## VISTA

- Implement congressional restrictions placed upon political and organizing activities by VISTA volunteers.

  ACCOMPLISHED.

- Eliminate the national grants program within VISTA. Alternatively, VISTA should redirect such funding away from political activist recipients.

  ACCOMPLISHED. VISTA IS BEING PHASED OUT TOTALLY.

- Strengthen the Inspector General's office, and establish procedures to ensure the implementation of the recommendations of the Inspector General.

  NOT ACCOMPLISHED.

- Redirect the emphasis in VISTA volunteers from generalists to specialists, and avoid using VISTA volunteers in administrative and supervisory positions.

  VISTA IS BEING PHASED OUT TOTALLY.

- Establish referral procedures within ACTION to ensure that senior citizen volunteers who cannot be placed within ACTION are placed in other volunteer programs.

  IN PROGRESS.

- Encourage the use of joint sponsorship agreements where several projects are administered by a single sponsor.

  ACCOMPLISHED.

- Maintain the Older Americans Program as a small and non-political program.

  ACCOMPLISHED.

- Restructure VISTA to ensure that it provides a well-trained and well-equipped corps of skilled workers to assist low income groups.

  VISTA IS BEING PHASED OUT TOTALLY.

- Restructure VISTA substantially or subject to significant reductions in funding.

  FUNDING CUT BY ONE-HALF. TERMINATION SCHEDULED IN FY 1983.

### Peace Corps

- Maintain the Peace Corps within the administrative framework of ACTION.

  SUPPORTED BY ADMINISTRATION. CONGRESSIONAL ACTION PENDING.

- Redirect the Peace Corps toward objective of providing well-trained professional and technical people for developing nations.

  NO MAJOR SHIFT.

- Ensure that the Peace Corps is non-political and non-ideological.

  NOT ACCOMPLISHED.

### Legal Services Corporation

- Repeal the Act authorizing the Legal Services Corporation.

  SUPPORTED BY ADMINISTRATION; CONGRESSIONAL ACTION PENDING.

- Eliminate funding for the Legal Services Corporation. Alternatively, limit such funding to provide individual client representation, not broad class actions aimed at changing public policy.

  PROPOSED BY ADMINISTRATION. CONGRESSIONAL ACTION PENDING.

### Community Services Administration

- Limit lobbying of Congress and state legislatures by grant recipients.

  ACCOMPLISHED.

- Increase the size and strengthen the effectiveness of the Inspector General's office.

  ACCOMPLISHED THROUGH HHS.

- Give CSA Project Review Board final authority to terminate grants, consistent with applicable law.

  ACCOMPLISHED THROUGH ABOLITION.

- Redirect the policy emphasis of the CSA by placing in leadership positions individuals favorably disposed toward Administration policies.

  ACCOMPLISHED.

- De-politicize the CSA and weaken the influence of the professional anti-poverty lobbyists.

  ACCOMPLISHED THROUGH ABOLITION.

- Provide the CSA with greater flexibility to shift grant monies from advocacy-oriented grantees to service-oriented grantees through changes in the Community Services Act.

  ACCOMPLISHED THROUGH BLOCK GRANTS.

- Restructure the Community Action Agency's Boards of Directors by eliminating the present legislatively mandated method of representation.

  SUPPORTED BY ADMINISTRATION. PARTIALLY ACCOMPLISHED THROUGH BLOCK GRANTS.

- Amend present requirement in the law mandating an administrative hearing before re-funding can be denied.

  ACCOMPLISHED THROUGH BLOCK GRANTS.

- Establish new means of spending oversight for CAAs, as well as new sanctions for CAAs which have spent significant amounts of funds in an unauthorized manner. An incentive system should be established that would reward those CAAs conducting themselves in the most fiscally responsible manner.

  ACCOMPLISHED THROUGH BLOCK GRANTS.

- Strengthen the ability of state governors to veto grants directed toward their states.

  ACCOMPLISHED THROUGH BLOCK GRANTS.

- Abolish the Community Food and Nutrition Program. Alternatively, direct its activities toward genuine anti-hunger activities, rather than political advocacy.

  ACCOMPLISHED THROUGH BLOCK GRANTS.

- Redirect the focus of Community Development Corporations from funding larger business ventures to assisting in the training of employees for smaller, local businesses. Explore demonstration projects where CSA funds are used to provide inducements to businesses to relocate in targeted areas. Consolidate all major economic development activities within CSA within the Office of Economic Development, including those promoted by the Community Action Agencies.

  TRANSFERRED TO HUD DISCRETIONARY FUNDS.

- Maintain the Senior Opportunities and Services Program at its present level of funding.

  INCLUDED IN BLOCK GRANTS.

- Maintain the National Youth Sports Program at its present level of funding.

TRANSFERRED TO HHS DISCRETIONARY FUNDS.

- Abolish administratively the State Economic Opportunity Program, unless there is a major transfer of program funding, control, and administration to the states.

  ACCOMPLISHED THROUGH BLOCK GRANTS.

- Reduce levels of funding for CSA Research and Demonstration Programs. Place particular emphasis, however, on programs designed to devise technological solutions to the problems of the handicapped.

  ACCOMPLISHED THROUGH BLOCK GRANTS.

- Maintain reduced levels of funding for CSA Training and Technical Assistance Programs, unless evidence is shown that they are effective.

  ACCOMPLISHED THROUGH BLOCK GRANTS.

- Enact a two percent reduction in the total budget for FY 1981 of the Community Services Administration. Enact a five percent reduction for FY 1982.

  ACCOMPLISHED AND EXCEEDED BY A SUBSTANTIAL MARGIN.

- Scrutinize such programs as the Community Food and Nutrition Program, the Economic Development Program, and the State Economic Opportunity Offices, if selective reductions of programs are made within CSA.

  ACCOMPLISHED AND EXCEEDED BY A SUBSTANTIAL MARGIN.

- Avoid false economies in the reduction of CSA administration and oversight activities.

  ACCOMPLISHED THROUGH BLOCK GRANTS.

# Chapter Twenty-Two
# THE NATIONAL ENDOWMENTS FOR THE ARTS AND THE HUMANITIES
### By Michael S. Joyce and Samuel Lipman

The Reagan Administration has not publicly announced policy for the National Endowments for the Arts and the Humanities. The President has named, and the Senate has confirmed, Francis S.M. Hodsell as chairman of the NEA. William J. Bennett awaits Senate confirmation as chairman of the NEH. Because of undue delays in the nomination of Endowment chairmen, the emergence of a new Administration policy is unclear. It is therefore impossible at this time to make a concrete examination of the Endowments' actions over the past year in terms of *Mandate for Leadership* recommendations.

The Administration has indicated its attitude toward the federal role in the arts and the humanities, despite delays in the appointments process. Immediately after the election, transition teams for both agencies were appointed. While the teams were of different composition, the Arts team seemed establishment-oriented, while the Humanities group seemed ideological in focus. The fate of both unpublished reports was the same: once filed, they were forgotten.

Little action was forthcoming until May 1981, when the President appointed a Task Force to study the problems of funding the arts and the humanities. Its members were a distinguished group of private citizens, among them a selection of American arts patrons, philanthropists, foundation executives, and cultural and academic administrators. Also on the task force were a few celebrities, and a smattering of intellectuals and artists. The group met in various sessions across the country during the summer of 1981, assisted by a staff drawn, in many cases, from cultural and educational administration, and on loan from the Endowments themselves. The Task Force report has now been filed, and in fact constitutes the first serious statement of a possible Administration philosophy (if not yet a policy) in the cultural field. As such it deserves close scrutiny.

The original charge from the President envisioned a study of the funding of the arts and the humanities in the United States, rather than a specific study of the basic goals and cultural policies of the Endowments. The main burden of the Report, therefore, is financial. Because the Administration emphasizes voluntarism in philanthropy, the Report is also more concerned with conditions of giving in the private sector than with the operations of the two federal agencies.

The Report comes to important conclusions about the past and present functions of the Endowments. The Report states, "Basically, the National Endowments are sound and should remain as originally conceived." It then concludes, "It is the consensus of the Task Force that the Endowments have functioned well in their present structure." The Task Force reaffirms the present professional panel review process, and implies its acceptance of past and present methods of affirmative social and geographical selection for choosing panel members.

The Report does make a new recommendation for altering the present policy-formation process at the Endowments. It suggests a transformation of the Federal Council on the Arts and the Humanities, from its present relatively unimportant status as a coordinating body of government officials, to a mixed private-public group with a private citizen as chairman. This revitalized body would help develop policy and mechanisms for federal support, increased private contributions, and improved federal, state, and local coordination.

Outside the specific area of the Endowments, the Report recommends the creation of a program of Presidential Fellows, composed of young "artists and humanists" to be assisted in the early stages of their careers. The Report suggests no numbers for either the size of the program or its cost. The implied significance of this recommendation is the demonstration of presidential leadership in culture. Such leadership is a major goal of the Task Force.

Because the details of the Presidential Fellowship Program are not spelled out in the Report, any discussion of the proposal must treat it as a part of the general entreaty for presidential leadership in funding culture. As an abstract principle, this concept is difficult to challenge; under favorable circumstances, it might lead to benign results. It does not square with the Task Force's evident desire to reduce the role of the federal government in the arts and humanities, a goal espoused by the Reagan Administration itself. Presidential leadership in this area might not seem quite so desirable in the hands of another President. Similar questions are raised by the evident plans of the present Administration to use celebrities as standard-bearers for culture. In politics, after all, one must not count on institutions retiring along with their inventors.

Other substantive proposals in the Report are financial, suggesting the use of government tax policy to encourage larger and more frequent private contributions to the arts and the humanities. The Task Force recommends increasing the tax advantage from donations of works by creators; providing limited tax credits for individual and corporate contributions; increasing the length of the charitable contribution carryover; improving the treatment of donative sales, and treating the contributions of appreciated property in the same manner as cash gifts to a private foundation.

The final section of the Report suggests subjects for later discussion by the reconstituted Federal Council on the Arts and the

Humanities. The most significant of these calls for the development of ways to use federal money to encourage private donations through the use of matching grants with a larger ratio of private to public funds. The Report states that some on the Task Force suggested that this Challenge Grant concept be extented from its present use (for capital and endowment projects) to cover program funding as well.

Any consideration of the work of the Task Force from the standpoint of *Mandate for Leadership* cannot fail to note the Report's blanket endorsement of both Endowments as currently constituted. Although the Report states that "Task Force members and staff solicited comment on the issues posed by the President from individuals and organizations in both the public and private sectors concerned with the arts and the humanities," the Report provides little evidence that the basic purposes and nature of the Endowments were either considered or challenged. While the Report disclaims any responsibility for examining "programs and personnel of the Endowment," the Task Force's words have been widely interpreted by the press and in less public comment by the present Endowment leaders as a vindication of current policies.

Despite this verdict, the issues raised by *Mandate for Leadership* remain, and deserve discussion. The problems of politicization, the use of programs to achieve social goals, and the treatment of serious culture as entertainment remain, despite recent budget cuts. Because these policies are entrenched both in precedent and in Civil Service personnel who advocate them, any change will require serious public examination. This examination has not yet been attempted.

The transformation of the Federal Council from a governmental to a mixed body seems relevant only from a fundraising standpoint. The purpose of fundraising itself becomes troublesome in the absence of a determined policy. Goals must be established before fundraising mechanisms can be decided. Artists, patrons, administrators, academics, corporation executives, bureaucrats, and politicians will clamor to set these goals. Assuming a consensus where none exists will not obviate the need for deciding the nature of the governmental cultural enterprise and the proper means for its support.

Many of the tax proposals made by the Task Force, insofar as they encourage private contributions made on the basis of private decisions, are laudable. The potential loss of tax revenue (especially since these changes would apply to charitable contributions in general) at a time of persistent budget deficits is worthy of an examination not attemped in the Report.

*Mandate for Leadership* recommended that "the present exploitation of the device of matching grants as a means of directing private funds to the accomplishment of government goals must be ended." The Task Force suggested increasing the use of the matching principle, a particularly disquieting development. This reliance on coordination of governmental and private decison-making is a prime example of the concept of partnership, which is urged by those concerned with the funding of social programs. It is not a concept which should be accepted without discussion. Although superficially attractive, this invocation of cooperation links essentially different governmental and private functions. Actions such as these inherently involve government coercion, a clear threat to the sovereignty of the individual. Liberty depends on private individuals making private decisions. The use of government funds to influence the spending of private money constrains private decisons. A reliance on the governmental *imprimatur* for the arts, by establishing *de facto* governmental standards of taste, results in an erosion of private responsibility. In addition, because the amount of private funds is limited, those applicants who have been rejected for government matching grants will likely be deprived of equal access to private funding.

The Task Force Report does not focus on the fact that the support of the arts and the humanities, no less than any other decision facing government, needs fundamental reconsideration. A general review of this issue must not be based on commissioned studies with largely preordained results, nor have as its result the initiation of the most convenient and customary short-term actions. New policies must be developed which are based upon the consideration of diverse viewpoints and a wide range of alternatives. The Task Force Report should not be allowed to foreclose discussion of the very real problems involved in governmental support of culture. The Administration should reject the concept that only the government can adequately lead to funding of the arts and humanities and look closely at the recommendations in *Mandate for Leadership* and other documents urging a return to true private support of culture.

# Chapter Twenty-Three
# REGULATORY REFORM
### By James E. Hinish, Jr.

President Reagan has initiated an impressive regulatory reform program. It may be less than fully successful because too few individuals committed to deregulation are being appointed to key positions and because, in congressional battles, the Administration is opposing wholesale reform if it in any way limits the powers of the Executive Branch.

This process began quite impressively. Immediately upon taking office, the President issued a memorandum to the heads of executive departments and agencies, imposing a strict freeze upon the hiring of federal civilian employees. On January 21, 1981, he issued an Executive Order creating the Presidential Task Force on Regulatory Relief under the chairmanship of the Vice President, with responsibility for implementing the Administration's regulatory reform program. Members of the task force are the Chairman of the Council of Economic Advisors (Murray Weidenbaum, himself an expert on regulatory issues), the Attorney General (William French Smith), the Secretaries of the Departments of the Treasury (Donald Regan), Labor (Raymond Donovan), and Commerce (Malcolm Baldrige), the Director of the Office of Management and Budget (David Stockman), and Vice President George Bush. The President named James C. Miller III, a prominent conservative economist, as executive director of the task force. Upon his appointment as Chairman of the Federal Trade Commission, Miller was succeeded by Christopher C. DeMuth, lecturer in public policy at the Kennedy School of Government and director of the Harvard Faculty project on regulation. He has written extensively on regulatory issues.

On January 28 and 29, 1981, President Reagan issued two Executive Orders: 1) eliminating federal controls on U.S. oil production as "a first step toward a balanced energy program" and 2) terminating the Council on Wage and Price Stability and its wage-price standards program which had been totally ineffective in controlling inflation. This latter action would save taxpayers about $1.5 million and relieve businessmen from the burden of submitting voluminous reports. The President also ordered on January 29 a freeze on all pending "midnight" regulations that had been rushed through during the closing days of the Carter Administration. Department heads were directed to delay for 60 days (until March 30) the effective dates of all federal rules not yet effective, and to refrain from issuing any final regulations unless they were mandated by court order, involved an emergency, or were essential for economic activity to go forward. By all of these actions taken early in his new Administration, President Reagan indicated his determination to carry out his campaign pledges and to make regulatory relief an important part of the Administration's economic recovery program.

On February 17, the President signed Executive Order 12291 setting forth the regulatory principles of his Administration. Under E.O. 12291, all executive agencies are mandated, to the extent permitted by law, to set regulatory priorities to maximize net benefits to society, to undertake regulatory action only when the benefits of a proposed rule outweigh its costs, and to select the cost-effective alternative among those considered to achieve the regulatory objective. The responsibility for carrying out these principles rests primarily with the Director of OMB, under the overall direction of Vice President Bush's Regulatory Relief Task Force.

Under the order, executive agencies must prepare a Regulatory Impact Analysis for each major rule, including 1) a statement of the need for and consequences of the proposed rule; 2) a description of the expected costs and benefits of the proposed rule, quantified to the extent possible; 3) a description of less costly alternative approaches to achieving the regulatory goal; 4) an explanation of the legal reasons why such alternatives should not be adopted; and 5) a determination that the proposed action is within the agency's statutory responsibility. All executive agencies must submit all proposed and final rules to OMB prior to publication in the *Federal Register*, unless prevented by statutory deadlines or court orders. This order affects only executive agencies. Independent agencies such as the Federal Trade Commission are exempt. If OMB determines that a rule does not adhere to the order's principles, the agency must respond to the Director's comments before publishing the rule. The OMB Director is authorized to 1) identify duplication, overlap and conflict in rules and make agencies rectify those problems; 2) develop procedures for estimating annual benefits and costs of regulation; 3) require a regulatory analysis of any "major" rule, i.e., one which would likely have an annual impact on the economy of $100 million or more, lead to a major increase in costs or prices, or have significant adverse effects on industry or the economy; 4) review and comment on the agencies' regulatory analyses; 5) determine which new and existing rules should be so analyzed and waive the analysis if he deems it appropriate; and 6) prepare recommendations for changes in the basic laws that authorize regulatory activity. Under the Paperwork Reduction Act of 1980 (P.L. 96-511), OMB also is responsible for reviewing and reducing federal paperwork burdens.

In addition to reviewing proposed rules, OMB and the Task Force have authority to designate existing rules for review. To this end, Vice President Bush sent out letters to the members of the business community soliciting advice in identifying regulations which they consider particularly burdensome. The response, through the Chamber of Commerce and other groups, was enthusiastic, and those regulations most often mentioned were targeted for review.

In the first four months of the review, OMB received from agencies 881 proposed and final regulations. Of these, 91 percent were judged to be consistent with the President's regulatory principles set forth in E.O. 12291; the remaining nine percent were returned to the agencies for review and modification. During the freeze ordered on January 29, OMB received 172 pending regulations which had been proposed in the final Carter days. Of these, 100 proposed rules were approved and put into effect at the end of the 60 day period; of the remaining 72, 35 were withdrawn and 37 were postponed pending further consideration. Some major examples: 1) the Secretary of Education withdrew the proposed bilingual education rules estimated to cost up to $1 billion over the first five years of the program, plus an annual maintenance cost of between $72 million and $157 million thereafter; 2) the Secretary of Transportation proposed a one-year delay of a regulation—thereby killing it—which would have mandated the installation of automatic seat belts and airbags, adding as much as $800 to the price of a new car; 3) the Secretary of Labor withdrew an Occupational Safety and Health Administration rule requiring labeling of certain chemicals, which would have cost between $643 and $900 million initially and between $338 and $473 million each year thereafter; 4) the Secretary of Energy announced the deferral, pending review, of national energy standards for major household appliances, which would have cost $500 million annually, resulted in sharply higher prices for consumers, and, according to the Department, would have driven most small appliance manufacturers into bankruptcy.

On March 25, Task Force Chairman Bush announced that the Administration was "indefinitely postponing" 36 of the 172 regulations already postponed and 27 other federal regulations already in effect were to be reviewed and possibly modified or eliminated. On August 12, OMB announced that another 30 regulations were targeted for review.

Federal departments and agencies have begun to undertake their own programs of regulatory relief under E.O. 12291. For instance, on March 14, Labor Secretary Donovan proposed cancellation of an OSHA rule requiring employers to pay "walk-around" funds to workers who accompany Occupational Safety and Health Administration inspectors on their visit to a workplace. He also postponed a revised rule on lead exposure and stopped efforts to terminate

Indiana's own OSHA program. Assistant Secretary of Labor Auchter indicated he plans to accomplish administratively many of the goals of the Reagan regulatory reform program by de-emphasizing standard-setting and emphasizing enhanced state-run OSHA programs, enforcement, voluntary compliance, labor-management inspection teams, consultation, and employee training.

On April 6, the Administration announced an automobile industry recovery package including a program to ease, delay, or eliminate 34 federal safety and environment regulations for cars and trucks. The proposed changes were estimated to save the troubled industry $9.3 billion over the next five years, or about $150 off the price of a car or truck. As part of this package, the National Highway Traffic Safety Administration initiated a series of regulatory actions including a one-year delay in requiring the installation of air bags and automatically closing seat belts in 1982 model full-size cars; a modification of crash standards for front and rear bumpers; rescission of rules regulating tinting of window glass and positioning of roof pillars; simplification of consumer information rules on tire quality; eliminating a requirement for interlock standards to prevent the ignition key from being removed while a vehicle is in motion and delaying proposed theft protection standards; and reconsideration for new rules on braking safety for vans, buses, and trucks. The Environmental Protection Agency's actions included the abolition of special emissions testing procedures for vehicles sold in high-altitude cities; relaxation of emission standards for carbon monoxide to the extent permitted by Congress, and changing measurement standards for hydrocarbon pollution; giving greater authority to manufacturers to check on their own compliance with vehicle pollution controls on new cars; reconsideration of proposed regulation of freon in vehicle air conditioners; easing carbon monoxide and hydrocarbon emission standards for 1984 model year heavy-duty trucks to eliminate the need for catalytic converters.

In his March 10 budget package, President Reagan made clear that he intended to cut back on the regulatory activities of executive agencies and departments. For instance, OMB reduced the Federal Trade Commission's FY 1982 budget from the $77.9 million proposed by the Carter Administration to $69.4 million, a reduction of 10.9 percent, which would eliminate 317 staff positions and close all FTC regional offices. Although the Administration, in the wake of consumer group protests, backed away from its earlier position in favor of eliminating the agency's anti-trust enforcement duties, OMB indicated that the proposed budget cuts would be "largely at the discretion of the agency rather than explicitly eliminating a given function." The agency got the message. Moreover, with the appointment of regulatory task force head James Miller as the new FTC chairman, it is unlikely that the Commission will be overzealous in its anti-trust mission.

Looking back on the first 100 days following issuance of E.O. 12291, OMB reported proudly that it had reviewed promptly more than 700 proposed regulations; the average regulation was reviewed in eight calendar days; the daily length of the *Federal Register* had declined 33 percent below the 1980 average; the volume of proposed rulemakings declined almost 50 percent; the federal paperwork burden was being substantially reduced; and a good working relationship had been established between agencies and OMB and the task force. The OMB staff report of June 13 concluded that "implementation of the President's program of regulatory relief appears to be off to a good start. ... Given the magnitude of the problems being addressed and the reversal of historic trends envisioned, one should be reasonably optimistic. ..."

Following is a statistical summary of OMB's review of agency regulations and paperwork under E.O. 12291 and a brief discussion of cost savings.

## OFFICE OF MANAGEMENT AND BUDGET
## OFFICE OF INFORMATION AND REGULATORY AFFAIRS

### Statistical Summary of Reviews of Regulation and Paperwork
through October 24, 1981

| Review of Regulations(*E.O. 12291*) | Year to Date |
|---|---|
| Regulations received for review: | 2336 |
| Reviews completed: | 2248 |
| Found consistent with E.O., no change | 2021 |
| Found consistent with E.O., minor change | 97 |
| Withdrawn by agency | 41 |
| Returned to agency | 69 |
| Exempt from E.O. | 20 |
| (Reviews extended and completed) | (110) |
| Reviews pending: | |
| Beginning of period | N/A |
| End of period | N/A |
| **Review of Paperwork** (P.L. 96-511) | |
| Clearance requests received for review: | 3490 |
| Reviews completed: | 3022 |
| Approved | 2459 |
| Not approved | 563 |
| Reviews pending: | |
| Beginning of period | N/A |
| End of period | N/A |

## SAVINGS FROM REGULATORY RELIEF

### Realized Savings
### (millions of dollars)

| Agency | Regulation | 1st Year or Annually Recurring | Investment (one-time) |
|---|---|---|---|
| Education | Nondiscrimination on the basis of national origin (bilingual education) | 72-157 | 900-2950 |
| EPA | Suspension of BCT Standards for secondary industries | N/A | 60 |
| | Deferred compliance date for electroplating | N/A | 20 |
| | Deferral of noise regulations | 150 | N/A |
| | Approval of Armco bubble | 15 | N/A |
| Labor | Walkaround compensation suspended | 5.3 | 0 |
| | Adverse effect wage rates suspended | .7 | 0 |
| | FLSA salary tests | 53.0 | 0 |
| Transportation | Passive restraint delay | — | 100 |
| | Fields of direct view | 25 | 174 |
| | Nondiscrimination on the basis of handicap | 139 | 2600 |
| | Total (millions of dollars) | 460 to 545 | 3854 to 5904 |

The Reagan Administration's assault on overregulation is a long-range and, for the most part, carefully targeted program. It is designed to lead to a more cautious, cost-conscious approach to government regulatory activity. Clearly, the Administration is intent on changing the federal government's basic method of regulating the economy, not on eliminating regulation altogether. Realizing that some of its favorite campaign targets (e.g., abolishing OSHA and EPA) might have to be abandoned, the White House nevertheless began its efforts early, while the Administration's economic program still enjoyed broad popular and congressional support. Working through a highly centralized operation at OMB, it has moved decisively, satisfied with the realization that the impact of its immediate actions might not be felt through the economy or in the society for months or even years. Whether the Reagan regulatory reforms will prove lasting or effective in the long run remains to be seen.

The Reagan program can be judged by standards proposed by one of its chief architects, Dr. Murray Weidenbaum, Chairman of the Council of Economic Advisors. In an article which he wrote for the American Enterprise Institute's *Regulation* magazine, prior to his appointment, he said:

296

When Ronald Reagan is sworn in as President on January 20, 1981, he will have the opportunity to embark on a new approach to government regulation that pursues two objectives simultaneously: (1) doing a better job of achieving regulatory goals, while (2) reducing regulatory burdens. Not only is it *possible* to have it both ways, it is high time! ... Acting obviously within available statutory discretion, the Reagan Administration should promptly use the appointment power to install reform-oriented leadership at the various regulatory agencies in order to establish at the outset a new tone and a new direction. The importance of this cannot be overstated. ... Those regulatory agencies that are deemed to be worthy of continuation must be managed by people who are sympathetic with the important social objectives to be achieved—and who are equally concerned with minimizing the costs and intrusions. ... The fundamental shortcomings of government regulation result more from statutory than from executive deficiencies. After all, every regulation is issued pursuant to an Act of Congress, and every regulator is paid from a congressional appropriation. There is an urgent need to change the fundamental regulatory statutes. Here are some of the proposals that could be introduced: (1) Statutes phasing out economic controls that interfere with market-place competition ... (2) Statutes revising social regulation that pursue unrealistic goals or apply unreasonable methods ... (3) Statutes mandating benefit-cost analysis and cost-effectiveness studies before new regulations are issued ... (4) Greater attention in the congressional budget process to the managing of regulation ... (5) A one-year moratorium on new regulations. ... Even before and even without the foregoing legislative initiatives, there is much the President can do through the administrative powers vested in him and his appointees to help bring about the same results. ...

Clearly, the Administration has used its administrative power effectively so far and has accomplished its objectives. The control and direction of the Administration's regulatory program has been centralized within OMB, and the regulatory analysis and review process has been undertaken, apparently with success, by all executive departments and agencies.

Not everything has proceeded as the President may have hoped. Even Republicans have grumbled that the Administration has been slow to take full advantage of its appointment power. At the conclusion of the most expensive transition period in American political history, very few appointees of the top 300 were in place and ready "to hit the ground running" as promised. As of March 20, President Reagan had nominated only 113 persons to fill the 246 top-level department positions. Of these only 41 had been approved by the Senate and were beginning their official duties. As a consequence of this irresponsible delay, most agency heads did not start long-range plans and programs aimed at regulatory reform until very late in the year. In some cases, these plans and programs are still not in place and Carter appointees have not been weeded out. Moreover, the Carter holdovers and liberal career bureaucrats have used this time to their own advantage. Some have gone to Capitol Hill to plead the case for beefing up their agency's mission and to speak out against the Reagan Administration's proposed cutbacks; others have settled back comfortably into the bureaucracy, attempting to influence or resist the efforts of inexperienced appointees and to co-opt agency programs whenever possible.

The most troublesome deficiency of the Administration's effort has been its failure to find and appoint genuine Reaganites to policy-making positions. A large number of talented and able presidential supporters are available and eager to serve in a conservative administration. Yet, only a few persons who worked for the President's election and are strong, loyal believers in his policies and programs have been chosen to fill important vacancies. In fact, so few major policy-making positions within the departments and agencies are now occupied by Reagan loyalists that there is a joke circulating around Washington that President Reagan is "the mole" in his own Administration. Part of the problem must lie with the White House personnel office which seems to have an unhealthy distrust of "ideologues." Whatever the reason, the results are clear. According to a recent article in *U.S. News and World Report*, of the top 400 positions in the Executive Branch, 37 percent are filled by persons who worked in the Nixon or Ford Administrations, 14 percent are veterans of the Reagan campaign, and 12 percent are Carter Administration holdovers. These agency appointees are not incompetent or unqualified for service, but many are ideological eunuchs who are not really committed to Reagan's philosophy or dedicated to the President's goals of reducing or rescinding regulation, where possible, and eliminating their own jobs, where necessary.

A few appointments are commendable. The Administration made an excellent choice in selecting as FCC chairman a communications expert, who has pursued a program of increased deregulation within statutory limits, while instituting management reforms and hiring like-minded staff. However, at the ICC, the Administration picked as agency head a lawyer backed by both the trucking industry and the unions who, in the opinion of many observers, seems intent on reinstituting a policy of re-regulation of the surface transportation industry, contrary to the direction taken by previous administrations and in the face of convincing evidence of the inflationary impact of trucking price and entry controls. The battle is on within the agencies themselves as to whether real deregulation can be accomplished now, next year, or at all.

In fairness, the Administration's goals cannot be accomplished solely by administrative action even if solid conservatives are appointed to commission vacancies. In order to be permanent and effective, regulatory reform will require congressional action. This should not pose an insurmountable problem. The Senate is in the control of the Republicans who hold a 53-46 (one independent) majority. Although a number of these Republican Senators are liberal, they are not unsympathetic to regulatory reform. The House remains Democrat-controlled, but as one Georgia Democratic Congressman observed: "This will be the most deregulatory Congress in the last 30 years." With greater cooperation between the White House and deregulation-minded Members of Congress, and a well-coordinated lobbying effort on the part of Administration officials, this prediction could well come true. The 97th Congress should be an oversight Congress, devoting more time to examining existing programs and agency activities than in passing new legislation designed to expand the federal government's spending and regulatory powers. Congress does understand the message of the voters last November, perhaps even better than does the new Administration. While the White House has failed to exercise its legislative power and has yet to send to Capitol Hill its own legislative package of regulatory reforms, Congress has been busy fashioning its own set of proposals.

A number of bills have been introduced this year in both Houses aimed at particular regulatory problems. Two principal initiatives are embodied in S.1080, the Regulatory Reform Act, introduced by Senator Paul Laxalt (R-Nevada), and S. 890, the Regulatory Reduction and Congressional Control Act, the legislative veto bill introduced by Senator Harrison Schmitt (R-New Mexico). Both bills have bipartisan support and companion measures in the House. Senate passage of the Laxalt bill, which would mandate a cost-benefit or regulatory analysis of independent as well as executive agencies, is expected this year. The more controversial legislative veto may be included as an amendment to S. 1080. Despite strong congressional and industry support for the Laxalt bill, the Administration remains ambivalent about this and most other general efforts at across-the-board deregulation.

The Senate Commerce Committee, under the leadership of Chairman Bob Packwood (R-Oregon), has been working on a series of bills aimed at easing regulation in the communications industry. While several reforms were included in the Budget Reconciliation Act (P.L. 97-35), the most significant accomplishment to date has been Senate passage of the Telecommunications Competition and Deregulation Act of 1981 (S.898). Again, the Administration's attitude toward these reforms has been at times obstructionist, at best ambivalent. Under prodding, the Administration belatedly endorsed the provisions of S. 898. Without more vigorous White House (and industry) lobbying, this landmark bill and other Republican deregulation measures face an uncertain future in the Democrat-controlled House. Unfortunately, regulatory reform has not received high priority, as the White House had devoted its resources to winning its budget and tax battles. Regulatory reform remains a fundamental part of the overall economic program, but despite the number of White House, departmental and agency personnel who are assigned to regulatory matters, the Administration seems unable to concentrate on more than one issue at a time.

The Administration's regulatory reform program seems to be directed by a centralized, efficient, and intelligent group with Cabinet-level authority, but in practice the planning and execution has not been especially well coordinated. Little consultation or cooperation has been offered to Members of Congress. The effort has involved at various times staffers of the Regulatory Relief Task Force, OMB, the Department of Justice, and others. For certain proposed procedural reforms, such as the legislative veto, the Bumpers Amendment, and regulatory analysis, this disjointed effort has had two consequences: first, the different voices speaking for the Administration made it unclear what position the White House really held on different matters; and second, the role of staff members who are also career professionals gave a "business-as-usual" touch to the Administration's performance. Then, too, the Administration's effort has been directed only at Executive Branch regulation. Executive Order 12291 applies only to executive departments and agencies; the OMB cannot enforce its will on independent commissions without legislative authority or the voluntary cooperation of agency heads. To affect the independent agencies, the Administration must seek the aid of Congress more vigorously. In the wake of the Supreme Court's ruling in the cotton dust standards case (in which it held that the health of workers is involved, under the Occupational Safety and Health Act, the government may not automatically apply a strict cost-benefit standard to strike down regulations it does not like), it is clear that if its regulatory reform program is to continue and be successful, the White House will now not only have to actively support omnibus regulatory reform legislation, but also will have to seek the aid of its Republican allies on Capitol Hill in securing legislative changes of underlying agency statutes.

The Administration's attitude toward legislative reforms has been one of indifference bordering on stubborn opposition. Many Administration staffers have acted as if reform should be the exclusive tool of the Executive Branch. Once it became clear that the Congress was bent on passing some form of regulatory reform legislation, the Administration appeared reluctant to support any measure which threatened Executive Branch prerogatives, even those reforms advocated by its closest congressional allies. Although the Administration paid initial lip service to reform legislation, it has continued to work to halt the progress of such legislation and has even attempted to induce business groups to pressure Hill leaders not to advance regulatory reform bills. Such efforts have been counterproductive, however, as Republicans and businessmen see the need to codify regulatory reforms for future administrations. As a result, legislation continues to advance, but the Administration has been relegated to the role of a reluctant participant in the process.

The Administration has never unreservedly endorsed either the Laxalt bill (S. 1080) or the Danielson bill (H.R. 746) nor has it worked for their speedy passage. During mark-up, Administration staffers have worked to protect Administration interests. As a consequence, it is now opposing proposals drafted by conservative Republicans, including the legislative veto initiatives. Accordingly, Administration spokesmen have expressed the view that administrative procedures have generally worked well and that the Administrative Procedures Act should be modified only slightly; they adamantly oppose more innovative reforms, such as the one-House legislative veto, and have let it be known that they would urge the President to veto any bill containing the legislative veto. Much of the Administration's posture can be considered the institutional self-interest of the Executive versus the Legislative Branch—not unlike the position taken by previous administrations.

It would be a serious mistake for the Administration or the Congress to fail to act on regulatory reform and deregulatory initiatives. The electorate who brought the Republicans to power, in part because of their commitment to regulatory relief, will be watching to see if this Administration and this Congress are sincere in carrying out their promises. The time is right for action. As the President himself observed, "If not us, who? If not now, when?"

## RECOMMENDATIONS
(Action taken on 18 out of 42)

### Personnel
- Reduce drastically the number of government-hired consultants. UNDERWAY.

- Act promptly to fill vacancies and find persons of high quality and friendly persuasion.

  NOT IMPLEMENTED.

- Ensure that the appointee shares the general philosophy and outlook of the President.

  NOT IMPLEMENTED.

- Extend the federal hiring freeze imposed by President Carter in 1980.

  IMPLEMENTED.

- Concentrate on making better appointments to agencies like the FTC and CPSC to improve their efficiency.

  NOT IMPLEMENTED.

- End the federal pay freeze for the sake of making regulatory reform a smoother enterprise and to alleviate the fears and misunderstandings of civil servants whose ideas and energies will be needed to make reform succeed.

  NOT IMPLEMENTED.

## Government Reorganization

- Support block grants and revenue sharing as a means of returning power to state and local government.

  PROPOSED BY ADMINISTRATION; PARTIALLY IMPLE-MENTED BY CONGRESS.

- Establish a Hoover-type commission to recommend ways to reorganize and reduce the Executive Branch.

  NOT IMPLEMENTED.

- Consolidate agencies to end waste and eliminate red tape.

  NOT IMPLEMENTED.

## Regulatory Review

- Support specific reforms, including regulatory analysis, changes in the Administrative Procedures Act, and sunset legislation.

  IMPLEMENTED IN PART THROUGH ADMINISTRATIVE RATHER THAN LEGISLATIVE ACTION.

- Reduce federal paperwork and make agencies justify forms.

  IMPLEMENTED THROUGH PAPERWORK REDUCTION ACT OF 1980.

- Establish a temporary moratorium on new regulations, consistent with health and safety.

  IMPLEMENTED.

- Strengthen existing consumer safeguards. Oppose new consumer protection bureaucracy and intervenor funding.

  IMPLEMENTED.

- Impose a temporary moratorium on new federal regulations except:

  1. those mandated by law;

  2. those required by health and safety considerations; and

  3. those required by emergency situations.

  IMPLEMENTED.

- Improve existing and future regulations by directive to all Executive Branch agencies:

  1. to review and simplify their procedures for developing regulations;

  2. to compile and review all existing rules with a view to scrapping those which are unnecessary, contradictory, or no longer effective; and

  3. to submit all proposed regulations to a regulatory analysis.

  IMPLEMENTED THROUGH E.O. 12291.

- Initiate a regulatory moratorium lasting from perhaps six to nine months, giving sufficient time to assemble a blue-ribbon, bipartisan panel of distinguished citizens to study and make recommendations on ways to improve the operation of government, regulatory programs that should be abolished, and the like.

  MORATORIUM IMPLEMENTED. PANEL NOT FORMED.

- Formulate an immediate and medium-term regulatory reform program, based upon that group's recommendations.

  NOT IMPLEMENTED. STALLED IN BUSH TASK FORCE.

- Choose targets of opportunity carefully. Do not attempt to tackle all regulatory ills at once.

  IMPLEMENTED FOR MOST PART.

- Concentrate on seeking relief for hard-pressed industries, on situations which have a serious impact on business and the economy, and which also have the greatest likelihood of immediate success.

NOT IMPLEMENTED.

### Regulatory Limits and Deregulation

- Establish a federal regulatory budget setting annual limits on costs of compliance with the regulatory requirements of every agency.

  NOT IMPLEMENTED.

- Improve the oversight of regulatory and spending programs. Coordinate activities within the Executive Branch under a single policy office.

  IMPLEMENTED THROUGH E.O. 12291.

- Require agencies to weigh the costs and benefits of all existing and proposed regulations.

  IMPLEMENTED.

- Request Congress to extend similar requirements to the independent regulatory commissions across the board.

  SUPPORT FOR CONGRESSIONAL EFFORTS IS ONLY LUKEWARM.

- Deregulate the energy, transportation and communications industries.

  IMPLEMENTED IN PART IN COMMUNICATIONS, CRUDE OIL AND REFINED PETROLEUM PRODUCTS; TRANSPORTATION DEREGULATION SLOWED.

- Implement deregulation where possible, although the Administration may have to settle for showcase reforms instead.

  IMPLEMENTED ONLY IN DECONTROL OF OIL.

- Take example from airline deregulation and encourage the deregulation of other forms of transportation and communications.

  ONLY LIMITED PROGRESS.

### Political Participation in Regulation

- Promote stronger political parties and full participation in electoral processes, but oppose postcard voter registration and taxpayer financing of federal campaigns.

  NOT IMPLEMENTED.

304

- Strengthen congressional oversight functions, in part through "sunset" and legislative veto procedures.

ADMINISTRATION HAS NO FORMAL POSITION ON "SUNSET" PROCEDURES, BUT OPPOSES ALL FORMS OF LEGISLATIVE VETO WHICH BYPASS PRESIDENTIAL ACTION.

- Consult with Members of Congress of both parties, particularly party leaders of both Houses and the powerful chairmen of the appropriations and standing committees which have jurisdiction over targeted agencies or programs.

NOT IMPLEMENTED.

- Make Democratic and Republican leaders of Congress feel part of the reform enterprise from its inception. Seek out potential supporters on Capitol Hill and keep them well informed of plans.

NOT IMPLEMENTED.

- Identify potential advocates (on the Hill) early to carry the ball for the White House.

NOT IMPLEMENTED.

- Do not shun potential opponents; neutralize their opposition, if possible, at an early stage. Make efforts to meet their major objections in a spirit of goodwill and cooperation.

NOT IMPLEMENTED.

- Involve trusted outsiders in the planning and execution of a regulatory reform program as part of overall strategy.

NOT IMPLEMENTED.

- Nourish bipartisan support among leaders of affected business and labor groups, local government, consumer organizations, and other such groups.

NOT IMPLEMENTED.

- Encourage congressional leaders to schedule hearings on the subject during which persuasive testimony can be taken from Administration spokesmen, from scholars and experts, from business, consumers, and ad hoc citizen groups formed merely to educate the public on the issue.

NOT IMPLEMENTED.

### Citizens and Small Business

- Support management-worker health and safety committees, curbs on OSHA and exemptions for small and safe employers.

NOT IMPLEMENTED.

305

- Exempt small business from all regulatory and paperwork requirements, except those mandated by statute. Where exception is not feasible, subject small business to a less onerous tier of regulation.

  IMPLEMENTED IN PART BY CARRYING OUT "REGULATORY FLEXIBILITY" ACT OF 1980.

- Require the federal government to provide restitution to individuals and small businesses who prevail in actions brought against an agency.

  IMPLEMENTED.

- Simplify the procedures for persons seeking court review of agency actions.

  NOT IMPLEMENTED. ADMINISTRATION NOT ACTIVELY SUPPORTING THIS MOVE.

- Improve citizen participation in the regulatory process by providing adequate notice and lengthen uniformly the comment period for public citizens and groups affected by the outcome of an agency proceeding.

  NOT IMPLEMENTED.

- Support state "right-to-work" laws.

  NOT IMPLEMENTED.

- Guarantee fairness to workers through full employment.

  THIS IS GOAL OF THE ECONOMIC PROGRAM.

# Chapter Twenty-Four
# THE CIVIL AERONAUTICS BOARD
### By James I. Campbell, Jr.

The Reagan Administration has generally moved along the lines recommended in *Mandate for Leadership* concerning the Civil Aeronautics Board. The most important recommendations were to propose legislation providing for early "sunset" of the Board; to include in the high ranking officials of the Department of Transportation at least one person knowledgeable in the field of aviation; and to develop a careful review of U.S. international aviation policy. The first two have been accomplished. While the CAB is scheduled to be abolished by January 1, 1985, under current law, the Senate Commerce Committee is working on draft legislation which would terminate CAB on April 1, 1983. A review of U.S. international aviation policy is underway. With respect to the fourth recommendation, the Administration might be criticized for not moving more quickly and for taking the apparent position that its final proposals will be embodied in ephemeral administrative regulations rather than sturdier Congressional statutes. In 1978, a long history of political abuses surrounding the award of international aviation certificates led Congress to curtail Presidential discretion in this area.

Most other recommendations in *Mandate* were variations of a central theme—that for reasons of politics and justice the government should continue to offer some assistance and protection to small purchasers of a service as essential as air transportation. As *Mandate* recommended, the Administration is currently reviewing the essential air service program; this review should not necessarily be expedited since the program is the responsibility of the Board until it is abolished. The Administration has also concluded that no residual regulation of high prices should be maintained in monopolistic, small town routes. *Mandate's* recommendation to the contrary was as much political prognostication (written prior to November 1980) as policy, and the resulting resolution in favor of laissez faire should not displease conservatives. Finally, *Mandate* suggested that the traditional prohibition of unjust discrimination by airlines should be retained, but as a private right of action instead of a regulatory prerogative. The Administration has opposed any restriction on unjust discrimination on the grounds that it, too, would be contrary to "true" deregulation, a judgment supported by the large airlines, but one which seems more questionable in the light of history and one which is running into more skepticism in Congress.

# RECOMMENDATIONS
(Action taken on 4 out of 9)

- Appoint at least one high-level official at DOT who is familiar with aviation issues.

  ACCOMPLISHED.

- Prepare, in early 1981, legislation to do the following:

  1. Advance the sunset date of the CAB to December 31, 1981.

     PROPOSED SUNSET OF APRIL 1, 1983.

  2. Authorize the Secretary of Transportation to prevent unreasonably high rates in monopolistic markets.

     OPPOSED BY ADMINISTRATION.

  3. Provide a private judicial remedy to prohibit unjust personal discrimination.

     OPPOSED BY ADMINISTRATION.

  4. Provide for competitive allocation of slots at congested airports.

     NO ACTION BY ADMINISTATION, BUT CAB IS BEGINNING TO CONSIDER.

  5. Continue air carrier minimal reporting requirements.

     INCLUDED IN PROPOSED LEGISLATION.

- Cut the Section 406 subsidy.

  EARLY ELIMINATION PROPOSED.

- Continue or increase the service subsidy to genuine small towns.

  UNDER CONSIDERATION BY DOT.

- Initiate an early re-examination of U.S. international aviation policy.

  IN PROCESS THROUGH DOT AND STATE DEPARTMENT.

# Chapter Twenty-Five
# COMMODITY FUTURES TRADING COM-MISSION
By Terrance J. Wear

The Reagan Administration's general inaction on the Commodity Futures Trading Commission can be traced to the lack of timely nominations from the White House. No attempt was made to designate an interim chairman from among incumbent CFTC commissioners, although the Republican Commission member easily could have been moved to the chair. This fact was communicated to the White House, but was not acted upon. The incumbent Democratic chairman continued to serve in this capacity until June 8, 1981, at which time a Republican candidate was sworn into office. No known circumstances excuse this inaction.

Serious delays occurred in the nomination of candidates to fill other Commission vacancies. The first nomination was not made until May 1981, but was delayed because of unanticipated clearance delays and other priorities within the White House. Since May 1981, the Administration has had the opportunity to make two additional appointments to the Commission. These nominations were delayed because the White House and Senate could not agree on the requisite qualifications of nominees. One new commissioner was finally nominated on September 8, 1981, and was confirmed by the Senate on October 27, 1981. A third commissioner resigned effective August 31, 1981. Although no placement has yet been nominated, the appointment is expected to be filled by January 1982.

The new CFTC chairman and his staff have done well in taking the lead in the congressional reauthorization process scheduled to begin in early 1982. The Administration, however, does not appear to have established clear goals for the Agency nor has it developed the means to accomplish these goals. Neither this Administration nor its predecessor appears to have given any thought to the nature, purpose, or goals of the CFTC. The role and direction of the CFTC should be considered carefully in the years ahead.

## RECOMMENDATIONS
(Action taken on 1 out of 3)

- Designate a new chairman as soon as possible after January 20, 1981.

NO NOMINEE UNTIL MAY.

- Nominate a candidate to fill the Commission vacancy existent on January 20, 1981, without delay.

  SERIOUS DELAYS IN APPOINTMENTS.

- Prepare for a leadership role in the congressional reauthorization process which will begin early in 1982.

  GOOD JOB SO FAR.

## Chapter Twenty-Six
# THE CONSUMER PRODUCT SAFETY COMMISSION
### By Anthony J. Coppolino

The Consumer Product Safety Commission was the first regulatory agency due for reauthorization after the Reagan Administration took office. This gave the new Administration a good opportunity to implement the primary recommendation made in *Mandate for Leadership*: abolish the CPSC entirely.

The Administration briefly advocated abolishing the CPSC but never pursued the idea in earnest. The Senate Commerce Subcommittee on Consumer Affairs held a series of hearings on the CPSC reauthorization early in the year. This would have been an ideal time and place for the Administration to propose abolishing the agency. Indeed, the subcommittee sought the Administration's position on the matter. An OMB official, James C. Miller III, testified at the hearings but did not indicate that the Administration favored abolishing the agency. Only on the day before the subcommittee was to commence mark-up on the reauthorization bill did the Administration publicly advocate abolishing the agency. This was done in a letter from Budget Director David Stockman to the subcommittee chairman, Senator Robert Kasten (R-Wisconsin). Although it received considerable publicity, the Adminstration's statement obviously came too late. A general agreement had already been reached to reauthorize the agency for at least one more year. Thus, after the committee voted to reauthorize the agency, the Administration appeared to have been rebuffed by the Senate. The Administration had not in fact made a strong attempt to abolish the agency.

In the Democrat-controlled House of Representatives, opposition to abolishing the CPSC was strong, as expected. The chairman of the House Commerce Subcommittee on Health and Environment, Rep. Henry Waxman (D-California), is a strong supporter of the agency. This subcommittee would not likely have approved a bill to abolish the CPSC. The Administration did support a proposal by Rep. Phil Gramm (D-Texas) to fold the CPSC into the Commerce Department. The Administration's efforts here were stronger than in the Senate. Commerce Secretary Malcolm Baldrige publicly endorsed the transfer of the CPSC's functions to his department. In addition, Vice President Bush reportedly called each Republican member of the subcommittee urging him to support the Gramm proposal. However, as the final vote on the measure was ten to ten, the proposal failed. The CPSC remains an independent regulatory agency.

A second major recommendation in *Mandate* was that the CPSC's budget be drastically reduced and that the agency be converted into an information clearinghouse. The Reagan Administration proposed a 30 percent budget reduction for the CPSC for FY 1982. This was ultimately adopted by Congress when it passed the budget reconciliation bill in July. Later in September, President Reagan proposed an additional 12 percent cut in the budgets of all agencies for FY 1982. Before the September budget cuts were announced, the Administration was rumored to be preparing another attempt to abolish the CPSC. An OMB Fact Sheet detailing the budget cuts did not specifically mention the agency, although it did indicate that a number of small agencies would be abolished. However, not only was the CPSC again spared from abolition, but it apparently also convinced OMB that it should be exempt from the additional 12 percent cut. The CPSC argued that an additional 12 percent cut in their FY 1982 budget (approximately $4 million) would seriously harm the agency because: (1) CPSC had already taken a 30 percent budget cut; (2) CPSC had to meet $3 to $4 million in severance pay for laid-off employees which effectively reduced the agency's FY 1982 budget by that amount; (3) a further 12 percent cut might have caused 200 additional layoffs and even more severance pay expenses. OMB was swayed.

The budget cuts did not reduce the CPSC to an information clearinghouse. It is still an independent agency regulating consumer products. The 30 percent budget cut was passed as part of the Consumer Product Safety Act Amendments of 1981, the legislation reauthorizing the agency for two more years. These amendments imposed several new restrictions on the rulemaking activities of the CPSC:

- The CPSC was directed to rely on voluntary safety standards developed by industry groups or individuals when it is likely that there will be substantial compliance with the voluntary standards.

- Before the CPSC can issue a mandatory safety standard, it must determine that: (1) a voluntary standard is not likely to result in adequate reduction of risk or will not meet with substantial compliance; (2) the benefits of the proposed standard must bear a reasonable relationship to the costs; (3) the rule must impose the least burdensome requirement in reducing the risk of injury.

- During rulemaking proceedings, the CPSC must seek proposals for voluntary standards and cease the proceeding if a voluntary standard is found satisfactory.

- The CPSC must notify a manufacturer in advance of releasing business information marked confidential. This gives a business time to seek an injunction on the proposed disclosure.

- The CPSC is barred from leasing information on new products submitted by a manufacturer unless a formal complaint has been issued, a settlement is agreed to, or the manufacturer agrees to the disclosure.

- CPSC safety standards are now subject to a congressional veto. Any rule can now be vetoed by concurrent resolution by both Houses of Congress within 90 days, or by one House within 60 days if the other chamber does not disapprove within 30 days.

A number of these provisions appear good on the surface, although it remains to be seen how the agency will interpret its new mandate from Congress. The basic structure of the agency has not been altered substantially, although a framework for better management seems to be in place, at least for the next two years.

## Internal Changes

A seat on the commission became available on January 20, 1981, but the Administration did not announce an appointment until the summer, and the seat was not filled until August. The President had no statutory power to appoint an acting chairman, and the position was filled by the commission's vice chairman. Initially, this was Stuart Statler, a Republican appointed by President Carter. However, in May, David Pittle, a liberal Democrat, became the commission's vice chairman, and hence acting chairman. The Reagan Administration could have filled the vacancy on the commission much sooner and begun to make changes at the agency.

President Reagan eventually appointed Nancy Harvey Steorts, a Republican, chairman of the CPSC. Steorts has worked on consumer issues throughout the 1970s, once as a special assistant on consumer affairs for Secretary of Agriculture Earl Butz. The public statements made by Steorts sound more favorable than those of past CPSC chairman. Steorts has said she favors more cooperation and consultation with business instead of the policy of confrontation often adopted by the agency in the past. Steorts has also embraced the concept of voluntary safety standards wherever possible, although she will support regulation when necessary.

A management review group at the CPSC appointed by Steorts has established several "operating principles" that support the ideas of cooperation with business and voluntary standards. One principle states: "Agency policies, procedures, and regulatory actions will be carried out to minimize regulatory and reporting burdens on industry." The operating principles are purely advisory, but do indicate the "game plan" that Steorts will attempt to influence the commission to follow. Steorts has also initiated a series of regular open meetings between businesses, consumer groups, users of products, and the CPSC to discuss particular products and any rules under consideration that affect them. Steorts believes that such meetings will result in a better understanding of the products, the causes of injuries associated with them, and the best way to regulate potential hazards.

The CPSC's consumer education programs will likely be upgraded by Steorts. This idea is consistent with *Mandate's* recommendation that the agency concentrate its effort on the dissemination of information to consumers. Ironically, Steorts abolished the agency's Office of Communication, the center of consumer education programs, because she regarded it as ineffective. That office was replaced by an Office of Public Affairs, which was given similar functions. The new office will provide information to four main groups: consumers, businesses, state and local governments, and the media. In addition to this organizational change, the Commission approved a Steorts proposal to increase the number of education and information personnel in the agency's field offices.

Finally, in accordance with another *Mandate* recommendation, Steorts has said that under her leadership the CPSC will "focus only on those products which pose a truly unreasonable risk of injury." The CPSC already is supposed to have such a "policy on priorities" which mandates that the agency deal only with hazardous products. That mandate is necessarily open to subjective interpretation, given the number of potential hazards that can be envisioned. Because Steorts did not arrive at the commission until August, she did not have an effect on the list of priorities the commission agreed to earlier this year. Upon taking office, Steorts established a task force that would help identify the most hazardous products that the CPSC should consider regulating. The commission will not likely change its established priorities for this year. The first year in which Steorts will influence the Commission's priorities directly will be 1982. Thus, more time is needed to judge whether this recommendation is followed.

The actual power that Steorts has to implement the general principles and specific recommendations discussed above is basically defined by her ability to influence and persuade her fellow commissioners and the agency's professional staff. She has, after all, only one vote on a commission of five. She is by far the only member of the commission whose views on regulation come close to resembling those of President Reagan. She can make several key appointments—for example, to the positions of executive director, general counsel, and the congressional liaison—and this will help her to influence policy. Not all of the appointments are as yet in place, and those that are have been there only since August. Again, more time is needed to judge whether Steorts and her appointees will be successful in directing the agency on a conservative course.

Since Steorts has been in office, a few favorable actions have been taken by the agency. The Commission refused to ban reversible bottle caps for medicine bottles. The caps, put on one way, are impossible for children to remove; but put on another way, are easy for the elderly or handicapped to remove. The CPSC staff suggested a mandatory ban, but had no data to support this action. The CPSC agreed to establish voluntary standards for manufacturers of upholstered furniture to make their products more fire resistant. Another voluntary standard was proposed to reduce the risks associated with the use of sulfuric acid drain cleaner. Also, the Commission voted to deny petitions to set mandatory standards for projectile toys and BB-guns, opting instead to encourage industry to follow the CPSC's safety suggestions and conduct consumer education programs. Finally, the agency is considering a voluntary standard for regulating the hazards of CB radio antennas.

It does not appear that the Administration was willing to face the political opposition to abolishing the CPSC. While lip service was given to this idea, it was not earnestly pursued. A more serious effort was mounted to fold the agency into the Commerce Department, but this failed in the House.

The legislation that reauthorized the agency for two more years contained sizeable budget cuts, as recommended in *Mandate*. The agency apparently was exempt from additional cuts in September. The legislation also contained several provisions which established a framework for better management of the agency.

Nancy Steorts should pursue a more conservative course at the CPSC than has been true in the past. She will encourage voluntary cooperation with business, concentrate the agency's efforts on the most dangerous products, and upgrade the agency's consumer education programs. The CPSC already appears to be moving in a better direction. Steorts's appointment came quite late. She has a considerable challenge before her.

## RECOMMENDATIONS
(Action taken on 3 out of 7)

- Abolish the CPSC entirely by legislation.
  ADVOCATED BY ADMINISTRATION, BUT NOT PROPOSED TO CONGRESS.

- Cut the CPSC budget drastically.
  BUDGET CUT 30 PERCENT.

- Concentrate efforts toward the dissemination of information and education.

  NOT ACCOMPLISHED.

- Narrow the regulatory range to the most potentially dangerous products.

  TASK FORCE APPOINTED TO DETERMINE THE MOST DANGEROUS PRODUCTS ON WHICH THE CPSC SHOULD FOCUS.

- Concentrate on evaluating the costs of regulations as opposed to benefits.

  AMENDMENTS PROPOSED AND PASSED WHICH REQUIRE A "COST-BENEFIT ANALYSIS" OF PROPOSED MANDATORY STANDARDS.

- Replace consumer advocates and lawyers at the agency, at least at the top levels, with managers and accountants who would be better qualified to make the agency more cost-effective.

  MORE TIME IS NEEDED TO EVALUATE APPOINTEES.

- Develop a system to determine the *causes* of injuries and not simply assume that a product is defective.

  NO FORMAL PROCEDURE IMPLEMENTED.

# Chapter Twenty-Seven
# THE FEDERAL COMMUNICATIONS COMMISSION
### By James E. Hinish, Jr.

Perhaps no independent agency has done a better job of carrying out its functions according to the spirit and letter of the Reagan program during the Administration's first year in office than the Federal Communications Commission. Chairman Mark S. Fowler was a good choice to head this agency: he is a former broadcaster and communications lawyer who is thoroughly familiar with the daily operations and regulatory problems of the industry. More important, Fowler is a Reagan loyalist. He was communications counsel for the Reagan organization during the 1975-76 and 1979-80 campaigns and for the Reagan-Bush Committee in 1980; he also served on the legal and administrative agencies transition team. He is oriented to a free market, committed to the President's policies and programs, and a strong advocate of deregulation—he prefers the term "unregulation"—of the telecommunications industry.

The Administration did not fill other Commission vacancies with Reaganites. Mimi Dawson was chosen primarily because she was administrative assistant to Senator Bob Packwood (R-Oregon), the Commerce Committee's Chairman, and had strong Senate backing; previously she had worked for liberal Democrats and has no communications credentials. James Quello, a prominent ex-broadcaster and a conservative Democrat, was reappointed because he has solid industry support. Henry Rivera was promoted by Senator Harrison Schmitt (R-New Mexico), a Commerce Committee member and telecommunications deregulation bill sponsor, and had the backing of Mexican-American groups. To date these commissioners have tended to support the Chairman's "unregulation" program.

Since his appointment last spring, Chairman Fowler has placed his own stamp on the Commission, filling important agency posts with like-minded deregulators, most of them conservative. He has placed new chiefs in ten of the thirteen offices and bureaus of the Commission. The people Fowler has picked are, in his view, "free market oriented and actively working towards unregulation." For instance, the general counsel was a volunteer communications counsel with the Reagan-Bush Committee, served as a member of the FCC transition team and headed the U.S. Railway Administration transition team; the Chief of the Office of Plans and Policy was an economist with the FTC transition team; the new public affairs director was Fowler's aide during the Chairman's transition duties; and the legislative affairs director was a Reagan delegate in 1976 and 1980 and chairman of the North Carolina Republican Party. Reagan supporters have been hired to fill lower positions at the agency as well.

Fowler started planning early for his regime with a series of meetings with his personal staff and members of the FCC transition team. Soon after his appointment, the Chairman delivered a series of well-publicized speeches to various industry groups which charted the course he intended the Commission to follow. From the outset, Fowler made clear that the agency should move forcefully to implement the President's campaign promise to remove excessive regulatory burdens from the communications industry. Henceforth, preference would be given to marketplace forces to provide a diversity of services through competition. "Let the players play" is his motto.

To carry out his pledge, the Chairman set up a Regulatory Review Working Group to examine every existing FCC regulation and to recommend for revision or rescission those rules which were not cost-beneficial, were harmful or unduly burdensome, or had outlived their usefulness. In one bureau alone, this working group found over 1,000 rules and regulations which could be eliminated or modified. (The Commission does not submit proposed rules to OMB for approval; OMB cannot force independent agencies to comply with its review requests.) At the same time, to improve the agency's performance to the public, the Chairman instituted a "Management by Objectives" program, giving the FCC a structured management system for the first time. Goals were set and standards of accountability were written for every Commission employee. Five overall objectives were proposed by the Chairman, adopted by the full Commission, and circulated to the staff. They are: (1) to create, to the maximum extent possible, an unregulated, competitive marketplace environment for the development and growth of telecommunications; (2) to eliminate unnecessary regulations and policies; (3) to provide service to the public in the most efficient and expedient manner possible; (4) to promote the coordination and planning of an international communications system which assures the vital interests of the American people in commerce, defense and foreign policy; and (5) to eliminate government action that infringes upon the freedom of speech and the press.

To implement this program, the FCC has undertaken a series of deregulatory actions designed to: speed up the processing of broadcast grant and renewal applications; modify existing ascertainment, programming, and log-keeping rules; cut back on licensees' paperwork requirements; improve the utilization of new technologies and existing spectrum allocations; and promote greater public access to the airwaves. A total of 47 actions was proposed between May and October. The Commission has moved to implement its

Computer II decision, speeding up the process of assuring greater competition in the common carrier field. In addition to endorsing existing congressional efforts to deregulate radio (S. 270) and the telecommunications industry (S. 898), the FCC Chairman and staff drafted, and the Commission approved and sent to Capitol Hill, its own legislative package aimed at updating the Communications Act of 1934. Included in this package are proposals to modify section 1 of the Act to redefine the public interest standard in terms of the efficient functioning of competitive market forces; provide for a demand system of allocation of radio service; codify the FCC's radio deregulation order; provide renewal expectancy to existing licensees who have adequately served the public; and repeal both the "equal time" rule and "fairness doctrine." (The "equal time" rule requires broadcasters to provide equal opportunities to all legally qualified political candidates who request access. The so-called fairness doctrine requires broadcasters to devote a reasonable percentage of their broadcast time to the coverage of significant community problems, and, in so doing, provide a reasonable opportunity for the presentation of contrasting points of view on controversial issues of public importance.)

At the same time the FCC is complying with OMB's recommendation that all agencies cut an additional 12 percent from their budgets. The 1982 FCC budget, originally set for $77 million, would be cut more than $9 million. Although Congress may not approve the added cuts, the FCC has set up a task force to evaluate every program on the agency's books, to rank them by priority, and to determine which could be reduced or eliminated. The Commission plans a reduction in force of 296 employees as of March 31, 1982, another 79 would be lost through attrition, and all 125 non-permanent employees would be terminated. A hiring freeze would remain in effect throughout the year. Those still on the payroll would be furloughed without pay for ten days during this year. The agency has also ordered a freeze on all discretionary spending, including travel and purchases. Cuts in expenditures would save another $2 million. Since under the law commissioners' pay cannot be cut, as a goodwill gesture, Fowler has offered to contribute to charity his pay for the number of days employees will be furloughed and indicated he expected the other commissioners to do the same. Although he testified in favor of these reductions, Chairman Fowler has written to Budget Director Stockman complaining that the proposed budget cuts might be "unsound" since they could impair the agency's efforts to eliminate regulations and carry out its mandated responsibilities.

# RECOMMENDATIONS
(Action taken on 4 out of 5)

- Appoint a new Chairman of the FCC, and make two other top appointments to Commission within the first six months.
  ACCOMPLISHED.

- Allow FCC flexibility to deregulate under specified conditions (where competition is sufficient to protect the public interest).
  ACCOMPLISHED IN PART. CONGRESSIONAL ACTION PENDING.

- Scrutinize FY 1982 budget request of $91,782,000, as it appears inconsistent with deregulation.
  ACCOMPLISHED. BUDGET CUT BY MORE THAN $20 MILLION.

- Support efforts to revise the 1934 Communications Act. Provide the Commission and the Courts with up-to-date congressional guidance.
  EFFORTS UNDERWAY.

- Develop proposals for telecommunications legislation in coordination with interested Members of House and Senate Committees; encourage revision and improvement in S. 2827 and H.R. 6121.
  NOT DONE. ADMINISTRATION SEEMS CONTENT TO LET CONGRESS TAKE THE LEAD.

# Chapter Twenty-Eight
# FEDERAL ELECTION COMMISSION
## By James F. Schoener

The actions of the Administration and, for that matter, Congress, toward the Federal Election Commission (FEC) can best be characterized as "benign neglect." The nature of the FEC and the sensitive area it deals with are prime causes of this neglect. Moreover, the imbalance created by a Senate controlled by one party and the House by another precludes the legislative changes that might appear to benefit solely Republicans or Democrats. Thus, a standoff continues.

The Administration has acted with extreme caution in dealing with the Commission, perhaps as a result of the ongoing FEC audit of the Reagan campaign. This audit is currently the subject of litigation in the D.C. Federal Courts, and the Administration appears reluctant to make appointments while these matters are pending.

Questions raised by some Members of the Senate in the continuing resolution for funding the FEC also contributed to the delay of the appointments, which were due in April 1981. Senators Armstrong, Humphrey and Jepsen, in particular, questioned the need and utility of the elaborate bureaucracy at the FEC. They have suggested reestablishing the obligation for full disclosure to the General Accounting Office, and transfer of with enforcement to the Justice Department.

The Administration has, perhaps unwittingly, caused considerable unhappiness in Republican ranks over the proposed appointments to the Commission. The present Commissioner, Joan Aikens, was not re-appointed to a full six-year term, but instead was given the remainder of the term of Commissioner Max Friedersdorf. The other potential appointment did not follow the Reagan transition team recommendations, and is seen as a weakening of the conservative viewpoint on the Commission. The need for a conservative with legal background to offset the liberal leaning of the General Counsel's office has been overlooked. This failure will undoubtedly cause further problems.

Several specific recommendations were made in the original *Mandate*. First, the conflicts among the IRS, FEC and the Ethics in Government Act should be resolved. The Senate, in little-noted action, removed the annual limit on honoraria paid to Senators, and removed the cap on deductions for living-away-from-home expenses for all Members in filing their 1982 income taxes. These changes will elimiate some problems that were raised by inconsistent rulings. Other problems will continue unless Congress acts.

The White House has not suggested any change in FEC legislation.

The Senate Rules Committee has not yet produced any changes, nor has the House Committee on Administration. Drafts of proposals have circulated on the Hill but, with the exception of the provision removing *ex officio* Members of the Commission, these drafts do not address critical problems such as those contained in *Mandate for Leadership*. The Supreme Court has assumed jurisdiction of part of the independent expenditures question, so some direction may be given in forthcoming opinions.

The 1982 FEC budget was finally approved at $9.4 million. The House had voted $9.66 million and the Administration recommended $9.75 million. The Commission had asked for $13.25 million.

When Congress and the Administration are cutting many other governmental functions, the utility of the Federal Election Commission should be placed in the balance; its overall *good* for the nation certainly is open to question. Reform could well be replaced by abolition, a prospect which seems more politically feasible now than when *Mandate* first examined the Commission in the fall of 1980.

## RECOMMENDATIONS
(Action taken on 3 out of 10)

- Require uniformity of interpretation between the IRS, FEC, and the Ethics in Government Act; require joint advisory opinions, if necessary.
  NOTHING HAS BEEN DONE IN THIS AREA.

- Cut budget request for FY 1982 from $13,259,078 to $10,000,000, eliminating $1,000,000 outlay for new building.
  BUDGET WAS PASSED FOR $9.4 MILLION.

- Amend the Federal Election Commission Act to get rid of *ex officio* members.
  HOUSE PROPOSAL DRAFTED TO ACCOMPLISH THIS; ACTION IN 1982 AT BEST.

- Abolish point-of-entry filings with the Secretary of the Senate and the Clerk of the House, and direct the filing of all candidate and committee reports to the FEC.
  HOUSE PROPOSAL DRAFTED TO ACCOMPLISH THIS.

- Revise the election law's hearing, investigation, and enforcement provisions, placing them under the jurisdiction of hearing panels composed of an administrative law judge and two commissioners (of different parties).
  NOT IMPLEMENTED.

- Require greater regard for First Amendment rights to prevent the development of a political bureaucracy.

  NOT IMPLEMENTED.

- Allow appearance by counsel and oral argument by counsel before the hearing panel, effectively curtailing growth in power by the General Counsel's office.

  NOT IMPLEMENTED.

- Urge Congress to amend the Act to allow entertainers to volunteer to appear at political rallies, but prohibit them from contributing proceeds from regularly scheduled performances to a candidate's campaign.

  NOT IMPLEMENTED.

- Clarify basic right of citizens to know voting records of Members.

  NOT IMPLEMENTED.

- Amend FEC Act to clarify independent expenditure rates and define areas of permitted but unreported party committee activity.

  NOT IMPLEMENTED.

# Chapter Twenty-Nine
# FEDERAL MARITIME COMMISSION
### By Douglas R. Graham

The Reagan Administration has failed to set clear guidelines for the FMC. This lack of direction ignores the recommendations in *Mandate for Leadership,* and is the result of a long and drawn-out appointment process, as well as the low priority given to the Agency.

The Reagan Administration has been very slow in appointing personnel. *Mandate* recommended that either of two Republican Commissioners—Peter Teige or James Day—be designated as the new Chairman. The Reagan Admnistration had someone else in mind. This required a long wait for an opening on the board. In the interim, the Administration designated Democratic Commissioner Kanuk as the temporary Chairman. When Commissioner Kanuk's term ended on June 30, 1981, the Administration appointed Alan Green, Jr., as the new Commissioner and Chairman of the FMC.

During this reshuffling process, Commissioner Teige resigned his post. The Reagan Administration was then faced with the task of finding and appointing another Republican Commissioner. They chose James Carey, who was sworn in on October 8, 1981. During this nine-month transition period, the FMC has been without effective leadership.

Some reform measures were considered by the FMC during this period. The Commission has examined the recommendation to transfer functions falling under the Federal Water Pollution Control Act and the Passenger Vessel Certification Act back to the Department of Transportation, and it welcomed the possibility of resulting monetary savings. These actions would not eliminate tariff filing or environmental statements, nor would they effect the closure or consolidation of the five FMC field offices.

The Reagan Administration reduced FMC's budget to $11.4 million, down from the Carter budget figure of $12.5 million. Under the recommended twelve percent across-the-board reductions, that figure would be cut to $10 million. Since 83 percent of the FMC budget goes toward personnel costs, some reductions in staff can be expected. The Administration did not follow the *Mandate* recommendation to reduce the FY 1982 budget to $2 million. A reduction of this magnitude would require a total overhaul of the agency, something the Administration has been reluctant to attempt.

The FMC raised approximately $3 million last year through penalties and fees. Following the Reagan Administration's directive about "user fees," this program is expected to expand.

Aside from these housekeeping measures, the Administration has given little guidance to the Agency. The Administration is currently trying to resolve this matter. However, a difference of opinion exists among the most senior players. The Department of Justice wants greater anti-trust authority over the FMC in the name of promoting competition. The Department of Transportation is calling for the extension and clarification of the anti-trust immunity-granting authority of the FMC. They have not been able to reach a compromise. One year after his election victory—on November 3, 1981—President Reagan chaired a meeting of the Cabinet Council to address this dispute. Each side presented its case to the Council, but no decision was made. President Reagan is expected to announce his decision sometime in the near future.

With the ultimate disposition of the FMC unknown, it is difficult to give a full evaluation of the Administration's action. The Administration's willingness to wait for an opening to appoint Chairman Green indicates that he represents the Administration's basic ideological attitude toward the FMC. This assumption implies that the Reagan Administration does not intend to abolish the FMC at this time.

*Mandate* recommended that the authority for regulating the steamship industry be placed under the Maritime Administration, constituting a return to pre-1961 policy, when the promotion and regulation of the U.S. maritime industry was conducted by the same government entity. The Administration apparently feels that these activities should remain separate because foreign carriers would not accept regulation by the same body responsible for promoting the interests of the U.S. maritime industry.

Chairman Green feels that an autonomous FMC can and should play an important role in maritime affairs. He is a firm believer in competition. In a speech before the Propeller Club in Washington, D.C. on October 7, 1981, he said, "I firmly believe that competition, not direct government regulation, achieves in most cases the most efficient allocation of labor and capital resources." Although the FMC is a regulatory agency, Chairman Green does not feel that the shipping industry is overburdened by regulation. There are no restrictions on entry or participation in the trade. While Chairman Green supports the general trend towards deregulation, he believes that the steamship industry is an exception. In his testimony before the Senate Commerce Committee on September 21, 1981, Green said the assumption of deregulation "breaks down in the area of international shipping because most foreign steamship lines play by a totally different set of rules than those imposed by our anti-trust laws." Chairman Green continued by stating what may become the Reagan Administration goal for the FMC:

Our job is to fashion a regulatory scheme which curbs the abuses which are inherent in an industry where competition is restricted or controlled by cartels or by other governments, but which imposes no undue administrative burden on those being regulated.

The nature of this regulatory scheme has not been decided. There are currently two pieces of legislation before the Congress—S. 1593 and H.R. 4374—which seek reforms along the line of those advocated by the Department of Transportation. The FMC itself endorses these bills with some reservations about certain specifics, but the Administration has not yet taken a stand. The Administration's stand, and the future of the FMC itself, now hinges on President Reagan's decision following the Cabinet Council debate.

## RECOMMENDATIONS
(Action taken on 1 out of 12)

### Reorganization Options

- Transfer functions under the Federal Water Pollution Control Act and the Passenger Vessel Certification Act to other agencies.
  UNDER CONSIDERATION, BUT NO ACTION TAKEN.

- Designate either of two Republicans, James V. Day or Peter N. Teige, to be Chairman of the FMC under Section 102(b) of Reorganization Plan No. 7.
  REJECTED.

- Reduce the FMC's operating budget to assure that only the most vital functions of the Commission are performed.
  BUDGET CUT BY ONLY $2.5 MILLION.

- Reduce personnel from 360 to 75 in 1982.
  NO DECISION TO DATE.

### Abolition Options

- Abolish the FMC.
  NOT FOLLOWED.

- Transfer all present FMC statutory authority to the Secretary of Commerce to be delegated to the Assistant Secretary of Commerce for Maritime Affairs.
  NOT FOLLOWED. MARITIME AUTHORITY TRANSFERRED TO DOT.

- Concentrate on the regulatory aspects of maritime administration.
  NOT FOLLOWED.

327

- Repeal the current general orders of the FMC which result in red tape in filing tariffs and environmental statements.

  NOT FOLLOWED.

- Eliminate the offices of Hearing Counsel, Freight Forwarders, Certification and Licensing, and General Counsel, along with the Chairman, four Commissioners and their staffs.

  NOT ACCOMPLISHED.

- Transfer the twenty employees and those functions performed under the Federal Water Pollution Control Act and the Passenger Vessel Certification Act to the Departments of Transportation and Commerce.

  NOT FOLLOWED. HOWEVER, THESE RECOMMENDATIONS ARE BEING CONSIDERED SERIOUSLY.

- Move to repeal the freight forwarders' licensing function of the FMC, tariff filing on ocean common carriers, and the International Shipping Act of 1933.

  THE FREIGHT FORWARDER FUNCTION IS INCLUDED IN PENDING LEGISLATION; OTHER RECOMMENDATIONS HAVE NOT BEEN FOLLOWED.

- Implement reductions in staff and budgets.

  PREVIOUS RECOMMENDATIONS NOT FOLLOWED; THUS, NO SAVINGS POSSIBLE.

# Chapter Thirty
# FEDERAL TRADE COMMISSION
### By Anthony J. Coppolino

The Reagan Administration's efforts to make immediate changes at the Federal Trade Commission have been limited. Although a vacancy occurred on the Commission in April, the Administration did not announce its nominee for chairman until June. James C. Miller, III, executive director of the Vice President's Task Force on Regulatory Relief, was President Reagan's choice for chairman of the FTC. Miller did not assume office until October—nearly eight months after inauguration. Technically, Miller filled a seat that was vacated on September 25, when the term of Commissioner Paul Rand Dixon expired. Thus, the seat that was vacated in April has still not been filled. Because of these personnel problems, the Administration has had little chance to directly affect internal policy at the FTC.

The Administration did attempt to use the budgetary process to control the agency indirectly. The Office of Management and Budget initially proposed a 13 percent budget cut for the FTC in FY 1981 and a 25 percent cut for FY 1982. These cuts would have necessitated the elimination of the agency's field offices and its anti-trust division. Because of strong congressional opposition to these proposals, the budget cuts were lowered to 4.8 percent in FY 1981 and 11 percent in FY 1982. In October, the FTC voted to accept an additional 12 percent cut in their FY 1982 budget, as requested by President Reagan for all agencies. The FTC was one of the few agencies that agreed to take further budget cuts. Chairman Miller, who has appeared willing to accept budget reductions, has said that the FTC can fulfill its functions despite a more limited budget. However, the Commission's vote is obviously non-binding and the budget cuts have to be approved by Congress. In late October, a Senate appropriations subcommittee, chaired by Senator Lowell Weicker (R-Connecticut), refused to cut the FTC's FY 1982 appropriation by an additional 12 percent as the President requested. Final congressional action on many appropriations bills has been delayed.

The main recommendation of *Mandate* was that the FTC should stop misusing Section 5 of the Federal Trade Commission Act which makes "unfair or deceptive acts or practices" by business illegal. Also under this section, the FTC may prohibit advertising that has a "capacity or tendency" to deceive a "significant" number of consumers. By broadly construing this vague part of the law, the FTC undertook many questionable cases against business. To curb this abuse, two specific recommendations were made in *Mandate*. The first was to propose legislation to directly amend Section 5 to eliminate the word "unfair" and substitute in its place a more precise term such as "fraudulent" or "false." The second remedy suggested was more indirect, namely to appoint individuals to key positions at the FTC who would not interpret this section so broadly.

The Administration has not yet proposed a legislative remedy to amend Section 5. Such an effort would be appropriate early next year when Congress considers the FTC reauthorization bill. Since Miller did not take office until October 5, and his own appointments shortly thereafter, no specific examples of a different interpretation of Section 5 can be cited. It should be noted that Miller was the director of the transition task force on the FTC whose report derided the abuses that occurred under Section 5.

*Mandate for Leadership* also recommended that the FTC develop new philosophical underpinnings for the fraudulent advertising cases it considers. In those instances in which a consumer of normal competence reasonably could be expected to discover misstatements of fact in advertising, the FTC should not issue prohibitory rules. Any cases that required technical expertise to discover the duplicity of advertisers would be more suited for a prohibitory rule. Miller has publicly agreed with this viewpoint on many occasions. This idea was endorsed in the FTC transition report. Miller has said that the FTC will review its advertising substantiation program which is the source of the problem. Again, no specific actions can as yet be cited as evidence of a shift in philosophy on these cases.

Another major recommendation of *Mandate* was that the FTC's anti-trust division, the Bureau of Competition, be abolished. This would end the dual enforcement of the government's anti-trust laws that currently exists between the FTC and the Justice Department. The Reagan Administration considered eliminating the Bureau as a means of achieving budgetary savings. Strong congressional opposition prevented this proposal from being adopted. Miller does not advocate eliminating the Bureau at this time and has said that the Administration would probably not propose the elimination of dual enforcement for at least a few years.

Although dual enforcement still exists, Miller plans to review the FTC's anti-trust policies. He has characterized the FTC's anti-trust efforts in the past as misdirected. This was a reference to the FTC's bizarre interpretation of anti-trust laws to encompass the notions of "shared monopoly" and "price signaling." It is likely that Miller will attempt to move the agency away from these controversial ideas and focus its anti-trust efforts on horizontal mergers. A horizontal merger usually involves a takeover of competing firms or price-fixing among competitors. Both result in higher prices for consumers.

Since Inauguration Day, the FTC has halted several cases. The Commission ended anti-trust suits against the nation's eight largest oil companies as well as against the nation's largest automakers. Both suits began in the early 1970s. In addition, the FTC has ended its much-publicized probe of children's TV advertising. An FTC administrative law judge has urged the Commission to drop its nine-year-old suit against three of the nation's largest cereal companies who were accused of a "shared monopoly."

These are positive signs from the agency, although the Reagan Administration had no direct input into the decisions. They most likely resulted from a reaction by the FTC to the bruising reauthorization battle with Congress last year in which the agency's powers were weakened, and from a recognition that a new consensus hostile to over-regulation had develped in the country.

The Reagan Administration can seek substantive changes at the FTC when the agency's reauthorization proceedings begin next year. This would be an appropriate time to amend Section 5 and to make other needed changes.

President Reagan's appointed chairman, Jim Miller, is a highly respected scholar of economics and regulatory issues. He will likely make a thorough review of each agency program before seeking sweeping changes. He has made statements supporting changes in the agency's anti-trust policies and fraudulent advertising cases which are consistent with recommendations made in *Mandate for Leadership*. In addition, Miller plans to integrate economic analysis into the work of the FTC's enforcement bureaus so that regulatory decisions are based on sound economics.

Miller is, however, only one of five commissioners on an independent agency. Because he is also accountable to Congress, he cannot appear to be a public spokesman for President Reagan's economic policies nor be expected to take orders from the White House. His success in redirecting the agency is based fundamentally on his ability to persuade fellow commissioners to follow a new course. He can also make several appointments to key positions within the agency, and will receive a boost when the President's nominee to fill the Commission's vacancy is confirmed by the Senate. Since Miller's own appointment came so late, his success in directing the agency on a conservative course cannot be judged. The White House can be faulted for delays in appointments.

### RECOMMENDATIONS
(Action taken on 1 out of 4)

- Stop FTC misuse of Section 5 of the FTC Act, the section making "unfair" practices by business illegal. Substitute "fraudulent," "false," or some other term in place of "unfair."

NO LEGISLATIVE REMEDY HAS YET BEEN PROPOSED.

- Make personnel changes in the General Counsel Office and the Bureaus of Competition and Consumer Protection.

  APPOINTEES TOOK OFFICE ON OCTOBER 5, 1981. THEIR PERFORMANCE CANNOT YET BE EVALUATED.

- Eliminate the FTC's anti-trust division, the Bureau of Competition.

  ELIMINATION CONSIDERED, BUT NOT PROPOSED.

- Develop new philosophical underpinnings for fraudulent advertising and rulemaking proceedings.

  NO ACTION TO DATE.

# Chapter Thirty-One
# INTERSTATE COMMERCE COMMISSION
### By Matthew V. Scocozza

In recent months, the Interstate Commerce Commission has been active in reducing the regulatory burdens on motor and rail carriers and in helping to formulate new bus legislation. Entry barriers have been significantly reduced and carriers have been afforded substantial rate flexibility. At the same time, the Commission has been taking steps to ensure that rates are provided on a non-discriminatory basis and that all shippers, regardless of size, continue to receive reasonably adequate service.

Consistent with the goals of reducing burdensome and unnecessary federal regulation, the Commission has streamlined many of its procedures to reduce regulatory delay and minimize the cost of its administrative proceedings. The new leadership at the Commission currently is undertaking a major program to identify all Commission regulations which no longer serve the public interest. The goal of this program is to eliminate or modify all unnecessary or outdated regulations as well as those which cannot be justified through cost/benefit analysis.

## Rail Industry

The Commission has been particularly active in the rail area. Numerous steps have already been taken, and several additional measures are now under active consideration to reduce the regulatory burdens on rail carriers and to afford these carriers increased rate flexibility.

The Commission has adopted a cost recovery index which modifies the past procedures governing the filing of general rail rate increases. The new rules simplify and expedite the recovery of cost increases for rail carriers through the use of a "zone of reasonableness." The new Commission has announced its interest in the active use of its new powers to exempt rail services from economic regulation in those instances where regulatory controls are unnecessary to protect against abuses of market power. This would be consistent with the *Mandate* recommendations. The Commission has already exempted various miscellaneous agricultural commodities as well as all rail and truck service provided by rail carriers in connection with trailer-on-flatcar (TOFC) and container-on-flatcar (COFC) service. The Commission currently is considering a proposal which would expand that exemption to TOFC/COFC services provided by rail-affiliated motor carriers and all other motor carriers. The Commission is also in the process of establishing simplified procedures governing the filing of rail contract rates, which should facilitate the use of this new marketing tool by the rail industry.

In recent decisions, the Commission has demonstrated a general tendency to encourage consolidations that are not contrary to the public interest. The Commission has simplified its consolidation procedures and reduced significantly the amount of information required of parties participating in such proceedings. Most important, the Commission has consistently been well within the new statutory deadlines for deciding merger proceedings. In a similarly important area, the Commission recently streamlined its procedures governing rail abandonments and terminations of service. Under the new procedures, the Commision will be able to render a final decision in contested cases within 255 days filing of the abandonment application. This is a significant improvement over the past handling of such cases, which generally averaged two and one-half years.

## Motor Carrier Industry

The Commission has adopted several rules and policies which significantly ease the ability of new trucking companies to enter the regulated motor carrier industry and of existing companies to expand their operation. The Commission has also adopted special procedures to process expeditiously applications by carriers seeking to remove operating restrictions or broaden their commodity and territorial authorizations. In line with the new eased-entry policies, the Commission has revised its procedures to make it substantially easier and less costly for those seeking motor carrier operating authority.

The new Chairman of the Commission recently announced that he is seriously considering seeking additional reform legislation which would eliminate the "public need" standard from existing motor carrier entry provisions. Such a proposal, if adopted by Congress, would lead to a substantial increase in competition in the motor carrier industry.

In recent months, the Commission has been the subject of controversy concerning its policy towards new entrants in the motor carrier markets. Applications which were handled in a routine fashion in the months following passage of the Act are now the subject of closer scrutiny and more detailed paperwork. The Commission has been criticized widely for "reversing the liberalized entry policy" established in the Motor Carrier Act of 1980. The Commission continues to pledge adherence to the new policies set out in the 1980 legislation. The difference in interpretation appears to be based on the current Commission's belief that the new law requires a thorough review of applicants.

Under the new Chairman, the percentage of authority applied for and granted actually exceeds the ratio prior to the new Chairman's taking office. No statistics are available to determine how much authority requested in each application is being granted.

The new Commision is young. Two nominees are awaiting Senate confirmation as of early November. For all intents and purposes, the "deregulation jury" is still out on the Commission.

The new Chairman, Reese H. Taylor, is the only Reagan appointee to date, and has been the only conduit for Administration policy thus far. His appointment came late in the year (June 16, 1981). Two Republican nominees are currently awaiting Senate confirmation. In his early days, numerous press reports and trade journals portrayed Taylor as an ardent regulator. These press reports were given some degree of credence when a senior ICC advisor testified on Capitol Hill, articulating numerous pro-regulatory appoaches to government policy. The Chairman has since conferred with the authors of the Motor Carrier Act of 1980 and disclaimed much of the substance of the testimony in question and has taken issue with resulting press reports.

The Chairman recently announced his intention to submit legislation that would drastically relax the motor carrier entry standard. The Commission appears to be on the right track. Critics remain doubtful. Official rulemakings and procedures by the Commission, and not press conjecture, will be the true litmus test of the regulatory policy of the ICC under Chairman Taylor.

### Bus Industry

The new leadership at the Commission has been working closely with the House Public Works Committee on the reform of bus legislation. In helping to formulate the new legislation, the Commission has suggested innovative procedures to ease entry and exit standards, increase pricing flexibility, and remove unnecessary and burdensome operating restrictions imposed on bus carriers.

One of the most important features of the reforms advocated by the new Commission is a liberalized entry policy. The new Chairman has come out in support of a new entry standard which would focus on an applicant's fitness, willingness, and ability to perform bus service. Under this standard, the submission of supporting evidence to establish a public demand or need for a carrier's service would no longer be required.

Taylor also believes that new legislation should supersede all counterproductive state regulations which inhibit price and service flexibility and revenue adequacy in the bus industry. For example, Taylor has advocated a freer exit policy which would supersede state laws and permit the elimination of bus service, except where essential last-bus intercity scheduled service is involved. In the latter case, the

ICC would have authority to review the actions of state commissions.

The Chairman also supports a new zone-rate freedom for bus carriers. Under this proposal, individual bus carriers would have greater freedom to raise or lower rates without government interference to meet the needs of their markets. Finally, Taylor has supported the adoption of a provision, similar to the one contained in the Motor Carrier Act, which would require the Commission to eliminate all unnecessary and wasteful restrictions traditionally imposed on bus carriers.

## RECOMMENDATION
(Action taken on 9 out of 18)

- Move aggressively to implement rate freedoms provided for in the Staggers Act.
  ACCOMPLISHED.

- Move to ensure that the railroads have greater freedom in raising or lowering their rates within acceptable confines.
  RULEMAKING IN PROGRESS.

- Ensure that the transition period for the three-year phase-out of rate increases does not result in abrupt price increases for shippers or loss of revenues by the carriers.
  MONITORING IN PROGRESS.

- Ensure that the ICC does not frustrate implementation of the new contract rate authority to deal with freight car shortages.
  CONTRACT RATEMAKING REGULATIONS NOT YET PROMULGATED.

- Review all commodity classes for potential total deregulation.
  UNDER REVIEW.

- Retain special service orders since they proved to be some relief to many small shippers during periods of extreme car shortages.
  NO ACTION.

- Devise a system to encourage railroad to invest in rolling stock and benefit from the incentive per diem charges.
  NO ACTION.

- Enact tax incentives to benefit railroads which purchase rolling stock — at the same time a disincentive to speculators.
  NO ACTION.

- Develop policies to expedite mergers following procedures established by the Staggers Act.

  DONE.

- Develop policies to encourage consolidations and restructuring of the industry.

  IN PROGRESS.

- Develop legislation to reform abandonment proceedings to provide that no proceeding shall take longer than nine months.

  UNDER STUDY.

- Relax entry standards in the motor bus industry; encourage motor bus operators to improve their market share with innovative pricing practices and marketing techniques.

  REGULATORY REFORM LEGISLATION IN PROGRESS.

- Provide direct subsidy to maintain rural bus service.

  NOT LIKELY TO BE INCLUDED IN BUS REGULATORY REFORM PROPOSAL.

- Develop innovative procedures to relieve the inter-city motorbus industry from tight rate, entry/exit, and operating restrictions.

  ACCOMPLISHED.

- Undertake a program to allow senior ICC attorneys to be designated as deputy U.S. attorneys for the purpose of processing ICC enforcement cases.

  NO ACTION.

- Review practical effects of rigorous enforcement of the Motor Carrier Reform Act of 1980.

  UNDER REVIEW.

- Either sponsor a stronger enforcement and compliance program, or seek additional legislation to eliminate rules which have a counter-productive impact.

  ENFORCEMENT PROGRAM UNDER REVIEW.

- Continue funding at the same level for FY 1982 due to the ICC's increased oversight responsibility under motor carrier and rail legislation, and revision of outdated regulations.

  FY 1981 APPROPRIATIONS CUT SLIGHTLY.

# Chapter Thirty-Two
# NATIONAL TRANSPORTATION
# SAFETY BOARD
### By Matthew V. Scocozza

The membership of the Board has not changed since the previous administration. James Burnett has been nominated to fill the next vacancy and to succeed the incumbent as the next Chairman. Senate action is expected in late November 1981. Accordingly, the Reagan Administration has not yet been able to influence the policies and procedures of the Board reviewed in the previous *Mandate* report.

Many of those recommendations noted the redundancy of NTSB functions. It concluded that the NTSB should be abolished, with those few functions not duplicated transferred to appropriate agencies. *Mandate* noted that after five years, the NTSB had little to show for its efforts. This observation, and the recommendation that the NTSB be abolished, have not changed.

The Board was requested to provide information on actions taken or not taken as a result of the first *Mandate* report. It chose not to respond.

This chapter does not include an audit. The Reagan Administration cannot be held accountable for the failure of an independent NTSB to implement needed reforms.

# Chapter Thirty-Three
# SECURITIES AND EXCHANGE COMMISSION
### By Robert J. Kabel

The Securities and Exchange Commission, under the leadership of Chairman John Shad, has outlined an impressive list of objectives in the areas of capital formation, regulatory reform and investor protections. This agenda is a marked departure from the past. Previous Commissions frequently have been viewed as a "friendly" adversary to the capital markets and business community, acting more as a restraining agency rather than in conjunction with the private sector to achieve a common set of goals.

In contrast to previous commissions, the current SEC has indicated its intent to enhance capital formation through its regulatory powers. Chairman Shad has stated that the SEC can contribute to the Administration's capital formation objectives by rationalizing its disclosure and reporting requirements. Specifically, the SEC has published for public comment what has been termed "The SEC Integration Package," the intent of which is to integrate and simplify registration and reporting under the various securities acts. Implementation of these would reduce paperwork and grant corporations and their investment bankers greater flexibility in structuring and timing future public offerings. This could be accomplished without compromising the full disclosure of material information to the investing public.

The SEC has also proposed exempting from registration certain limited securities offerings. This proposal was developed in consultation with state securities officials and, if implemented, would constitute the first such state-federal registration exemption effort.

The Commission also announced its intent to review all of its accounting rules and regulations with the objective of simplifying them. Some recently have been withdrawn; those retained will be codified. In the enforcement area, the Commission and its chief enforcement officer have pursued insider trading activities with exceptional fervor. Their stated intent is to put everyone involved in the securities industry on notice that profiteering on insider information will not be tolerated. Insider trading is a major infraction of the rules governing an industry, the success of which is based largely on public trust.

The budget cuts recommended by the Reagan Administration were handled forthrightly by the SEC. While one commissioner published an article critical of any additional cuts in the Commission's budget, Chairman Shad testified where the cuts would be made and indicated that the Commission could live with them if necessary.

Specifically, Shad stated that a twelve percent cut would result in a 20 percent cut in staff, as most of its costs are in personnel. While not overtly opposing the cuts, Shad clearly indicated that such a reduction would slow the Commission's response to registration statements and other filings, and perhaps affect its enforcement activities as well.

The SEC has established a commendable agenda during the first months of the Reagan Administration. Beyond this initial step, the SEC has given concrete support to several of its own initiatives. For example, Chairman Shad testified in support of legislation to modify the Foreign Corrupt Practices Act, an objective recommended in *Mandate*. Several other items are in progress and considerable efforts remain to be made before these proposals become final.

## RECOMMENDATIONS
(Action taken on 2 out of 4)

### Foreign Corrupt Practices Act

- Develop specific amendments to the Foreign Corrupt Practices Act in order to mitigate any harmful effects of the Act, including:

  1. Pursuing multilateral agreements in which other industrialized countries might join in adopting a code of commercial conduct.

  NO LEADERSHIP AT SEC.

  2. Continuing to implement Department of Justice review procedures; possibly involve other departments (i.e., Commerce) in the process.

  PROPOSAL HAS ADMINISTRATION SUPPORT.

  3. Targeting amendments to the Act designed to minimize ambiguities in the Act. Include opinions of attorneys and accountants regarding compliance.

  SENATE BANKING COMMITTEE HAS COMPLETED ACTION ON CORRECTIVE LEGISLATION.

  4. Considerng the removal of SEC jurisdiction to enforce the Act.

  ALL OF THE ABOVE ISSUES UNDER GENERAL LEGISLATIVE REVIEW.

### General

- Urge Congress to take action to increase fees in order to cover more of SEC's expenses by either increasing specific fees on securities transactions or by authorizing the SEC to increase fees sufficiently to collect a specified percentage of its annual appropriations.

LEGISLATION DRAFTED BUT NOT YET INTRODUCED.

- Oppose federal legislation to create federal chartering of corporations, or federal minimum standards for various aspects of corporate structure. Encourage state jurisdiction.

NO ACTION. IN THIS CASE, NO ACTION IS TO BE DESIRED.

- Encourage self-regulating organizations such as the New York Stock Exchange to develop their own policies to improve corporate accountability.

NO LEADERSHIP FROM SEC.

# Chapter Thirty-Four
# THE POSTAL SERVICE AND POSTAL RATE COMMISSION
By James I. Campbell, Jr.

Commendably, the Reagan Administration moved quickly to make dramatic cuts in the federal subsidy to the Postal Service. The new budget bill reduced appropriations for FY 1982 by more than half, saving $956 million. Through FY 1984, total savings will amount to just over $3 billion.

Unfortunately, the Administration has not yet addressed other, more fundamental postal problems; it has not developed an overall postal policy as part of a comprehensive approach to national communications. *Mandate for Leadership* outlined the logically necessary starting point of such a policy, a policy of deregulation. First, the Postal Service must be subject to the discipline of competition in order to cure its number-one problem—uncontrolled costs. The postal monopoly must be terminated and other federal protections eliminated. Second, Postal Service management must be given more freedom to operate their business on a rational, business-like basis, including pricing freedom (now regulated by the Postal Rate Commission). Third, public support for rural mail delivery must take the form of direct subsidy, supplied on a contract basis. Contrary to the belief of rural congressmen, the present system of undifferentiated subsidies and protection from competition offers little financial incentive for the Postal Service to provide better rural service. Although the Administration has been slow, there are signs that it is now beginning to consider these matters.

The Administration's slowness to develop a new approach to the postal industry has been matched by a slowness to discharge its limited responsibilities under the current scheme. The Postal Service's recent increase in postal rates, including the increase in the basic first-class rate from 18 cents to 20 cents, could have been blocked by one new appointment which the Administration simply failed to make. Two vacancies in the Postal Rate Commission also remain unfilled. The Attorney General has done nothing to embrace a narrow reading of the current statute creating a governmental monopoly in the document delivery business. Without comment from Justice, Congress has been busily working on a criminal code revision that would effect a thirty- to two hundred fold increase in the penalty for providing a competitive delivery service. In an especially troublesome development, postal inspectors have been demanding customer lists from private carriers under the guise of administering the current postal monopoly regulations.

The Administration is moving in one important area, albeit under pressure from events beyond its control. Pressure is building to allow the Postal Service to get into the telecommunications area. As long as the Postal Service receives a government subsidy, it will be challenged whenever it attempts to move into telecommunications. This issue has been raised continually since 1844, when Samuel Morse established the first telegraph line. The Administration is working out a new policy which will recommend firm limits on the authority of a governmental post office to encroach upon the generally private telecommunications industry. (If the Postal Service becomes a private company, this might no longer be an issue.)

## RECOMMENDATIONS
(Action taken on 1 out of 5)

- Issue an Attorney General's opinion narrowly construing the scope of the postal monopoly.
  NOT IMPLEMENTED.

- Develop a new policy in the Commerce Department on postal telecommunications.
  ACCOMPLISHED, ALTHOUGH NOT YET MADE PUBLIC.

- Develop a new postal policy that would attempt to lessen government participation in the document delivery industry, including:

  1. Abolition, or at least updating, of the postal monopoly.
     UNDER CONSIDERATION.

  2. Allowing the Postal Service greater control over its prices.
     UNDER CONSIDERATION.

  3. Elimination of the general subsidy and replacement of all indirect subsidies with direct subsidies, if appropriate, including subsidy for rural mail delivery.
     LEGISLATION ENACTED TO CUT GENERAL SUBSIDY BY $394 MILLION (TO $250 MILLION) IN FY 1982, WITH PLANS TO ELIMINATE BY FY 1984. OTHER SUBSIDIES REDUCED BY $562, $575, AND $627 MILLION, RESPECTIVELY, IN NEXT THREE FISCAL YEARS.

  4. Re-examination of the need for any government participation in the national document delivery industry.
     NO ACTION.

- Fill a vacancy on the Postal Rate Commission with a person who

346

will work to moderate price and cost increases and prevent actions inappropriate to a state corporation.

NO ACTION. TWO VACANCIES REMAIN.

- Fill a vacancy on the Board of Governors with a person who will support attempts by the Postal Rate Commission to moderate price and cost increases or prevent actions inappropriate to a state corporation.

NO ACTION. ONE VACANCY REMAINS. AN APPOINTMENT COULD HAVE BLOCKED THE 20-CENT FIRST-CLASS RATE.

## THE PRESIDENT AND EXECUTIVE OFFICES
### Office of Presidential Personnel

WILLA A. JOHNSON is Senior Vice President of The Heritage Foundation. She is Director of the Resource Bank, an outreach program which involves more the 1,600 U.S. and foreign scholars in public policy issues. She also manages a liaison program with more than 350 other policy groups in the United States and worldwide. From January until July 1981, she served as Deputy Director of the Office of Presidential Personnel. She had responsibility for recruiting national security and foreign affairs personnel; she also helped to staff the presidential boards and commissions. Previously, she has had extensive experience as a legislative aide on Capitol Hill. She was educated at the University of Arizona at Tuscon and at the University of Geneva, Switzerland.

### Office of Management and Budget

CATHERINE ENGLAND is a policy analyst at The Heritage Foundation specializing in regulatory reform. Before coming to Heritage, she was on the faculty of the economics department at American University in Washington. She received a B.S. from Tennessee Technological University and an M.S. from Texas A&M University and is a Ph.D. candidate at Texas A&M.

### Executive Orders

MARGARET D. BONILLA is the assistant to the Department of Government Information at The Heritage Foundation. She was formerly associated with Energy Decisions, Inc., as a regulatory and legislative analyst. Mrs. Bonilla received her B.S. in foreign service from Georgetown University in 1980. Mrs. Bonilla also provided editorial assistance for *The First Year*.

## CABINET DEPARTMENTS
### Agriculture

WILLIAM C. BAILEY is an economist for the Senate Committee on Agriculture, Nutrition, and Forestry. Educated at the University of Idaho, Pepperdine University, and the University of Missouri (Ph.D.), he served five years in the United States Marine Corps. He has worked at the Department of Agriculture and is the author of a number of articles on topics which include water resources, transportation, and agricultural policy.

## Commerce

**CHARLES H. BRADFORD** is Assistant Director of the Joint Economic Committee. He has served on the staff of the Senate Committee on Banking, Housing and Urban Affairs; as economic advisor to the American Banker's Association; and as deputy chief, Division of Research and Statistics for the Federal Deposit Insurance Corporation, among other legislative and governmental positions. Educated at the University of Utah and Harvard University, Dr. Bradford is the author of numerous articles in the fields of economics and taxation. He was chairman of the Commerce Department team in the *Mandate for Leadership* project.

**WILLIAM R. WORTHEN, ESQ.**, vice-chairman of the Commerce report, is the Special Assistant for Domestic Policy Research at the Republican National Committee. He served as attorney advisor to an administrative law judge in the Federal Mine Safety and Health Review Commission, and worked as a criminal defense attorney in the District of Columbia. He holds a B.A. *magna cum laude* in history from the University of New Hampshire and received his J.D. from Georgetown University. Mr. Worthen is a member of the American Bar Association, Federal Bar Association, the Bars of the District of Columbia and the State of New Hampshire.

## Defense

**WILLIAM C. GREEN** is currently the editor of the *National Security Record*, a publication of The Heritage Foundation. He is completing his doctorate in International Relations at the University of Southern California. His dissertation, "Contrasts in U.S. and Soviet Thought on the Political Utility of Military Force," will be completed by late 1982. He also holds an appointment as research associate with the University of Southern California Defense and Strategic Studies Program, of which he was the former coordinator. Mr. Green speaks Russian and has lived and studied in the Soviet Union. He has published numerous articles on international relations and Soviet affairs.

## Education

**ONALEE McGRAW** is an education consultant to The Heritage Foundation, specializing in family and education issues. She is the editor of *Education Update*, a newsletter on education and family matters. Dr. McGraw was appointed to the Reagan transition team on education after serving on the Family Policy Advisory Board during the Reagan-Bush campaign. She was appointed by former Virginia Governor John Dalton as a delegate to the 1980 White House Conference on Families. Among papers Dr. McGraw has written for Heritage are the monographs *Secular Humanism and the Schools: The Issue Whose Time Has Come; Family Choice in Education: The New Imperative,* and *The Family, Feminism and the Therapeutic State.* Dr. McGraw received her Ph.D. in government from Georgetown University.

### Energy

MILTON R. COPULOS is currently Director of Energy Studies at The Heritage Foundation. Prior to joining the Foundation, he served as legislative assistant to Maryland State Senator Victor L. Crawford. Mr. Copulos served on the transition team covering Energy and Natural Resources and worked with both the Synthetic Fuels Corporation and the Department of Energy. He was recently appointed to the National Petroleum Council. Mr. Copulos has written a number of major studies for The Heritage Foundation's Critical Issues series including: *Confrontation at Seabrook, Closing the Nuclear Option,* and *Domestic Oil: The Hidden Solution.* He also edited *Energy Perspectives,* an anthology of energy-related articles. In addition to his duties at The Heritage Foundation, Copulos writes a weekly column which is distributed nationally by the Heritage Features Syndicate. Mr. Copulos did his undergraduate and graduate work at The American University. He was chairman of the Energy Department team in the *Mandate for Leadership* project.

### Health and Human Services

PETER G. GERMANIS is a policy analyst at The Heritage Foundation, specializing in labor economics and Social Security. While at Heritage, he has authored studies on the budget, tax policy, the minimum wage, and the Consumer Price Index. Mr. Germanis holds a B.S. from George Mason University an M.A. in economics from the University of Pennsylvania.

### Housing and Urban Development

STUART M. BUTLER, British-born economist, is policy analyst at The Heritage Foundation, has authored numerous Foundation studies on "enterprise zones," rent control, nationalized health, and other urban policy matters. Among his published works are *Enterprise Zones: Pioneering in the Inner City; Philanthropy in America: The Need for Action;* and his newest book, *Enterprise Zones: Greenlining the Inner Cities.* In 1981, Dr. Butler received the George Washington Honor Medal from the Freedoms Foundation at Valley Forge, Pennsylvania, for his pioneering efforts to promote "enterprise zones." Prior to joining Heritage, Dr. Butler was an instructor in economics at Hillsdale College in Michigan. He has been Secretary of the Adam Smith Institute and Honorary Research Fellow for the Institute of United States Studies at the University of London. Dr. Butler was educated at St. Andrews in Scotland, where he received a B.S. in physics and mathematics, a M.S. in economics, and a Ph.D. in economic history.

### Interior

ROBERT L. TERRELL is a professional staff member on the Senate Energy and Natural Resources Committee. Prior to serving on the Senate Committee, Mr. Terrell was a professional staff member on the Energy and Environment Subcommittee of the House Interior and Insular Affairs Committee. He also served as a professional staff member of the Public Lands Subcommittee of the House Interior and Insular Affairs Committee. He has worked with the U.S. Bureau of Land Management as a minerals specialist and as a district minerals examiner in Montana. He has worked with the U.S. Bureau of Mines as program assistant to the Coordinator for Wilderness and River Basin Program. Mr. Terrell, a geologist, was educated at the University of South Alabama. He was chairman of the Department of the Interior team in the *Mandate for Leadership* project.

### Labor

GEORGE PRITTS is chief counsel on the Senate Labor and Human Resources Committee.

### State

JEFFREY B. GAYNER is Director of Foreign Policy Studies at The Heritage Foundation. He was foreign policy advisor to President Reagan during the 1980 election and member of the International Department Cooperation Agency transition team. Educated at Washington and Lee and the University of North Carolina at Chapel Hill, he has led student groups in Taiwan, Korea, and Japan. Mr. Gayner has written several articles for both foreign and domestic journals and newspapers. He is a contributing author to books on East Asia, Latin America, and Southern Africa, and he was chairman of the State Department team in the *Mandate for Leadership* project.

### Transportation

JACK R. WIMER is Director of Media Relations for the Synthetic Fuels Corporation. He worked previously as a legislative assistant for Senator William L. Armstrong of Colorado, where he was the principal staffer for the Economic Policy Subcommittee of the Senate Banking Committee. He was press secretary for Representative Mickey Edwards of Oklahoma, a city editor for the KTUL-TV News Department, and a reporter for *The Tulsa Tribune*. In 1975 he was a nominee for the Pulitzer Prize in the Meritorious Public Service category, and in 1977 he was the recipient of the Society of Professional Journalists Award for investigative reporting. Mr. Wimer received his B.A. from the University of Tulsa.

## Treasury

BRUCE R. BARTLETT is a Washington-based economist, writer, lecturer, and political consultant. He currently serves as Deputy Director of the Joint Economic Committee. He was a former chief legislative assistant to U.S. Senator Roger W. Jepsen of Iowa, and an economic consultant to the Honorable Perry B. Duryea, Minority Leaders of the New York State Assembly and Republican candidate for Governor of New York. Mr. Bartlett worked on the staff of Congressman Jack F. Kemp of New York, where he helped draft the famous Kemp-Roth tax bill. Prior to that, he was legislative assistant to Congressman Ron Paul of Texas. Mr. Bartlett is the author of *Reaganomics: Supply-side Economics in Action; The Politics of Pearl Harbor, 1941-1946; The Keynesian Revolution Revisited*, and many other popular and scholarly articles. Mr. Bartlett is a graduate of Rutgers University, and holds a master's degree from Georgetown University, where he was a Richard M. Weaver Fellow.

## EXECUTIVE AGENCIES
### ACTION, Legal Services Corporation, and Community Services Administration

STEPHEN MARKMAN is general counsel for the Senate Judiciary Subcommittee on the Constitution where he has worked for Senator Orrin G. Hatch of Utah since 1978. He has worked on constitutional, civil rights, and criminal law matters for the Judiciary Committee. He previously worked as legislative assistant to Rep. Tom Hagedorn of Minnesota. He was educated at Duke University and the University of Cincinnati Law School, and is a member of the Michigan Bar.

### Environmental Protection Agency

LOUIS J. CORDIA at the time of this writing was environmental policy analyst for The Heritage Foundation. He is now special assistant to the administrator of EPA. He was a member of Ronald Reagan's transition team effort on the Environmental Protection Agency. He has worked as a researcher for the House Republican Research Committee. He has been a city planner in Orlando, Florida, and State Youth Coordinator for the President Ford Committee in Florida in 1976. He was also an assistant in the editorial office of the *Buffalo Evening News*. Mr. Cordia received a B.A. in government and English. He served as chairman of the EPA team in the *Mandate for Leadership* project.

## Intelligence

SAMUEL T. FRANCIS is a legislative assistant for National Security with Senator John East of North Carolina. He was formerly an international affairs policy analyst with The Heritage Foundation. Dr. Francis was educated at Johns Hopkins University and at the University of North Carolina at Chapel Hill, from which he received a Ph.D. in modern history. He has written over twenty research papers on various aspects of European and African affairs, and on problems of intelligence, internal security and terrorism. Most recently, he authored *The Soviet Strategy of Terror*, which deals with Soviet support for terrorism in different areas of the world. Mr. Francis was chairman of the Intelligence team in the original *Mandate for Leadership* project.

## National Endowments for the Arts and Humanities

MICHAEL S. JOYCE is Executive Director of the John M. Olin Foundation, Inc. He has worked in the past as Director of the Institute for Educational Affairs, and as Executive Director of the Goldseker Foundation in Baltimore, Maryland. He spent seven years with the Educational Research Council in America, first as research assistant, then research associate, senior research associate and then assistant director; he has taught history and political science at the secondary and undergraduate college levels, and has lectured widely on public policy issues. Mr. Joyce also served on President Reagan's National Endowment for the Humanities transition team, and he was chairman of the NEH/NEA team in the *Mandate for Leadership* project.

SAMUEL LIPMAN is a pianist and a writer. He is a member of the Artist Faculties of the Aspen Music Festival in Colorado and the Waterloo Music Festival in New Jersey. As a writer he is music critic for *Commentary* and the author of *Music After Modernism* (Basic Books, 1979). He has received three ASCAP-Deems Taylor awards for critical journalism. Mr. Lipman holds a B.A. in government from San Francisco State College, and an M.A. in political science from the University of California at Berkeley.

## Senior Executive Service

ROBERT M. HUBERTY is Assistant Director of the Resource Bank at The Heritage Foundation. He taught history at the University of California, Irvine, and was a research assistant to former President Richard M. Nixon in the preparation of his *Memoirs*. Mr. Huberty holds a B.A. and an M.A. in history from the University of California, Irvine. He was a co-chairman for the SES team in the *Mandate for Leadership* study.

## INDEPENDENT REGULATORY AGENCIES

### Federal Communications Commission & Regulatory Overview

JAMES E. HINISH, JR. is counsel to the Senate Republican Policy Committee. He has worked in the past with Manufacturers Hanover Trust Co., King Broadcasting Co., Storer Broadcasting Co., and the Federal Communications Commission. During his eight years on Capitol Hill he served as legislative assistant to Senators Edward Gurney of Florida, Roman Hruska of Nebraska, Paul Fannin of Arizona, and Harrison Schmitt of New Mexico. Mr. Hinish was educated at Yale University and the University of Colorado School of Law. He was chairman of the Regulatory Reform team in the *Mandate for Leadership* project.

### Civil Aeronautics Board & Postal Service

JAMES I. CAMPBELL, JR. is an attorney with Cook, Purcell, Hansen and Henderson. Previously, he dealt with governmental affairs for DHL Corporation, and was with the Senate Judiciary Committee's Subcommittee on Administrative Practice and Procedure as assistant counsel. Mr. Campbell was educated at Princeton University and the Georgetown University Law Center. He was chairman of the CAB and USPS teams in the *Mandate for Leadership* project.

### Commodity Futures Trading Commission

TERRANCE J. WEAR is assistant counsel on the Senate Committee on Agriculture, Nutrition, and Forestry. Prior to 1981 he served as a member of the Division of Enforcement, Commodity Futures Trading Commission, as a special assistant United States Attorney, and as a member of the Office of General Counsel, USDA. Mr. Wear received an A.B. degree from Benedictine College, Atchison, Kansas, and an M.A. in economics and a J.D. from the University of Iowa.

### Consumer Product Safety Commission & Federal Trade Commission

ANTHONY J. COPPOLINO is a research associate for the House Republican Study Committee. He graduated from Holy Cross College in Worcester, Massachusetts, in 1981, receiving his B.A. *magna cum laude* in history. He is a member of the Phi Alpha Theta (National History Honors) Society.

### Federal Election Commission

JAMES F. SCHOENER practices law in Washington, D.C., with the firm of Miller, Canfield, Paddock and Stone of Detroit, Michigan. He graduated from the University of Michigan Law School in 1950 and practiced law in Michigan for twenty years before being appointed to the Michigan Circuit Court Bench. He resigned from that post to become minority counsel to the Committee on Rules and Administration of the United States Senate in July 1974. As minority counsel, Mr. Schoener worked on the 1974, 1976, and 1977 amendments to the Federal Election Act. In private practice he specializes in election law matters and represents the National Republican Senatorial Committee and other political organizations and candidates. Mr. Schoener was chairman of the FEC team in the *Mandate for Leadership* project.

### Federal Maritime Commission

DOUGLAS R. GRAHAM is defense and strategic affairs specialist for the Republican Study Committee. He was a researcher on defense and national security affairs for Senator Jake Garn of Utah. Mr. Graham was a co-author and co-editor of *A Program for Military Independence* as a member of the Capitol Hill Staff Group. He also worked on defense and international commercial issues for Dr. John Lehman at Abington Corporation. Mr. Graham received his B.A. in history from Amherst College, with emphasis on Russian/Soviet history and politics.

### Interstate Commerce Commission & National Transporation Safety Board

MATTHEW V. SCOCOZZA is senior counsel for the Senate Committee on Commerce, Science, and Transportation. He was formerly minority counsel to the Subcommittee on Transportation of the House Appropriations Committee and chief legislative assistant to Congressman Silvio Conte of Massachusetts. He has served as a trial attorney in the Interstate Commerce Commission's Bureau of Enforcement. Mr. Scocozza is a graduate of the University of Tennessee Law School. He was chairman of the ICC and NTSB teams in the *Mandate for Leadership* project.

### Securities and Exchange Commission

ROBERT J. KABEL is legislative director for Senator Richard Lugar of Indiana. Educated at Denison University, Vanderbilt Law School (LL.M. in taxation) and the Georgetown Law Center, Mr. Kabel is former staff assistant to Governor Dunn of Tennessee and legislative assistant to Senator Paul Fannin of Arizona. He was chairman of the SEC team in the *Mandate for Leadership* project.

### EDITORIAL ASSISTANTS

LYNN E. MUNN is a staff assistant with The Heritage Foundation. She has produced and edited several editions of the Foundation's monthly *Insider Newsletter*, and served as liaison with many organizations cooperating with The Heritage Foundation's Resource Bank. She edited the *Annual Insider 1980: An Index to Public Policy,* published by Heritage in 1981. She received her B.A. in international relations from Brigham Young University in 1979, and currently is pursuing an M.B.A. from George Mason University. Miss Munn also served as editorial assistant for the original *Mandate for Leadership* project.

BOBBIE BREWSTER SCARFF is a staff assistant in the Department of Legislative Information at The Heritage Foundation. She was a copy editor at Doubleday and Company from 1968-1976, and received her B.A. in English from Colby College.

## THE EDITOR

RICHARD N. HOLWILL is Vice President and Director of Government Information and Special Projects at The Heritage Foundation; he has been the editor and coordinator for *A Mandate for Leadership Report: The First Year.* Prior to joining the Foundation in 1981, Mr. Holwill was Vice President of Energy Decisions, Inc., in Washington, D.C., a consulting firm on energy policy. He was named director of the corporation in November 1980. From 1977 to 1978 he was managing editor of "Monday Morning Report," a weekly analysis of energy economics and regulation, published by Energy Decisions, Inc. He has served as a White House correspondent for National Public Radio, producing major reports on presidential politics and national energy policies. Mr. Holwill received his B.A. in history from Louisiana State University in 1968.

# Selected Heritage Foundation Policy Studies

*The Inter-American Foundation*
 by Cleto DiGiovanni, Jr. (1981, $4.00)
*The Annual Insider 1980: An Index to Public Policy*
 edited by Lynn E. Munn (1981, $4.00)
*U.S. – Japan Mutual Security: The Next 20 Years*
 edited by Edwin J. Feulner, Jr. and Hideaki Kase (1981, $5.00)
*Mandate for Leadership*
 edited by Charles L. Heatherly (1981, $21.95, hardcover; $12.95, paperback)
*Agenda for Progress: Examining Federal Spending*
 edited by Eugene J. McAllister (1981, $11.95, hardcover; $6.95 paperback)
*Earth Day Reconsidered*
 edited by John Baden (1980, $4.00)
*The SALT Handbook*
 edited by Michael B. Donley (1979, $3.00)
*Energy Perspectives: An Advocates Guide*
 edited by Milton R. Copulos (1979, $6.95)
*Forty Centuries of Wage and Price Controls*
 by Robert L. Schuettinger and Eamonn F. Butler (1979, $4.95)
*The Welfare Industry*
 by Charles D. Hobbs (1978, $3.00)

## Fiscal Issues

*Philanthropy in America*
 by Stuart M. Butler (1980, $2.00)
*The Value Added Tax: Facts and Fancies*
 by Norman B. Ture (1979, $2.00)

## Critical Issues

*Strategic Minerals: The Economic Impact of Supply Disruptions*
 by James T. Bennett and Walter E. Williams (1981, $3.00)
*Corrigible Capitalism, Incorrigible Socialism*
 by Arthur Seldon (1981, $3.00)
*East Germany: Marxist Mission in Africa*
 by John M. Starrels (1981, $3.00)
*Reforming the Military*
 edited by Jeffrey G. Barlow (1981, $3.00)
*The Economics of Education Tax Credits*
 by E. G. West (1981, $3.00)
*The Soviet Strategy of Terror*
 by Samuel T. Francis (1981, $2.00)
*Domestic Oil: The Hidden Solution*
 by Milton R. Copulos (1980, $2.00)
*The Family, Feminism, and the Therapeutic State*
 by Onalee McGraw (1980, $2.00)
*Strategy and the MX*
 by Colin S. Gray (1980, $2.00)
*The Failure of Socialism: Learning from the Swedes and English*
 by Arthur Shenfield (1980, $2.00)
*Balancing the Budget: Should the Constitution Be Amended?*
 edited by Phillip N. Truluck (1979, $2.00)
*Congress and the Budget: Evaluating the Process*
 by Eugene J. McAllister (1979, $2.00)
*Verification and SALT: The State of the Art and the Art of the State*
 by Amrom H. Katz (1979, $2.00)
*Family Choice in Education: The New Imperative*
 by Onalee McGraw (1978, $1.00)

**For a complete list of publications – or to order any of the above – write:**

Dept. G, The Heritage Foundation, 513 C Street, N.E., Washington, D.C. 20002